Rural Discontent in 19 C. Britain

RURAL DISCONTENT
in Nineteenth-Century Britain

J. P. D. DUNBABIN

Faber and Faber
3 Queen Square
London

First published in 1974
by Faber and Faber Limited
3 Queen Square London WC1
Printed in Great Britain by
Butler and Tanner Limited
Frome and London

ISBN 0 571 08813 9

Acknowledgements

My thanks are due, in the first instance, to Pamela Horn (of the Oxford Polytechnic) and to A. J. Peacock (of the York Educational Settlement) for the chapters they have contributed to this volume. These chapters are an integral part of the book. But they are also individual studies in their own right; and they in no way commit their authors to any responsibility for sins, errors and omissions in other parts of the book. I am grateful to my publishers, not only for undertaking the book in the first place, but also for accepting this slightly unusual arrangement.

Next I should like to thank the many libraries in which I have worked while assembling material for this book, notably the Bodleian and Christ Church Libraries, Oxford; the British Museum Library; the National Library of Wales; Register House, Edinburgh; the National Library of Scotland; and the Ashridge repository of the Public Record Office. I am indebted to them for much efficient helpfulness. I am equally indebted to those who have deposited papers in them. And I am particularly grateful to the following for access to, and permission to quote from, their papers: the Marquess of Lothian; Viscount Harcourt, K.C.M.G., O.B.E.; Eric J. Ivory, Esq.; and the Dean and Governing Body of Christ Church, Oxford.

Lastly I must record my great debt to my wife. She has not only encouraged me throughout, but also given me perceptive help with the organization and expression of all my scholarly writing.

St. Edmund Hall, Oxford   J. P. D. DUNBABIN
December, 1973

Contents

Maps, graphs and tables

I

Introduction

This book is about rural unrest. But we must not assume that open unrest or discontent was the sole, or even the normal, condition of the late Victorian countryside. A decade after the turn of the century the wheel-wright and novelist George Sturt wrote of his neighbours,

They have no sense of oppression to poison their lives. The truth which economists begin to recognize, that where there are wealthy and idle classes there must as an inevitable result be classes who are impoverished and overworked, has not found its way into the villager's head.

So supported by an instinctive fatalism, the people have taken their plight for granted, without harbouring resentment against the more fortunate. It may be added that most of them are convinced believers in those fallacies which cluster around the phrase 'making work'. It were strange if they were not. The labourer lives by being employed at work; and, knowing his employer personally . . . he sees the work he lives by actually being 'made'. Only very rarely does it occur to him that when he goes to the shop he, too, makes work. The idea is too abstract to be followed to its logical conclusion. The people do not see the multitudes at work for them in other counties, making their boots and ready-made clothes, getting their coal, importing their cheap provisions; but they do see, and know by name, the well-to-do of the neighbourhood, who have new houses built and new gardens laid out; and they naturally enough infer that labour would perish if there were no well-to-do people to be supplied.

Against the rich man, therefore, the labourers have no sort of animosity. If he will spend money freely, the richer he is the better. Throughout the south of England this is the common attitude . . . the labouring folk . . . [are] not exacting as to the sort of person—lunatics, fox-hunters, Bishops—anybody would be welcome who could spend riches in a way to 'make work'. And so here. This village looks up to those who control wealth as if they were the sources of it; and if there is a little dislike of some of them personally, there has so far appeared but little bitterness of feeling against them as a class.

Sturt's Surrey 'village' was a straggling settlement with no 'great house' or resident squire. Flora Thompson's *Lark Rise* (in

Oxfordshire) gives a slightly different picture. Though her ham-
let accepted the importance of gentry in providing work, 'For
wealth without rank or birth they had small respect.' But 'They
took a pride in their rich and powerful country-house neighbours, especially when titled. The old Earl in the next parish
was spoken of as "our Earl" and when . . . [his] flag . . . could
be seen floating above the tree-tops they would say: "I see our
family's at home again".' In other parts of the country, this
sense of identification might be far stronger. Norman Maclean
continually emphasizes the fierce loyalty felt by the Braes towards their landlord and clan chief, Lord Macdonald, and their
vicarious pride in his ability to travel by special train, and still
more in the magnificence of his yacht, *The Lady of the Isles*.
And even in Wales, where the position of the Anglican upper
crust of rural society really was being deliberately challenged,
it could still be said that 'the squires in Montgomeryshire are
personally liked by voters, as far as is compatible with the
wide difference in politics and religion'.[1]

No account of the late nineteenth-century rural scene can
ignore such sentiments. Equally nobody could maintain that
the rural poor looked on, say, the Guardians and the workhouse
with any degree of affection. And, as Dr. Peacock will show in
Chapter III, in parts of East Anglia at least, the first half of the
century was marked by an undertone of violence, sometimes
ritualized. Admittedly this never achieved quite the same dimensions as in Ireland;[2] and it declined sharply after the middle
of the century. But some of the sentiment behind it must have
lingered on, even if it was now suffered in silence, or forced to
find less violent forms of expression.

The Victorian countryside can therefore be painted both black
and white. Neither picture is wholly correct, and the choice
between them depends partly on the sources and criteria used.
But there is a sense in which, for the latter part of the century,
the brighter picture is the more important. For the countryside
in Britain was not hard to govern; indeed it mostly ran itself,
and consumed only a fraction of the political attention that was
commanded by rural Ireland. Also the more articulate members

[1] George Bourne (pseudonym), *Change in the Village* (1912),
pp. 104ff.; Flora Thompson, *Lark Rise to Candleford* (World's
Classics edn.), pp. 59, 321; Norman Maclean, *The Former Days* (1945),
esp. pp. 131–2; K. O. Morgan, *Wales in British Politics* (Cardiff,
1963), p. 56.
[2] For which see e.g. Sir G. Cornewall Lewis, *Local Disturbances in
Ireland* (1836).

of rural society were fairly happy with it. Causes for dissatisfaction naturally remained in plenty, and might well be briefly
reported in the local press; but on the whole this gave far more
coverage to local festivities or to euphoric agricultural dinners.
So whenever there really was trouble, it always came as a shock,
and it was commonly ascribed to a few external agitators who
had misled a simple, but basically well-disposed, populace. In
other words the established classes seldom anticipated unrest,
and so they reacted consciously to it only after it had occurred.

This is not, of course, to say that the nineteenth-century
countryside was free from landlord (and farmer) coercion, or
from social pressure and conditioning. Volumes have been written about *The Tyranny of the Countryside*[1]—estate regulations
(whether over-paternal or dictatorial), concerted refusal to employ 'trouble-makers', threatened or actual eviction, the choice
of tenants along sectarian or political lines, and the like. It is
difficult to say quite how extensive such practices were, for
specific allegations often produced denials or explanations that,
in their turn, generated more heat than light.[2] But there can
be no doubt that the nineteenth-century landed system had an
'unacceptable face'; and the fear this inspired naturally tended
to discourage the open expression of discontent.[3] Such fear was

[1] By F. E. Green (1913); see also e.g. Adfyfr (T. J. Hughes),
Landlordism in Wales (Cardiff, 1887), and Edmund Vincent, *Tenancy
in Wales. A Reply to 'Landlordism in Wales' by Adfyfr* (Caernarvon,
1889). The whole question of coercion was much ventilated by the
Royal Commissions on the Condition of the Crofters and Cottars,
and on Land in Wales and Monmouthshire, to which we shall return
in due course.

[2] There was probably most scope for overbearing or coercive
behaviour in the Highlands, where estates were largest and social
relationships most old-fashioned—unpaid harvest work on the lord's
farms sometimes survived until the agitation of the 1880s. Equally
many Highland townships depended on periodic aid from the landlord in time of destitution. At the other extreme, English tenant
farmers (mostly men of some capital) had little to complain of.
Between these two poles came English farm labourers (who were
especially subject to supervision in paternalistic 'closed villages' in
the south), and the small Welsh farmers. Land hunger placed these
last at a disadvantage when dealing with large landlords: and some
landlords responded coercively to the new political and religious
challenges of the third quarter of the century; but, by the final
quarter, such responses had become too dangerous, and were largely
discontinued.

[3] Also, as Reginald Lennard pointed out in 1914, 'to assert that

13

most influential before discontent 'went critical' and emerged
into the open. For it was difficult (and often counter-productive)
to coerce a whole community. And though individual ring-
leaders might be victimized, they could—if they were sufficiently
determined—find alternative accommodation and employment
in the reasonably close vicinity;[1] in any case these leaders often
came from backgrounds that gave them a degree of independence.

Unlike coercion, social conditioning was seldom regarded as
reprehensible. The landlord and the parson performed many of
the functions that have since been assumed by local government; and it was widely accepted that they had a responsibility
for promoting the general good of their community—Lord
Salisbury was somewhat unusual in believing the personal
morality of his cottagers to be no concern of his.[2] Included in
the 'general good' was the concept of social harmony; and this
was buttressed, both deliberately and sub-consciously, in a
variety of ways ranging from preaching to charity. Of course
they were sometimes resented; but they also often established
or confirmed ties of affection or belief in the common interest
of all stations in society. In normal times these ties may have
had considerable influence and have inhibited the development
of unrest. But if discontent ever did become overt, social conditioning had, by definition, failed (at least for the time being).
At such moments one of the commonest complaints of the
established classes was of the 'ingratitude' for past favours that
led people to concentrate on present disputes, or to prefer
solidarity with their peers to a continuance of the old relationship with their superiors. So however important acts of charity
were in the normal pattern of rural relationships, only very

---

the labourers fear the disapproval of the squire if they join a union,
is not necessarily to accuse the squire of intolerance. It may be only
to accuse the labourers of ignorance' (*English Agricultural Wages*,
p. 17 n.).

[1] Thus George Edwards tells us he lost (or gave up) a number of
jobs in the 1860s, 1870s and 1880s, but was always able to switch
from farm work to brick-making and back. His worst period was after
he had been evicted for political reasons in 1886, when he had to
walk twelve miles a day for eighteen months. But eventually another
Liberal patron came to his rescue, and found him not only employment but also a cottage (*From Crow-Scaring to Westminster* (1922),
chaps. ii and iv).

[2] Lady Gwendolen Cecil, *Life of Robert Marquis of Salisbury*, ii
(1921), pp. 4–5.

occasionally did their continuance (or curtailment) serve to quell an actual outbreak of unrest.[1]

These outbursts of discontent were less violent and less dramatic than those of the earlier part of the century, and have accordingly attracted less attention from historians. But in a sense they were more important. For the earlier protests had generally been rear-guard actions, not necessarily unsuccessful —indeed the Swing riots of 1830 put back mechanization in much of southern England for some twenty years—but with little prospect of development. In the course of the second half of the century English agricultural labourers, Scottish farm servants, Scottish crofters, and Welsh anti-tithers (mostly small farmers) all mounted a major challenge to some aspect of their living conditions. These challenges were not devoid of an element of reaction, but in their various ways they all groped towards positive changes, and some achieved them. They represented, too, an adaptation by the rural poor to the vast but unnoticed changes of the mid-Victorian years—the spread of railways and of literacy, the extension of the franchise and of political activity in a national rather than a local context, and the conscious emphasis on sobriety and orderly behaviour. Also, unlike their predecessors, these movements came to be adopted by urban politicians; and so they were at least partially fused to create a 'Rural Question', whose rôle in the general late nineteenth-century climate of opinion has been somewhat neglected. Nevertheless by 1900 they had, for the time being, all died down; and this in itself is a testimony to the basic strength and durability of the rural social system.

No general history of this process has yet been written; indeed some of the individual movements have not previously been chronicled; and this book is an attempt to fill the gap. Its principal theme is the development of rural unrest from purely local and spontaneous demonstrations to organized and articulate movements, drawing on external assistance and deliberately appealing to public opinion at large. This change in horizons led to participation in national politics. And, in the 1880s, the range of possibilities open to reformers appeared to be transformed by the growing readiness of the State to intervene, in rural problems, with legislation to set aside the previously sacrosanct principle of freedom of contract. So the expectation grew that

[1] It was suggested, however, that the promptitude with which subscriptions were raised in 1886 for the widows of two accident victims was one of the causes of the decline of the 'Land League' in the Skye Parish of Strath (Scottish Record Office, GD 40/16/32, p. 42).

it would react to pressure by compelling change. In fact this expectation was often to be disappointed; but it did mean that unrest was increasingly channelled into politics, and that gains were looked for from political action by groups too weak to achieve them in any other way. This transition to politics was materially assisted by the extension of the franchise in 1885 to include all rural householders, and by the readiness of the Liberal Party, always loosely knit and now leaning increasingly towards the left, to offer the new elements at least a foothold within it.

In our survey we shall confine ourselves to Great Britain, though some references to Ireland will be necessary to explain the developments of the 1880s.[1] We shall also restrict ourselves to movements within rural society, as opposed to attempts, by such organizations as the Chambers of Agriculture, to defend rural interests as a whole in what was becoming an increasingly urbanized state.[2] Nor shall we be concerned with purely urban movements for small-holdings or land reform except in so far as they evoked a significant rural response.[3] Lastly we shall have to pass over most purely local disputes, even though these could sometimes assume considerable dimensions.[4]

[1] The evolution of rural unrest in Ireland (and, indeed, elsewhere) presents many parallels with Britain. But it took place against a different background and on a far larger scale.

[2] For which, see A. H. H. Matthews, *Fifty Years of Agricultural Politics* (1915).

[3] Many urban movements from the Anti-Corn Law League onwards sent lecturers out into the countryside, though often to little purpose. We shall encounter the Land Nationalization Society and the Land Restoration League in connection with the crofters' agitation of the 1880s, and the latter also played a considerable rôle in the revival of agricultural trades unionism in southern England in the 1890s. A more marginal case is the Birmingham politician Jesse Collings's Allotments Association, set up to work the 1882 Allotments Extension Act and to enlist support for the Liberals, and his later Rural Labourers' League, designed to perform the same service for the Unionists.

[4] Grazing disputes and squatting on crown land and unenclosed Welsh mountain pasture were recurrent sources of disturbance. Better known, though only as a curiosity, is the 1838 rising in rural Kent of a lunatic (claiming to be the Messiah) and a band of some 40 followers. He committed one murder, and attacked troops sent to intercept him; eleven people were killed in the resultant skirmish. The Government was able to use the credulity with which he had been accepted as an argument for increasing the State grant to education. (P. G. Rogers, *Battle in Bossenden Wood*, Oxford, 1961.)

Such exceptions apart, nineteenth-century rural disturbances fall conveniently into two groups, divided by an interlude that was to become known in retrospect as the 'Golden Age of British Agriculture'. The earlier group will be passed over rather more rapidly, for the individual movements have already been described by other historians. So what is attempted in the next chapter is a synthesis of their work, and an exposition of the different forms that unrest might take. Dr. Peacock will then show, in a detailed local study, just how disturbed East Anglia could be even in the superficially calm periods between the more celebrated outbreaks. From the middle of the century such violence gradually declined. This was one of the greatest achievements of the Victorian age, but also one of the most elusive. Chapter IV attempts to provide some explanations, and also to give a general picture of the rise and fall of a new vehicle for the expression of farm workers' grievances—trades unionism. This picture is filled out and brought to life in the next chapter by Dr. Horn's study of rural trades unionism in Oxfordshire.

We have thus reached the second group of disturbances; and we now proceed to discuss the other formal movements that 'set class against class' in the later nineteenth-century countryside on a more than local scale and with some political consequences.[1] This second group of movements was, as we have seen, better organized, more articulate and more ambitious than the first; so it is possible to construct a general picture of their techniques, ideas and aspirations. But, to succeed, they, like their predecessors, had to win over, or intimidate, the holders of power, local or national. And the concluding chapter seeks to examine the reasons for the success or failure of the various rural outbreaks throughout the century, a hitherto surprisingly neglected topic.

[1] The (Tenant) Farmers' Alliance will, however, be described only briefly since it confined itself to action as a conventional and parliamentary pressure group. Many of the other movements eventually developed in this direction, but they had all at some stage operated outside the established political structure.

II

The First Half of the Nineteenth Century

In 1794 it was said that an agricultural labourer permitted to keep a cow or pig 'has a stake in the common interest of the country, and is never prompt to riot in times of sedition, like the man who has nothing to lose'.[1] Riots were clearly fairly frequent, and farm workers were becoming increasingly involved. They had not figured much in English riots in the eighteenth century, though they had in French. But a number of factors were now drawing them in. As food prices rose, farmers were abandoning the practice of boarding their labourers in their own houses,[2] and they were also less likely to pay in kind or to sell grain privately to their employees at traditional prices. Instead cash wages were becoming the rule. Agricultural labourers were therefore no longer shielded from price fluctuations, except perhaps through the Poor Law. And sharp price rises had for centuries sparked off riots designed to force the sale of food at normal rates in accordance with Tudor legislation.

Such riots had once been a more or less accepted part of life. Local magistrates sometimes anticipated them by intervening in the market to stabilize prices; and if trouble did break out, the justices might not be unsympathetic towards the coercion of grain hoarders and merchants. However by about 1800 this tradition was being undermined. The eighteenth century had had a fairly high tolerance of violence; but the upper classes were now coming to appreciate its dangers—London had been shaken by the destructiveness of the 1780 Gordon riots, Birmingham by that of the 1791 Priestley ones, and the whole kingdom by the example of Paris during the French Revolution. Also the central Government was now becoming converted to the new political economy of Adam Smith, which held State interference with trade and prices (as demanded by the rioters) to be counter-productive. So magistrates who still sought to invoke the old Tudor laws, or to turn an indulgent eye while the 'mob' did, might now be lectured and rebuked.

[1] Nathaniel Kent, *A General View of the Agriculture of the County of Norfolk* (1794), p. 46.
[2] Other reasons for the change were the rising prosperity and social status brought to the farmers by the high food prices of the Napoleonic wars.

But all this took time—occasional price fixing and hunger riots can be traced as late as 1847. Moreover though the authorities were less and less inclined to interfere with trade, they remained ready to supplement wages on occasion through the Poor Law. So the riot retained some relevance. In 1816 East Anglian rural mobs put to local magistrates not only traditional demands for flour at a fixed price (2s. 6d. a stone), but also requests for a wage of 2s. a day and a Poor Law allowance of 2s. per head per week. As time went on, prices moved increasingly into the background—their long-term trend after the Napoleonic Wars was downward—and the labourers' attention was concentrated on wages and unemployment. So in 1830 the most widespread demands were for wages of from 2s. to 2s. 6d. a day.

But there were, of course, other grievances that could be settled at the same time and in the same way. Thus in 1830 nine Sussex villagers wheeled the local overseers of the poor out of the parish and dumped them over the boundary. Parsons were often made to promise to cut their tithes so as to leave more money for wages. Above all, some 390 threshing machines were smashed. These machines intensified winter unemployment, and both magistrates and farmers had qualms about them on this score; so their destruction was generally performed openly, for a standard fee of up to £2 each, and might well be regarded by the labourers as a meritorious act—in parts of Dorset they expected the Government to pay for it.

Nineteenth-century English riots perhaps only assumed really considerable dimensions in 1816 and 1830, both of which were thought to warrant Special Commissions of Assize as a deliberate deterrent. But there were, of course, many more local disturbances. In general they were fairly standard affairs. They might well be preceded or accompanied by threatening letters and arson. There would be discussion in pubs, and perhaps in the houses of local sympathizers. When tension had risen sufficiently a small crowd would assemble—it might even be summoned by the village cryer or, on at least one occasion, by handbills. The crowd would go through the fields, or from village to village, forcing men to join. And the resultant 'mob' would then visit the local farmers and worthies with its demands, and perhaps descend on the nearest town to insist on the local authorities satisfying it. On the way there might be some looting, or in 1830 more usually the levying of cash contributions for food and drink. And the demands themselves were backed up by threats and strong language; but matters seldom went much further.

All this involved some organization, but of a very rudimentary nature. Individual mobs often had leaders, who might ride on horseback and assume the style of 'Captain'; if contributions were levied, they might go to a 'treasurer'; and messengers or 'delegates' might be sent to treat with magistrates or to summon aid from neighbouring villages. Very occasionally such delegates might meet as a committee. But there is no evidence of a plan on a more than local scale: riots spread partly by rumour, and partly by contagion from individual villages, which operated over a radius of at most half a day's journey in each direction. And riots of this kind were all ephemeral, to be measured in days rather than weeks. This was partly because they were put down by force if they were serious enough; but in any case the labourers did not have the resources to give up many days' work, and indeed the whole purpose of the exercise was to obtain work not lose it.[1]

An instructive contrast is provided by the Otmoor (Oxfordshire) disturbances of 1830–5. The enclosure of the moor in the early nineteenth century had clearly been very unpopular. But trouble only really came to a head some fifteen years later, when farmers were brought to trial (for destroying ill-designed drainage works that flooded their lands) and formally acquitted. The verdict was locally taken to mean that the whole enclosure was invalid, and hedges and fences were promptly levelled. This was done mostly at night, often by men with blackened faces or wearing women's clothes. But on 6 September 1830 about a thousand people openly circumambulated the moor as of old, 'possessioning' it and breaking any obstacles in their path. A number were arrested, but they were rescued as they were being conveyed to prison through the streets of Oxford, some eight miles away. So troops were sent to the moor and military detachments stationed there for much of the next two years; they were succeeded by a small force of police. Neither had much success in preventing the nocturnal destruction of fences and bridges, which seems to have been organized by

[1] For the above, see e.g. E. P. Thompson, 'The Moral Economy of the English Crowd in the Eighteenth Century', *Past and Present*, 1 (1971); R. B. Rose, 'Eighteenth Century Price Riots and Public Policy in England', *International Review of Social History*, vi (1961); G. Rudé, *The Crowd in History* (New York, 1964); A. J. Peacock, *Bread or Blood* (1965); E. J. Hobsbawm and G. Rudé, *Captain Swing* (1969); Barbara Kerr, *Bound to the Soil* (1968) chap. V; S. W. Amos, *Social Discontent and Agrarian Disturbances in Essex, 1795–1850* (unpublished M. A. thesis, Durham University).

fairly well-known militants at local beer-shops. And when re-sistance collapsed, it did so largely for other reasons—notably the authorities' conscious conciliation of the larger farmers.[1]

So, unlike ordinary riots, nocturnal raids could be sustained for a considerable period, even in the face of military opposition. This was to be shown still more clearly by the Rebecca riots in south-west Wales.[2] These seem to have developed out of the traditional *ceffyl pren* processions, the parading of unpopular figures on a wooden pole, accompanied by a noisy mob with blackened faces and wearing women's clothes. Such processions always happened at night, and often involved a mock trial of the victims. And they become more frequent in the late 1830s. Then in 1839 two newly erected turn-pike gates on the Pem-brokeshire–Carmarthenshire border were cut down by nocturnal gatherings of this type. When replaced, they were again des-troyed. On one occasion the mob's leader was addressed as 'Becca' after the woman whose clothes he had borrowed, and the name stuck. Eventually the turn-pike trust gave in and abandoned the gates. But in the winter of 1842 it again erected a new gate, and a 'Rebecca' appeared to destroy both this and its neighbour (the latter after 'trial'). This time the trust made no concessions, and the destruction of gates and toll-houses continued, gradually spreading outwards into neighbouring counties. It was discriminating in the sense that certain gates were accepted and permitted to remain; but it became increas-ingly violent, several gate-keepers being beaten, two blinded by blank gun-shots, and one murdered.

The riots were certainly planned locally at nocturnal meet-ings, and we know the names of a number of men who led raids in the guise of Rebecca. Some clandestine advice and general assistance may have been given by a Carmarthen solici-tor, Hugh Williams. But the riots' historian, Professor David Williams, feels that there was no master-mind behind the move-ment, which spread rather through the independent imitation by one area of another. Crowds were raised partly by pressing, as in England, and partly by the despatch to farmers (and even gentry) of letters demanding their presence on pain of vengeance or death. Such crowds were considerably more formidable than English mobs, since the farmers had guns, and were prepared to use them. And in June 1843 disturbances reached such a

[1] Bernard Reaney, *The Class Struggle in 19th-Century Oxfordshire: The Social and Communal Background to the Otmoor Disturbances of 1830 to 1835* (Oxford, 1970).

[2] For which see David Williams, *The Rebecca Riots* (Cardiff, 1965).

pitch that the local Yeomanry were supplemented by the despatch of considerable numbers of troops. Rebecca still managed
to elude pursuit with surprising ease for the rest of the summer,
but in the process her doings became increasingly hurried and
secret.

Toll-gates accounted for most of her activities, but by no
means for all. Rebecca was also a great writer of threatening
letters, some displaying a marked anti-English animus: they
commonly demanded reductions of rent or tithe, and promised
attacks on workhouses. There were several assaults on informers
and bailiffs.[1] The ricks of magistrates and of land-grabbing
farmers were fired. In a lighter vein, Rebecca acted as moral
censor, making men care for their illegitimate children or marry
girls they had made pregnant, and even forcibly reconciling a
vicar and his estranged wife. In short 'Rebecca' might be used
to deal with any grievance or scandal about which there was
strong local feeling.[2] But from righting public wrongs to intervening in current feuds was a short step; Rebecca had always
levied collections for her 'expenses', and the movement eventually spawned a couple of gangs ready to sell their services for
private vengeance. These were not popular with the local
farmers. But more serious were the openings that the disturbances offered to the farm servants, who had begun to hold
meetings to discuss their wages in anticipation of the autumn
hiring fairs—one farmer was to declare that Rebecca herself
had become 'the greatest grievance in the country' as she now
'burned the corn'.

Farmers therefore turned against the riots, once actually replacing a gate that had been destroyed; and by the autumn of
1843 it was again possible to swear them in as special constables.
Another restraint was the scale of the eventual military deployment—150 metropolitan police and 1,800 troops, 'enough' (the
Home Secretary wrote) 'to conquer the country, let alone keep
it in order'; by contrast the 1839 Chartist rising had succumbed
to a single volley at Newport. So the movement was gradually
transformed into a political one of open meetings. It had
already occasioned a fair number of hostile pamphlets and handbills. So it is perhaps not altogether surprising that two clan-

---

[1] One bailiff was punished for distraining on a farmer's goods by
being bound hand and foot and placed in the local pound. He was
released the next morning only on payment of the 4d. fine for stray
beasts, and the experience is said to have made him a strong opponent of cruelty to animals.

[2] Around Llanelli it was adopted to express industrial unrest.

destine gatherings admitted a sympathetic *Times* correspondent to hear their side of the case. The Carmarthenshire magistrates made the transition easier by persuading the Government to look into the affairs of the turn-pike trusts. For this led to legitimate assemblies to prepare evidence. And these in turn developed into mass meetings, attended by some of the men who were also active in the rioting, and strongly influenced by Hugh Williams's Chartist rhetoric. Further scope was provided in the autumn when the Government appointed a fully fledged Commission of Inquiry, which spent seven weeks taking evidence from all and sundry. Its report in 1844 resulted in legislation to regroup the trusts and reduce the tolls; so through Rebecca the Welsh farmers had achieved a success, albeit at substantial cost to their rates.[1] But by that time the riots had sputtered out, the troops were being withdrawn, and a rural police set on foot.

A third type of disturbance is to be met with in the Scottish Highlands.[2] By 1800 these were being swept by a tide of agricultural improvement that had been building up further south for almost a century. In southern Scotland this break-up of the open-field 'run-rig' system had sometimes involved the sweeping away of the small cot-houses that clustered round farms, and had thus occasionally caused a drop in population. But there had been available such safety-valves as migration to towns, the growth of rural villages, and the extension of agriculture to employ more labour. So, apart from a minuscule rising in Galloway in 1724, the process led to little trouble. However, the further north and west one went, the less the safeguards applied. For if agricultural improvement demanded that the people be cleared from the land, there might be nowhere for them to go and little else for them to do.[3] And agricultural improvement did demand this in a big way—the profits of, therefore the rents from, large-scale sheep farming far outweighed the meagre produce of crofting 'townships'. So many considerations tempted landlords to substitute the one for the

[1] For the toll-houses had to be re-erected, and the metropolitan police paid, by the county.

[2] Of course, these saw more conventional forms of riot too, notably the food riots of 1847.

[3] In some districts a temporary alleviation was offered by the kelping industry, which boomed during the Napoleonic war but subsequently collapsed, leaving its labour force stranded. In all areas the strain was increased, at the turn of the century, by an unprecedented population growth.

other—pressure of debts, greed, mania for 'improvement', even the belief that the crofting population could only be delivered from recurrent destitution by being thinned or redeployed. The substitution was piece-meal, and could be effected in many ways. A landlord might take over the hill grazings for sheep, thus ultimately making unviable townships that had depended on pasturing cattle on them. Alternatively the small tenants (and still more the landless squatters) might simply be cleared off and left to shift for themselves; many would then drift as 'incomers' to townships with more tolerant landlords, and congest them. Or clearance from one part of an estate might be accompanied by resettlement on another, generally by the sea so that the crofters might supplement their food by fishing (and incidentally take up less land)—this was the pattern of the notorious Sutherland clearances, which represented ambitious and rather Stalinist social engineering, backed by massive investment, but in many respects gone sadly awry.

In most cases the clearances were accepted with remarkable docility,[1] but not in all. Where there was resistance, it usually took the shape of 'deforcement', that is of mobbing sheriff's officers to prevent them from serving the formal legal writs of removal. Such deforcements were generally the work of the women of the township, and were almost always spontaneous. Very occasionally they led landlords to have second thoughts, but more often the authorities merely provided their officers with an armed escort; and in any case the crofters might have repented in the meantime. But opposition could also assume more systematic forms. In 1792 there was an unplanned and simple-minded attempt literally to drive the sheep out of Ross-shire. Some twenty years later the Sutherland clearances encountered more developed resistance. First there were petitions to the Government, and to the Marquis of Stafford.[2] The Marquis referred the petitioners to the courts; and when his agent, Patrick Sellars, was arrested for his part in the 1814 Strathnaver clearance, the whole valley eagerly gave evidence and collected money to bring him to trial. In this it was prompted by the local Sheriff Substitute,[3] and also by a London newspaper, the

[1] They were unprecedented in scale, but not in nature. They took place piece-meal. They were undeniably legal, and legal authority was generally reinforced by spiritual. Lastly they were at least partially covered by the remainder of clan loyalty.

[2] Husband of the last Countess of Sutherland.

[3] He was a tacksman who stood to lose by the changes, and he also had a personal grievance against Sellars.

Military Register. But Sellars was acquitted. And thoughts subsequently turned to emigration—in 1819 a 'Sutherland Transatlantic Friendly Association' was founded. Admittedly this may have been a largely paper organization, revolving round its secretary; but he is recorded as having intervened in another strath to try to persuade it to resist removal.

Events in Sutherland gave rise to pamphlets on both sides, and a major part in the attack on Sellars was played by the *Military Register*, which circulated among retired Highland officers disappointed at not having been rewarded with land for their services, as under the old clan system. But, with this exception, it was not until the second cycle of clearances in the 1840s and 1850s that their opponents began to make any very extensive appeals to public opinion at large. One catalyst was the 1841 Committee of Inquiry into Highland destitution and emigration. The evidence given to it about Sutherland so incensed Donald Macleod, a stone-mason who had been driven out of the county, that he wrote to the *Edinburgh Weekly Chronicle*; when challenged to substantiate his statements he embarked on a series of letters; and, once launched, he continued to write copiously, ultimately embodying his views of events since 1807 in his *Gloomy Memories in the Highlands of Scotland* (published from Canada in 1857). Much publicity also resulted from the long-drawn-out clearances of 1842–5 in Glencalvie, Ross-shire. These were resisted not only by the people in the traditional manner, but also by a committee of gentlemen perhaps inspired by the local minister. This committee sought to place an advertisement in the London *Times*, and to check their assertions *The Times* sent down a Special Commissioner. As a result questions were asked in Parliament, and a 'Society for the Protection of the Poor' was formed in Edinburgh to prevent a recurrence of such evictions.[1] None of this came to much, and clearances continued, especially in the aftermath of the great 1846 Destitution. For the most part they were still passively accepted. But they had become recognized subjects for letters to the newspapers and for pamphleteering—one

[1] The Society was still in existence in 1851, and may well have been active in sponsoring petitions in Skye. These petitions were principally concerned to assert the inhabitants' moral right to receive poor relief from the Government, but they also touched on clearances. The Society itself seems to have favoured leases, as giving 'proper fixity of tenure' to the small occupiers and thereby encouraging them to improve their lots—*P(arliamentary) P(apers)* 1851 xxvi, pp. 902, 1103–5.

Glasgow lawyer wrote six pamphlets in four years in the 1850s. So by now there were clearly some outsiders prepared to take up the cause of the crofters. And the Highlanders themselves surprised the country by showing a marked reluctance to volunteer for the Crimean War; indeed they explained why, both at recruiting meetings and in at least one meeting of their own, which drew up an address to the newspapers on the subject. It is possible that in the 1850s discontent was on the verge of becoming articulate and even, to some extent, organized. But it had not yet passed over to the offensive. And the next twenty years gave it little stimulus, since clearances died away and were succeeded by a measure of prosperity.[1]

[1] For the above, see e.g. John Prebble, *The Highland Clearances* (1963); Philip Gaskell, *Morvern Transformed* (Cambridge, 1968); J. E. Handley, *Scottish Farming in the Eighteenth Century* (1953); Robert McLellan, *The Isle of Arran* (Newton Abbot, 1970) chap. vi; Eric Richards, 'The Prospect of Economic Growth in Sutherland at the Time of the Clearances, 1809 to 1813', *Scottish Historical Review*, il (1970); Malcolm Gray, 'The Abolition of Runrig in the Highlands of Scotland', *Economic History Review*, second series, v (1952–3); J. H. G. Lebon, 'Old Maps and Rural Change in Ayrshire', *Scottish Geographical Magazine*, lxviii (1952).

III
Village Radicalism in East Anglia 1800-50

by A. J. Peacock

It is a commonplace of nineteenth-century history that the agricultural worker only rarely asserted himself, and that when he did there was a time-lag, often a considerable one, before the waves of unrest that affected the urban workers stirred those in the villages; or, the same thing, that it was much longer before the rural worker kicked against appalling conditions than it was before the town dweller began agitating. The general reason given is that the farm labourer worked much more in isolation than his urban counterpart and was more difficult to organize. And it is also usual to cite the 'special' kind of working relationship that the labourer receiving his cottage or his rent-free potato patch often had with his employer. There is more than a little in this—though not by any means as much as is sometimes claimed. Equally important, however, is the fact that, until the appearance of efficient police forces halfway through the century, the labourer had, as the town dweller did not have, ample means of squaring his scores with his employer. The labourer was adept at slacking in the most effective and undetectable ways. More serious, he could steal his employer's fruit, corn or game almost with impunity. Stacks could be fired, farm buildings lit, animals maimed, fences destroyed, banks breached. This went on continuously in rural England, a check on the farmers without doubt, a psychological release for the labourer for certain. Usually vengeance of this kind would be wreaked, as far as one can tell, by individuals or small groups. Only when conditions became really overpowering, as in 1816 or the early 1830s, did the labourers unite on the grand scale; then they appear in the pages of the history books. But they appeared all the time on the pages of the local press. The usually immovable, completely cowed, soporific Hodge is a figment of imagination—at least in East Anglia. He protested *all* the time, and most of the time very effectively indeed.

Very rarely, again except where conditions were so bad that villages and villagers united, were the rural 'criminals' caught, and so Home Office, Treasury Solicitors and Assize papers reveal little about what went on in the 'peaceful', normal years of the nineteenth century. The major source of information for this study and any similar one is, therefore, of necessity the local press. Fortunately press coverage was good and enables a fairly comprehensive picture to be built up of what went on in the villages of the east.

Most of the examples cited will be taken from the fenlands and the marshland, that area of reclaimed land around the Wash where 'The soil is a rich ooze,' highly productive of arable crops and, in particular, rape seed. '. . . one of the richest districts in the kingdom', a correspondent to the Board of Agriculture called it. Writing about the area recently, a guide book said that 'The Marshland . . . although to a slightly lesser extent than Fenland, is pure gold.'[1] In the first half of the nineteenth century much of this marshland, like indeed much of the fens, was given over to sheep farming, which meant that labourers there would not be required in vast numbers, and that the pickings from a midnight venture into the pastures would be good.[2]

The condition of the fenlands at the beginning of the nineteenth century was dismal, as Arthur Young recorded in his *General View of the Agriculture of Norfolk*. In the period covered by this chapter enclosure went on apace with a consequent gain to the efficiency of agriculture and the consequent losses, real or imagined—or both—to the rural poor. Young's dictum about the losses of the poor has often been quoted; a writer on the marshland uttered similar sentiments. 'The poor people who turned cows, geese, and ducks upon the common, without possessing *rights*, have suffered, as in so many other cases.'[3] The process of enclosure was a continuing background to the violence of the eastern counties, a constant unsettling reminder to the labourer of the process of disinheritance.

Appalling housing conditions existed throughout the area,

[1] W. Marshall, *A Review and Abstract of the County Reports to the Board of Agriculture* (York, 1818), pp. 282–3; J. Seymour, *The Companion Guide to East Anglia* (1970), p. 267.
[2] On the farming of East Anglia in the nineteenth century, see e.g. G. E. Fussell, ' "High Farming" in the East Midlands and East Anglia, 1840–80', *Economic Geography*, xxvii (1951); S. Jonas, 'On the Farming of Cambridgeshire', *Journal of the Royal Agricultural Society of England*, vii (1846), and J. A. Clarke, 'On the Great Level of the Fens, including the Fens of South Lincolnshire', *ibid.* viii (1848); W. Gooch, *Agriculture of the County of Cambridge* (1813); W. Watson, *Historical Account of Wisbech* (1827); H. C. Darby, *The Draining of the Fens* (Cambridge, 1956); E. Kerridge, *The Agricultural Revolution* (1967).   [3] Marshall, *op. cit.*, p. 287.

with the farmer who benefited from enclosure appearing, more often than not, as a dreadful landlord. Disease was rife; life expectation low. In 1850 Mayhew reported on villages in the east for the *Morning Chronicle*. His descriptions of Cambridge, Ely and St. Ives were harrowing, but outdone by those of the surrounding villages. In Welch's Dam, near Chatteris, there were 16 cottages with a population of 81, 'among whom there were last year not less than eleven fatal attacks of cholera, besides a number of cases of diarrhoea'.[1]

Enclosures, bad housing, ill health and the sight of increasing prosperity among the farmers as the fens were improved, the sight of which made men 'doubly poor' as George Crabbe said— these were the constant background to half a century of violence. But only on rare occasions did that violence take on a more than purely local character, and most of those occasions have been studied in considerable detail. In 1816 the east was the scene of serious rioting that ended in severe repression, and the area was similarly the scene of serious trouble during the heyday of Captain Swing.[2] The story of Swing has been told superbly, but the authors recognized that research among local records might revise their story in detail. This is certainly the case in East Anglia.

For example, the presence of (and hostility to) itinerant Irish workers may have been greater, as a cause of unrest, than has hitherto been realized. At Walton, near Peterborough, a crowd of 30 labourers armed with sickles assembled in July 1831 to attack the Irish. 'There is a strong feeling existing among the labourers against the employment of the Irish, and several petty outrages have occurred', said the *Cambridge Chronicle* on 5 August. The same issue reported that labourers at St. Ives, seeing Irishmen at work, had threatened to 'split their skulls'. Later James Stearn, Thomas Whinnel and William Harradine were charged at the Cambridgeshire Sessions with 'conspiring to raise the rate of wages in the parish of Trumpington'. Stearn was said to have declared during the harvest that the labourers would 'drive all the Irishmen from the village, and . . . that a quantity of hedge and fold stakes in his possession were for that purpose'. Later, a crowd waited on Colonel Pemberton's overseer and 'demanded of him to turn the Irishmen from his barn'.[3]

---

[1] Quoted in the *Cambridge Chronicle*, 5 Oct. 1850.
[2] For which see A. J. Peacock, *Bread or Blood* (1965), and E. J. Hobsbawm and G. Rudé, *Captain Swing* (1969).
[3] *Cambridge Chronicle*, 26 Oct. 1832. The incidents had occurred in July.

The Irish only seemed to rouse the ire of the labourers in years of great stress (like 1821, 1830, 1838 and 1842), and do not seem to have been a continuous object of attack. They were a relatively new (post-war) phenomenon, like the threshing machines. During the reign of Swing, however, more traditional forms of 'political' activity were still present. For example, in February 1830 the 'very improper custom' of 'forestalling the market' was said to be prevalent at King's Lynn, and in September the market was thrown into confusion when

a host of coal-porters assembled for the purpose of causing the millers to reduce the flour 10s. per sack. The attack was very formidable, and had, in part, the desired effect. Some of the millers had the good fortune to escape, but others of them fell into the hands of the lawless band, who, by threats and menaces, forced a reduction of 7s. . . .[1]

After the suppression of Captain Swing the more traditional forms of protest—like those above—declined and eventually disappeared. They were replaced by other forms of protest. But the more one reads the local press, the more one realizes that many of the rick burnings and farm fires were simply the result of personal pique. How many? It is impossible to tell, except when the culprits responsible were caught, but the proportion must be very high—perhaps as high as a third or a half. And if this is so it must affect one's interpretation of working class solidarity, and 'political' behaviour.

When Richard Knights, a 53-year-old pauper, set fire to an overseer's stacks at Guilden Morden in December 1832, he was carrying out an oft-uttered threat, because he had been refused relief. He had had a personal hate against Butterfield, the overseer, and had been heard to say that Butterfield 'was a d——d bad one to the poor' and that 'he . . . wished all the farmers were in h—l, he wished they were all to be hung, and he was to be Jack Ketch over them.'[2] Dozens of people like Knights were caught and tried in the east in the first half of the nineteenth century. There are obvious difficulties in interpreting their behaviour. Should incidents like that at Guilden Morden, for example, be used in an assessment of the amount of 'political' activity in an area? The answer in this case is probably that it should—Knights was expressing generally held views about the administration of the Poor Law. Stephen Spicer (aged 24),

[1] *Cambridge Chronicle*, 12 and 26 Feb. and 3 Sept. 1830.
[2] Knights was alleged to have done £1,500 worth of damage; but he was acquitted. Butterfield's property had already been attacked earlier—*Cambridge Chronicle*, 7 Dec. 1832 and 15 March 1833.

who wrote a moving 'Swing' letter threatening to set fire to the property of two farmers in Wicken 'for Fallen pore mens wages to nine shillings a wheak', was doing so too.[1] They were behaving in a way their class behaved frequently, adopting methods that were effective and reasonably free from the possibility of detection. Inarticulately, maybe, but they were expressing in their personal actions the feelings of resentment of their class.

Two of the best known arsonists in Cambridgeshire, William Reader (aged 26) and William Turner (aged 22) were of this kind. They were tried at the Cambridgeshire Assizes in August 1829 for setting fire to a haulm stack and a barn, the property of William Chalk of Linton. Reader was denounced to the authorities by one of the few informers there were, Robert Casbolt, his brother-in-law, who received a reward of £300. Chalk, the farmer, was an overseer who had once employed both Reader and Turner, the latter as a bricklayer's labourer, until he received 'certain information' and discharged him 'from that work'. According to Casbolt the labourers 'stood under the vestry window of the meeting-house and heard . . . Chalk say he was not afraid of any man', whereupon Reader said that as 'Turner and himself had agreed to have a blaze somewhere, and as Mr. Chalk had offended them, they determined on setting fire to his stacks'. Reader and Turner were found guilty, but owing to legal arguments were not sentenced until March 1830. They were executed in Cambridge in the following April. 'No earthly motive can be ascribed for this diabolical revenge', a pamphlet account of the executions said, 'but that Mr. Chalk had made himself obnoxious while in the character of overseer of the poor.'[2]

But there must have been, among the labourers never discovered and brought to trial, many who committed their crimes for reasons which, by *no* stretch of the imagination, can be interpreted as 'political' or as being a part of a running protest against society. The researcher looking at the village of Great Shelford, Cambridgeshire, in 1833 would be impressed, initially, by the extraordinary amount of arson that went on there. At the Cambridgeshire Assizes in August of that year, however, it was revealed that no less than a dozen fires at Great Shelford

[1] *Cambridge Chronicle*, 15 March 1833.

[2] *William Reader, William Turner, and David Howard, who suffered on Saturday, April 3, 1830, in front of the County Gaol at Cambridge, for wilfully and maliciously destroying several stacks of corn.* Also the *Cambridge Chronicle*, 7 Aug. 1829, 26 March and 9 April 1830.

had been started by one man, John Stallan, a pyromaniac. Stallan was executed in December 1833, after giving the reasons for his actions: '. . . he had no malice or ill will against any of the persons whose property he set on fire, . . . his only object was to occasion a necessity for working the [fire] engine, for which, as one of the assistants, he received 6s. 6d. each time.'[1]

The case of John Stallan, in itself insignificant, might perhaps serve to correct a tendency to assume that all violence had a basis of social criticism. A look at two fenland villages, rather later in the century, might equally correct the tendency to assume, as contemporaries did, that all the arson was committed by the rural poor. Waterbeach, on the edge of the fens, was a village with 814 inhabitants at the time of the 1821 census. Nonconformity was strongly established there, and from early in the century there had been attempts (well publicized in the press) to provide allotments and smallholdings for the labourers.[2] From about 1843 fires started with awful regularity, often on property belonging to the Densons, a family long well-disposed towards the poor. By the end of September 1845 there had been nine incidents, reported the *Chronicle*. And on 16 October there were two fires in one night, one on property belonging to William Denson. Suspicion fell on William's son-in-law, Robert Fromant, who had insured the cottages and out-buildings that had been destroyed for £120. An 'inquest' was held at the request of the Royal Farmer's Insurance Society, which brought in a 'verdict' that Fromant had acted 'reprehensibly', but Fromant does not appear to have been prosecuted.[3]

Events in Soham were even more striking. Although surrounded by riotous villages, it was a relatively quiet place, by local standards, until late 1845. In December a stackyard attached to a brewery was destroyed; in May tremendous damage was done to a five-storey mill, and two weeks later the same property was fired again. Suspicion naturally fell on the

[1] *Cambridge Chronicle*, 24 May, 7 and 14 June, 2 and 16 Aug., 13 Dec. 1833. As the years passed, Stallan gained stature as a folk hero: in 1845 Charles Mayes was bent on imitating him; when caught, he committed suicide, but before he died said, 'Stallion [sic] set fire to 10 stacks before he was found out, and then the —— confessed when at the station-house'—*ibid.*, 14 June 1845.

[2] *Cambridge Chronicle*, 20 Oct. 1820 and 23 Aug. 1822; A. J. Peacock, 'The Revolt of the Field in East Anglia', in *The Luddites and Other Essays*, ed. Lionel Munby (1971), esp. pp. 177–9.

[3] *Cambridge Chronicle*, 20 Sept. and 18 Oct. 1845, 3 Jan. and 14 Feb. 1846.

labourers, and at the Summer Assizes no fewer than five were tried (and acquitted). In July the village was devastated—a pub and 13 houses were burnt down, 79 people made homeless and five acres laid waste. Again an inquest was held, a fortnight later, by the local vicar, several farmers and a deputation from the Suffolk Fire Office. Before them appeared Cornelius Harvey (aged 50), said to have property worth £6,000, and his nephew James Harvey (aged 30), 'yeoman and shopkeeper'. They were charged with attempting to defraud the insurance company; and at subsequent committal proceedings it was established that James had insured some of his property for £350, and that the fires had started in neighbouring buildings. Tried at the Assizes they too were acquitted for lack of conclusive evidence.[1]

Soham not only had its insurance swindlers; it also had its pyromaniacs. At the July Assizes, as has been said, seven people were charged with arson in Soham, yet during the hearings of their cases more fires took place. In August the *Chronicle* reported that a barn had been lit, and only just discovered in time to prevent massive damage—'The town . . . is still under the baleful influence of the incendiary spirit.' In September a stack was fired in 'this dreadfully scourged town' and £400 worth of damage was done. Later in the same month barns and other property belonging to Charles Fyson were destroyed. Although 'the town is rigidly watched every night, and a reward of £200 offered for the conviction of the offender or offenders, not the slightest clue is to be obtained of the malignant and cowardly perpetrator,' reported the *Chronicle*. In March 1847 property worth £1,600 was destroyed and Sarah Munson was arrested. She was the mother of Josiah Munson (aged 24), a local basket maker then in gaol charged (under 9 and 10 Victoria cap. 25) with firing a haulm stack. He was tried at the Cambridgeshire Assizes a week after his mother's arrest, and was found not guilty. At the following Assizes he was charged again with firing a wheat stack in November, and again acquitted for lack of evidence. The grand jury found no true bill against Sarah.[2]

The cases of the Munsons, the Harveys and Fromant show that one has to be cautious in jumping to conclusions about the people responsible and the reasons for much of the arson in rural England. During the forties, when the east's railway

[1] *Ibid.*, 20 Dec. 1845, 16 and 30 May and 4, 11, 18 and 25 July 1846.

[2] *Ibid.*, 8 Aug., 5 and 26 Sept. 1846, 20 and 27 March, and 24 July 1847.

system was being built, railway navvies were employed in large numbers in the area. Their propensity to violence is well known, and they may well have been responsible for more than a little of the unsolved crime in the eastern counties. On 14 June 1844 haulm stacks and property were destroyed at Snailwell, and five railway labourers, all strangers to the county, were committed. A few days later, at the same place, labourers on the Norwich and Brandon line were suspected of more stack fires.[1] In that year no less than 1,200 men were employed on the line between Cambridge and Norwich.

During the trials care was taken not to publicize information that would be of help to incendiaries. Nevertheless we can sometimes learn something of their methods. Munson used peat ('turf coal' that would smoulder for hours) mixed with brimstone and tar. So did David Howard and John Bulman at Badlingham in 1830.[2] A note in the *Chronicle* of 13 January 1844 drew attention to the fact that the advent of lucifer matches had made the tasks of people like Munson simpler. 'The old tinder-box, the flint and steel', it said, 'have been discarded, and a sufficient quantity of these matches may be purchased for a penny to lay a whole parish in ruins.'

The chances of detection were remote, and the village arsonist was able to enjoy (usually) the pleasure of acting with impunity. The possibilities of causing tremendous damage added to the effectiveness of his actions. The files of the local papers show how unwilling the labourers were to help their employers douse the fires, how they made a spectacle of their employer's embarrassment, and how rudimentary fire-fighting equipment was— if it existed at all. Very few engines are reported active in the villages before the 1840s. Thereafter they are reported a little more frequently. In January 1843 an incendiary set fire to property at Moulton and a fire-fighting appliance was sent from Spalding—the first fire engine ever seen in the village. Stretham was devastated in May 1844 (this was not a case of arson) and there was no fire engine in the village. One eventually arrived from Haddenham—too late, and after £15,000 to £20,000 worth of damage had been done. Later in the same year fire-fighting equipment was sent from Cambridge to Harlton—only to find, a common occurrence, that there was no water available. A week later engines were sent to Whepstead—without pipes. Eaton Socon was a village that was continually ravaged by

---

[1] *Ibid.*, 22 June 1844.
[2] *Ibid.*, 26 March 1830, and 24 July 1847 (supplement).

incendiaries throughout the whole period covered by this chapter, and it obtained an engine by the 1840s. In August 1846 this was sent to St. Neot's where a steam mill and warehouses had been fired, and it would not work. Rather worse, in the following month it was sent to a barn fire in Eaton Socon itself —and again it refused to function.[1]

Until fire-fighting equipment became more efficient and more plentiful there was little hope of the farmer saving his property —and the labourers massed, to enjoy the spectacle of watching their employers' wealth go up in smoke, in the same ritualized way, very often, that they had destroyed machines in Swing's time or broken open the shops and mills in 1816. The labourers of Coton, and some of their neighbours who had gone to enjoy the sights, simply 'looked on with apathy and indifference' as flames destroyed property there. At Great Barford, in 1838, farm buildings and stacks were completely destroyed, and £1,000 of damage was done, while a crowd of 1,500 watched, and did nothing more—'one-fourth . . . in a state of intoxication'. In November 1838 there was a serious fire on a farm belonging to the Duke of Rutland at Wood Ditton; '. . . we regret to [say] that there was not a general willingness on the part of the parishioners to exert themselves', commented the *Chronicle*. At Keysoe, 'The most disgraceful scenes occurred' at a fire as 'not only men, but women, rejoiced in the work of destruction'. And at Gravely 'The conduct of most of the labourers [at the scene of a fire] was most disgraceful; they not only refused to work, but indulged in the grossest language and jests, and appeared to delight in the calamity; many of them assembled at the public-house, and were drinking and singing during the raging of the fire.' It was not unknown for the hoses feeding the engines to be cut, as at Elm in 1832.[2] Also, though plundering was comparatively rare, it sometimes took place.[3]

Indeed it was so rare for the labourers to help douse the fires that, when they did, it was regarded as an indication of guilt! Gilpin Reynolds, an agricultural labourer who had been employed on the roads, was arrested for setting fire to property of a Mr. Hase, a farmer at Corpustye and an overseer of the poor, in November 1833. The jurors, 'all farmers but one', found Reynolds guilty and he was executed before a crowd of between

[1] *Ibid.*, 14 Jan. 1843, 4 May and 5 and 12 Oct. 1844, 22 Aug. and 5 Sept. 1846.
[2] *Ibid.*, 10 Dec. 1830, 30 Nov. 1832, 27 Oct. and 10 Nov. 1838, 10 Dec. 1842, and 6 Dec. 1845.
[3] See e.g. the *Chronicle's* report of 22 June 1844.

30,000 and 40,000 on 12 April 1834. Reynolds had helped with the fire fighting. 'This assiduity was', the *Chronicle* recorded, 'according to the practice of late years, pressed as a suspicious circumstance against him, and a cover for guilt.' Poor Reynolds confessed his guilt for the Hase fire, and he may well have had claim to a record longer than Stallan's. 'Nor ought it to be forgotten that there have been about 20 fires in the immediate neighbourhood of Corpustye', a report said, 'of most of which he has been very strongly suspected. . . . No fire has taken place since his committment'.[1]

How much rural crime of this kind was there, and were there peaks of violence? It is well known that the answer to the second question is that there were. 1816 was a violent year. The early 1830s, the age of Captain Swing, were violent years. And so were the years when the new Poor Law was being implemented. An oft-heard generalization is that the new Poor Law was introduced peacefully into the south, at a propitious time, and while the labourers were cowed from the vengeance doled out after Swing, but violently in the north. Whatever the truth as regards the south, in the east the Poor Law was opposed, no more effectively, but just as violently, as it was in the north.

Poor Law riots, and attacks on Poor Law officials *before* the 1834 reform, were as common in East Anglia as they were anywhere; not as common as other forms of riot perhaps, but common nevertheless. The Speenhamland system of relief had spread throughout the whole of East Anglia by the early years of the nineteenth century, with all the consequent effects of demoralization, and those effects were well catalogued in reports of the time. The labourers regarded relief as a right and they were prepared to act violently to assert or obtain those rights. At Mildenhall, in 1828, a Mr. T. Kitchener was fired at. Kitchener was an overseer who had 'no doubt excited the ill-will of' some of the unemployed (who engaged 'in poaching, thieving, and all the other violations of the law which idleness engenders') in his 'difficult task of administering the parish funds, and in endeavouring to put down their disorders'. At the Cambridgeshire Assizes in August 1833 William Peachey (aged 42), James Poulter (aged 40), William Billett (aged 26) and Nathaniel Billett (aged 23) all received one month's hard labour after being found guilty of riotous assembly and assault on William Polley, 'a person who contract[ed] for farming the poor at Newport, Essex'. The incident took place at Hinxton where Polley had gone to act as security for one Jenkins, 'who was

[1] *Ibid.*, 4 and 18 April 1834.

going to farm the poor of that parish at so much a-head per week'. Polley said he did 'the same at Newport, for which he got £700 per annum'. Polley was at the Red Lion Inn when a crowd assembled outside shouting 'Old Polley, carrion, dead horse!' and 'Old Polley, fetch him out.' Some of the crowd carried a halter saying, 'He shall have it—it's for Old Polley.' Eventually a gun was fired at him through a window of the inn.[1]

One of the very worst of the Poor Law riots occurred at Bassingbourn in 1832 and led to the appearance at the Cambridgeshire Assizes of four labourers and a woman on charges of assaulting James Unitt, a superintendent to the poor at Baldock. The parish officers had met and decided to enter 'into a plan to better the condition of the poor', and called in Unitt for advice. The poor let it be known that they would not allow him to stay in the village 'as they were certain he had come to take away their children, &c.'. A huge crowd met the superintendent and escorted him to the Black Bull where he met the magistrates. Eventually the doors were broken down and a crowd, led by Martha Cubiss (aged 50) 'with a spade in her hand', entered the inn. They

immediately seized Mr. Unitt, and dragged him into the street were [sic] he was assailed by pelting and persecution, and cries of 'murder him! Burke him! take him to the horse-pond and finish him.' [They pursued Unitt] assailing him, for two miles. His coat was torn from his back, he was pelted with missiles of the most offensive kind, and beaten severely. Several persons . . . wished to receive him in their houses, but the mob formed barriers which prevented his availing himself of their friendly shelter. His horse was brought, but they swore, 'that if he got on him, the horse should die as well as he', and he desisted from mounting him. He was bruised from head to heel, and kept to his bed 3 days, in consequence of the injuries he received.[2]

By midsummer 1835, Poor Law riots against the new system took on a serious aspect in the east. In June prolonged disturbances occurred in north-west Norfolk. The Poor Law authorities there directed that persons applying for relief 'should receive at least part of their allowance in kind'. Five or six labourers of Great Bircham 'were offered tickets for shop-goods and flour which they swore they would not receive, and declared that the system would be resisted by the whole parish'. This

[1] *Ibid.*, 25 Jan. 1828 and 2 Aug. 1833.
[2] *Ibid.*, 10 Feb. and 16 March 1832.

was on a Saturday. On the following Monday all the labourers struck and the important tasks of haymaking and turnip sowing were held up. On 29 June a blackleg was sent to Great Bircham, but both he and his prospective employer were severely beaten up. Eventually, the governor of Walsingham Bridewell was sent with a caravan to arrest the leaders, but he and his officers were brutally attacked and forced to retreat from the village, leaving a Mr. Tilney, one of their injured, behind. Later a pitched battle took place and 'after great efforts [Tilney] was rescued in a dreadfully injured state, having received seven wounds on the head alone, one of them three inches long.'

Following the battle with the prison officers the windows of many farm houses at Great Bircham were broken, and eventually the 'Rainham and Melton troops of Yeomanry and the Preventive men from the coast were sent for'. Between 11 and 12 o'clock some 800 to 900 men 'marched under order to the house of Mr. Kitton, one of the overseers; every door and window was immediately demolished, the furniture broken into pieces and piled on the floor, and set on fire by means of books. The inmates fled', leaving Tilney in a back room. Later the house of the second overseer, Hegbin, in bed and also injured, was attacked and destroyed, as was other property. The crowd then marched to Bircham Tofts where Kitton's son-in-law's house was destroyed. The Preventive men arrived the day after these disturbances and kept the peace until the Wednesday, when a detachment of Inniskillen dragoons from Norwich arrived and were stationed in the village.[1]

In May 1835 a Poor Law riot took place at Ampthill. A union had been formed of which Ampthill was the central parish, and on 14 May the guardians met there 'for the purpose of hearing the complaints of the paupers residing within the union, and transacting the general business of the confederation'. A crowd of between 200 and 300 assembled, angry because, like the labourers at Bircham, they had heard that the guardians 'were inclined to act upon that portion of the new statute which authorizes the giving of relief in clothing and food, and not in money'. The guardians addressed the crowd and were met with shouts of 'Blood and bread,' 'All money,' and 'No bread.' H. Musgrave, a guardian and a J.P., read the Riot Act; but notices saying that 'any one remaining in a state of riot or tumult for one hour would be guilty of a capital felony' were pulled down. Arrests were made, rescues effected, and the work-

[1] *Ibid.*, 10 July 1835.

house windows broken. Eventually John Burgoyne, William Setting, Richard Warner and John Buxford 'were capitally indicted' at the Bedfordshire Midsummer Assizes, 'for feloniously remaining in a state of riot for the space of one hour after proclamation made and the reading of the Riot Act'.[1] At the end of the year there were 'tumults' at Ipswich which 'spread their contagious influence amongst the pauper population of the adjoining districts'. Labourers in the villages of the Hoxne and Blything Unions also caused serious disturbances and did great damage.[2] But the Poor Law riots died away as quickly in the rural areas as they did in the northern industrial districts, although conditions in the workhouses and the behaviour of some officials kept hatred of the new system alive.

There were peaks of riotous activity, then, in the east—in 1816, in the early 1830s and in 1835 and '36. On all these occasions general causes of dissatisfaction were present—extremely bad harvests, for example, like those of 1829 and '30, or the creation of Poor Law unions. But they were only exceptional years in the *amount* of violence that took place. No year in the first half of the nineteenth century was a quiet year in the east. Every year was violent, and the amount of violence that took place was very great indeed. It may have been localized, and it may have been a reaction against local conditions—conditions that were changing rapidly and, of course, at an uneven rate over the area. It may even have been simply the result of the fact that objects to attack were more abundant in some places than in others. Some villages became known as trouble spots and conditions in them would be worth studying in detail (though they might only reveal the existence of a John Stallan). Exning, for example, where the great lock-out of the 1870s started, was such a place. In 1819 and '20, the *Chronicle* repeatedly reported cases of arson at Exning, and on one occasion printed a long list of incidents that had occurred there between 1808 and August 1821. In one month in 1818 there were five incendiary fires in the village, and a barn worth £400, the parsonage, and several cottages were completely destroyed. A Bow Street officer was taken down; but no one ever seems to have been brought to book.[3]

The causes of discontent were those described by Dr. Hobs-

[1] *Ibid.*, 24 July 1835.
[2] *Ibid.*, 1 Jan. and 6 May 1836.
[3] *Ibid.*, 28 Aug. 1818 and 14 Sept. 1821; see also e.g. 23 July 1819 and 23 June 1820.

bawm and Professor Rudé: unemployment—or underemployment—which varied from place to place and occurred at different times in different places; machinery, which, of course, became more odious when unemployment became severe; and that general feeling of alienation and insecurity which the labourers must have felt as they lived through the transition from a paternalistic form of society to that based on the economics 'of the free market'.[1] Machine smashing, Poor Law rioting and arson were common forms of protest (strikes were extremely uncommon except during the Swing era) throughout the first half of the last century. But these do not exhaust the list by any means. There were other forms of protest—sheep stealing for example, which reached epidemic proportions by mid-century.

It has already been mentioned that parts of the eastern counties—and the Norfolk marshlands in particular—were noted for the fine sheep reared there in the nineteenth century. The crime of sheep stealing was by no means non-existent in the east in the early years of the century,[2] but it was relatively rare. It does not make its appearance, really, until after the suppression of Captain Swing. It is almost as if the labourers, thwarted in their attempts to obtain redress by overt means, consciously decided to adopt guerilla tactics to cow or repay their employers for docking their pay, for using machinery, or for helping in the administration of poor relief under the hated new system. Henceforth rick burning, that old remedy, would replace striking, and sheep stealing was an addition to the labourers' repertoire of social crime. But there was another reason for the increase. In 1832 the reformers in Parliament succeeded 'in securing the abolition of capital punishment for horse, sheep or cattle stealing'.[3]

Sheep stealing had its 'high season'—when the creatures were grown and when the nights were long—and nowhere was affected worse than the villages near Wisbech in the marshland, places like Elm, Outwell, Emneth, Walsoken and Newton. The files of the *Cambridge Chronicle* contain dozens of reports of incidents there. (And not only of sheep stealing.) Take the period from 23 November 1832 to the end of 1834 for example.

[1] See E. P. Thompson, *The Making of the English Working Class* (1963), p. 67.
[2] See e.g. the report from Long Sutton in the *Cambridge Chronicle*, 11 Dec. 1829.
[3] L. Radzinowicz, *A History of Criminal Law*, iv (1968), p. 305.

23 November 1832
    Elm. Three stacks of oats fired. 'There is no doubt but that
    it is the work of an incendiary.' Report of sheep stealing.

30 November 1832
    Elm. Thursday, 22 November, a day of thanksgiving 'for the
    removal of the pestilential disease with which this town and
    neighbourhood has been visited'. Straw stacks belonging to
    William Dow burnt. 'During the time the engine was
    playing upon the fire, one of the pipes was cut.'

14 December 1832
    Upwell. Fifth attempt to fire the corn stacks of Thomas Wiles.

1 February 1833
    Newton. Three men named Claypole arrested for sheep stealing.
    (Two were subsequently sentenced to transportation for life.)

1 March 1833
    On Saturday, 17 February two banks belonging to the North
    Level Commissioners were cut. Wednesday, 'a dam which
    protects a farm of Mr. John Marshall's from the inundation
    of the Old Elm Leam, was cut through, which did very great
    damage to his property'.

29 March 1833
    Wisbech. Drainage water mill, the property of Joseph New-
    sham, fired and destroyed on 19 March.

10 May 1833
    Sheep stealing still prevalent around Wisbech.

5 July 1833
    Wisbech. 'Sheep-stealing continues unabated in this neigh-
    bourhood; so much so indeed, that many farmers are obliged
    to hire men to watch their flocks at night.'

30 August 1833
    'Sheep stealing continues to be practised in Marshland to an
    alarming extent, and so cautious are the depredators that
    they invariably elude detection.'

4 October 1833
    'The midnight sheep-slaughterer has been again at work in
    the parish of Elm. On Saturday last, Mr. John Dow, who, we
    have before recorded as a sufferer, lost a valuable wether.'

13 December 1833
    Walpole St. Andrew. Fire in stack-yard.

31 January 1834
    Downham Market. Robert Verguson, William Kent and Robert
    Rust, all of Hilgay, caught and charged with killing sheep.

28 February 1834
    'Extensive as the practise of sheep slaughtering has been in

this neighbourhood, we never had a more dreadful catalogue to present than the following.' 17 and 18 February incidents at Outwell. 22 and 23 February incidents at Upwell, sufferer John Hodson. 24 and 25 February incidents at Elm, sufferer John Dow, 'who, we have several times before recorded as a sufferer'.

4 April 1834
Elm. Trees cut down.

25 April 1834
Elm. Sheep stealing.

16 May 1834
Thomas More of Whitehall, 'who had previously suffered much from damage done to his hovels and fences, had a sheep slaughtered' in one of his fields and a cow maimed.

30 May 1834
Report that the crime of sheep stealing, notwithstanding the offering of rewards, 'increases both in extent and audacity'. Incidents at Outwell and Newton.

8 August 1834
Report saying the local correspondent had been silent on the question of sheep stealing for some time. New outbreak now at Murrow and Needham Hall, and rewards of 10 and 15 guineas offered.

5 September 1834
Sheep killed at Newton.

26 September 1834
Sheep killed at West Walton.

10 October 1834
Sheep stolen at Tydd St. Mary.

24 October 1834
Thomas Jackson arrested for the above offence, given away by a child. (He was subsequently sentenced to transportation for life.)

7 November 1834
Wisbech. 'The system of thieving in this neighbourhood seems to be so well organized that nothing comes amiss or to have any apprehension of detection.' 28 fleeces of wool taken at West Walton.

21 November 1834
Stack fire at Tydd Marsh, Friday last.

These were not exceptional times in any way at all. 'Few days pass over without some account' of sheep-stealing, it was reported from Elm on 17 April 1835; 'the number of severe examples which have of late been made, seems to have given it but a very short check.' Three years later the Elm Association [for the Prosecution of Felons?] confessed that theirs was 'a neighbourhood where lawless depredators [had] continued their nefarious practices till locality and crime [had] become, as it were, identic'.[1] So it went on into the 1840s, with people like John Dow of Elm[2] and William Bell being regularly robbed—Bell of Wisbech was referred to on 14 May 1842 as 'an extensive and frequent sufferer'.

The Marshland quietened down around 1843. Could it have been because the labourers found employment on the railways then being built there? But by that time sheep stealing had spread over all the eastern counties. Whittlesea became as violent a centre of the crime as Elm had been. 'Scarcely a night passes without a depredation of this nature being committed' in Whittlesea, it was reported in January 1845. 'We regret to find the continuation' of sheep stealing during a season when 'labour is more abundant', and when there was opportunity for work on the railroads, another report from Whittlesea said. There was an Association offering a reward of £45 for information that would lead to a conviction for the offences, but 'no one has ever yet "peached"', moaned the *Chronicle*. Whittlesea was a large centre of population with some 7,000 inhabitants; Elm, Outwell and Emneth were small (with between 1,000 and 2,000); Walsoken and Upwell had over 2,000 each. Sheep stealing was common to them all, and it spread throughout all the eastern counties—Huntingdonshire, Cambridgeshire, Suffolk and Bedford (where Eaton Socon was prominent). It spread with alarming rapidity and it remained an everyday occurrence right up to 1850 and beyond. At the Cambridgeshire Assizes of March 1846 no less than 12 men were charged with sheep stealing, receiving sentences ranging from ten years' transportation to six months' hard labour.[3]

But is it reasonable to classify the crime of sheep stealing as a crime of protest? Certainly there were gangs at work, like the one which worked in Burwell and Wicken and had an arrangement with local butchers who gave 10s. apiece, 'if they got the

[1] *Cambridge Chronicle*, 21 April 1838—the reports do not give the Association's full title.

[2] On 21 Jan. 1837 the *Chronicle* mentioned that Dow had lost a sheep 'under the usual circumstances', and the same report recorded the killing of three sheep the following night at Emneth and of one at Terrington.

[3] *Cambridge Chronicle*, 25 Jan., 7 June and 30 Aug. 1845, 21 March 1846 (supplement).

skins off clean', and the Hatfield Broad Oak gang. The latter operated around Eastwick (Hertfordshire) and consisted of two farmers and their servant. Sheep stealing was prevalent in Bedfordshire in 1834, particularly near Ampthill. '. . . from the workmanlike manner in which the animal is skinned, &c., it is generally thought', the *Chronicle* said, 'they are stolen for sale in the London markets.'[1] Then again there must have been scores of incidents, perhaps the vast majority, when animals were stolen simply to feed a labourers' family. But, although the labourers stole to feed themselves and their families, this does not rule out the possibility of the act becoming one of protest as well. And this is the way the crime must be seen. The methods used make the point.

In the first years after 1832 sheep were simply slaughtered and taken away from the fields; but within a very short time a new method came into existence—as much the result of work study as radicalism, it must be admitted, but having the same pleasurable effects as the threatening letter left at the side of a burning haystack. By this method the creature was killed, skinned, and only the best cuts of meat were taken—the head, skin, fat and entrails were left as an awful reminder of the power of the labourers. '. . . the new system of sheep stealing was practised upon Mr. Stranger, of Tid St. Mary; by carrying away only the legs and shoulders,' the *Chronicle* reported on 10 October 1834. 'Mr S. has been a considerable sufferer.' 'As the season advances the thieves become more dainty' a report from Wisbech said. 'Our thieves continue to live delicately' the same correspondent wrote a few weeks later. Sometimes the creatures were simply killed and left lying in the fields. Henry Smith of Gamlingay had eight sheep slaughtered and left on his farm; 'The offence [was] supposed to have been committed out of malice, Mr. Smith being a guardian.' The throat of Robert Sear's breeding ewe was cut at Upwell. Sometimes threatening or mocking letters were left behind. In Bedford, where sheep stealing was 'very prevalent' in 1836, sheep were stolen at Tempsford and a note was left affixed to a gate:

> *Sir, your mutton's very good*
> *And we are very poor,*
> *When we have eaten this all up*
> *We'll then come and fetch some more.*[2]

[1] *Cambridge Chronicle*, 12 Dec. 1834, 21 March 1846 (supplement).
[2] *Ibid.*, 4 Dec. 1835, 15 Jan., 13 and 20 May, 3 June 1836.

If there could be arguments about sheep stealing being a crime of protest, there can be none concerning the hideous business of cattle maiming. There is no other way of explaining some of the dreadful incidents that occurred. Again the crime increased in the early thirties, and was widespread—though the marshlands once more saw it at its most bestial. 'The diabolical practice of cutting and maiming cattle seems in the western part of this county [Norfolk] to have in some degree taken the place of incendiarism,' the *Chronicle* reported in November 1834. At Littleport a cow belonging to William Gillett, an overseer, was disembowelled. A shepherd going round a farm at Counter's Doles, one mile from Whittlesea, found that 36 lambhogs had been driven into a fold and stabbed, many to death, and three horses and six bullocks had had their hind legs cut between the hock and the fetlock. And at Worlington, early in 1836, on William Poulter's farm, it was discovered that 'two cows and a filly had been stabbed, a sheep's throat cut, a donkey much injured, and a number of implements cut in pieces.' At Walsoken, in one week, John Patrick's poultry were all stolen and found with their necks broken, and a few nights later horses were bled. William Shelton (aged 36) was charged with drowning fifty sheep, the property of his employer, Samuel Bradford of Downham, in February 1839. W. Layton, acting chairman of the Ely Union, had three bullocks poisoned at Woodhouse.[1] Horses were 'docked' or 'tailed' at Elm and Ely, and in February 1841 the tails were cut off two cows belonging to a farmer at Outwell and the leg of another was 'nearly severed'.[2] At the Assizes for Cambridgeshire in March 1848 William Barlow (aged 22) received 12 months' hard labour for maiming cattle belonging to William Gittus of Snailwell.[3] Barlow, one of very few persons caught and tried for maiming, 'said he did it when the devil was in him'.[4]

The crimes of sheep stealing, cattle maiming and arson were all forms of protest, and were clandestine. The Poor Law riot,

[1] *Ibid.*, 10 Jan. and 14 Nov. 1834, 11 Dec. 1835, 15 Jan. 1836, 30 March 1839 (supplement), 1 Feb. 1840.

[2] *Ibid.*, 24 Feb. 1838, 6 Feb. 1841, 14 Jan. 1843—horse hair from the dockings was sold (12 Feb. 1830).

[3] Gittus was a 'regular sufferer' (see also e.g. *Cambridge Chronicle*, 22 June and 3 Aug. 1844). Another such was William Ball, a farmer of Stapleford; some of his sheep were killed on 12, 14, 16 and 18 May 1836, and the following September he was severely beaten up while riding home (*ibid.*, 27 May and 9 Sept. 1836).

[4] *Cambridge Chronicle*, 25 March 1848 (supplement).

the bread riot, the machine smashing and striking of the 1830s, were overt crowd activities. There were still other forms of overt violent protest in the east. If the labourers' traditional rights were threatened in the matter of gleaning, for example, serious trouble could flare up—and did.

Gleanings were an important item in the labourer's existence, particularly in a bad year. They were a right he had had from antiquity, he reckoned, and the practice was regulated by custom. In August 1842 Hannah Turner, Hannah Lusking, Mary Ann Perkins, Mary Perkins and Emily White were charged with assaulting Thomas Simmons, a farmer, in a dispute over gleanings from his land. Simmons argued with 'divers females' of the parish of Little Badow who, he said, had begun gleaning before the corn was cleared. Simmons declared he would 'dew-rake' his fields and collect up what normally went to the gleaners, and this he proceeded to do. The women decided to exert rough justice on the farmer, 'who they considered had deprived them of their long-established right'; and when he rode into one of his fields he was met by a crowd of over 100 and stoned. The ladies decided 'to unhorse' Simmons 'and inflict punishment upon his person—indeed something shocking to ears polite was more than once mentioned'. Each of the accused was fined one shilling and costs, a total of 6s. 10d. In August 1844 there was an affray between the gleaners of Ely and Witchford which ended disastrously—'There is a great jealousy of gleaners going out of their own parish,' the *Chronicle* noted. In 1846 Richard Webb (a rag and bone man) and others contravened gleaning customs by entering an allotment before permission had been given. 100 women and children forcibly took the day's gleaning from them and ceremoniously threw it around the field. At the Saffron Walden petty sessions in 1847 six women were charged with breaking a hedge and doing 3d. worth of damage. They had been told not to glean in the field and they and 40 others had forced their way through a hedge. The case was dismissed and a great victory was reckoned to have been won.[1]

Enclosure riots were also a common feature of life in the eastern counties. By its very nature enclosure was not likely to start a general movement of protest. It often came unexpectedly and village by village—but in many places the labourers protested, as ineffectively as they did against the machines, in the

[1] *Cambridge Chronicle*, 27 Aug. 1842, 31 Aug. 1844, 15 Aug. 1846, 25 Sept. 1847.

only way they knew. Labourers of Cowlinge were indicted at Assizes in 1817 for 'assembling in a body on the Green in that parish, and breaking down the fences of several inclosures on the wastes or green'. In 1825 and 1826 there was trouble in the large village of Chesterton, which led to the appearance at Quarter Sessions of four labourers who were fined between £5 and £20 and ordered 'to enter into securities for their good behaviour for two years' in sums of £50 and £100. '. . . in their zeal to remove what they considered to be an encroachment upon the waste lands of the parish', said the *Chronicle*, they 'not only levelled the fences, &c, but committed a violent assault upon John Cross, Mary Cross, and William Cross, by whom they were resisted.' When the enclosures of Stretham and Thetford commons were proposed, 12 or 14 armed men prevented the requisite notices being posted on the church door at Thetford. The official went back to Ely where special constables were sworn in and taken to the village. They were met by a crowd of 150. 'After a variety of attempts to obtain an entry into the chapel yard, all of which were ineffectual, the police were forced to retreat . . .' As late as 1844 fences enclosing two acres at Folksworth were broken down.[1]

Enclosure officials were an obvious object of hatred, as were the overseers. Village pinders also featured as the objects of bitter attacks. The pinder often acted in disputes over rents, church rates and tithes and was hated as much by nonconformist farmers as by the working class. In June 1832 horses had been taken from the village of Tydd in the marshland, 'in consequence of a seizure for rent', and had been impounded in Wisbech. This had thrown 'a considerable number of men out of work', and on the 15th a crowd of bankers had marched on Wisbech 'for the purpose of recovering' the impounded animals. 'Their patience . . . failing them . . . they attacked the stables, and after forcing off the lock . . . seized and gallopped off with them . . .' Three months later, at the same place, 'one of those disgraceful scenes of Irish origin occurred in the Sheep Market' when four sheep belonging to Joshua Bland ('a weak, litigious old man', the *Chronicle* called him, 'the tool of crafty designing knaves') were seized for tithe. A great crowd turned up and stopped the sale.[2]

Six years earlier, in a village in Huntingdonshire, a pounding gave rise to a serious riot which showed how easily one incident could trigger off another. The pinder impounded 24 geese

[1] *Ibid.*, 8 Aug. 1817, 20 Jan. 1826, 29 Nov. 1833, 30 Nov. 1844.
[2] *Ibid.*, 22 June and 14 Sept. 1832.

belonging to Edward Barnes, not for any great issue of conscience, but for 'feeding about the Town Street'. Mrs. Barnes had to pay 2s. to get them out; and then events took a very nasty turn. Mrs. Barnes told the pinder that 'he might put sixpence to [the fine], and buy a frock for his father's bastard'; and the following day

a mob assembled before his father's door, with an effigy representing a man carried on a pole. Some kept throwing it on the ground, others cried out don't hurt the old fellow, he will be able to get another child. On the Monday night following, the mob again assembled when an effigy representing a child and carried by boys, was brought with great shouting and noise before his father's house.

Evidence was given that the old man who had caught the backlash of feeling against the pinder had been responsible for a 'natural child' when he was over 60. John Blackman, a witness, said he had heard there was a *'maulkin* at Sarah Stretton's house . . . it represented a man—and a mob was crowding round the house crying "Bring him out ".' The crowd dropped the maulkin on the ground and pulled it to pieces. Then 'George Saunders coming up with a brush in his hand, said let us whitewash the old fellow, and bring some string, we will tie him together—they did so, and carried on the effigy.' Mrs. Barnes seems to have been behind all the trouble, and she had organized the making of the maulkin—'calling it her servant Bridget's bastard'. The unfortunate Bridget seems to have approved of what went on since she 'put a saucepan and [a] spoon in the child's hand'.[1]

A report from the Isle of Ely Sessions of April 1839 suggests that the kind of traditional behaviour meted out to people like the virile old man at Yaxley was not uncommon well into the century. Matthew and Isaac Glitherow, James Brown and John Timms were charged with riot at that trouble spot of Whittlesea. '. . . a procession of idle boys and young men went round the town', the *Cambridge Chronicle* recorded, 'on the occasion of some misconduct of a married man, for which it is customary in many places to what is called "ride for them", beating kettles, canns, &c.' On this occasion a horse had taken fright, and had bolted and killed a bystander. All those charged, however, were acquitted.[2]

At the beginning of the century heavy sentencing was the

[1] *Cambridge Chronicle*, 16 Jan. 1824.
[2] *Ibid.*, 13 April 1839.

principal, almost the only, check on unlimited crime and law-lessness. At major trials some defendants were deliberately selected for exemplary punishment and a great show of mercy then made to the rest—of 65 prisoners arraigned before the Norfolk County Sessions in January 1831 for machine smashing, one was sentenced to 14 and eight to seven years' transportation, while the rest were admonished and let go.[1] In cases of arson judges with frightening regularity warned the convicted that they could expect no mercy, as they were to be made an example of as an awful warning to their confreres. William Reader and William Turner were found guilty of firing haulm stacks. Their indictment was shown to have been wrongly drawn, and this necessitated a second trial. But the judge warned them to pre-pare for death:

I earnestly recommend you to employ all the time thus afforded in repenting your sins. The crime of which you have been convicted is of the deepest dye; it is easily perpetrated, and almost impossible for society to provide against. Rely upon it that if the indictment is found to be good in point of law, the Judge who shall preside at the next assizes will pass upon you the sentence of death, and you will assuredly be executed. If, however, it shall be otherwise, a new and correct bill will be framed, upon which the same evidence as has been given to-day will be adduced against you, and I will leave it to you to say whether you anticipate the same result. I therefore earnestly entreat you to prepare yourselves.

Reader and Turner spent 12 months in prison and eventually received the promised sentence. 'You cannot expect mercy this side of the grave—you *must not* expect it; the gates of mercy are forever closed,' they were told.[2] Dying confessions and scaf-fold repentences were also reported at great length to impress the labourers. George Pulham (aged 22) was executed at Bury in 1835, and addressed the crowds saying, 'Good bye, good bye, and God bless you all—I hope my fate will be a warning to you all, and I hope you gentlemen farmers will give the young men work; it was the want of work that brought me to this.'[3]

On 24 September 1824 the *Chronicle* reminded its readers that

[1] *Cambridge Chronicle*, 21 Jan. 1831. Similarly, in sentencing the Tolpuddle Martyrs, Mr. Baron Williams laid great stress on the deterrent function of punishment: 'The use of all punishment is not with a view to the particular offenders or for the sake of revenge... ; it is for the sake of example'—*The Times*, 21 March 1834, p. 6.

[2] *Cambridge Chronicle*, 7 Aug. 1829 and 26 March 1830.

[3] *Ibid.*, 17 April 1835.

'The *Code Napoleon* awards the punishment of death to six cases only; that of England to 200.' Subsequently the law was softened and the number of capital crimes decreased. Sheep and horse stealing ceased to be capital offences in 1832, and arson followed in 1837 (Lord John Russell choosing to ignore hysterical protests from the rural areas).[1] The usual sentence became something like 20 years' transportation, though transportation for life was not uncommon. As the change was not complemented by better police methods, the result was a sharp rise in the incidence of certain types of offence.[2] Sheep stealing increased, as has been said. There was no comparable growth of arson— many areas had been at saturation point for years. But horse stealing—though this certainly cannot be classified as a crime of protest—definitely increased. It was 'very prevalent', the *Chronicle* reported in 1834, mentioning incidents at Reepham and Tittleshall. Two weeks later it declared that 'horse and sheep stealing is getting to an alarming extent' in Huntingdonshire. The previous month it was stated at a trial that the culprit was a 'horse-fancier' who had personally 'nipped up' 20 horses during his last two years of freedom; these his gang disposed of at from 10 to 40 guineas apiece, sharing the proceeds equally. And in December two members of another gang were

[1] Radzinowicz, *op. cit.*, pp. 305, 321.
[2] Concern for the consequences of the change led to the publication of a number of comparative statistical tables. Thus *P.P.*, 1846 xxxiv, p. 761, gives figures for commitments and executions (in England and Wales) for various offences before and after they ceased to be capital, e.g.:

| | Five years before change | | Five years after |
	Committed	Executed	Committed
Cattle stealing	144	3	119
Sheep stealing	1,221	11	1,320
Horse stealing	990	37	966
Arson	391	42	183

(For more detailed statistics on arson over a slightly longer period, see also *P.P.*, 1844 xxxix, p. 263.)

For an interesting list of rural crimes committed in Leicestershire, see a letter in the *Cambridge Chronicle*, 12 Oct. 1844; and for similar tables before the lifting of the death penalty, see H. W. Woolrych, *The History and Results of the Present Capital Punishments in England* (1832).

taken at Osbournby, near Falkingham (Lincolnshire); they were said to have stolen from 80 to 100 horses in the previous three months, taken them to rented stables and altered their appearance, before selling them (often to the Continent).[1]

That the whole system of policing the villages was hopelessly inefficient was recognized by Charles C. Bailey, the Chief Constable of Cambridge, in a survey of rural police in 1844. To expect the village constable, probably a reluctant shop-keeper or tradesman, to pursue the business of detecting the arsonists and cattle maimers—at great peril to himself, his property and his business—was to be hopelessly naïve. An annual salary of £5, the *Chronicle* pointed out early in 1845,[2] was not enough for rural constables—they would serve summonses, but would definitely not go out looking for fire raisers.[3] The dangers were obvious to everyone. James Weston, the constable of Downham Market, was murdered when he was too diligent in tracing the 'lawless banditti of poachers . . . who . . . infested' the neighbourhood in the late 1820s. The papers are full of such incidents. At Cheveley a constable who had stumbled on a gang of sheep stealers at work was seriously assaulted, and at Hilgay another person was murdered by a poaching gang. A well-known poacher called Adams, who operated in the Flitwick area of Bedfordshire, was said to have met a farmer and told him that it was 'a foolish thing' for farmers and constables 'to interfere with us poor fellows, who go on to your land to shoot a few birds—you may have some injury done to you'. Told of the creation of Protection Societies Adams replied, 'But as yet there is no society to protect a man's life; I would as soon shoot a man as a bird.' True to his word Adams fired at the farmer, half an hour later, from the window of a beer-house. (Taken to task about it Adams cursed himself as 'a d——d fool' for not having shot him in the dark, instead of the light.) Small wonder that, as the *Chronicle* said, 'little or no inquiry is made', in many cases, 'or made only in such a loose manner as leads to no profitable result'.[4]

To supplement the inadequate forces of law and order, private

[1] *Cambridge Chronicle*, 31 Oct., 14 and 28 Nov, 12 Dec. 1834.

[2] *Ibid.*, 17 Aug. 1844 and 4 Jan. 1845.

[3] Nor, of course, could they rely on people flocking to their assistance—Edward Jackson of Bassingbourn was fined for refusing to help a village constable during a riot against the employment of Irish harvesters, *Cambridge Chronicle*, 26 Oct. 1821.

[4] *Cambridge Chronicle*, 31 Dec. 1830, 19 Sept. 1834, 11 Dec. 1835, 3 March 1838, 14 Sept. 1844.

methods were resorted to. Occasionally Bow Street officers were sent for (as at Bishop's Stortford in April 1825, and at Werrington in December 1833), but only occasionally. Protection Societies of the kind that were common in the north of England receive hardly a mention in the press in the east until the early 1830s. But in the wake of Captain Swing—and of the increase in rural crime that came with the reforms of 1832—societies cropped up all over the place. During the Swing era special constables had been sworn in in hundreds, the military called in and horse patrols established, but they were exceptional times. In the 'quieter' years organizations like the Wisbech St. Mary's Association for Pursuing and Prosecuting Horse Stealers and the St. Ives Association 'for the prevention and detection of incendiarism' came into being. Like their northern counterparts they relied on offering (often substantial) rewards for information leading to a conviction. But they were, on the whole, very ineffective. The village community could keep its secrets, and the arsonist, the machine breaker or the sheep stealer was not regarded as an outsider. He was as safe from the informer as was the poacher. Thomas Clarke was convicted of arson in 1844. Clarke had set fire to farm buildings in Billington and had asked two other labourers to help him. They had refused. But, a report of the trial said, although they would not go with Clarke, 'Neither . . . appeared to consider the proposal itself as an insult, or objected to it as containing anything wicked or wrong *per se.*' On very rare occasions informers were found. Robert Casbolt (who had denounced William Reader in 1829) was one. And a labourer also gave evidence against Samuel Stimson at the Bedfordshire Assizes in March 1844. Stimson 'gave me half a pint of purl not to tell', he recorded. 'I did not tell before', he went on, 'because so many people said "damn a fellow as would split": I did not like to tell of it: I was frit at it, I thought I should be interrupted if I did.'[1] The informer was right to be afraid; the punishment meted out to people who broke the code of silence was sudden and severe. Three informers due to give evidence in a minor case at Great Berkhamstead were set upon by a crowd and dragged to a pump. One was so seriously injured that the case could not proceed.[2]

So the system of rewards offered, before the 1830s by individuals, and afterwards by Protection Societies of various kinds,

[1] Clarke and Stimson both appeared before the same Assizes, *Cambridge Chronicle*, 23 March 1844.

[2] *Cambridge Chronicle*, 12 Jan. 1839.

produced only rare results. An hysterical article in the *Cambridge Chronicle* on 13 January 1844 recorded how ineffective the system was.

Agrarian outrages are of very frequent occurrence in the neighbourhood of Ely: two or three times the crier is employed every week to announce some destruction to someone's property. The farmers complain of their fences being broken, and pigeons being shot: within a few days Mr. Jas. Cheesewright had his potato heap robbed three times, and on Wednesday evening last all of the potatoes of Mr. Mark Manchet were stolen from out of his pit. Offering rewards proves . . . useless . . . in bringing the parties to punishment.

Nightly watches, which must have been very expensive and just as ineffective as the offering of rewards, were often started to combat the terror. At Terrington St. Clement, another of the ravaged marshland villages, a subscription was entered into early in 1832 to establish a nightly watch on agricultural premises. Its fund and members were said to have been incorporated with the Hundred of Freebridge Marshland, and the Bishop of Peterborough was a subscriber. Rewards of as much as £300 were offered. Farmers around Wisbech were forced to hire men to watch their flocks—again with what effect will be obvious from what has gone before. During the period when Soham was the number one trouble spot in the fens the town was said to have been 'rigidly watched every night, and a reward of £200 offered for the conviction of the offender or offenders, [yet] not the slightest clue [could] . . . be obtained of the malignant and cowardly perpetrator'. As the century reached its halfway mark the town of Ramsey became the east's greatest trouble spot. Week after week, from 1848 onwards, fires were reported, to the consternation and surprise of the *Chronicle*. Why Ramsey? it asked. Both daily wages and piece rates were as good there as elsewhere. A volunteer watch was started, but again to no effect. The fires went on, started in places 'selected for [their] dangerous situation[s]', and doing enormous damage.[1]

'Inquests' (of the kind which exposed insurance swindles at Waterbeach and Soham) were another attempt to enforce some kind of law and order on the area. They became fairly common in Cambridgeshire and Huntingdonshire in the 1840s—in the winter of 1845–6 three were set up in as many months to investigate fires at Ellington, Ramsey and Upwood. But, by the

[1] *Ibid.*, 6 Jan. 1832, 5 July 1833, 26 Sept. 1846, 1 and 15 Jan., 5 and 26 Feb., and 30 Dec. 1848.

time these were held, rural police forces of a centralized, modern type had come into being in some parts of eastern England. The inquests were held in counties which had, until then, refused to adopt new legislation passed by the Whigs.

The need for efficient forces had been obvious for years, and Suffolk seems to have had a pioneer county force from about 1830. After recording an assault on the village constable of Cheveley in 1838, a correspondent of the *Cambridge Chronicle* looked enviously at the police forces a few miles away across the border in Suffolk, where, he said, 'the appointment of a rural police, . . . has had, in the parishes of Wickhambrook, Lidgate, Ouseden, Dunstal Green, and Hargrave, the desired effect in preventing crime.'[1] Throughout the mid-'30s, as the Whigs set about gathering information about rural crime, arguments on the pros and cons of an organized police force were heard everywhere; and in 1839 and 1840 Acts were passed which enabled county police forces to be brought into existence. These were the hated 'Rural Police Bills' which so aroused the passions of physical force Chartists like Peter Bussey, and which were opposed by Disraeli in a most extraordinarily ill-informed way. Norfolk adopted them almost immediately, and Suffolk and the Isle of Ely shortly thereafter.[2] The magistrates of the Isle decided on the desirability of a force in February 1841. But it was not universally welcomed, as a report of opposition from Wisbech shows. Nor did it have the immediate beneficial effect that some may have expected. For, in reporting sheep stealing at Elm in June 1842, the *Chronicle* observed that that particular offence had in fact 'greatly increased' since the establishment of the force, while 'the mischievous practice of breaking down fences is more prevalent than before'.[3]

Cambridgeshire, or at least its northern part, was among the worst areas for crime, yet there was tremendous opposition to the creation of a police force. The opposition was basically the usual selfish one of antagonism to the increased expense a force would necessitate. A meeting of County magistrates for Cambridgeshire was held in October 1844 to consider the creation of a rural police force, and a committee was set up. The deliberations at that meeting make interesting reading. One person said (surely with some truth) that wages of 18s. a week for the agricultural labourers would keep the countryside quiet, another that the crime of sheep stealing had been drastically cut where

[1] *Cambridge Chronicle*, 10 Dec. 1830 and 3 March 1838.
[2] Radzinowicz, *op. cit.*, chap. vii *passim*.
[3] *Cambridge Chronicle*, 20 Feb. and 3 April 1841, 18 June 1842.

the new forces had come into existence. Great concern was expressed about the railway navvies (who could only have been responsible for a small proportion of crime in the area), and a partial police force operating eight miles on either side of the lines was suggested. Essex, Hertfordshire, parts of Suffolk, the Isle, Cambridge town and Bedfordshire had forces, it was pointed out, while the county of Cambridge was unprotected and becoming a refuge for the crooks from other areas.[1]

The files of the *Chronicle* contain many letters arguing for or against the creation of a Cambridgeshire police force. A magistrate wrote instancing the enormous decline in sheep stealing in Leicestershire: commitments in the year before the force was established were nearly five and a half times as high as in 1842 and 1843; so a proper police would actually save money, by lessening the number of prosecutions. But his views did not go unchallenged. A week later 'K.N.' called the new rural police 'the worst kind of standing army'. And William Metcalfe of Foulmire cited the parliamentary returns of criminal statistics to deny that there had been a reduction in crime.

I would ask have Bedfordshire, Essex, Herts, Suffolk and Norfolk been protected by their Rural Police from the dark deeds of the incendiary? Have the inhabitants of Stortford and its vicinity escaped by having a policeman in every parish?

Metcalfe's views were echoed again and again. The new police force had *not* brought any diminution of crime, some contended, and the files of the newspapers surely bear them out.[2]

After mid-century the new police forces were, with improved conditions, the greatest factors in the reduction of crime. But their influence had hardly been felt by the late 1840s. Scarcely any improvement had occurred during the fifty years covered in this study. In fact conditions had got worse in the years following the criminal law reforms of the early 1830s. An enormous amount of crime went on, most of it clandestine, most of it capable of being regarded as crime of protest, and most of it

[1] *Ibid.*, 26 Oct. 1844.
[2] *Ibid.*, Oct.–Nov. 1844. One writer asserted that, before reform, Haddenham (a large village in the Isle of Ely) had been well policed by a single constable responsible to a parochial committee of inspectors, but that it was now served more expensively but less efficiently by two. The police reply was that under the old system the parochial inspectors' property had been cared for, but little else. (See also *ibid.*, 19 and 26 Oct. 1850 for a most unsatisfactory report to the Cambridgeshire Quarter Sessions on the police in Soham.)

undetected. These were the crimes of the closed village community. In later years trouble among the labourers was to be put down to 'travelling delegates' bent on causing strife in the countryside. As late as the early 1850s, however, the villages were still, most of them, isolated and self-contained. Were there any 'outside influences' at work in the first half of the century that could have contributed to—or lessened—the discontent that so often led to fires and cattle maiming?

The only two movements which did penetrate into the countryside were Chartism and the temperance movement. The former made a great impact in Norwich, Wisbech and some other of the larger towns in its early phases,[1] but hardly outside them. The temperance movement, on the other hand, did, and temperance organizations were extremely active in the early forties. From 1841 the newspapers are full of meetings addressed by famous temperance advocates at places like March, St. Neots, Soham, Ramsey, Upwell and Outwell, but by 1845 the movement was almost a spent force. Before this it had split into warring factions, the temperance advocates and the teetotallers. At Wisbech, and this must have happened in many places, one of the factions joined forces with the Chartists. '. . . a considerable number of one', the *Chronicle* reported, 'have embraced Chartism.'[2] Socialist organizations appeared, also, in the larger places, like Wisbech;[3] and in an earlier period the Grand National Consolidated Trades Union had an extremely active branch in Cambridge.[4] But again these did not infiltrate into the countryside. Even earlier there had been a famous Owenite settlement established in the fens, but it ended its short life in bitterness and mutual recriminations.[5] None of these 'outside influences' had any discernible effect on softening attitudes in the villages or in lessening violence. Not until the 1870s did the urban 'emissaries' stirring up trouble in the villages become more than a figment of imagination.

[1] *Cambridge Chronicle*, esp. 10 and 24 Aug. 1839.
[2] *Ibid.*, esp. 22 Feb. 1842.
[3] *Ibid.*, esp. 4 July 1840, 22 Jan. and 11 June 1842.
[4] The President and Secretary of the Union were charged with 'conspiracy to raise wages' and tried at the Assizes—*ibid.*, 4 April and 25 July 1834.
[5] W. H. Armytage, 'Manea Fen: An Experiment in Agrarian Communitarianism', *Bulletin of the John Rylands Library*, xxxviii (1956), and *Heavens Below* (1961), chap. viii; E. Porter, 'The Manea Society', *Cambridgeshire, Huntingdonshire and Peterborough Life*, July 1968.

Throughout the whole of the first half of the nineteenth century, then, the countryside was violent. There were peak years when violence became more open and unified, but there were no such things as quiet years. By 1850 rural police forces had been set up in many places, and these—and better times— were eventually to have a decisive influence in pacifying the villages. The crime they were confronted with was traditional (the rick burning, the food rioting and forced sales), ritualized (the sheep stealing and machine smashing) and vicious (the cattle maiming). It was sometimes effective in a demonstrable way (it held up the introduction of machinery in many places), and it was certainly always a check on the forces of authority. Its causes are eloquently spelled out in threatening letters, and statements in court and from the scaffold.

James Friend (aged 27) had sent to a former employer (who had bought a threshing machine) a letter addressed, or endorsed, 'Farmar, yure primsas wil sone be set fire, 1844'; it read:

Farmers, we are starven, we wol not stan this no longer; this gang is 600 and 80. Rather than starv we are tormint to sit you on fire. You are roges and robbs the pore of their livin by imployan thrashmans sheans. this primsas will sone tak plase fire if you donot olter. You must note be surprised if you see your primsas on fire, and stock al burnt, there will be six on fire in one time.

Edmund Botwright was tried at the Suffolk Assizes at the same time. Near the barn he had set alight was found this letter.

Mr. Watkin, Sir,—This come as a warnin for you and the police. it is the entenshun if an alteration is not made verry quick you shall have a totch of Carlton, [a nearby village where there had been fires] for wee hav prepared ourselves for you all. i understand you have got a wheat hoe and we have got a life-hoe prepared for you and not you alone, but you will be the first if you do not make an alterashun, we will make an exampel of you enstead of your making an exampel for the pore to be kept alive, your Exampel is, to have them all starved to deth you damnd raskell. You bluddy farmers could not liv if it was not for the poore, tis them that keep you bluddy raskells alive, but there will be a slauter made amongst you very soone. I shood verry well like to hang you the same as I hanged your beastes. You bluddy rogue I will lite up a little fire for you the first opertunity that I can make, and I shood like to have their at the present time. If the pore be not employed different to what they have bin, it shall be as the promes is made.[1]

[1] *Cambridge Chronicle*, 3 Aug. 1844.

William and Henry Stigwood were prompted to arson by their employer Charles Giblin telling them 'three or four days before the fire . . . that they must try to work for rather less, as he must lower their wages a little until corn fetched a higher price.' A paper was found at the scene of the fire saying:

this is to ghive notts if you take the men of thir whas you may exspak som fires fore long giblin and chimbs lik wiss ebis min your filds stiks for thay shill shouly be burnt if you dew.[1]

John Monsey was found guilty of firing wheat stacks belonging to Robert Porter, 'a considerable farmer' at Rolesby. Monsey also complained about low wages, and said:

he did not care what became of him . . . he did not mind so long as he should not be hanged, for he wished to leave the country, as he never should live with his wife again . . . Porter gave him only 8d. a-day, and besides owed him for two or three days work.

Monsey was transported for life. Thomas Hills, who got 20 years' transportation, uttered similar heart-rending sentiments. Hills had said:

he would do something . . . before the assizes, in order to be transported, for he believed that transports fared better than he did, and he should not have long to lay in gaol.[2]

The unfair way village charities were manipulated has often been commented on. In Milton there was a charitable fund for coal for the poor; and when it was decided in 1843 to deprive able-bodied single men of the benefit, two letters were picked up threatening local farmers:[3]

you shall see a good blase before Christmas day old David i will give five or six a tase the coles for that.
you may prepare your selfs for a fire old David yard shall be on fire before nex Mondy old Nix Lawson Webster Adam Jennings they shall all have tast before winter gone for taken me of coles.

John Turpin was an extensive farmer and parish clerk and pinder of West Wickham. He received the following frightening letter:[4]

Jack,—You are a cuzzen to Dick Turpin, and a worser muck than ever he wor. You are a rode-looker and pounder, you bull-headed fule! There ain't 20 in the parish but wot hates you bull-hed. You must

[1] *Cambridge Chronicle*, 15 March 1833.
[2] *Ibid.*, 7 April 1838 and 22 March 1845.
[3] *Ibid.*, 16 Dec. 1843.   [4] *Ibid.*, 27 July 1844.

git hoam good time o'nites, and wen you are at hoam keep your ize open, or els your braynes will be nockt out, els burnt out, you bull-hedded varmin.

At the Huntingdonshire Quarter Sessions in January 1835 Ephraim White, a pauper, was indicted for writing anonymous letters to Joseph Goodman, William Brown and Fullard Fyson, all overseers of Whitton. White's letters said:

To Joseph Goodman and Fullard Fyson:— I hear that you are the overseers of Whitton and I hope you will behave better for the future, as assuredly you will have your stacks burnt down before next moon. To Fullard Fyson, Brown and Goodman at Whitton:—You are starving the poor as fast as you can you may expect that your farms will be set on fire soon mark this my name is not here.[1]

William Watts was a returned convict, who appeared at the Norfolk Quarter Sessions charged with killing cattle at Buxton, a place where scarcely a day passed 'without a horse, ox, or cow being found dead, or in a dying state'. Watts (who was transported for life) was one of the few labourers who spoke on their own behalf in court. He

said that the cruel Poor-laws and the rates and taxes now imposed upon the poor labourer drove him to dishonesty. He would not see his children starve, while he was called on to support full-fed relieving officers and other folks connected with them and the unions.[2]

A Mr. Kisby in Huntingdonshire employed both machines and Irishmen. He was threatened by a notice put up on a church door:

Warning—to those that imply the Irish—and use meshines while our countrymen and neibours are starving for food, we do assure the farmer we as Labourers cannot bear it no longer, as we would as willing die as live this oppress condition; therefore if the farmers do not act defernt they may expect the town [Godmanchester] to be very hot soon, with many other calamities.

John True Blue.[3]

The period between the end of the Napoleonic Wars and the onset of the 'golden age' of British farming was the most dreadful time of the English agricultural labourer's existence—many

[1] In sentencing White the Chairman of Sessions assured him that the court had behaved 'very leniently . . . in sentencing him to only 14 years' transportation'—*ibid.*, 16 Jan. 1835.
[2] *Cambridge Chronicle*, 26 Oct. 1839.
[3] *Ibid.*, 27 Aug. 1842.

more written protests against the Poor Law, enclosures, machines, high prices, low wages, and that ever present fact of life, unemployment, could be found. Against those evils the labourers protested in a multitude of ways. Eliot Yorke, M.P. for Cambridgeshire, talked, in a speech opposing the repeal of the Corn Laws, of widespread discontent and the labourers' predisposition to violence.

If gentlemen think that there is nothing to be dreaded from our rural labourers, I fear they are greatly mistaken. I do not believe there is a village in my neighbourhood that would not be ready to assert by *brute force* their right (as they say) to eat fully the fruit arising from their own labour. . . . Every parish in this neighbourhood is . . . ripe for any outbreak.[1]

Yorke did not exaggerate. Any village at almost any time was a powder keg. He spoke in 1846, but it is possible to produce reliable documentary evidence of the deplorable state of the peasantry for any time during the first five decades of the century. *The Agricultural State of the Kingdom*, a volume produced just at the end of the wars with France, gives the background to the troubles of 1816. Yorke's speech indicates feelings in the 1840s. A petition to Parliament from the farmers of Ely described the degradation of the labourer in 1830.[2] The petitioners said they were unable to find employment for the labourers, 'a circumstance which has been mainly instrumental in reducing' them 'to their present wretched and degrading means of subsistence'. They went on to paint a roseate picture of yesteryear, and accredited too much blame for the state of the labourers to the unreformed system of poor relief. Nevertheless, they did sketch out the kind of depressing conditions that are the backcloth to all the trouble and the incidents mentioned in these notes. They sighed for the days of living in, and the pace of pre-enclosure days. They longed for the quiescent working class of the eighteenth century. 'When the tillage of the land afforded a fair remuneration to the farmer', they said

the labourers reaped the due reward of their toil, and with their earnings maintained their families, and trained them in habits of industry and sobriety. Then they filled their stations in society with credit to themselves and advantage to the community . . . now no longer able to maintain themselves by the sweat of their brow, . . . their spirits have become broken, and they are constantly repining at

[1] *Cambridge Chronicle*, 28 March 1846.
[2] *Ibid.*. 8 Jan. 1830.

their hard condition, and inciting each other to vicious courses, while their employers are regarded as taskmasters, and the ties of attachment to the land of their birth becomes gradually torn asunder.

The farmers of Ely purported to believe that Poor Law reform would end their troubles. Reform came within four years, but the violence and the antagonism went on and even got worse. The 'tyranny of the countryside' was a very real thing. But, though shut out from the body politic, though allegedly 'broken in spirit', though reduced to a landless wage earner, though threatened by machines and unable to get regular employment, the labourer was not without his means of redress, and would not be for many years to come.

IV

The Rise and Fall of Agricultural Trades Unionism in England

Only further studies based, like Dr. Peacock's, on the local press could determine just how typical the Fens were. But the evidence given to the Select Committee on Police in 1852 suggests that the sort of sheep stealing Dr. Peacock describes had been widely prevalent—reference was even made to thieves nailing their trophies' heads to the church door at Heckington, Lincs.[1] Nor was any county wholly immune from incendiarism. Large scale arson, however, appears to have been something of an East Anglian speciality, at least in the 1840s and 1850s. The outbreak of 1843–4 was sufficiently distinctive to cause the despatch of a *Times* 'Special Commissioner' to Essex and Suffolk; he observed that, within these counties, the line of these fires corresponded closely with that of low wages,[2] and he also found direct evidence for regarding them as a protest against poverty, unemployment and the Poor Law. But two years later the 'Commissioner' investigating conditions in the at least equally depressed county of Dorset noticed nothing comparable in the way of resistance—'The labourer confines himself to mere complaint' (if that).[3] And early in the next decade one writer claimed that arson was 'to some extent peculiar to Suffolk . . . Cambridgeshire is the only county in England that exhibits an equal number of offences'. This last is confirmed by Caird's

[1] *P.P.*, 1852–3 xxxvi, p. 239.

[2] For Essex this impression is largely confirmed by S. W. Amos, thesis cited, pp. 96, and Conclusion.

[3] *The Times*, esp. 7–28 June 1844 and 18 June–3 Aug. 1846. Similarly Sidney Godolphin Osborne held in 1849 that 'The cases of incendiarism which have occurred of late years [in Dorset] have been few, though there have been some symptoms lately of a disposition to display discontent by this means.' He also felt that 'the peasantry' was not much given to assault or to burglary, their 'most common crimes being fuel stealing, barn robbing [in small quantities], sheep and poultry stealing'; at least 60–70 sheep were stolen each year. Poaching was also 'very common' 'wherever there is a field for it'; but, unlike barn robbing, it was commonly detected, and, if detected, prosecuted. A. White (ed.), *The Letters of S.G.O.*, i (1891) pp. 38–43.

account of his tour of England in 1851, for he singles out the
Cambridgeshire–Huntingdonshire borders as infested with incendiarism, and notes that corn ricks were spaced widely apart
in the fields to prevent the spread of fire (as they had been in
the disturbed parts of Suffolk in 1844).[1]

But perhaps even more important than the geographical incidence of crime is its general trend. The first part of the nineteenth century saw a rising crime rate. This was sharply checked
during the prosperous years of 1843–5; and thereafter, apart
from a bulge in the late 1870s, the number of commitments for
trial in England and Wales declined, either absolutely (especially in the late 1850s and in the 1880s), or relatively to the
population as a whole.[2] Of course this decline did not affect all
offences equally—outside East Anglia the volume of arson
known to the police did not greatly diminish, though it may
well have become increasingly the work of vagrants rather than
a direct way of paying off grievances against one's employer.
Again serious poaching offences (like assaults on keepers) certainly declined in the 1850s and 1860s; but new legislation
(pressed for principally by Cheshire) and greater police vigilance
actually raised the number of summary convictions in the 1860s,
and they did not really begin to diminish until the late 1880s.
However witnesses before the Select Committee on Police repeatedly asserted that sheep stealing had been sharply curbed;
and similar (though less emphatic) claims were made that the
property of rich and poor alike now enjoyed greater security.
Most of the credit was given to the institution of a rural
police.[3] And this must have been an important factor, for

---

[1] Stacks had been set in the fields in Suffolk for the same reason
during the 1844 outbreak of incendiarism—J. Glyde, *Suffolk in the
Nineteenth Century* (1856), pp. 125–6; James Caird, *English Agriculture in 1850–1* (1852), pp. 467–8.

[2] See the annual tables of 'Criminal Offenders' and of 'Judicial
Statistics' in the *Parliamentary Papers*; also *P.P.*, 1893 cviii, p. 119
(for a diagrammatic representation of the period 1874–93) and p. 75
for a table of offences tried summarily.

[3] Thus the Chief Constable of Wiltshire proudly cited the decline
of serious crimes in his district between the first year of his police
force in 1841 and 1852 (by which time it covered not only the
original rural areas but also all the county's boroughs except Salisbury):

	1841	1852
Highway robberies	12 (3 arrests)	—
Burglaries	19 (8)	3 (3)

vagrants were moved on into the unpoliced counties and criminals often preferred to operate there, sometimes mounting raids over county borders. But a fall in crime was noticeable also in some unpoliced areas, so other explanations must be found too.

An important, if intangible, factor was the growing Victorian emphasis on order, respectability and law-abidingness. This was constantly being inculcated at almost all levels of society, by Radicals and Nonconformists as well as by Tories and a revivified Established Church. And it was effective: in the 1850s it had been regarded as something of a triumph that the Crystal Palace was not smashed up by its thousands of visitors; by the 1860s such good behaviour was taken for granted. The change was mostly the result of indirect social conditioning. But on occasion this was complemented by the deliberate modification or suppression of practices and institutions that gave scope for trouble. Thus in Oxfordshire the unenclosed forest of Wychwood, and its great autumn fair, were being attacked from the beginning of the century as a 'fertile source of crime'. An attempt was made to discontinue the fair in 1830, largely for this reason; but local determination secured it two more decades of life, and its final demise after 1855 was only achieved by digging trenches across its site to prevent the access of vans; the same period also saw the enclosure of the forest itself.[1] Again we are told that, in the early 1850s, Norfolk 'Parsons and squires combined to attack the custom of holding harvest suppers at public-

Housebreaking	4 (0)	12 (6)
Cattle stealing	9 (9)	2 (2)
Horse stealing	12 (6)	3 (2)
Sheep stealing	95 (26)	8 (3)

The number of people charged with offences of any variety had fallen from 3,006 to 2,350. And in 1852 only 283 prisoners had had to be committed for trial in Wiltshire, as against 585 in unpoliced Somerset (*P.P.*, 1852–3 xxxvi, pp. 148–9). But not every police force could claim such success.

[1] *Victoria County History, Oxfordshire*, ii, pp. 218, 299; M. Sturge Gretton, *A Corner of the Cotswolds through the Nineteenth Century* (1914), chap. vii—Mrs. Sturge Gretton notes that by then the general standard of behaviour was far better than it had been at the late eighteenth-century Burford races, 'even though it differed very widely from the demeanour of' the early twentieth century, by which time 'the case for out-of-doors places of amusement in villages and country towns' had been 'much strengthened by the fact that rustic civilization has reached a point now at which little or no policing would be necessary'.

houses, of [begging for] largesse, and of uncontrolled drink and frolic in barns.' Many parishes tried to substitute more decorous public dinners, but these never really caught on, and the result was a general decline in village feasts.[1] Such developments may have impaired the spirit of local community, and, for a time,[2] have increased the monotony of rural life; but they also contributed towards a marked reduction in violence and brutality.

The reduction owed much, too, to a gradual improvement in wages and employment—Joseph Arch, indeed, regarded this as the explanation of the decline in poaching by agricultural labourers.[3] Fuller employment is obviously difficult to quantify. But returns made in 1832 to the Poor Law Commission suggest an excess of labourers in 60 per cent of the rural parishes in Speenhamland counties and in 45 per cent of parishes elsewhere. Various devices were used to mitigate this excess, notably employment on the roads (for which we have no figures), and the 'roundsman' and 'labour rate' systems reported by 25 per cent of Speenhamland and 16 per cent of other parishes. Nevertheless many villages clearly had massive winter unemployment —at Pulborough in Sussex over a third of the labouring population was out of work for nine months and over a half at the worst part of the year. The introduction of the New Poor Law in the mid-1830s coincided with a marked improvement in employment. But, at the end of his 1850–1 tour, Caird still noted the prevalence of the system whereby the parish ratepayers agreed 'to divide amongst them the surplus of labour, not according to their respective requirements, but in proportion to the size of their farms'.[4]

However Caird believed that this surplus was 'apt to be

---

[1] L. Marion Springall, *Labouring Life in Norfolk Villages 1834–1914* (1936), pp. 71–2; see also Richard Jefferies, *The Toilers of the Field* (1892 edn.), pp. 98–100, and A. F. J. Brown, *English History from Essex Sources, 1750–1900* (Chelmsford, 1952), p. 176. Of course not all such interventions were failures—in Lerwick 'Up Helly Aa' still survives as a successful nineteenth-century canalization of indiscriminate drinking into a picturesque festival.

[2] As the century wore on, they were counterbalanced by, for instance, more frequent excursions and the rise of sports clubs.

[3] *P.P.*, 1873 xiii, pp. 390–1—Arch was then President of the National Agricultural Labourers' Union.

[4] Mark Blaug, 'The Poor Law Report Re-examined', *Journal of Economic History*, xxiv (1964), pp. 235–7; N. Gash, 'Rural Unemployment, 1815–34', *Economic History Review*, vi (1935), pp. 90–3; Caird, *op. cit.*, p. 515.

exaggerated', and he proved correct. The 1851 census saw the peak of the purely rural population of England; and in the ensuing decade the situation was eased in many areas by a slight fall in population accompanied by a continued rise in the demand for labour from a more intensive agriculture. Of course things were not transformed overnight, and the need to spread employment continued to colour farmers' attitudes for decades. But the dimensions of the problem changed—in the winter of 1868–9 unemployment on Oxfordshire and Berkshire farms was a little below 4 per cent of adult males, mostly concentrated in 'open' villages for which no single landlord had responsibility. In 1873 Arch remarked that he could 'remember some winters when there were 10 or 12 men out of employ, but for the last three or four winters we have not had a man out of employ during all the year, they have all been taken up on one job or another'. Arch was admittedly talking of a boom period. But nevertheless, as a Suffolk writer put it, 'the day has happily gone by when the farmer could find half a score of men on the village-green waiting for a job, to be set on, or paid off, at his convenience.'[1]

Of wages it is possible to speak with a little more precision, but not with much. For few farmers and even fewer labourers kept detailed accounts. So we usually know only the basic wage-rates said to be current in any particular area. Actual earnings might be reduced below this by sickness and (especially in Lincolnshire) wet weather, or boosted above it by piece-work and harvest rates: in the second half of the century they are generally taken as being nearly 20 per cent above the basic wage-rate, but this varied from county to county, and can only be regarded as an approximation.[2] There is, too, considerable difficulty in putting a value on payments in kind, which might range from free housing in the north to the more doubtful benefits of 'scrumpy' cider[3] and of low quality grist-corn at a fixed price in the south and west. So it is not surprising that whenever the question of agricultural wages was ventilated, it always occasioned heated disputes as to their real value. This was true even before the days of agricultural trades unions. But their advent naturally gave the matter a more immediate edge; and, then, as

[1] *P.P.*, 1868–9 xiii, pp. 155–7, and 1873 xiii, pp. 390–1; *Journal of the Royal Agricultural Society of England*, 2nd series, xi (1875), p. 88.   [2] *P.P.*, 1905 xcvii, pp. 382–4.

[3] However the provision of drink was popular with the labourers themselves (if not with their spokesmen), and attempts to commute it for money tended to be resisted.

now, the unions tended to rest their case on the basic unskilled wage-rate, employers on their own estimates of real earnings.

Lastly, to form any idea of the true position of the labourer, one would need to take into account such factors as earnings on the side, the value of his garden or allotment produce (if any) and, above all, the income of other members of his family. In some circumstances this could be considerable, though elsewhere it is probable that wives' earnings only served to make possible the continuation of unreasonably low wages for men. They do, however, explain why in so many 'specimen budgets' expenditure exceeds the income claimed. And since they might be derived from employment at home as washer-women, seamstresses or glovers (rather than from agriculture), they are virtually unquantifiable.

But if the precise figures are debatable, the general trend seems reasonably clear. Almost all our series suggest a substantial increase in money wages in the third quarter of the nineteenth century (and one which outstripped the rise in prices); in the fourth quarter money wages remained fairly stable, but prices fell sharply.[1] The effect can perhaps best be illustrated by a graph (see p. 68).

Weekly wage rates, wheat and bread prices (1900=100) (Derived from *PP.*, 1905 xcvii, p. 416, and B. R. Mitchell with P. Deane, *Abstract of British Historical Statistics*, pp. 488–9, 498)

Note: In 1850 both prices and wages were rather low by comparison with previous years.

The London bread prices may serve, in the absence of any cost-of-living index for agricultural labourers, to illustrate general trends. But they cannot be used as the basis of any very precise calculations—bread formed only a part, though a large part, of the labourers' expenditure—and some labourers were at least partially insulated from external price changes by their method of payment, or by the possession of potato ground or allotments.

[1] See e.g. *P.P.*, 1905 xcvii; B. R. Mitchell with P. Deane, *Abstract of British Historical Statistics* (Cambridge, 1962), which derives its wage date from A. L. Bowley, 'The Statistics of Wages in the United Kingdom in the last Hundred Years, Agricultural Wages', *Journal of the Royal Statistical Society*, lxi and lxii (1898 and 1899); G. E. Prothero, *English Farming Past and Present* (1961 edn.), pp. 524–6; L. M. Springall, *op. cit.*, p. 140; F. Clifford, *The Agricultural Lock-out of 1874* (1875), pp. 324–5.

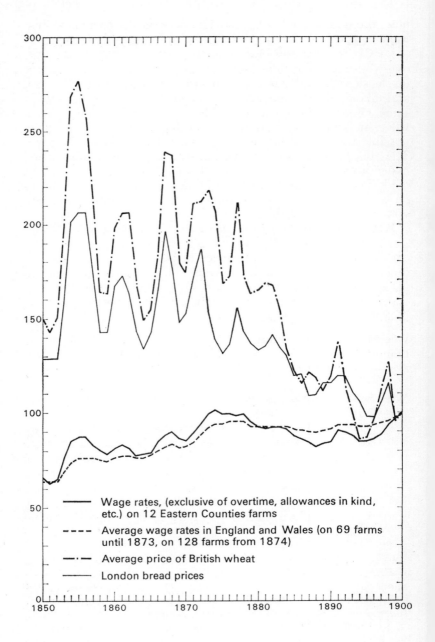

Wage rates, (exclusive of overtime, allowances in kind, etc.) on 12 Eastern Counties farms

Average wage rates in England and Wales (on 69 farms until 1873, on 128 farms from 1874)

Average price of British wheat

London bread prices

For the money value of weekly *earnings* in 1902, see the map on page 239.

Too much should not be made of this improvement, for it still left the labourers very poor. Nor does a simple increase in wages remove all occasions for conflict. Urban wages rose too, and as time went on farm workers were better able to compare their conditions with those in the towns. Moreover in an inflationary situation, like that of the great boom of the early 1870s, rising prices prompt wage demands often in excess of the actual increase in the cost of living. Also the spread of education tended both to deprive families of their children's earnings and (until 1891) to extend their liability for school fees—this was in fact mentioned at a number of the labourers' meetings in 1872.

But higher wages might nevertheless help to change the nature and context of disputes. Before about 1850 the usual form of 'industrial action' in the countryside was, as we have seen, the wage or price riot, which was associated with distress, not prosperity. Riots were supplemented, as Dr. Peacock has shown, by crimes of protest. These are harder to classify, since the occasions for them were often personal, but again they are usually to be linked to adversity: many of the culprits gave this explanation; and those we are best informed about, the East Anglian incendiaries of 1843–4, were disproportionately young and unmarried, and were therefore more liable to be laid off than were men with family responsibilities.[1] By the last third of the century, however, the chief periods of unrest among agricultural labour, 1872–4 and 1890–2, were years when work was plentiful and wages rising. In these conditions trades unions could spring up to help the process on; but their membership always declined when the cycle turned down, as indeed did that of urban trades unions too. In other words, if rural unrest in the first part of the century was mainly the product of desperation, in the second half it was mainly that of hope.

There was, of course, something of a transitional period. A *Times* leader of 5 March 1862 conceded that arson was no longer on the scale of former times, but deplored the apparent reappearance of 'the old spirit . . . on the old scenes'. In 1870 there was an old-fashioned outbreak of fires and threatening letters in two Leicestershire villages. And in the far west of

[1] *House of Lords Papers*, 1844 x, pp. 199–203; *The Times*, esp. 7, 10, 11 and 21 June 1844. But it must, of course, be remembered that crime rates are always highest among this group.

Dorset fires were common enough during the post-1885 depression to have an appreciable impact on everyday life. Even the adoption of trades unionism did not constitute a complete break: there was a certain amount of arson in the aftermath of the labourers' defeat by the 1874 Eastern Counties Lock-out; and in 1914 stacks built by black-leg labour were set alight in two north Essex villages.[1] Again, though the labourers in Swanbourne, Buckinghamshire, were unionized in 1873, they seem to have expected to secure their wage increase by pressuring the leading landowner very much in the old style:

> One of the unionists told me that they never imagined it would go to a strike. They quite thought that you with your usual kindness would have given in directly and that the farmers would have been obliged to follow your example.

This was not to be, and the unionists proceeded (unsuccessfully) to invoke the new tactic of striking; but they also paraded the village constantly, as men had always done in times of tension, though they now acted with greater sobriety and sported union ribbons.[2]

Equally, if traditional practices survived into the 1870s and beyond, the unions of that date were not altogether unprecedented. 1830 itself saw no purely rural strikes, but there were a number in subsequent years. Most were informally managed village 'turn-outs', but some were more institutionalized. There was a union, or unions, in Hampshire in 1832, possibly an off-shoot of the London National Political Union: it aimed at defending existing wage rates, supporting its members when unemployed, and perhaps also at the acquisition of arms. Better known is the branch of the Grand National Consolidated Trades Union at Tolpuddle in Dorset in 1833–4; interestingly, this was founded only after a more traditional approach to the magistrates to fix wages had proved fruitless. And in April 1836 a full-blown 'Tendring Agricultural Labourers Union' was formed in Essex, with published rules and objectives and the high

---

[1] Pamela Horn, *Joseph Arch* (Kineton, 1971), pp. 17–18; Barbara Kerr, *Bound to the Soil* (1968), p. 61; A. J. Peacock, 'The Revolt of the Fields in East Anglia', cited above, p. 165; S. W. Amos, thesis cited, p. 162.

[2] Actually it was not the case that the farmers were obliged to follow the Fremantle example, though some members of the family (as well as some labourers) believed it was. For the Swanbourne strike, see the Fremantle MSS, Bucks. Record Office, D/ER/109 and D/FE/133.

subscription of a shilling a month. It apparently claimed a membership of 1,200, and sought to expand into the neighbouring hundred; but by the end of July it had collapsed, its members fearing that the union funds were insufficient to support them if they were dismissed.[1] Subsequently we hear less of organization. But both Chartism and the Corn Law agitation woke occasional, though certainly no more than occasional, echoes among the rural population—the former sought unsuccessfully to mount a harvest strike in south Essex in 1839,[2] and the latter led to meetings of agricultural labourers to publicize their conditions.[3] In 1852 we hear of men going from farm to farm in Wiltshire to raise wages, and about this time there was a short-lived combination at Montacute in Somerset.[4] Further research will doubtless produce more examples; but it is a matter of looking for a needle in a haystack, and the instances are important only as anticipations of a new style of industrial relations.

By the 1860s we are on slightly firmer ground. It was now sometimes difficult to get sufficient workers at peak seasons, and this could lead to sudden strikes to push up wages—even in the poor county of Dorset farmers were, by 1868, afraid of being deserted at busy times, and a self-consciously good employer recommended specifics 'for keeping our labourers, and for preventing them striking and giving trouble.'[5] And from the middle of the decade, formal organization became commoner: in the summer of 1866 (a year of marked labour shortage) a Kent Agricultural Labourers' Protection Association temporarily raised wages around Maidstone but then melted away, and a union was also formed (unsuccessfully) in a village near

[1] Hobsbawm and Rudé, *op. cit.*, esp. pp. 283–4, and Appendix III; *Lord Melbourne's Papers*, ed. Lloyd C. Sanders (1889), esp. pp. 147–52; George Loveless, *The Victims of Whiggery* (1838 edn.), pp. 5–6; S. W. Amos, pp. 152–4.

[2] S. W. Amos, pp. 154–6.

[3] See e.g. E. L. Jones, 'The Agricultural Labour Market in England, 1793–1872', *Economic History Review*, 2nd series xvii (1964–5) p. 327; G. E. Fussell, *From Tolpuddle to TUC* (Slough, 1948), pp. 53–6; *The Times*, 27 Jan. 1847 p. 7.

[4] *Victoria County History, Wilts*, iv p. 81; *Dorset County Chronicle*, 6 June 1872 p. 16.

[5] *P.P.*, 1868–9 xiii, pp. 249–252. One such strike on the part of 20 men near Newbury led to letters to *The Times* (21 and 25 April 1866) and a notice in the *Economist* (reprinted in the *North British Agriculturalist*, 16 May 1866).

Leicester. Next year a union was organized in north Bucking-hamshire; it led to a strike at Gawcott, which was reported by the press, and the movement was taken up briefly in a number of the surrounding villages: there were also combinations in south Lincolnshire that for some months collected subscriptions and sought to reduce hours. And in 1870 disputes over charities and riots over enclosures in Norfolk led to the formation of an Association for the Defence of the Rights of the Poor, later restyled the Eastern Counties Union.[1] The scale of these activities was still small—only 28 labourers were involved at Gaw-cott, and the affair must have been reported partly for its novelty value.[2] But they are evidence of stirrings among the agricultural labourers, and indications that these might well assume trade union form.

Conditions were now in many ways more propitious for such activity. We have already noted changes in economic circumstance and in attitudes towards crime. It is also of importance that the urban trades union movement was now far more highly developed, and therefore a more attractive model and a more generous patron. The Tolpuddle martyrs had indeed got in touch with the Grand National Consolidated Trades Union; but even had this link not branded them as subversives, the G.N.C.T.U. was itself to collapse the following year and could have offered them little financial assistance. By the 1870s urban unionism was securely established, and was able to offer help running into tens of thousands of pounds. The law, too, had changed. During the inflationary period of the Napoleonic Wars there had been some incipient combinations, but their leaders were liable to be jailed. In the early 1830s the Home Secretary, Melbourne, had some difficulty in persuading local magistrates that combination as such was no longer an offence, partly because certain types of combination still were.[3] But Acts of

---

[1] E. L. Jones, article cited, pp. 335–6; Pamela Horn, *op. cit.*, p. 18; *P.P.*, 1868–9 xiii, p. 105; G. E. Fussell, *op. cit.*, p. 58; L. M. Springall, *op. cit.*, pp. 79–81.

[2] The account in the *Berwick Warder* begins 'A novel strike—a strike among the agricultural labourers—has just occurred in the north-west portion of Buckinghamshire . . .' (22 March 1867, p. 7).

[3] Not only were the Tolpuddle martyrs transported for administering illegal oaths (albeit with entirely innocent intentions), but corresponding societies were arguably still illegal; it also proved possible to imprison two men in Essex in 1834 for conspiring together to compel the increase of wages, while in Cambridgeshire 'The number of labourers committed to the county jail under the Vagrancy

1869 and 1871 had removed all doubt as to the legality of trades unions, a point often stressed by speakers in 1872. This is not to say that unions now found the state of the law altogether satisfactory, or that their opponents could not bring vexatious prosecutions for obstruction or breach of contract.[1] But these could not seriously hamper the conduct of trades unionism by workers engaged on a weekly basis. (Farm servants engaged by the year were another matter, and where these predominated, as in Scotland and Northumberland, agitation necessarily assumed very different forms.)

Also the isolation of the countryside was beginning to break down. Admittedly it had never been absolute. But by the 1870s migration and emigration agents were actively seeking to recruit villagers by holding out prospects of better pay, and they lost no time in latching onto rural trades unions when these appeared in 1872. Cheap newspapers were also starting to make an impact: Richard Jefferies describes the trumpet-blowing itinerant vendor as 'a product of modern days, almost the latest'; and, as one Dorset M.P. remarked in 1872, '. . . you can't suppose those papers are not read; and the people see full well that the wages of mechanics and artizans in different towns have been raised considerably.' Nor was this the only way in which rural horizons were expanding. Benefit societies had played an important rôle in the life of the southern English labourer throughout the century, insuring him against sickness and thereby to some extent against old age. But in the first half of the century they were mostly independent village clubs; these often continued to exist, but by the 1870s they had generally been overhauled by lodges affiliated to the national fraternal orders and conducted on more or less uniform principles; the transition had been particularly rapid in the 1860s. Lastly it is perhaps worth mentioning two further Victorian innovations, the railways (built very largely in the 1840s and 1850s) and the penny post. For without them it is hard to see how rural trades unions could have operated on a more than local scale.[2]

Law for "refusing to work for the customary wages" rapidly increased from the twenties onwards.'—*Lord Melbourne's Papers*, pp. 151–2, 156–62; S. W. Amos, thesis cited, p. 127; *Victoria County History, Cambridgeshire*, ii p. 117.

[1] For examples, see e.g. A. J. Peacock, *op. cit.*, pp. 166–7.

[2] *Hodge and his Masters* (1890 edn.), pp. 281–2; *Dorset County Express*, 5 Nov. 1872, p. 2; Hobsbawm and Rudé, *op. cit.*, pp. 295–6, 301–2.

By the 1870s, then, the necessary conditions existed for wide-spread unionism in the countryside. Its sudden appearance need not, I think, surprise us. There was, for instance, a fairly similar development in 1871–2 in the previously unorganized London docks. And, as Ensor remarks, in 1872 'came an epidemic of strikes—by builders and by agricultural labourers, who succeeded; by gas-stokers and by Metropolitan police, who failed.' There was even a would-be combination of domestic servants in Dundee. The actual origins of agricultural trade unionism varied from place to place. In Herefordshire a Primitive Methodist school teacher was inspired, by a local controversy between farmers and landlords, to start a labourers' movement sympathetic to the farmers but determined that the workers' interests should not be overlooked. In south Warwickshire the initiative came primarily from the labourers themselves, prompted perhaps by newspaper reports of agricultural unions elsewhere; and militants in Wellesbourne made what proved to be a most successful choice of leader in Joseph Arch, an independent-minded jobbing workman and hedger who owned his own cottage in the next village. Sometimes, especially in the east, the immediate stimulus was a dispute over village charities—at Leverton in Lincolnshire a local republican agitator, William Banks, was called in too late to prevent the diversion of funds from the poor lands to the support of the school, but he proceeded to organize a local union and then to extend it through evangelization and mergers. Perhaps the commonest single catalyst was the widespread and largely successful urban movement in 1871–2 for a nine-hour day: this clearly inspired similar demands on the part of farm servants in Scotland, in north Warwickshire, and above all, in Lincolnshire, where one local union was even named the 'Long Sutton Nine-Hours Labour League'.[1]

The upshot was the sudden mushrooming of local combinations over wide areas of southern and eastern England. The process was self-reinforcing, as can be shown from developments in Dorset. Here labour unrest seems to have been in the air in 1872, just as student unrest was to be in 1970. Certainly 'The Labourers' Strike' was already being discussed in the press and

[1] John Lovell, *Stevedores and Dockers* (1969), chap. iii; R. C. K. Ensor, *England 1870–1914* (Oxford, 1936), p. 133; *Oxford Journal*, 4 May 1872; J. P. D. Dunbabin, 'The Incidence and Organization of Agricultural Trades Unionism in the 1870's', *Agricultural History Review*, xvi (1968), pp. 126–7, 130; Pamela Horn, below, chap. V; *The Labourer* (Boston), 15 Jan. and 29 Aug. 1876; R. Olney, *Agricultural Labourers' Unions in Lincolnshire, 1872–3* (unpublished MS).

at the Dorchester Farmers' Club in early April, before any such thing had manifested itself locally. Then in May newspaper accounts of events in Warwickshire prompted one man to ask for higher wages; an unsuccessful village strike ensued. This led to an appeal for funds in the London trades union paper, the *Bee-Hive*, and this in turn to the despatch, by the newly formed National Agricultural Labourers' Union, of strike funds and of deputation to evangelize and organize.[1]

Once established, local movements soon tended to crystallize into larger units. Most entered into communication with, and ultimately affiliated to, Joseph Arch's Warwickshire union. For Arch had established himself by mounting the first sizeable agricultural strike in March 1872; this soon drew the attention not only of the local press, but also of the *Daily News* and *Daily Telegraph* (both of which sent special correspondents); it was generously supported by the Leamington, Birmingham and London Trades Councils; and it was at once patronized by advanced politicians like George Dixon (the senior member for Birmingham) and the republican Auberon Herbert, M.P. All this went far beyond Arch's original expectations; he had become a national figure, and he had little choice but to continue his work on a national basis. At its peak in 1874 his National Union came to number over 80,000 members.

Some combinations, however, held aloof. This might merely reflect local bickering—when Old Buckenham in Norfolk was not permitted to form a district in itself, it largely seceded to the rival Lincolnshire League. It might reflect different approaches to labour relations: the Kent and Sussex Labourers' Union was alienated by Arch's 'firebrand policy of strikes and disruption', and preferred to press claims only by persuasion and by sponsoring migration to create a labour shortage. Local conditions, too, might affect the outcome. With Warwickshire wage levels in mind, Arch's union did not sanction claims for a basic wage of more than 16s. a week: in Lincolnshire this effectively confined it to the poorer south of the county, since elsewhere combinations had already been formed to press for 18s., a figure that became the minimum envisaged by the rules of Banks' Lincolnshire League.[2]

The common denominator of these unions was a wish to retain independence, and in particular financial independence, from

[1] *Dorset County Chronicle*, 4 April 1872, p. 10; *Dorset County Express*, 16 April 1872, p. 2; Dunbabin, article cited, pp. 127–30.
[2] Springall, *op. cit.*, p. 85, *P.P.*, 1882 xiv, questions 59, 318–36; Olney, MS cited.

the National Union's central office at Leamington. But, in the (justified) belief that they secured less publicity than the N.A.L.U., and therefore fewer contributions from outsiders, they allowed the London Trades Council to bring them together in the late 1873 into a far looser 'Federal Union', which claimed 49,000 members, though of these only 35,000 at the most can have been agricultural labourers. Inter-union rivalry was often ferocious. And the existence of different models provided a standing invitation to men discontented with their own union to press for changes or break away altogether—as Dr. Horn will show below, when the Oxford District Secretary seceded from the National Union he immediately sought support from what remained of the Lincolnshire League. Such splits, of course, only occasioned more controversy. And it is possible that, after the tide had turned against the unions in 1874, they devoted as much energy to internecine disputes as to fighting anybody else—Josiah Sage recalls that 'Weekly letters by the leaders of the unions attacking each other used to appear in the public Press', and these feuds sometimes became the chief concern of the unions' own newspapers.[1]

Until 1874, however, the 'Revolt of the Field' experienced quite unlooked-for success. It has been described by a number of writers; and in the next chapter Dr. Horn will give a detailed account of events in Oxfordshire, not the most highly unionized county but perhaps the one for which we have the fullest information. So I shall here confine myself to sketching the general outlines of the movement's rise and fall.

The agricultural unions were launched, as we have seen, on a rising market. And wages increased in areas where they did not penetrate—in West Somerset, for instance, the rise was attributed partly 'to the example of the principal proprietors and farmers, who have given way to public opinion, and whose example the smaller holders of land have followed', and partly to joint requests by the labourers 'on one or two farms' for an extra shilling or couple of shillings, which usually had to be granted since no other men could have been found to work at the old rates.[2] Such processes would no doubt have served to raise wages elsewhere, even had there been no unions. But I doubt whether the increase would have been as great. For the unions certainly sent speakers round the villages encouraging

[1] *The Memoirs of Josiah Sage* (1951), p. 36; see also e.g. the inaugural article of *The Labourers' Herald, The Organ of the Federal Union of Agricultural and General Labourers* (Maidstone), 27 Nov. 1874.   [2] *The Times*, 19 Dec. 1872, p. 5.

the men to make demands. These demands were quite often rejected, and only conceded after a brief strike. And even when the unions were less directly involved, some of the advances 'spontaneously' conceded by the farmers were designed, in part at least, to pre-empt claims or to keep the men from joining. Of course not all union branches demanded, still less obtained, increases; but those that did might well get distinctly more than the national average.

However it soon became clear that the unions would have difficulty in resisting a concerted lock-out. For they relied on the contributions of men still at work to finance those on strike. In East Anglia local strikes soon led to the formation of anti-union Farmers' Associations; and in April 1873 one of these on the Essex–Suffolk border discharged about 1,000 union members. Dispute pay could only be maintained for a little over a month, and in the end the men either gave in or left the district. 1874 saw conflict on a more extended scale. In Lincolnshire demands and local strikes for a further advance of three shillings a week led to counter combinations by farmers, pledged not to employ any union member until the strikers returned to work at the old wage. Some hundreds of men were locked out. And the dispute lasted from March until May, when a settlement was mediated on the basis of a return to work at the old rates, and an alteration of the Lincolnshire League's rules to extend the notice that had to be given before strikes.

Many Lincolnshire farmers would have liked to go further and destroy the League. But the chief issue remained that of wages. In East Anglia this was not so. Here strikes at Exning and Woodbridge in Suffolk were converted, in fairly similar fashions, into lock-outs in parts of Suffolk, Cambridgeshire, Essex and Norfolk. The Farmers' Associations were interested not in the actual wage claims, which might have been conceded had they been made directly rather than through the National Union, but in the principle of the thing. For they had persuaded themselves that, as long as unions existed, they would be exposed to a constant sequence of wage demands and lightning strikes at harvest time. They also maintained that it was impossible to run a farm on the basis of union rules—and the National Union unwisely tended to accompany its wage claims with a demand for 'a general conformity' to its (actually quite innocuous) rules. So the East Anglian farmers rejected mediation on the Lincolnshire model.[1]

[1] After the Lincolnshire settlement, too, the National Union

Because the lock-out was therefore a direct attack on the right to combine and also because of the special emotions still evoked by agriculture, the dispute speedily became of national concern, despite the relatively small numbers involved—perhaps about 5,000,[1] as against some 70,000 ironworkers out in South Wales the previous year. Both the National and the Federal Unions bent all their efforts to support their locked-out members in East Anglia, and they received substantial assistance from urban unions and the public at large. In all some £18,000 was contributed, and £29,000 spent on strike pay and the promotion of migration and emigration.[2] But by the summer the farmers were clearly winning. For the unusually dry weather had reduced the need for hoeing. And in any case they had previously employed too many people, partly to find jobs for men past their prime, and partly because they had been farming too high. They were therefore able to make do with considerably fewer workers. Also, though the unions had managed to enrol virtually the entire labour force in some villages, on a

---

withdrew its earlier offers of mediation, and declined to go back without a pay rise.

[1] Precise figures are hard to come by, since not all the unions' claims can be taken at face value. In any case they gave not the total number dismissed, but the number they were currently having to support. And as the dispute progressed, new groups of men were locked out, while some of those originally involved left the area or drifted back to work. The best source is the reports in the *Bee-Hive*.

In mid-April the unions claimed to be supporting over 6,000 men, but this is probably an exaggeration. Earlier that month Banks had said 1,200 Federal members were locked out in all (of whom some 200 must have been in the Louth area of Lincolnshire—*Stamford Mercury*, 17 April); by mid-May the Federal total was down to 1,075; and in early June (after the end of the dispute in Lincolnshire) a careful count gave the East Anglian total as 829. In addition over £400 is said to have been spent on the support of men locked out for union membership in Kent. The most detailed National Union count gave 3,324 members as in receipt of strike pay (mainly, but not entirely, in the east)—*Labourers' Union Chronicle* (Leamington), 13 June 1874; by the end of the dispute in early August this had shrunk to rather over 1,000.

[2] Again claims are conflicting, and the discrepancies were to occasion the unions serious trouble. See esp. the *Labourers' Union Chronicle*, 13 June 1874 and 29 May 1875; F. Clifford, *op. cit.*, p. 21; The Federal Union of Agricultural and General Labourers, *Report to the Trade Societies and General Public of the United Kingdom* (1874); and the *Bee-Hive*, 19 Dec. 1874, p. 3.

county basis they never accounted for as much as half; so there remained a substantial pool of non-union labour to draw on. As the summer continued, many of the locked-out men found other jobs or left the district; but the remainder hoped that they would prove indispensable at least during the harvest. In fact this was got in by women, tradesmen, townsmen and coprolite diggers (whose mines were specially closed to release them). So in August the National Union suspended dispute pay, thus effectively conceding defeat; and the Federal followed suit.[1]

Only a minority of the unions' members even in the counties concerned had been directly involved in the lock-outs. And of those who had, a surprising number were able to retain their membership after the dispute was over.[2] But the psychological effects were more widely felt—they led, for instance, to the rapid disintegration of the National Union's outpost in Northumberland. More seriously the personal frictions and financial deficiencies high-lighted by the dispute split both the Federal and the National Unions. Thus by March 1875 the Lincolnshire League had pulled out of the Federal Union, and had itself lost a couple of districts in Norfolk. Trouble in the National Union came to a head at its May Council; it led to the alienation of the Union's newspaper, which proceeded to foster a small breakaway body that turned its back on strike tactics in favour of the acquisition of small-holdings.[3]

Not only was the movement now bitterly divided, but its priorities were changing. We have seen that one of the terms for ending the Lincolnshire lock-out was a change in the League's rules to de-emphasize strikes. Thereafter the League

[1] For the above, see esp. F. Clifford and A. J. Peacock, works cited; Rex C. Russell, *The 'Revolt of the Field' in Lincs.* (n. pl., 1956), chap. iv; and *The Annual Register*, 1874, pp. 113–21.

[2] The *Labourers' Union Chronicle* of 24 October 1874 claimed that of 3,116 N.A.L.U. members locked-out, 402 left the union, 415 were still unemployed, 1,123 migrated or emigrated, and 1,176 returned to work retaining their union membership. The figures do not tally exactly with the paper's other statements. But they suggest that some of the locked-out men found work with other farmers locally, and that others were taken back by their original employers— Clifford mentions an instance, p. 63. The Farmers' Associations were constantly pressed to be magnanimous in victory, and they may have been the more inclined to take this advice since the men in question were usually good workmen.

[3] The *Bee-Hive*, 24 Oct. 1874, p. 5; *The Labourer* (Boston), 13 March 1875, p. 4; Horn, *op. cit.*, pp. 111–15; *Labourers' Union Chronicle*, 24 July 1875.

TABLE I. *The Membership of Agricultural Trades Unions*
(Figures with asterisks are taken from the Press. The remainder relate to the end of the year and derive from the returns in the *Parliamentary Papers*.)

A	1873	1874	1875	1876	1877	1878	1879	1880	1881	1882	1883	1884	1885	1886
N.A.L.U.	71,835*	86,214*	40,000	55,000	30,000	24,000	20,000	20,000	15,000	15,000	15,000	18,000	10,700	10,366
Lincoln, &c., Amalgamated Labour League	c. 18,000*	n.a.	10,000	5,500	4,000	3,400	3,072	n.a.	1,020	850	n.a.	94	154	99
Kent Agricultural and General Labourers Union	8,000	9,000	9,500	10,000	11,500	12,000	12,500	10,300	10,200	10,300	10,400	10,500	11,000	10,300
Peterborough District Labourers' Union	4,020	n.a.	n.a.	n.a.	2,000*									
West of England	c. 3,500*													
West Surrey Agricultural Labourers' Union	179													
Botesdale (Suffolk) Agricultural Labourers' Union	213	subsequently incorporated into N.A.L.U												
Gloucestershire Agricultural Association	n.a.													

This table does not quite cover all the rural trades unions of the period. No Scottish union registered until 1887. In 1884 there was also a 'Dorset Agricultural Workers', Union', which republished Thomas Hardy's article on 'The Dorset Farm Labourer Past and Present'. And a number of the districts that broke away from the National and Federal Unions continued independently for a greater or lesser time—for examples from Norfolk, see Springall, pp. 99–100.

For an attempt to plot the geographical distribution of the unions in the 1870s, see Dunbabin, article cited, pp. 115–18.

B	1887	1888	1889	1890	1891	1892	1893	1894	1895	1896	1897	1898	1899	1900
N.A.L.U.	5,300	4,660	4,254	8,500	15,000	15,000	14,746	1,100	n.a.	dissolved				
Amalgamated Labour League	68	78	90	295	148	104	51	50	42	40	40	37	30	21
Norfolk Federal Union, Harlestone District				n.a.	n.a.	136	98	32	10	dissolved				
Norfolk & Norwich Amalgamated Labour League				n.a.	840	675	700	400	20	dissolved				
Eastern Counties Labour Federation				2,183	8,409	16,881	11,432	2,500	4	dissolved				
Wiltshire General & Agricultural Workers							1,500	1,500	330	200	merged with Gasworkers & General Labourers			
Agricultural Farm Labourers' League of Dorset				n.a.	n.a.	400	548	500	589	533	229	134	122	150
Berkshire Agricultural and General Workers							245	120	21	dissolved				
Warwickshire Agricultural and General Workers							562	450	dissolved					
Herefordshire Agricultural and General Workers' Union							500	n.a.	n.a.	dissolved				
Hertfordshire and Bedfordshire Land and Labour League								membership never reported						
Scottish Farm Servants, Carters and General Labourers' (Aberdeen)	464	644	265	400	456	257	223	157	merged with the Ploughmen's & Labourers' Union					
Ploughmen's & Labourers' Federal Union			n.a.	n.a.	n.a.	at most 6,000*	n.a.	n.a.	1,300	1,541	2,390	875	807	dissolved
London & Southern Counties Labour League	9,040	8,500	10,000	13,000	13,000	10,900	8,900	4,620	dissolved					

This was a continuation of the Kent Agricultural and General. But it had shifted its emphasis, and when the two classes were first distinguished in 1895, it was listed under 'General Labour'.

concentrated increasingly on fostering emigration, on offering friendly society benefits, and on the politics of the day. And the National Union in fact followed a similar course. In so doing the unions were clearly responding to the wishes of their members. And the slide of agriculture into depression in the latter half of the decade discouraged further strikes for the improvement of wages. But the functions the unions now assumed could all be performed by other agencies,[1] and in sponsoring migration they may also have deprived themselves of key supporters. As table I (on pages 80 and 81) shows, the result was a gradual decay in membership, punctuated by the occasional catastrophe (like the return to Worcestershire and Herefordshire in 1877 of ex-union migrants disillusioned by the industrial slump[2]). And by the 1880s the unions had largely ceased to count except in the sphere of politics (which we shall discuss in a later chapter).

But there was a marked revival at the end of the decade. This, too, is in line with the pattern of trades unionism in other unorganized occupations. Indeed it was to a considerable extent the consequence of the 'New Unionism' of urban unskilled labourers. Thus the London Dockers sought to extend their organization back into the countryside, in part at least to prevent farm workers competing in the docks. And the Eastern Counties Labour Federation (which temporarily overhauled the old N.A.L.U.) had its origins in the ferment inspired in Ipswich by the celebrated 1889 London Dock Strike.[3]

The revival was, however, very largely confined to East Anglia. Even in the 1870s the east had accounted for a disproportionate share of rural trades unionism, probably because of its large-scale arable farming, perhaps too as a result of the prevalence of large agricultural villages. But there had also been a high degree of union membership in parts of central and southern England. Twenty years later membership briefly approached the old figures in East Anglia. But though new unions were again quite widely founded in other parts of the country, only in Wiltshire did they attain any very significant

[1] Farm labourers could not readily afford the subscriptions of the better friendly societies, so there might have been considerable scope here for the unions had their schemes been financially sounder.

[2] Joseph Arch, *The Story of his Life* (1898), p. 281.

[3] A. J. Peacock, *Land Reform 1880–1919: A Study of the Activities of the English Land Restoration Leagues and the Land Nationalisation Society* (unpublished M.A. thesis, Southampton University), pp. 173–4.

size. This difference is no doubt partly due to the much greater impact the agricultural depression had had on wages in East Anglia. Also it was still usual for wage-rates there to fluctuate with the price of corn; and this volatility may have encouraged combinations and counter-combinations.

In general the unions of the 1890s were less militant and more political than their predecessors. But, politics apart, their fortunes were fairly similar, though less dramatic. The East Anglian unions were founded, or in the case of the N.A.L.U. refloated, on a rising market. They grew rapidly, local branches often springing into existence and almost immediately making wage claims. These were often conceded, sometimes enforced by small strikes; and over the period 1890–2 the unions generally succeeded in raising wages slightly in the spring and in preventing serious cuts after the harvest. As before, their success led to the formation in July 1891 of a Farmers' Federation for mutual assistance in disputes, and this eventually secured over 700 members in Norfolk and Suffolk. In due course the cycle turned; wheat prices fell in 1892 and by 1893 were lower than for over a century; and farmers insisted that wage rates should also come down. This led to a number of disputes—the Farmers' Federation claimed success in 18 out of the 22 in which their members had been engaged during the year 1892–3. Sometimes the process dragged on for a considerable period; but the scale never remotely approached that of the 1874 lock-out.[1]

In themselves these defeats did not seriously impoverish the unions. But men came to question the value of subscribing to organizations that could not keep up wages. And such doubts were sedulously encouraged by the unions' opponents. Here politics also entered into the matter. For all the unions had worked actively for the Liberal Party. And the Conservatives seem to have responded here as elsewhere by promoting a rival 'Ipswich Mutual Working Men's Independent Federation', run by A. L. Edwards, 'a recent convert from ultra-Radicalism to hyper-Toryism'. From the beginning of 1893 Edwards pursued the unions through their balance sheets; these did indeed show that by far the greater part of their expenditure went on administration, and the fact was none too scrupulously broadcast in leaflets on 'How the Labourers' Money is Spent'. The tactic is said to have been effective; and in 1894 the major unions collapsed, the disintegration of the Eastern Counties Labour

---

[1] *P.P.*, 1893–4 xxxvii Part 2, esp. pp. 163–4.

Federation being further accelerated by internal disputes over an abortive attempt at co-operative farming.[1]

This was not quite the end. For in 1898, a year when farm labour was scarce, the Workers' Union recruited briefly in the countryside until the enterprise was cut short by the decline of its urban base. A small union founded in Dorset in 1890 survived into the twentieth century. And the last vestige of the 1872 Lincolnshire League still had a score of members in one Norfolk village in 1910. But for practical purposes all organizational continuity had ceased, though some of the individuals and the families involved in the earlier cycles of agitation were to take part also in the next one (which began in 1906, gathered momentum shortly before the First War, and was then transformed by the War itself).

[1] George Edwards, *From Crow-Scaring to Westminster* (1922), pp. 75–6; *Bury Free Press*, 11 Feb. 1893, p. 5; *The Memoirs of Josiah Sage*, pp. 37–8; A. J. Peacock, thesis cited, esp. pp. 182–5.

V

Agricultural Trade Unionism in Oxfordshire

by Pamela Horn

Effective trade union agitation amongst farm workers began in Oxfordshire—as in most other counties—during the year 1872. Admittedly, slight manifestations of discontent had occurred before this in 1867, when at a time of high food prices and of political pressure from urban workers for the passage of the Reform Bill, labourers in the very north of the county had become involved in a small-scale union which had been established in Buckingham (largely for the benefit of Buckinghamshire farm workers). A few Oxfordshire men paid their membership entrance fee of 1s. and took advantage of the union's offers to provide details of better-paid employment elsewhere. For example, labourers from the village of Mixbury took positions in Yorkshire under this scheme.[1] Nor was the discontent confined to the men, for about the same time some of the women field workers in the nearby Bicester area went on strike for an increase in their wage rate from 6d. to 8d. per day. But their protest was a purely local and spontaneous affair and was not backed by any formal organization.

Nevertheless, these events of the 1860s were merely straws in the wind and were not of any real significance in their own right; it is noticeable that they soon petered out. The story in 1872 was very different.

It was from the activities of the South Warwickshire farm workers that their Oxfordshire counterparts drew direct inspiration. The strike in the Wellesbourne area of Warwickshire had caught the public imagination and, at the same time had

[1] See *Buckingham Express*, 25 May 1867, and also P. L. R. Horn, 'The Evenley Strike of 1867' in *Northamptonshire Past and Present*, iv, no. 1. The main storm centre of the 1867 agitation was the Buckinghamshire village of Gawcott, however, and it is interesting to note that a well-supported Reform meeting was held in the village about a month before the local labourers went on strike. A number of the officers of the Buckingham Union were also prominent in the Reform agitation in the town of Buckingham and had addressed labourers at the Gawcott reform gathering in late Feb. 1867. See *Buckingham Advertiser*, 23 Feb., 2 March, 23 March, 30 March, 27 April and 18 May 1867.

shown agricultural labourers that by determined action they could focus attention on their economic and social problems. In certain parts of Oxfordshire, particularly in the northern area bordering on Warwickshire, this interest was shown by establishing branches in direct association with the South Warwickshire Union. Thus the *Oxford Journal* for 9 March 1872 mentions 'a good deal of agitation' among the agricultural labourers of the Banbury district and reports that at Bloxham and Milcombe this had led to a 1s. a week rise being secured; in the following weeks there are accounts of meetings at Salford, Mollington, Turweston and a number of other nearby villages. But in communities in the central and southern regions of the county, needs were catered for by the formation of an independent union.

The first meeting to establish this was held in mid-April on the recreation ground at the village of Milton-under-Wychwood, in the west of the county, just over twenty miles from Oxford. The meeting was enthusiastically supported and at its close about fifty of those present agreed to form their own union. Four days later (20 April 1872) the first committee meeting of the Milton Union was held, and on this occasion it was decided to appoint a local carpenter and Methodist lay preacher, named Joseph Leggett, as secretary.[1] However, at this time interest in the new union appears to have been largely confined to three villages only (viz. Milton-under-Wychwood itself, and the two nearby communities of Shipton-under-Wychwood and Lyneham); and the six-member committee of labourers initially appointed to direct its affairs in fact came from these villages. Nevertheless plans were soon in hand to extend its scope, and it was quickly decided that some of the union's funds should be specifically set aside for the purpose of financing meetings; at the same time the rate of contribution for members was agreed at 2d. per week.

But although the Milton Union had been set up as an independent organization, its leaders felt deep admiration for their Warwickshire counterparts, who had done so much to pave the way for future progress. Consequently when Edwin Russell, the

---

[1] Leggett was born in Windsor, Berkshire, although his wife was a Milton-under-Wychwood girl. He had lived in Milton at least from the end of the 1850s and at the time of the formation of the union was aged about 35. At that date he was employed by Alfred Groves, carpenter and builder, of Milton. See 1861 Census Return for Milton-under-Wychwood at Public Record Office, R.G.9.910, and *Oxford Chronicle*, 18 May, 1872.

latter's corresponding secretary, wrote to Leggett early in May, inviting his members to join the Warwickshire Union 'as a branch', and offering advice and help, the Oxfordshire men responded warmly. Indeed, they stressed 'the desirableness of forming a National Union'.[1] Messages were exchanged between the two, and, at a Whit Monday demonstration held by the Warwickshire Union at Wellesbourne shortly afterwards, Russell announced that Charles Cox of the Milton Union was among those attending. In the course of his speech, Russell noted that the Milton Union had thirteen branches and over five hundred members. He also pointed out that, as yet, these branches were still quite independent of the branches in Oxfordshire connected with his own organization.[2]

That independence was not to survive much longer. When the Warwickshire Union called their Congress at Leamington to discuss the formation of a National Union, the Milton leaders readily agreed to send three representatives to the meetings on 29 and 30 May, and to pay any expenses incurred from the union's funds. At that May Congress the momentous decision was taken to establish the National Agricultural Labourers' Union, and the Milton representatives returned to report this to their executive. At a meeting held on 1st June it was unanimously agreed that the union 'should be joined to the National Union as a district, having Leamington as the centre'.[3]

Nevertheless formal affiliation was delayed until 23 October, when a delegate meeting (attended by the N.A.L.U. President, Joseph Arch) was held for the purpose at Oxford Town Hall. The district became known as the 'Oxford District' and at the time of affiliation claimed about 2,500 members. However, this was not the sum total of Oxfordshire membership. Those

[1] Milton Union Minute Book, 7 May 1872, preserved at Nuffield College, Oxford.

[2] *Royal Leamington Chronicle*, 25 May 1872. Cox, the Milton Union representative, was aged about 31 and was an agricultural labourer from the village of Shipton-under-Wychwood. He was a member of the original six-man committee appointed at Milton on 20 April 1872. The others were John Hollyock, a 36-year-old labourer from Lyneham; William Tripp, labourer, aged 42, from Lyneham; from Shipton, William Wright, labourer, aged 50; James Mills, labourer, aged 43, from Milton-under-Wychwood; and William Barnes, aged 37, woodman from Milton-under-Wychwood. See Milton Union Minute Book at Nuffield College, Oxford, and also 1871 Census Returns for these parishes at the Public Record Office, R.G.10.1455 and R.G.10.1456.

[3] Milton Union Minute Book, 1 June 1872.

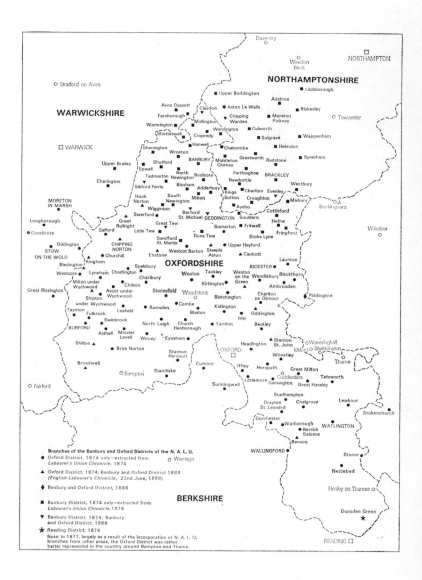

Branches of the Banbury and Oxford Districts of the N. A. L. U.

- ● Oxford District, 1874 only—extracted from ○ Wantage
  Labourer's Union Chronicle, 1874

- ▲ Oxford District, 1874; Banbury and Oxford District 1888
  (*English Labourer's Chronicle*, 22nd June, 1889)

- ◆ Banbury and Oxford District, 1888

- ■ Banbury District, 1874 only—extracted from
  Labourer's Union Chronicle, 1874

- ▼ Banbury District, 1874; Banbury
  and Oxford District, 1888

- ★ Reading District, 1874

Note: In 1877, largely as a result of the incorporation of N. A. L. U.
branches from other areas, the Oxford District was rather
better represented in the country around Bampton and Thame.

branches which had been established in the north of the county —together with some in Northamptonshire and a few in Warwickshire—were formed into a separate N.A.L.U. district centred around Banbury. But as about half of its branches lay outside the county borders, it was less typically an Oxfordshire organization than its southern counterpart.

One of the main aims of the union movement was to secure an improvement in the wages and conditions of employment of members. It is, therefore, scarcely surprising that demands for payment of overtime, etc., were quickly incorporated into the rules of both the Milton and the Warwickshire unions, and as early as 23 May discussions were taking place in Oxfordshire on the wages to be demanded at harvest time. On this occasion it was decided that the payment should be 4s. per day 'without beer' and 6d. per hour overtime; but the decision was subsequently amended in late July to '5s. per day . . . the hours for labour to be 13, 2 hours to be allowed for meals.'[1] The basic wage rate of the ordinary labourer in the county was at that time in the region of 11s. to 12s. per week, and although it might be augmented by piecework earnings or by perquisites, by no means all labourers shared in these advantages. With the coming of the union, however, a basic minimum of 15s. or 16s. per week was aimed at. The demand was not in itself an unreasonable one, but the size of the weekly increase which it involved, plus anger at the union's interference, helped to create bad feeling between Oxfordshire farmers and the union branches. Out of this feeling there developed a determined opposition to the trade unions—and its clearest manifestation in 1872 was at the village of Wootton in the vicinity of Blenheim Palace, the seat of the Duke of Marlborough.

A union branch had been formed in Wootton in May 1872, under the leadership of Christopher Holloway, a local farm worker and Wesleyan lay preacher.[2] Less than a month after

---

[1] *Ibid.*, 25 July 1872.

[2] Christopher Holloway was born in 1828. His first wife, Susan, had at one time been a schoolmistress and gloveress in Wootton, while his own interests in the Wesleyan Church were of long standing. In 1864 he was appointed a trustee of the local chapel, and in 1870 he is recorded as attending Local Preachers' meetings in Oxford, held in connection with the Oxford Methodist Circuit. His connection with the union was later to bring him into conflict with some of his fellow preachers, and at a Local Preachers' meeting held on 25 Sept. 1872, an unsuccessful attempt was made to censure him. Holloway later became an emigration agent, and by 1880 had also

its establishment the branch had a membership of 185, and in late June the men decided that, unless they were paid wages of 16s. per week from 6 July (in accordance with the rules of the Warwickshire Union), they would come out on strike. This proposal had been previously discussed by Holloway and members of the Milton Union Executive Committee at a meeting on 27 June, and it had received the Committee's blessing.

In the face of a strike threat, the local farmers met together and decided to respond in kind by locking out all trade unionist labourers. At the same time they formed themselves into a Property Protection Society in case 'damage should arise as a consequence of the agitation.' On the Friday following the meeting all workers belonging to the union were dismissed, and it was announced that they would not be re-engaged until they had left it.

The hostility of these Oxfordshire farmers towards trade unionism was underlined on 9 July, when forty of the principal agriculturists in the area met at Woodstock to discuss the situation. Perhaps part of their resentment can be attributed to the fact that the workers had threatened to strike at a time when the demand for their labour was greatest—at harvest time. Four days later a further meeting was held—this time at Oxford Corn Exchange—when about two or three hundred people attended, and it was decided to establish a society to be known as the Oxfordshire Association of Agriculturists, whose objective would be the protection of the interests of employers of agricultural labour. No member was 'to engage a labourer without a character from his last employer', or 'to employ a labourer belonging to a Union, unless he [was] already a hired servant'.[1] Annual subscriptions of 10s. for membership of the Association were agreed upon, payable in advance. But despite this early enthusiasm, the Association never seems to have really got off the ground, and within two months it had finally collapsed.

---

set up as a shopkeeper in Wootton. At the time of his death on 6 Dec. 1895, he was described as a grocer and coal merchant, although, as his Will shows, his worldly possessions were not very great. His property was valued at only £174. See P. L. R. Horn, 'Christopher Holloway—An Oxfordshire Trade Union Leader' in *Oxoniensia*, xxxiii (1968).

[1] *Oxford Journal.* 20 July 1872. See also P. L. R. Horn, 'Farmers' Defence Associations in Oxfordshire, 1872–74' in *History Studies*, I, no. 1 (1968).

In the meantime the lock-out in the Wootton area continued and some of the labourers affected decided to migrate or emigrate. On Wednesday, 17 July, forty men left Wootton with their families to seek employment in ironworks near Sheffield, for example, and further cases could be quoted. On the other hand, despite their opposition, a number of the farmers were obviously becoming concerned as the lock-out stretched into August. Although they had the support of the Duke of Marlborough (who offered to transfer control of the cottages and allotments rented by labourers on his estate to the tenant farmers, to strengthen the latter's bargaining position), it was appreciated that if the farmers were not to give way they would have to take further steps in order to get in the harvest.[1] Eventually it was decided to apply to the military authorities at Aldershot for soldiers to work in the harvest fields. Although this was not the first time soldiers had been used for agricultural strike breaking,[2] their intervention on this occasion aroused considerable ill-feeling in trade union circles. Both the secretary of the National Agricultural Labourers' Union and the secretary of the London Trades Council wrote to the Secretary of State for War about the use of soldiers during a civil dispute; and as a result of their efforts the Queen's Regulations were subsequently amended to prevent a repetition of the affair. Nevertheless, the farmers' immediate problems were solved. The harvest was gathered in, and at the same time the dispute fizzled out—although unionist activity in the Wootton area did not.

Yet if the fate of the Oxfordshire Association of Agriculturists indicated that farmers lacked the determination and persistence to combine *together* to oppose the unions, this did not mean that

[1] It should be noted, however, that the Duke's decision did not always cause problems for the labourers. Christopher Holloway of Wootton rented an allotment at a rent of 16s. 8d. per annum from the Duke of Marlborough before the trouble began, and he was still in occupation of his holding and paying the same rent by Michaelmas, 1873, when the movement had become well-established (see Allotments Account Book—His Grace, the Duke of Marlborough's Oxfordshire estate). On the other hand, at Whitehill and Tackley (and even at Wootton) some of the land formerly let as allotments was, by 1873, being rented in blocks to tradesmen, instead of separately to individual labourers.

[2] In Aug. 1867, for example, striking labourers in Essex were replaced by 200 soldiers sent from Colchester barracks. See *Midland Free Press*, 31 Aug. 1867.

their opposition had itself disappeared. Reactions varied, but in these early days the more embittered employers used any weapon they could to penalize those workers who had dared to join the union. In particular, breaches of the contract of employment by unionists were frequently brought before Petty Sessions. In this connection waggoners, cowmen, shepherds and others hired by the year or the month were especially vulnerable if they ceased work after giving only one week's notice. Even in the South Oxfordshire/Berkshire border area, where agricultural trade unionism was not very strong, the number of cases of breach of the contract of employment brought before Henley Petty Sessions showed a considerable increase at this time:

Year	*Number of breaches of the contract of employment per annum*
1870	3
1871	2
1872	7
1873	10
1876	2

(Calculated from Minute Book of Henley Petty Sessions at Bodleian Library, Oxford.)

It will be seen that by 1876, when the first fever of agricultural unionism had abated, the number of farm servants charged with absconding had returned to the 1871 level.

In other instances, eviction of unionist labourers from their cottages was the weapon employed. Thus the *Oxford Journal* of 23 March 1872 noted that: 'Many labourers have already received notices to quit their cottages in consequence of their connexion with the Union, or sympathy with those out on strike', and the policy was continued thereafter. Still more extremely, in the north of the county at the village of Tadmarton, a local farmer was charged with having thrashed a labourer (Isaac Bodfish) because he had joined the union.[1] This

---

[1] The Bodfish family's brushes with the law were not happy ones. During the 1830 Swing riots in the Banbury area, Isaac's uncle, James Bodfish, had been found guilty of machine breaking and sentenced to fifteen months' imprisonment. With regard to eviction, the *Oxford Chronicle of* 10 Aug. 1872, reported that Richard Brain of Bletchington, a tenant of Lord Valentia, and 'a local preacher among the Primitive Methodists, . . . a good workman, had been obliged to go away into Warwickshire because he had joined the Union.' And

affair was complicated by allegations that the magistrate whom Bodfish had first approached had advised settlement out of court, with the farmer paying Bodfish £4. Although the union provided a solicitor to represent Bodfish in the eventual court case, his claim was dismissed on the grounds that the publicity which had been given had already compromised the matter, and 'no satisfactory evidence had been adduced that any attempt was made to coerce the man from joining any Union . . .' And though the question was raised in the House of Commons on 7 June, no further progress was made from Bodfish's point of view.

Nevertheless, if agricultural trade unionism aroused serious hostility among certain Oxfordshire farmers and landowners in its early months, it bestowed worthwhile benefits upon its supporters as compensation. Basic wage rates were raised by 2s. or more per week as a result of the agitation—sometimes without a strike but in other cases (as, for example, at Minster Lovell) only following industrial action. And even where the farmers were more determined and men were dismissed, the union funds could provide out-of-work benefit until they found fresh employment, or else migration payments to enable them to move elsewhere. Nine shillings per week was the sum agreed by the Milton Union for payment to any man 'thrown out of work on account of connection with the Union, so long as he may be out of work', while varying sums were paid to men wishing to migrate to the north of England, the Midlands and even Wales. Some of the other benefits which the unions were eventually to provide (like the investigation of local charities) took longer to organize. But even at the end of their first year unionists in Oxfordshire had cause for satisfaction. Both the Oxford and the Banbury districts had been firmly established and appeared well set to make progress in the coming months.[1]

---

in July 1876, the secretary of the Weston-on-the-Green branch (William Dumbleton) was evicted from the cottage in which he had lived for sixteen years. Dumbleton was a very active member of the Oxford District Committee. Many other cases could be quoted. *English Labourer*, 29 July 1876; and Oxford District Minute Book, 7 June 1876.

[1] Incidentally, not all of the District officials were agricultural labourers. Apart from Joseph Leggett, the Oxford District Secretary, who was a former carpenter, the District treasurer, Mr. G. G. Banbury, was a Woodstock draper. Mr. Banbury and his son, John (who was also active in the union) provide a further example of the links between the union and Methodism, for both were leading

During the winter of 1872/3 branch meetings continued to be held, but in general the union remained quiescent. The relative calm was partially due to the fact that during the winter employment was always in short supply, and the farmers could therefore more confidently have withstood a lock-out or strike. Then, too, the unionists were still engaged in planning their future strategy, collecting information on wage rates within the county, etc. It is noticeable that at a meeting on 25 November 1872 the committee of the Oxford district refused to support men in the village of Chadlington who had given in their notice following wage cuts.

But with the approach of the spring sowing season, unionist militancy became more obvious, with disputes taking place in a number of villages. Undoubtedly the most significant of these —at least from a publicity point of view—occurred in Ascott-under-Wychwood. Although the village concerned was a small one (population 462 in 1871), the details of the case received national coverage, both from the press and through Parliament, on account of its special features.

The strike arose out of a demand by labourers employed by farmer Robert Hambridge, of Ascott, for a rise of 2s. per week in their basic wages. Hambridge, who was the largest farmer in the village, declined to raise the wages of *all* his men, although he agreed to give the advance to his 'efficient labourers, and observed that the others, from age or infirmity, must for the present remain at 12s. per week . . .'.[1] These terms were rejected by the men and on 14 April 1873, after the expiration of their 'due notice', they came out on strike. A week later labourers employed by other farmers in the village followed suit.

Hambridge was in particular difficulty because of the large scale on which he farmed,[2] and he immediately set about recruit-

---

members of the Methodist Church. Indeed, when Mr. Banbury, senior, died many years later, it was reported to the meeting of the Oxford United Methodist Trustees on 14 March 1912, that 'most of the Chapels belonging to this Trust were built' at his instigation; John Banbury became treasurer of the United Methodist Trustees until his own death in 1907.

[1] *Midland Free Press*, 7 June 1873. See also *The Times*, 26 May 1873.

[2] According to a letter he wrote to *The Times* of 2 June 1873, Hambridge occupied a 'Government farm of 400 acres'. He complained that the men had left him 'in the middle of a backward barley sowing, with 12 agricultural horses, four working bullocks, a superior flock of 500 sheep at turnips, milking cows, bullocks,

ing non-unionist replacements for the strikers. After some efforts he obtained the services of two young men named John Hodgkins and John Millen, from the nearby village of Ramsden. And it was at this point that the wives and daughters of the strikers decided to intervene, to support their menfolk and to prevent the two lads acting as strike breakers. On 12 May (while Hambridge was absent at a fair) about thirty of them went to the field where the youngsters were due to start their day's work, to try to persuade them to stop. Although some of them carried sticks and also 'jostled' the men, it was generally agreed that their attitude was not very dangerous. Indeed, at one stage they offered to buy Hodgkins and Millen a drink if they would cease work, but the offer was refused. It was further admitted that though the men left the field at the time of the 'intimidation', they freely returned to work there afterwards, under what *The Times* ironically called, 'the powerful protection of one police constable'.[1]

Shortly afterwards 17 of the women were charged at Chipping Norton Petty Sessions with a breach of the Criminal Law Amendment Act, and two clerical magistrates sentenced 16 of them to imprisonment—seven receiving 10 days', and nine receiving 7 days', hard labour. A great outcry followed since two of the women had babies, who were also taken to prison with their mothers. Indeed, following the announcement of the sentence a large crowd of union supporters gathered in front of Chipping Norton police station, where the women were confined prior to their removal to Oxford Gaol. Stones were thrown and union leaders later claimed that only the presence of Christopher Holloway, the district chairman, prevented a serious riot.[2]

---

and young stock, with only a head shepherd and a youth (yearly servants)'. See also the *Oxford Journal*, 7th June 1873. At the 1871 Census of Population Hambridge employed 10 men and 4 boys. P.R.O. R.G.10. 1455.

[1] An anonymous correspondent, writing to the *Oxford Journal* of 7 June 1873, under the dramatic nom-de-plume 'One of the Threatened', claimed that this was not the first time that women had intervened in an agricultural dispute in Oxfordshire. During the summer of 1872 'a party of women drove four men out of a field of turnips, at Barton, near Wootton', where they had been employed by a Mr. Thomas Tims of Dun's Tew.

[2] According to the *Oxford Journal*, 24 May 1873, there were fears that an attempt would be made to rescue the women from the police station by force. 'As night still further set in, an attack was made on the station, stones being thrown, and most of the windows of

Public opinion on a wider front was also aroused, and questions were asked in the House of Commons concerning the case. Ultimately the Lord Chancellor requested the Duke of Marlborough, as Lord-Lieutenant of the county, to investigate the conduct of the two J.P.s. In the event, the duke's report supported their action, and his letter was 'backed by a testimonial, signed by 298 occupiers of land, and others from 29 Oxfordshire parishes, expressing entire satisfaction with the action of the justices'.[1] But if the landed classes of Oxfordshire approved of the J.P.s' actions, many other people did not; even the Lord Chancellor expressed reservations and the N.A.L.U. leaders certainly used the case as propaganda and as an example of the tyranny of both farmers and clerical magistrates. Not only was the occasion of the women's release from prison turned into a large union demonstration, but about three weeks later (on 20 June) each of them was presented with £5 in cash and a dress in the union colour—blue—by Joseph Arch, the N.A.L.U. President and Joseph Leggett, the Oxford district secretary.[2]

Superintendent Larkin's house were smashed, and a few in the station, also the street lamps. A telegram in the meantime was sent to Oxford for a van to take the prisoners direct from the station and for further assistance. The Mayor urged the well-disposed to leave, and announced that unless the crowd dispersed he should be obliged to read the Riot Act. Ultimately most of them went away . . . About two a brake from Oxford, with a reinforcement of police arrived, and the prisoners being placed therein, started under a strong guard for gaol, a number of additional men being left here, should their services be required.'

[1] *P.P.*, 1873, liv, pp. 27–31, and Diana McClatchey, *Oxfordshire Clergy 1777–1869*, (Oxford, 1960), pp. 199–200. The last survivor of the imprisoned women—Mrs. Rathband (née Fanny Honeybourn)—died in 1939 at Chipping Norton. She was aged 16 at the time of the imprisonment and was sentenced to 10 days' hard labour. She was the daughter of an Ascott labourer and at the time of the 1871 Census of Population was employed as a domestic servant in the parish. See Census Return for Ascott-under-Wychwood, 1871, at P.R.O., R.G.10.1455. Another of the imprisoned women, Mary Pratley, emigrated to New Zealand in Sept. 1875, with her husband and 6 children. I am indebted to Mr. R. Arnold for this information.

[2] See also P. L. R. Horn, *Joseph Arch* (Kineton, 1971), pp. 86–8. According to the *Labourers' Union Chronicle* of 5 July 1873, the governor of Oxford gaol received the Queen's Warrant to remit the remainder of the women's sentences and to release them forthwith. Unfortunately, the Warrant only arrived on 31st May—the date when the last of the women were due to be released anyway, so they derived no benefit from it.

The involvement of the clergy in this matter may incidentally have reinforced the growing hostility of unionists towards the Church of England. Many Oxfordshire incumbents attributed dwindling Church attendance by labourers during the 1870s to the influence of the union. For example, during 1875 it was reported from the village of Swinbrook that: 'Congregations [had] considerably fallen off since the formation of [the] Agricultural Union and the propagation of its literature,' while at Fifield the *Labourers' Union Chronicle* was blamed: 'It slanders the Clergy and indeed every class of society, it is circulated on the Saturday so as to furnish reading for the Sunday. The Church has provided no antidote in any new form to meet the new evil.' And at Weston-on-the-Green the incumbent sadly reflected that: 'Since the Agricultural Labourers' Union *my* attendance has *sadly decreased*; three years ago the Church was quite filled but now there are many empty benches . . .' In all, during 1875, 16 incumbents out of a total of 237 directly blamed the N.A.L.U. for their smaller congregations, while many of the remainder noted a decline without giving any particular reason for it. Significantly, too, as the union weakened towards the end of the decade, so the complaints of non-attendance at Church by labourers became muted. By 1878, for example, it was claimed at Chesterton (among others) that: 'The attendance at Church has increased during the last three years; and the Union influence which affected us for a time has quite disappeared.'[1]

The favourable publicity which the Ascott-under-Wychwood case secured may well have assisted in the improvement in union recruitment figures which occurred during this period. By November 1873 the Oxford district claimed a membership of 3,800 divided among 62 branches, while the Banbury district,

[1] Clergy Visitation Returns for Oxford Diocese, at Bodleian Library: for 1875, MS. Oxon. Dioc. Pp. c. 341; for 1878, MS. Oxon. Dioc. Pp. c. 344. As late as 1884 the incumbent of Milton-under-Wychwood could report that Church attendance had increased, 'Now that the distrust of the church and clergy which was very strong here through frequent meetings of the Labourers' Union and fomented by Mr. Arch has apparently passed away. The men formerly *surly and uncourteous* are now cheerful and polite to me . . .' Clergy Visitation Returns for Oxford Diocese, 1884. See also P. L. R. Horn, *Joseph Arch*, p. 71, for the attitude of the vicar of Minster Lovell, who had been initially sympathetic to the union movement but had then objected to it being made 'a nail upon which to hang an attack upon the Church . . .'.

in the north of the county, had one of over 3,000, divided among 54 branches. Nevertheless, it is worth remembering that even this progress was not sufficient to bring the *majority* of agricultural workers into the trade union movement. According to the 1871 Census, there were 18,771 male agricultural labourers, 534 male farm servants, and 875 shepherds employed in the county. The 7,000 or so trade unionists who had been organized in the two districts by the end of 1873 fell very far short of being a majority of these—and in any case around half of the Banbury district's branches lay outside the county boundaries. This failure to secure a high level of support was, in the long run, to prove a point of great weakness to the entire movement. Although the incidence of membership was rather patchy, with some villages better organized than others, it was fairly easy for farmers to carry on even in the face of union opposition, by the use of non-unionist or 'blackleg' labour.[1] Naturally union supporters bitterly resented this and there are several accounts in the early 1870s of clashes taking place between unionists and non-unionists. One typical example may be quoted. In July 1874 a labourer from Toot Baldon was charged (before Bullingdon Division Petty Sessions) with threatening to run a pitch-fork through a fellow labourer who would not join a strike, and also with using bad language towards him. The offender was fined 2s. and required to pay 13s. costs, or to face 14 days' hard labour.

Indeed, although the Ascott-under-Wychwood affair was the most dramatic dispute involving agricultural workers in Oxfordshire during 1873, there were many conflicts of a lesser nature, which were of considerable local significance to the long-term improvement, or otherwise, of the labourer's standard of living. The Oxford district minute book records that between January and early April 1873 20 disputes were reported to the district committee. In other cases, wage rises were secured (as in 1872) without resort to such action. For example, within a week of

[1] Sometimes, too, union men would 'betray' their fellow members. At Lyneham, near Milton-under-Wychwood, when unionists were locked out, two labourers and a foreman, all unionists themselves, agreed to work in their place, and were duly fined 5s. by the Oxford district committee 'and cautioned for the future'. Oxford District Minute Book, 18 March 1873 (Nuffield College, Oxford). With regard to the incidence of union membership, it is impossible to give any clearcut explanation as to the difference in membership levels between villages. However, it does appear that membership was rather more widespread in 'open' villages than in 'closed' ones, and in the arable areas of the county than the pastoral ones.

the formal establishment of the Horspath branch, application was made to the Oxford district secretary for permission to give notice to three local farmers who were paying lower wages than a fourth in the area. The requisite permission was given and notice served—with the gratifying result that the men's wages were increased by 2s. per week, as had been demanded.[1]

During the following year, strikes and lock-outs continued to play their part. Although the disturbances in Oxfordshire were insignificant compared to the major conflict in the eastern counties, they were clearly important to the men concerned. During 1874 it was the Banbury district which was more directly involved, on the whole, than the Oxford one; and if the unrest lacked the propaganda appeal of the Ascott case, it did at any rate cause a drain on the union's funds. At the time of the N.A.L.U's annual conference in June 1874, there were 30 men reliant on union funds in the Banbury district—compared with 1,963 in Suffolk and 376 in Cambridgeshire. In all, the sum of £283 was granted from the funds for relief to the Banbury district during the spring and summer of 1874. But this hardly compared with the £14,985 spent in the most seriously affected Suffolk district over approximately the same period.

In order to cope with expenditure on this scale in the eastern counties, fund raising became a vital part of the N.A.L.U.'s activities during 1874. Financial contributions were collected extensively from areas outside the major seat of conflict, and in this work Oxfordshire proved a generous helper. The Oxford district alone sent, in all, the large sum of £1,281 to the fund, while within the same county assistance was also secured from Oxford University, £26 being forwarded from undergraduates at Balliol College.

The methods adopted to raise money varied considerably. One very popular device was the holding of religious services on Sundays. After each service collections were taken; for example, the fairly small Horspath branch (with a membership of 42) collected 14s. 10d. following an afternoon service in the village church on 17 May 1874. But, given the preponderance of Methodists amongst the union leadership, it was more common for the services to be held in Nonconformist chapels, or else out of doors under the direction of local preachers. Thus, the Oxford District Committee organized a series of services at Chipping Norton. At the

---

[1] Horspath Branch Minute Book, 8 and 11 March, 1873. The Minute Book is preserved at the Bodleian Library, Oxford, MS. Top. Oxon. d.533.

first, held on Sunday, 19 April, a crowd of some 2,000 attended, coming from villages as far as 12 miles away, and the service was conducted from a waggon 'kindly lent for the occasion'. Sermons were preached by three of the district officials—including Thomas Bayliss, who was at this time a district delegate, but who became district secretary early in 1875. Bayliss was a tall, commanding figure, standing well over six feet, and his interest in giving public dramatic recitations, plus his Methodist lay preaching experience, ensured that his speeches held the attention of the audience.[1] In the account of this first Chipping Norton service published in the *Labourers' Union Chronicle* (the N.A.L.U. newspaper), strong words of exhortation were given: 'Working men, fight to the death! We are waging a social war. Stand up for the future liberty of defenceless women and children!' The quotation indicates the attitude of many of the labourers towards the eastern counties lock-out, and at the close of the service £5 were collected for the dispute funds.

Unfortunately, despite this wholehearted support, the large scale on which relief funds had to be distributed, the ability of the farmers to secure 'black-leg' labour, and the migration away from East Anglia of many of the most active leaders, led ultimately to N.A.L.U. defeat. At a meeting of the Union's Executive Committee on 27 July the decision was taken to advise those still on strike to return to work. Although no doubt inevitable in the light of the union's financial condition, this decision caused great dissatisfaction to be expressed in some quarters, whilst a sense of betrayal was undoubtedly felt by many members, particularly in the eastern counties.

Amongst those who felt especially strongly was J. Matthew Vincent, a Leamington newspaper proprietor who owned the *Labourers' Union Chronicle*, and who was also the N.A.L.U. treasurer. Vincent's hostility—although partly caused by a personal feud with the union's secretary, Henry Taylor—was primarily directed against the ending of support for the locked-out men without any safeguards for those who were unemployed and perhaps likely to remain so. In addition, he had a growing belief in the importance of co-operative farming (on land provided by the union), seeing it as a direct method of improving

[1] Pamela R. Horn, 'Methodism and Agricultural Trade Unionism in Oxfordshire: The 1870s' in *Proceedings of the Wesley Historical Society*, xxxvii Part 3 (Oct. 1969), p. 70. Bayliss was reported in the press as addressing union meetings at least from Jan. 1873, (*Oxford Journal*, 1 Feb. 1873).

the social and economic status of farm workers. These various internal problems came to a head at the N.A.L.U.'s annual conference held in May 1875, and shortly afterwards Vincent and some of his supporters decided to form an independent union, to be known as the National Farm Labourers' Union. Early in July they announced a preliminary organizing committee of labourers who had 'spontaneously come forward' to help with the new project. Only one was an Oxfordshire man— from the village of Hornton; of the remainder, five came from Warwickshire and two from Northamptonshire. The main objects of the new union were the acquisition of land for use as allotments or co-operative farms, the establishing of a sick and benefit society with the provision of some form of pension for the aged, and the building up of a strike fund to support members involved in industrial action. However, it was emphasized that as far as possible the latter fund should remain untouched, and any surplus revenue accumulated in it was to be used for the acquisition of more land.

The establishment of this union caused great conflict within the existing N.A.L.U. branches, as some members continued in their allegiance to the old union and some transferred to the new. In Oxfordshire support for the new organization was limited. But its emergence undoubtedly helped to weaken overall confidence in the agricultural union movement, especially when the leaders of the rival organizations began to abuse one another —the N.A.L.U. dubbed the new Union 'the Bogus'—and to cast aspersions on each other's personal probity. Two examples will perhaps illustrate how the split set branches against branches and members against members. At Great Tew, in the Banbury district, it was noted in October 1875 that the branch was divided 'part for the old Union, and part for the new', and the following January it was reported from Steeple Barton that 'A great many stand aloof from either Union, as they know they have been very much duped.'[1] Accordingly, membership of the Oxford N.A.L.U. district had fallen to 3,515 by May 1875, as compared with 3,800 in November 1873; by March 1878 the figure was just over 2,000. Over the same period membership of the Banbury district also fell from over 3,000 in 1873 to 2,300 in

[1] The Oxford District committee had from an early stage expressed concern at the development of internal rivalries. On 9 June 1875 it recorded deep regret at the 'angery [sic] recriminations . . . made at the Birmingham Council by the chief officers of the union against each other', and the theme was again taken up at a meeting on 4 Aug.

May 1875 and about 1,200 in March 1878. By 1879 the two districts had been further reduced to 930 and 1,000 respectively, although, as will be seen, the particularly severe cut in the Oxford district was due to rather special factors.

1879 also witnessed the abandonment by the rival National Farm Labourers Union of its trade union functions, and the transfer to its land section of its strike fund. Even before this —in 1877—some of the active hostility between the two unions had been removed when Vincent decided to sell the *Labourers' Union Chronicle*, ostensibly for reasons of health but no doubt also because the paper was losing money. It was bought and merged with the N.A.L.U.'s new paper, the *English Labourer*, to form the *English Labourers' Chronicle*, which represented the union's views until it ceased publication in 1894. With this newspaper amalgamation, and the decline of the National Farm Labourers' Union, it seemed that agricultural trades unionism might again enjoy a measure of unity, at least within Oxfordshire. But such hopes were soon disappointed—and on this occasion Oxfordshire proved to be in the van of the dissidents.

The new conflict arose over the rival merits of centralization and federalism as methods of union organization. Under the rules of the N.A.L.U. the various districts had to remit three-quarters of their annual income to the central executive, and the district officers were expected to manage their own local business on the remaining one-quarter, i.e. upon ½d. per member per week. The Oxford district, in particular, objected to this, especially when large sums of money were paid out of central funds for relief in other areas. As has been seen, their help at the time of the eastern counties lock-out was generous, but they nevertheless felt that since Oxford members did not go on strike, there was no reason why they should spend large amounts supporting those who did. This attitude was clearly shown by one of the leaders several years later, when he wrote to the *Oxford Chronicle* in 1889: 'We raised funds by paying our twopences; three parts of it was sent to Leamington and spent in high salaries for officers and strikes in the Eastern counties, and we, who were plodding on had neither funds to fall back on and no prospect of getting allotments.' In these circumstances some of the members began to demand greater autonomy for the districts and a reversal of the financial arrangements—three-quarters of the subscriptions to be retained in the district and only one-quarter to be sent to Leamington; in fact, the adoption of a federal system of organization.

Dissatisfaction with the *status quo* was not confined to

Oxford alone; among other areas concerned was the adjacent Buckinghamshire/Northamptonshire district. In these circumstances, Thomas Bayliss, the secretary of the Oxford district, and Leonard Clarke, secretary of the Buckinghamshire/Northamptonshire district began to discuss their common problems from as early as 1878. Discontent was also felt in other counties, and was at least in part a symptom of the growing unease at the financial weakness of the N.A.L.U. itself. Eventually, in January 1879, the National leaders realized that action must be taken to resolve the problems facing them, and a special conference was called in London to consider ways of reducing expenditure and ending the internal conflicts. The meeting proved stormy, with Bayliss and Willett (the Oxford district chairman) speaking out in favour of a federal system of management, to replace the existing centralized organization. Clarke seconded their motion, but when it was put to the meeting it was defeated by 35 votes to 19. Despite this rejection it was clear that feelings were running high and that many delegates were unhappy at the attitude of the leadership—and particularly that of Joseph Arch himself. When the conference finally broke up, Bayliss and Clarke decided to call a special meeting at Oxford on 28 January, to consider the issues raised.

It is clear from a study of the Oxford district minute book that the actions of their two representatives had the backing of the rest of the district committee. Indeed a committee meeting (held on 15 January just before their departure for London) unanimously agreed 'that the Central system of government in our union has completely failed to exercise a nice and judicious management of the funds under its control' and instructed its delegates to press instead for a federal system. It also resolved that, '... provided it is found necessary for the district secretary Mr. Bayliss to start a paper in the interest of the district, this committee will render him all the moral support in its delegates' power and bear the expense of a free circulation for two weeks.' Consequently when the rebel Oxford and Buckinghamshire/Northamptonshire districts had their meeting of 28 January, it soon became apparent that many delegates considered that the only possible solution to their problems lay in the establishment of an independent society. It was then agreed that a circular should be drawn up and sent to every branch, explaining the actions which the district committee had taken so far.

By early February the attitude of both sides had hardened. As was usual at these times, each party to the dispute began to abuse the other and to disagree with its rival's claims of support. For example, while Bayliss declared he had the allegiance of 50 branches and about 1,000 members, the general secretary of the N.A.L.U. pointed out that 47 of the branches and over 900 of the members of the Oxford district had expressed their support for the old union. As total membership in the district was only about 1,000, one (or both) of the claims was grossly exaggerated.

Despite the unrest, however, the disgruntled sections of the Oxford and Buckinghamshire/Northamptonshire districts did not *formally* sever their connection until after the Oxford district's annual conference, held in May 1879. In fact, only 22 representatives from the district's 60 or so branches actually attended—perhaps the absence of many was due to the fact that Joseph Arch had been invited to chair the proceedings. Bayliss embarked on a personal attack of Arch, and at the end of a somewhat unpleasant meeting it was announced that 40 branches in the district had seceded from the N.A.L.U. These dissidents, plus those from the Buckinghamshire/Northamptonshire district who supported them, decided to form an independent union, to be known as the National Land and Labour Union. This was officially inaugurated later in May, with Clarke as general secretary and Bayliss as president. Its aims were largely pacific; labour disputes were to be settled if possible by conciliation and arbitration rather than by strikes, although in the political field the union was said, rather vaguely, to support 'progress and reform'.

Both Clarke and Bayliss soon realized that their organization was too small to be effective, unless it could rely upon the support of other friends who shared their hostility towards the N.A.L.U. One such ally stood ready to hand—the Amalgamated Labour League, centred in Lincolnshire. Under these circumstances, William Banks, the secretary of the League, and Bayliss and Clarke soon established an understanding, and by the end of October 1879 there are reports of Banks speaking for the National Land and Labour Union in both Oxfordshire and Buckinghamshire. The Labour League and the new union were obviously working in close co-operation and so it is scarcely surprising that at a conference held by the latter on 12 November formal amalgamation with the League should be discussed and unanimously approved. As a consequence of the amalgamation a small committee was appointed to settle up the accounts of the National Land and Labour Union, and by the following January the League had assumed control of the Midland branches. Bayliss became district secretary for the League's

Oxford area—something of a demotion from the position of union president which he had occupied about six months earlier —, and shortly afterwards he withdrew from the union altogether.[1] Thereafter the League branches appear to have declined steadily, and within a few months the entire breakaway organization in the Midlands was dead.

Meanwhile those branches in the two rebel districts which had not supported the new organization were absorbed by existing N.A.L.U. districts—the Oxford branches being incorporated into the Banbury district. Such an overlapping of areas on the part of the N.A.L.U. and the National Land and Labour Union soon provided fertile ground for dissension, at least in the early days of the dispute. As with the previous split between the N.A.L.U. and Vincent's union, the net result was a reduction in general support for agricultural trade unionism. For example, at Wendlesbury it was reported that members had 'stood aloof' from the N.A.L.U. since the conflict began, although they had not given their support to the breakaway union either. Similarly at Bloxham, near Banbury, the delegate complained in March 1880 that there was 'no Union fire here. The soup can and old clothes are preferred before independence and self-help . . .' Here it is clear that membership had fallen off, not only as a result of inter-union hostilities, but also through the influence of the richer classes in the community, who were prepared to dispense charitable gifts to the rural poor, provided they were received in a suitably subservient spirit.

By 1880, therefore, these various problems had combined to reduce interest in agricultural trades unionism in Oxfordshire to a marked degree—and it will be remembered that even at its height in 1873/74 there had never been a majority of members among the farm workers of the county. During the 1880s affairs

---

[1] According to the 1883 Kelly's *Directory of Oxfordshire*, Bayliss was at that date employed as a newsagent and coal merchant in Oxford, but within a year or so he had disposed of these businesses. By the end of the decade (1890) he had become Liberal Party agent for the Horncastle division of Lincolnshire—a position he held for 20 years. He died in Oxford on 24 April 1939, aged 91—the last survivor of the original union leaders. In his obituary notice it was recorded that at the time of the Home Rule split in the Liberal Party he had been invited to join Chamberlain's Liberal Unionists, but had refused. Although his union career ended at the beginning of the 1880s, he remained an active Methodist local preacher until well into his 80s. See *Oxford Mail*, 26 April 1939.

were conducted on an ever-lower key. Furthermore, the failure of the unions to hold the advance in money wages gained in the early years of success disillusioned some supporters—especially when, as occurred from the second half of the 1870s, arable agriculture came under increasing pressure, as prices slumped following the increase in cheap grain imports. The difficulties which this situation created were recognized by union leaders. As the Banbury and Oxford district secretary declared in September 1880: 'Times must mend if we all try, and I know many of you don't want the sufferings of last winter repeated. Then every man join the Union and try and prevent it . . .' It was a bitter contrast with the years of heady success between 1872 and 1874.

But if the N.A.L.U.'s *main* concern in its early days had been to secure better wages, this had certainly not been its *sole* preoccupation. Linked with it were the efforts made to regulate the supply of labour by encouraging workers to migrate or emigrate to areas where employment prospects were brighter and wages higher. Then, too, attempts were made to satisfy the demands of members for allotments and for the provision of friendly societies connected with the union. Demonstrations in favour of franchise extension and efforts to secure the equitable administration of local charities were other features of N.A.L.U. activities during the 1870s and 1880s. It is now proposed to examine these additional aspects of union work in more detail, beginning with emigration.

Would-be migrants were given financial help by both local and central funds to enable them to move—although the bulk of the funds came from the latter source. For example, the Oxford district secretary, Bayliss, claimed in 1875 that his district had spent £400 on emigration during the previous year, and this was obviously deemed a large sum. Over the same period the Banbury district spent £234 2s. 11d. on emigration—but, unlike the Oxford district position, only £43 10s. 6d. came directly from its local funds.[1]

Those labourers who subscribed to the Oxford district's own special emigration fund received, in addition, a further grant when they actually moved away. At the district committee meeting on 8 July 1873, it was decided that those who had subscribed 1s. to the fund should obtain 10s., and those who had subscribed 6d., 5s. The N.A.L.U. central funds also gave

[1] In 1878 the total Banbury expenditure on emigration had fallen to £5 5s. 8d.

the emigrants financial support. In the early days no specific sum was mentioned, but by 1877 it had been established as the railway fare to the port of embarkation, plus 10s., where there were two or more children under 12 years in the family, or 20s., where there were four or more children under 12 in the family.[1] These small payments went some way to meet the inevitable expenses of emigration which occurred even where passages were granted free.

Information on free passages was widely distributed in the Oxfordshire villages during the period 1872–75, and special emigration agents toured the area for this purpose.[2] In some cases, too, union officials acted as agents—a policy of which the Oxford district committee approved. Where officials assumed this rôle, they of course benefited from the commission paid by colonial governments and others concerned with the migration schemes. Union funds were also boosted from the same source. Thus between April 1874 and May 1875, the National Union as a whole drew £1,933 from commission for procuring emigrants.

Eventually some of the union officials became *full-time* emigration agents on their own account. For example, Christopher Holloway became a 'special travelling agent' for the New Zealand Government from May 1875 until June 1880. During that period he seems never to have earned less than 35s. a week; in August 1877 an annual figure of £150 was suggested; and in 1876 he appears to have made no less than £312 from this

---

[1] Rule Book of the N.A.L.U., 1875 and 1877 editions. According to Rule 14 (2) of the 1875 Rule Book, members receiving help either to migrate or emigrate were supposed to sign a promissory note agreeing to repay any sums advanced 'in case the member returns without giving a satisfactory explanation to the Committee'. In practice, this proved almost a dead letter.

[2] For example, early in November 1873 Mr. C. R. Carter, an agent for the New Zealand Government, addresses a meeting of 'between five and six hundred persons' held in 'a very large tent' at Milton-under-Wychwood. And in 1875, Mr. A. B. Daveney, Special Immigration Agent for the Dominion of Canada, visited Oxfordshire (among other counties) 'delivering addresses on "Emigration to Canada" at public meetings, three, four and even five evenings in a week in village club rooms, chapels, barns, etc.' See Report of Minister of Agriculture for the Dominion of Canada, 1875, Appendix No. 22, p. 89; and information kindly provided by the New Zealand High Commission. Emigration to New Zealand is also discussed in R. Arnold, 'English Rural Unionism and Taranaki Immigration, 1871–1876' in *New Zealand Journal of History*, Vol. 6, No. 1 (April, 1972).

source.[1] Thomas Bayliss, too, after his break with the union continued to act as an emigration agent for both the Canadian and Queensland Governments for a number of years. In January 1882 he was advertising 'free passages to Queensland' for farm labourers and domestic servants—an offer he continued to make for at least another year.[2]

A number of union officials also took parties out to the colonies. In December 1873 Holloway escorted 400 labourers and their families (very largely from Oxfordshire) to New Zealand in the steamship *Mongol*. For this he was paid 'subsistence money' for his family at the rate of 25s. per week during his absence, plus £1 per day for travelling expenses during his stay in New Zealand.[3] And in the early spring of the following year the district secretary, Joseph Leggett, resigned his office in order to take out a second party. Leggett in fact settled in New Zealand, but Holloway returned to England in 1875, to take up his work as a full-time agent.[4]

Emigration, like unionism itself, was uneven in its incidence; one village particularly affected was Milton-under-Wychwood, where the Oxford union had originated. Here it was claimed that between 1872 and 1875 over 200 people had emigrated (out of a total of 962 at the time of the 1871 Census). This estimate may perhaps have been exaggerated, but it is significant that the 1881 Census *did* show a sharp fall in population—to 836. Quite considerable parties went from other villages, too; thus in August 1874 it was noted that 20 emigrants were preparing to leave the village of Wheatley for New Zealand, while at

[1] Information kindly supplied by the New Zealand High Commission.

[2] See advertisements in *Oxford Chronicle*, 31 Jan. 1880, 7 Jan. 1882 and 20 Jan. 1883.

[3] See Appendices to the Journals of the House of Representatives, New Zealand, 1874, on Immigration. Extract No. 26.

[4] Oxford district officials valued their personal commission for emigration work, and when the N.A.L.U. executive in Leamington suggested that this money should be placed instead to the use of the union movement as a whole, the Oxford district committee expressed their discontent. The national decision was reached on 1 March 1875, but at their meeting on 17 March, the Oxford district committee resolved to 'abide by the former regulations until after the general council', i.e. the annual meeting of all the union delegates held in May. Bayliss raised the matter at this meeting but the decision went against him. See *Labourers' Union Chronicle*, 6 March and 29 May 1875; and also Oxford District Minute Book, 17 March and 14 April 1875.

Burford, in September of the same year, 'thirty names were taken for Canada and New Zealand'.[1]

Unfortunately not all of those who went overseas were successful (although few were as unlucky as the 17 members of two Shipton-under-Wychwood families who perished, along with about 400 others, in a mid-ocean fire, which destroyed their ship, the *Cospatrick*, on the way to New Zealand in 1874).[2] Nevertheless, one particular field of emigration early on proved a fertile ground for discontent—namely Brazil. Oxfordshire was one of the counties most involved in the Brazilian emigration schemes of 1872/3.[3] However those who made the journey quickly discovered the unsuitability of Brazil, both climatically and otherwise, for British settlement. Contemporary newspapers contain many accounts of their plight—including extracts from letters written home. In one such letter William Brown, a labourer from Great Bourton, near Banbury, bitterly declared: 'They have deceived us very much. You may expect me back in a short time, as soon as I have the money; . . . we have nothing to eat but black beans and rice. There is no bread here. We have no bed to lie on here but the cold ground.' Government reports largely bear out these claims.[4] And one returned emigrant, a former coachman from Great Bourton, named William Stanton, felt so strongly over the matter that he addressed a number of meetings in Oxfordshire and elsewhere, describing the privations he and his fellows had endured. On 13 February 1873 he spoke in Banbury Corn Exchange and caused considerable confusion and disorder, as union supporters were also present in large numbers to dispute his criticisms. However, there is little doubt that by this time the Brazilian emigration bubble had been well and truly pricked.

Yet if the disappointment of the Brazilian enterprise deterred *some* labourers from emigrating, it did not, of course, provide a true picture of the emigration scene. Those who went to Australia and New Zealand, in particular, appeared well satisfied with their lot. For example, one Stadhampton farm worker who had

[1] *Labourers' Union Chronicle*, 22 Aug. and 19 September. 1874.

[2] For details of the disaster see *Labourers' Union Chronicle*, 12 Dec. 1874.

[3] For an account of another county which was deeply involved in Brazilian emigration see P. L. R. Horn, 'Gloucestershire and the Brazilian Emigration Movement—1872–73' in *Transactions of the Bristol and Gloucestershire Archaeological Society*, No. 89 (1970).

[4] *Thirty-third Annual General Report of Emigration Commissioners*, *P.P.*, 1873 xviii, p. 8.

emigrated to Queensland, wrote to his parents in September 1873: 'We have good living, as much mutton, beef and duff a week as we can eat . . . Dear mother, here is plenty of work . . .' A Weston-on-the-Green labourer, who had settled in New Zealand, wrote in a similarly optimistic vein, declaring that he wished he 'had come twenty years sooner'.[1]

Many farm workers emigrated without the help of the union, of course, just as their predecessors had done before the N.A.L.U. was established, and as their successors were to do when the movement had largely faded away. But there is little doubt that the large parties of unionists escorted by district officials did encourage some of the more timid to move who would probably never have otherwise done so.

If Oxfordshire members were active in union emigration schemes, they were equally so in respect to union-sponsored migration to other parts of Britain. Small-scale migration was carried on regularly, and during the lock-out at Wootton in the summer of 1872 (as noted earlier) about 40 men left with their families to seek work in the Sheffield ironworks. The Oxford district minute book reveals many other such examples of sponsored migration. On 18 February 1873, for example, the committee agreed to send William Wiggins 'to Manchester', while in June of the same year, men involved in a dispute at Longborough were to be paid one week's strike benefit 'and . . . assisted to migrate'.

Those labourers who received financial help to migrate were supposed to refund the money, but unfortunately few did so. In this way not only was the agricultural trade union movement robbed of many of its most able members—since it was those who had the greatest initiative who tended to move away—but also its funds were depleted by the same means. The Oxford district committee, at a meeting on 30 September 1873, complained of the imbalance in the finances of its migration fund, and declared that new members must be 'on the books two clear months' before they were eligible 'for the benefit of migration'. The following figures from the 1873 balance sheet would indicate that their dissatisfaction was justified: expenditure on

[1] *Labourers' Union Chronicle*, 10 Jan. 1874 and 12 Dec. 1874. For an examination of the rôle of the agricultural unions in regard to emigration during the 1870s see also, Pamela Horn, 'Agricultural Trade Unionism and Emigration, 1872–1881' in *Historical Journal*, xv, I (1972).

migration, £262 12s. 8d.; income from migration grants repaid, £3 18s. 4d.

Unfortunately, too, a number of those who did migrate returned quite quickly to their home village, as the minute book of the small Horspath branch amply demonstrates. Of nine labourers sent north by the branch at the end of March and the beginning of April 1873, seven had returned within about three months; indeed the majority came back within one month! Perhaps the most striking example was Henry Surman, who left home for the 'North' on 17 March and returned on 21 March. For this behaviour and because he had 'underworked a Fellow Member of the Union' he was deprived of his membership on 5 April, but appears to have been reinstated several months later.[1]

It cannot be said that the union-sponsored emigration and migration schemes were an unqualified success. First and foremost, they failed to achieve their objective of creating a shortage of labour—save in the short run in limited areas. This was largely because the majority of labourers remained outside the ranks of the movement, despite the various recruitment campaigns, while many who *were* members were unwilling to leave their home for little-known destinations in the towns or overseas. The farmers, for their part, countered the threat to the labour supply by economizing on their work force as far as possible and by the use of more machinery.

Another matter with which the unions concerned themselves was the provision of land for allotments. It is interesting to note that, as early as September 1872, the secretary of the Iffley branch had advocated the acquisition of land for allotments when addressing a meeting in the nearby village of Littlemore. But, despite this early interest, it was not until 1875 that the Oxford district committee began to make plans for a society to acquire land for its members' use. And even then the scheme was never adopted—largely because, as a member of the

[1] Horspath Branch Minute Book—Oxford district of the N.A.L.U. at Bodleian Library, Oxford, MS. Top. Oxon. d. 533. It was perhaps because of these problems connected with migration that the Oxford district leaders seem to have preferred emigration. Thus in 1873 Leggett declared, 'we believe emigration to be a more sufficient means than migration for our improvement.' Again in 1878, Bayliss spoke of migration or emigration and 'considered of the two the latter was preferable'—*Oxford Chronicle*, 1 Nov. 1873 and 11 May 1878.

committee subsequently claimed, Joseph Arch and the N.A.L.U. Executive Committee disapproved of it.[1]

Later in 1875 came the establishment of Vincent's National Farm Labourers' Union. And in the following March a special land company was registered for the explicit purposes of land acquisition, the fostering of co-operation, and the improvement of the 'moral and social condition of the shareholders'.[2] A summary of the capital and shares, made up to 15 December 1876, provides details of the support among Oxfordshire farm workers at this date. Out of the total of 144 shares at £1 taken up, only three were held by Oxfordshire men, while out of a total of 11 at £2 10s., two had been taken up in the country— one by a 'tradesman' from Steeple Barton. These figures do not, of course, indicate the true level of support for the company, since many labourers at this time were undoubtedly still subscribing their weekly pence towards a £1 share but had not yet saved the necessary amount.

The organization purchased its first estate in 1876, but since this was situated in Avebury, Wiltshire, and was let to local members, the purchase was of no benefit to Oxfordshire men; other purchases followed, but none within Oxfordshire. Perhaps not surprisingly, interest began to wane during 1877/8. Nevertheless, when a second list of subscribers was prepared, made up to 14 December 1879, it *did* show a remarkable increase over the 1876 figures. By 1879 the company had branches in 25 counties; all told, 689 shares at £1 had been taken up, and 15 at £2 10s. Out of these totals, Oxfordshire's share had increased to 46 at £1 and three at £2 10s. Some members held more than one share—for example, John Wyatt, a labourer of Great Barrington (Gloucestershire) held six £1

[1] The Oxford district land scheme was still under discussion in the spring of 1876, but nothing was achieved—see the Minute Book, 16 Feb. and 12 April 1876.

[2] The step had been made necessary by the fact that trade unions were unable legally to acquire land in the way Vincent and his fellow enthusiasts desired; the formation of a limited company to achieve their end had thus been the only alternative. The company had 12 directors, plus a chairman and managing director, and had nominal capital of £25,000, divided into 10,000 shares of £1 each and 6,000 shares of £2 10s. each—although nothing like this amount of money was, in fact, subscribed (or likely to be subscribed) at the time of registration. See records of the National Farm Labourers' Union Co-operative Land Company—Memoranda of Association, Public Record Office, B.T. 31/2240.

shares—and the largest 'branches' which can be identified in the county were at Wigginton (with eight paid-up members) and Steeple Barton (with seven). It will be noted that the most active branches of this union were in north Oxfordshire, close to Warwickshire, where the greatest support for the movement lay. But any lingering hopes which these members may have nurtured were soon to be dashed. For in September 1880 it was discovered that the company could no longer carry on its business. 'Finding that the liabilities exceeded the assets, the managers have stopped the concern,' as the notice read in the *Oxford Chronicle* of 18 September. By July of the following year the whole enterprise had been wound up.

It is clear that Oxfordshire members obtained little but disappointment from their efforts to acquire land through the unions, and it was only when the Liberal Party turned its attention to the allotments question in 1882 and the Conservatives and Liberal Unionists followed suit in 1887 that the number of allotments available showed an appreciable increase. According to one estimate, they grew from 9,088 in 1873 to 14,706 in 1886 and 17,947 in 1889.[1]

A fourth area in which the agricultural unions concerned themselves was the provision of friendly society benefits. In this respect they were following in the footsteps both of the ordinary independent small village benefit societies and of many well-established non-agricultural trade unions. Interest in a union friendly society was displayed by the Oxford district committee as early as the spring of 1873. At a delegate meeting held at this time it was agreed that the members 'think it necessary to form a Sick Benefit and Superannuation Society in connection with the Union and that the delegates be instructed to press the same on the attention of the National Congress'.[2] In the event, the N.A.L.U. annual council of 1873 did consider the matter, but without reaching any firm decision; and that was still the position 18 months later. But by then the Warwick district of the union had established a sick benefit society of its own and the Oxford committee began to think of following suit. At their meeting on 25 November 1874, it was decided

[1] Arthur W. Ashby, *Allotments in Oxfordshire* (Oxford, 1917), p. 34.
[2] This desire for a friendly society was perhaps due to the fact that allegations were made that in some areas poor law guardians had 'refused the ordinary privilege of parochial relief in necessitous cases' to members of the N.A.L.U. See *Oxford Chronicle*, 1 Nov. 1873 (Oxford District Meeting).

that rules of a proposed Sick Club should be circulated, while during the course of the following year a district benefit society was formally registered with the Chief Registrar of Friendly Societies. According to the *English Labourer* of 14 November 1875 it had a membership of 80, and a capital of £25 at district headquarters. Nevertheless, it does not appear to have had any real success; indeed from the district minute book one gains the impression, inexplicably, that no society had been established. Thus at a meeting on 12 April 1876 it was resolved that, if the national organization did not introduce a sick benefit society, 'the Oxford district will do so'. Yet, according to its official registration number and to the membership figure previously quoted, the district already *had* a friendly society.

Apart from this rather mysterious and ineffective district effort, some of the branches had their own small friendly societies (or 'incidental funds') modelled on the old village benefit clubs. One such was Milton-under-Wychwood. In 1875, despite the considerable emigration which had taken place, this local society was still flourishing. At the annual meeting on 20 April 1875, it was reported that during the preceding year income from subscriptions for sick and funeral benefits, etc., had reached £21 18s., while the expenditure had amounted to £2 1s. for funeral benefit and £2 12s. for sick members. However some branches preferred the more informal arrangement of an 'incidental fund', to which members made free-will contributions or for which collections were organized after meetings or religious services. From it were met any unusual outgoings, including payments to sick members. One village adopting this plan was Great Rissington, where sick members received £2 15s. 6d. in 1874 'out of the incidental fund'.

A similar interest was displayed in the Banbury district, but no attempt was made to set up an independent district benefit society. Indeed the Banbury district delegate declared in September 1875 that union members were 'looking forward to the time when [they would] have a well-established [national] sick fund . . .'. For, despite the existence of various local schemes, many members still wanted a central sick benefit society to be set up in connection with the N.A.L.U. This desire was eventually satisfied in 1877, when the Executive Committee agreed that the proposed rules for a sickness and burial society be put into operation. By the end of the year the Banbury district secretary was able to report that 'in several places members [were] joining the Sick Benefit Society', and to advise that 'all intending to do so [should] make up their minds at once'. We cannot tell how many Oxfordshire members did so, since no unequivocal figures were quoted in connection with the society in its early days. But at this time overall union membership in the county was less than 4,500, and it is most unlikely that all of these joined the new benefit scheme.

The weekly contributions payable varied according to age, from 6d. for the 16 to 21-year-old age group to 1s. for those between 40 and 50. In return the benefit paid out also varied, but for most groups it averaged around 10s. a week, with a funeral benefit of £5 for the member and £3 for his wife.[1] Unfortunately the continuing decline in national membership, plus the confused state of book-keeping at the N.A.L.U. central office, soon led the Sick Benefit Society into difficulties; and at the annual conference in 1888, the general secretary reported that 'the disbursements in the shape of sickness claims were still considerably in excess of the contributions, which had fallen off to a large extent.' A levy of 1s. 6d. per member was authorized in an attempt to make good the deficit, but without success, as the Annual Report for 1889 was to show. In Oxfordshire membership had slumped dismally by this time—formerly strong branches like Milton-under-Wychwood having only twelve members or less—but some of the surviving sick benefit branches were amongst the worst offenders as regards overspending. At Deddington, in north Oxfordshire, payments into the Sick Benefit Society over the course of the year 1888–9 amounted to £3 8s. 3d.—while payments out amounted to £21 8s. Similarly, at Chipping Warden, in the same area, receipts of £6 3s. 6d. were more than counterbalanced by expenditure of £19 12s. 8d. Even at Milton-under-Wychwood, although the position was more satisfactory, it was by no means ideal, with subscriptions standing at £11 6s. 3d. and withdrawals at £7 16s.[2]

Oxfordshire also made a very poor response to a second levy in 1889, remitting a paltry £1 2s. 9d.[3] By 1890 the process of decline had gone further, and it is at this time that the first proper indication of membership is given. In May 1890 there were 37 members in the county as a whole—of whom 22 had received some form of benefit from the friendly society during the previous year. In these circumstances it is not surprising

[1] Rule Book of the N.A.L.U., 1879, Public Record Office, F.S. 7/4/154.
[2] *English Labourers' Chronicle*, 29 June 1889.
[3] *English Labourers' Chronicle*, 31 May 1890.

that the N.A.L.U. Executive Committee was forced to wind up the enterprise; and this was finally completed in 1892.[1]

Although the sick benefit societies (with their concomitant funeral benefits) were the most significant forms of friendly societies for Oxfordshire members, at least one attempt was made in the Banbury district to set up a Widows' Society. This scheme had already been attempted, with modest success, in Northamptonshire, but although it struggled to survive for about three years in Oxfordshire, it achieved little. One of the reasons was undoubtedly the very casual way in which the rules were drawn up. Expenditure was planned without any real reference to the size of possible income, while no attempt was made to use actuarial tables which would take into account the age of members or of their husbands. The society was established in October 1878, and according to its rules, members were to pay an entrance fee of 6d., with 2d. per week contributions. In return they were to receive 'four shillings per week so long as the Member may live and remain the Widow, but if the Member change her situation by marrying again, or misconduct herself in any way contrary to decency and respect . . . all allowance from the Society's funds shall at once cease to be paid . . .'[2] As far as can be ascertained, the maximum membership recorded for the society was a mere 50, in May 1879.

As a consequence of their declining success in the industrial field during the later 1870s, therefore, the Oxfordshire branches of the N.A.L.U. turned their attention to such side issues as the Sick Benefit Society and also—perhaps more valuably—to the question of village charities. This sort of activity had, of course, also been carried out during the earlier, successful days, when local union officers had collected information relevant to the charities in their areas, so as to secure the proper administration of the money or land concerned. In January 1876 the Banbury district secretary announced that he had copies of the reports of the Charity Commissioners for Oxfordshire and Northamptonshire, which were open to the inspection of any member 'should they feel dissatisfaction about the distribution of their charities'.

Similarly branch officials often obtained information on their own local charities. At Horspath the minute book contains

[1] See, for example, *English Labourers' Chronicle*, 26 March 1890.

[2] Rule Book of the Widows' Society of the Banbury District the N.A.L.U., G.A. Oxon. 801255(7)—Bodleian Library, Oxford. The scheme was ended in June, 1882.

detailed information on the subject of charities; and in 1881 the secretary of the branch, who was also a churchwarden, approached the Charity Commissioners over an alleged maladministration. The matter was investigated and a proper distribution of the funds secured. Since the average labourer was often ill-equipped to obtain information of this sort, the union's intervention was obviously of benefit to its members.[1]

Concern for the proper administration of village charities also led to periodic efforts by union leaders to encourage labourers to seek election as churchwardens. The years 1876–8, for example, saw a 'battle for the vestries' on a national scale. In Oxfordshire some success was recorded, especially during the spring of 1877. Thus at Wootton, Christopher Holloway was elected churchwarden, and as he happily told the annual meeting of the Oxford district shortly afterwards: 'Who would ever have thought of such a thing as that . . . a wicked agitator in common with Mr. Arch . . . should have been chosen as churchwarden?' Several other 'working men' shared his success. And at Hanborough, where a local farmer had dismissed one of his labourers after he had voted for the 'working man' candidate at the vestry meeting, the branch secretary declared: '. . . we will not rest until every office that can be held by working men or their friends is wrested from the powers that are . . .'

Another matter with which unionists concerned themselves—and one linked with the anxiety for labourer participation in political life which had characterized the 'battle for the vestries'—was franchise extension. This had been a basic issue of the movement from its inception and was to remain so until the rural householder received the vote in 1884. In both 1876 and 1877 the Banbury and Oxford districts were active in sponsoring pro-franchise petitions, and at the end of June 1876 the secretary of the former district boasted that there had been 6,130 signatures on their petition. Next year the Oxford district secretary declared that upwards of 11,000 signatures had been sent from his area for the same purpose. As time wore on, these

[1] This was equally true of the legal advice which the union provided for members in other matters, notably over breaches of the contract of employment. A typical example is that provided by the Oxford District Minute Book entry for 9 June 1875, when it was agreed: 'That we defend John Hill at Chipping Norton in the breach of contract case.' On this occasion the labourer was charged with absenting himself from his service without leave, but his action was successfully defended by a London barrister appointed by the union, and the case dismissed (*Oxford Journal*, 19 June 1875).

petitions were also coupled with demands for wider changes. In August 1879 a meeting at the small village of Finmere, for example, passed a motion in favour both of a wider franchise and of land nationalization, while in the same year, at meetings at Churchill and Middle Barton, resolutions were passed deprecating the use of corporal punishment in the armed services.[1]

In the final push for the county franchise in the 1880s the impact of the unionists was weakened by their loss of numbers. But meetings were nevertheless held to support the cause during the last vital months, as the Franchise Bill wound its weary way through Parliament during 1884. It was also noted that at many meetings in Oxfordshire copies of Mr. Gladstone's speeches were sold; and there is no doubt that the statesman was regarded as a hero by most active agricultural unionists at this stage.

Interest in the union seems to have increased during these hectic days—in December 1884, shortly after the Bill was passed, a local delegate claimed that 107 new members had joined the N.A.L.U. within the county, and that five dozen additional copies of the union newspaper had been ordered. At the small village of Shabbington (population 351 in 1881) it was announced in January 1885 that a branch with 64 members had recently been established. And similar, if more modest, progress was recorded elsewhere. However, once the initial excitement had passed, and especially when the Liberal Party split over Irish Home Rule in 1886, this brief advance was rapidly lost.

During this period the union leaders were becoming increasingly identified with the Gladstonian line. It is certainly not fortuitous that Thomas Bayliss, the former Oxford district secretary, became a Liberal Party agent in Lincolnshire at the end of the decade. And in July 1887 a Banbury delegate wrote of the Oxfordshire farm workers,

I think in many places the men are opening their eyes to see their own folly. First they left the Union, and then they were promised if the Tories got into office they would have plenty of work and better wages, but now it is worse than ever; less work and lower wages, but where the Union is strongest wages are higher . . .

There is little evidence to support this last statement. Indeed

[1] This was a Radical campaign much favoured by Joseph Chamberlain and Joseph Arch. Arch, indeed, made it a plank in his political platform when he unsuccessfully contested Wilton for the Liberals in 1880.—P. L. R. Horn, *Joseph Arch*, pp. 152–6.

at that date there were *no* really strong branches within the county. The rivalries of union leadership, the difficulties of arable agriculture, and the failure to maintain wage increases won in the early and successful days of 1872–4 had all contributed to the general disillusionment. And though some labourers approved of a strongly pro-Liberal stance—the Horspath branch secretary wrote on page 27 of his minute book 'The Tories are responsible for all workhouse scardles [sic], to vote for the Tories is to insult the Wounded and Poor of the Working Classes'—there can equally be no doubt that other members resented the time and attention devoted by their leaders to the Liberal Party rather than to the economic position of the workers themselves.

For the majority of farm workers, therefore, the broad outlines of existence during the 1880s were altered only by the gaining of the franchise. In other respects life flowed along channels similar to those which it had followed in earlier decades—although the steady migration of workers away from agriculture continued. The total number of male farm servants and agricultural labourers employed in Oxfordshire fell from 19,305 in 1871 to 14,796 in 1891, while for women workers the trend was even more sharply downward. The female agricultural work force employed on a permanent (as opposed to an unenumerated part-time) basis decreased from 1,352 in 1871 to a mere 278 in 1891, many of the daughters of farm workers preferring to leave the villages for domestic service. The excitements of the early days of trade unionism had disappeared for men and women alike. Indeed just as the latter had frequently been among the most enthusiastic supporters of the union in its early days, during the years of decline they were often its most outspoken critics. They were anxious to keep hard-earned pennies in the family instead of paying them out 'to keep ol' Joey Arch a gennelman'.[1]

The labourer's concern with his small day-to-day affairs in this period is very vividly described by Flora Thompson in *Lark Rise to Candleford*. The book is primarily concerned with north Oxfordshire, but much of what it relates is relevant to other parts of the county. It is interesting to note that rearing the family pig was still a major feature of life—for those who were fortunate enough to have one to rear—just as it had been two decades earlier. In Flora Thompson's little community these

---

[1] Christopher Holdenby, *Folk of the Furrow* (London, 1913), p. 152.

domestic matters were far more important than trade unionism in the mid-1880s.[1]

The lengths to which the process of decline had gone within the N.A.L.U. by 1889 are indicated by the fact that the *national* membership of the union was a mere 4,254—far fewer than had been recruited in Oxfordshire itself in 1873–4. The size of membership within the county is impossible to ascertain—but obviously it was extremely small. In December 1888 there were about 25 Oxfordshire branches in existence, but some of these, like Steeple Aston, were so small that they scarcely warranted the title of 'branch', and none had any worthwhile membership. Almost all of these survivors were situated in the north of Oxfordshire, within the area of the old Banbury district.[2] By 1889, therefore, the early demise of the union seemed inevitable, but such was not to be the case. A brief reprieve was granted, and it now remains to examine the position of trade unionism in Oxfordshire during the last decade of the nineteenth century.

The much-needed resurgence of agricultural trade union membership came early in 1890, following the successful London dockers' strike in the previous August. There is no doubt that this, and other similar successful strikes amongst unskilled workers, gave encouragement to farm labourers and their leaders. Although the major revival took place in the eastern counties (particularly in Norfolk), Oxfordshire had some small share in the improvement. At the annual conference of the N.A.L.U. in May 1890, the county was represented by J. Cockbill, who had been a branch official and union delegate in earlier years.[3] And Joseph Arch, in his presidential address, intimated that modest progress had been made and that approximately eight or ten new branches would be formed in the near future.

One of the most active in the recruitment work at this stage was William Hines, a chimney sweep from one of the Oxford colleges, who had been an enthusiastic (if not always welcome) supporter of agricultural trade unionism in Oxfordshire from

[1] See, for example, the Oxford 1963 edn. of Miss Thompson's book. For a discussion of the home background of labourers in this period see also my forthcoming book, *The Victorian Country Child*, Chapter 1.   [2] *English Labourers' Chronicle*, 22 and 29 June 1889.

[3] In 1882 Cockbill appeared before the Royal Commission on the Depressed State of Agriculture to give details of his experience as a smallholder on a four-acre allotment at Minster Lovell, Oxfordshire. He obviously found his life there a most unrewarding one. Minutes of Evidence (*P.P.*, 1882 xiv, Q.64,595–64,680).

1872. In the early days it had seemed that some of the leaders resented his interference, but by 1890 this was obviously no longer the case.[1] Hines was a convinced Radical—indeed, in 1889, a fellow Liberal called him one of the 'fast trotters' of the Liberal cause—and less than a decade later he was to abandon the Liberal Party for Socialism. During the autumn of 1895, when an Oxford and District Socialist Union was established in Oxford, he became a member of the committee.

In his agricultural trade union work in the 1890s, Hines was able to secure help from some of the more Radical members of the University. One of the most enthusiastic in this connection was L. T. Hobhouse, a Fellow of Merton College, who was also a leading Liberal. Two other non-labourer supporters from early days included J. N. Godden and G. G. Banbury, both of Woodstock; the former was a leading glove manufacturer in the town and the latter a draper and former treasurer of the Oxford district of the N.A.L.U. in the 1870s.[2]

During the late spring and summer of 1890, Hines, Hobhouse and other members of the University held many meetings, but the spontaneous success which had attended the movement in 1872–3 was lacking. Certainly *some* of the early branches were revived—at Middle Barton, for example, 19 members were recruited, and the Lower Heyford branch secretary announced a membership of 37, while at Wheatley, 31 new members were enrolled. But the response was piecemeal and inadequate. It would appear that by the end of August even Hines was becoming disheartened. He wrote to the *English Labourers' Chronicle* of 30 August exhorting the Oxfordshire men to emulate those in Norfolk (where membership figures had reached over 7,000). He declared that Oxfordshire labourers were quite

[1] For example, at the Oxford District committee meeting on 15 April 1873, resolutions were passed 'that W. Hines shall not be employed as a delegate' and that 'each delegate be a bona fide labourer'. Hines also kept a herbalist's shop in Oxford, but another observer considered 'his real interest was in politics, and his hobby the organization of public meetings in the villages around Oxford . . . No orator himself, he made it his part to act as an impresario for others; arranging the meetings, and enlisting speakers wherever he could among the undergraduates and the younger Dons.'—Viscount Samuel, *Memoirs*, (1945), p. 14.

[2] Godden had also concerned himself with other social matters from the 1870s. For example, in April 1873, he successfully contested an election for Poor Law Guardians in Woodstock—the first time an election had been called for 15 years! (*Oxford Journal*, 12 April, 1873).

willing to attend union meetings and to applaud the speakers, but 'they do not attend to the one thing needful, that is, they do not join the Union in that earnest and systematical way they do in Norfolk and other districts'.

Perhaps Hines felt dissatisfied with the attitude of the union leaders towards Oxfordshire—although Arch did visit the county several times during 1890—or perhaps he was attracted by more Radical policies. The fact remains that, by the early part of January 1891, his allegiance (and that of his helpers) had been transferred from the N.A.L.U. to the Dock, Wharf, Riverside and General Workers' Union. The leaders of this organization, which had done much to inspire poorly paid workers elsewhere to establish unions, were drawn into agriculture because of the dangers which the labourers offered as strike breakers and as new recruits into urban industries where little or no skill was required. They therefore selected two counties to begin their operations—Lincolnshire and Oxfordshire. It is with the latter that we are concerned.

The first delegation left their London headquarters for Oxfordshire on 17 January 1891, duly armed with pamphlets, rule books, etc. Their objectives, apart from the obvious ones of establishing branches and seeking to improve wages and conditions of employment, included the acquisition of allotments. In a handbill prepared for the agricultural campaign it was also pointed out that special entrance fees of 1s. were to be accepted from the labourers, instead of the usual minimum of 5s. 6d. But the weekly contributions were to be set at 3d., as for other members. Finally, provision was made that where members were dismissed for obeying union instructions they would receive unemployment benefit in the form of 'a prompt payment of 10s. a week'.[1]

The main representative of the union in Oxfordshire was E. H. Nicholls, who had been active in the seamen's union prior to the 1889 dock strike, when he had undertaken organizational work for the dockers.[2] He and Hines soon started work. The first meeting was held at Burford on 26 January, just over a week after the arrival of the dockers' delegation. This was the precursor of many similar gatherings addressed by the indefatigable Hines and Nicholls, plus their Oxford University helpers (among them H. L. Samuel of Balliol). In his *Memoirs*, Viscount Samuel (as he became) described the work undertaken during

[1] Handbill—Webb Collection, London School of Economics, Coll. E. Sect. B.-CV.

[2] See his letter to *Oxford Chronicle*, 15 Oct. 1892.

this period—including efforts to establish not only branches but also co-operative stores in connection with the union.[1] The stores were frequently set up in members' cottages, and Samuel remembered taking supplies to them by dog-cart. However, in the village of Wootton a proper shop was established under a paid manager, H. Dawson. Dawson also became secretary of the Wootton and Tackley branches of the union. It is noticeable that Christopher Holloway, the former Wootton N.A.L.U. leader, played no part whatever in these activities; indeed, it is possible that his own small grocery business may have suffered from the competition of the co-operative store.

Despite the hard work, the movement was doomed to failure. By September 1891 a membership of only about 500 or 600 was being claimed—a very small response from the county's 15,561 male agricultural labourers, farm servants and shepherds. And the weak response is further emphasized by the fact that a number of the members were not farm workers at all. For example, in addition to Hines himself, several branch secretaries were employed in other spheres, like Price, the Islip branch secretary, who was a postman, and the Kirtlington secretary, Jessett, who was a boot and shoe maker. The low key reaction was no doubt partly due to the fact that the Socialist philosophy of the dockers' leaders proved alien to conservative country-men, while their urban background caused them to ignore the special problems of rural life. Then, too, agriculture was still affected by the long depression which had afflicted the arable sector since the end of the 1870s. The outlook seemed gloomy, and labourers who were dissatisfied tended to leave the industry altogether.[2]

The annual report of the Dock, Wharf, Riverside and General Workers' Union for 1891 revealed that, in all, 58 agricultural branches had been established. Approximately 22 of these were in Oxfordshire.[3] The largest was at Great Milton, where total

[1] Viscount Samuel, *op. cit.*, p. 16. Samuel noted 'tea, sugar and tobacco' as being among the items sold by these stores.

[2] When the Assistant Commissioner visited the Thame Poor Law Union, Oxfordshire, in connection with the 1892 Royal Commission on Labour, he was told by one labourer from Tetsworth that 'the feeling [was] not so good between the employers and men since the Dockers' Union came and set men against masters, and masters against men.' So perhaps the union's attempts to stir up class feelings were resented by some of the labourers.

[3] Exact numbers cannot be given as some of the names were equally applicable to villages in other counties where the dockers had agricultural branches. See Rex. C. Russell, *op. cit.*, p. 154.

receipts for the year amounted to £42 0s. 8d. The next was at Wootton, where the receipts were £24 6s. 3d., while Burford came third with a total of £23 5s. 4d. Other fairly large branches included Ickford, Kirtlington and Milton-under-Wychwood. The annual report also claimed that through the union's efforts allotments had been acquired, 'proper sanitary inspection of cottages' had been secured, while wages had been raised. Over-time hours had been fixed in some villages and 'proper contract prices' established for the harvest and other busy periods. Particular examples of these generalizations are difficult to isolate. But the Royal Commission on Labour was told in 1892 that at Worminghall (just over the Buckinghamshire border), a weekly wage increase of 1s. had been obtained through earlier industrial action on the part of members of the Dockers' Union, while Hines himself declared that the establishment of union branches in such villages as Great Milton, Haseley, Horspath, Cuddesdon, Tetsworth and elsewhere, had led to higher wages being paid 'without a man asking' for them.[1]

Yet if the progress made by the Dockers' Union had been very modest in 1891, it was to have still less success in the following year. In part, the failure was probably due to financial difficulties within the parent organization, where membership was declining rapidly, and in part to the fact that the London-based leaders were often out of touch with their rural audiences. By the middle of the year the number of Oxfordshire branches had dwindled to about 17, while branch receipts were showing a dramatic fall.[2]

Finally, at the Swansea conference of the Dockers' Union in September 1892, it was decided to abandon organizational work in the rural areas because of the 'heavy charges involved'. It might have seemed that this was the end of trade unionism among Oxfordshire farm workers. However, Nicholls, who was still organizing secretary for the county, was a tenacious character, and he decided to form a local union. He wrote to the weekly Liberal newspaper, the *Oxford Chronicle* of 17 September 1892, calling the labourers to organize 'until the co-operative and

---

[1] *Oxford Chronicle*, 19 Sept. 1891.

[2] For example, in the six months to 30 June 1892, Burford, which had recorded total branch receipts of over £23 in 1891, registered a mere £4 9s. for the following half-year, while Milton-under-Wychwood could only muster 4s. in respect of the latter period—as compared with £17 3s. 8½d. obtained in the preceding year. On the other hand, receipts for Wootton, Kirtlington and Lower Heyford were well maintained.

commonweal shall be established, and wagedom, capitalism and landlordism have ceased to exist.'

The new society was to be known simply as the Oxfordshire Labourers' Union. Its objects embraced the usual range of regulation of conditions of employment and of wage levels, plus the promise of dispute pay at 10s. per week In addition, provision was made for legal protection of members, the acquisition of land for allotments and small holdings, and the lending of 'small sums of money' on satisfactory security for the use of occupiers of allotments or small holdings. Weekly subscriptions were fixed at 2d., with an entrance fee of 6d., while every full member who, at the time of his death, was of six months' standing and 'clear on the books' was entitled to a funeral benefit of £4. Other minor inducements included the co-operative purchase of coal by the union for resale to members at cheaper wholesale prices and the making of a voluntary contribution, where this was felt to be justified, to any member suffering the accidental loss of livestock.

The finances of the new organization were to be administered by three trustees—and here the links with the Liberal Party (and Oxford University) were immediately apparent. The first three trustees were all active Liberals and two of them were members of the university, viz. A. Sidgwick, who was also chairman of the local Liberal Association, and Hobhouse, who had earlier assisted the N.A.L.U.

The *Oxford Chronicle* carefully recorded the efforts made to establish the union; in the early months of 1893 Nicholls even visited Lincolnshire in an attempt to promote links with those favourable to agricultural unionism in that county. His initiative met with some small success, and when the first formal meeting of the new union was held on 1 April 1893, it was announced that the name was to be changed to the Oxfordshire and Lincolnshire Agricultural Labourers' Union. Membership of approximately 500 was claimed for Oxfordshire, divided among 17 branches, plus eight branches established in Lincolnshire. The total income of the union for the half-year was nearly £100 —of which £40 had come from 'donations'. On the expenditure side, Nicholls, as secretary, had received £60, and only *one member* had secured any direct assistance. The prospect appeared a hopeless one and by the late summer of 1893 the whole enterprise had collapsed, the *Oxford Chronicle* sadly reporting 'that the present moment is not propitious for forming a stable trades union among our local labourers had been proved by the unfortunate end of the Oxfordshire Agricultural

Labourer's Union.' Thus concluded a genuine effort at co-operation between a union for urban labourers and the farm workers.[1]

With the demise of the Oxfordshire union in 1893 agricultural trade unionism disappeared from the county for the remainder of the nineteenth century—for the N.A.L.U. branches had faded away during the period of activity of the Dockers' Union. Nevertheless some spirit of Radicalism remained alive, and, when the elections for Parish Councils were held in December 1894, a number of former unionists offered themselves for election. Although the Oxfordshire farm workers did not match the success of their Norfolk and Suffolk counterparts, at least one contemporary, Richard Heath, considered that they had done well. For example, in 19 parishes which polled on 17 December and which were scattered throughout the county, he estimated that 23 councillors were agricultural labourers and 20 were concerned with 'other forms of labour'—out of a total of 135 councillors involved. Again, in 41 parishes in the southern division of the county, 97 of the 130 elected councillors were described as labourers and 'working men of all kinds'.[2]

If a descent is made from the general to the particular, the election results show that in parishes where the Dockers' Union (or its successor) had been active, labourers—or candidates selected by them—were often successful. For example, at Burford, three of the 11 councillors were labourers and one of them was J. Search, the former secretary of the Dockers' Union branch established there; at Wootton two of the seven councillors were labourers and a third had been manager of the union co-operative shop and branch secretary. At Horspath three of the five councillors were labourers, and again the former union branch secretary was elected.[3]

[1] See P. L. R. Horn, 'The Farm Workers, the Dockers and Oxford University' in *Oxoniensia*, xxxii, 1967, p. 68. It is perhaps worth noting that the Dockers' Union was not the only urban society to experiment in this field within the county. The National Labour Federation carried out a similar scheme on a small scale in the Banbury area during August and October, 1891, but with little success. *Workmen's Times*, 21 Aug. and 23 Oct. 1891. Branches were said to have been established at Bodicote, Bloxham, King's Sutton, Deddington and Hanwell.

[2] Richard Heath. 'The Rural Revolution' in the *Contemporary Review* (Feb. 1895), p. 123.

[3] Nevertheless in some villages where there had been no union branch in the recent past the labourers also did very well. One such village was Cuddington, where all five councillors were agricultural labourers.

This success was not, however, maintained in the elections of 1897, when out of 18 Oxfordshire parishes where the occupations of candidates were given in the local press, farm workers only secured 16 of the 116 seats available. On the other hand, former branch secretaries did offer themselves for election in six villages at the 1897 elections and four out of the six were successful. Some vestiges of Radicalism had thus survived, even if by the end of the 1890s they were very weak. Labourers, in general, took little part in the parish council elections at the end of the century—perhaps through indifference, or perhaps through fear of reprisals if they appeared over-zealous in the wrong cause.[1]

What then had the Oxfordshire farm worker to show for his earlier agitation? First and foremost, he was better off financially than he had been in the 1860s, even if wages had fallen from their 1872–4 peak. Of course, it may be argued that the rise in wages which occurred in the 1870s would have come anyway as agriculture was prosperous and the demand for labour buoyant at a time when employment in urban industry was at a high level. But it must be remembered that such prosperity had existed before without the labourers deriving any great benefit from it. Union agitation pinpointed the need for some redistribution of agricultural income in favour of the farm worker.

In other matters the contribution of the unions is clearer. There is little doubt that the extension of the franchise in 1884 owed something to their agitation. Even the *Economist*—a not very sympathetic source—declared in its 1877 article, 'A Positive Argument for Extending the County Franchise':

The existence and spread of labourers' unions supplies, therefore, a *prima facie* reason for giving the labourers votes. It is evidence that the class has, and it is conscious that it has, desires and interests peculiar to itself, and that it can no longer be treated as a mere appendage to some other class . . .[2]

The article referred to the country as a whole, but, as has been seen, Oxfordshire played its own particular rôle in forwarding petitions for enfranchisement and in holding pro-franchise meetings. Similar valuable work was also achieved in relation

[1] Redlich and Hurst, *Local Government in England and Wales* (London, 1903), ii, pp. 45–46.
[2] *Economist*, 17 Nov. 1877.

to the administration of local charities and in defending members in the courts, particularly in breach of contract cases in the early days of the movement.

Finally, and most significantly, the unions gave to the farm worker a greater sense of self-respect; after 1872 neither landowner nor farmer could forget that the labourer was a human being, even if sometimes an inconvenient one, who insisted on having his due rights and privileges. He was no longer a contemptible 'chaw bacon' or 'Johnny Raw'.

APPENDIX

SPECIMEN BALANCE SHEETS FOR THE OXFORD AND BANBURY DISTRICTS

Income and Expenditure of the Oxford District for the Year to October 1873

From: *Oxford Chronicle*—1 November 1873

INCOME	£	s.	d.	EXPENDITURE	£	s.	d.
Contributions from Branches	1,518	10	3	To National Agricultural Labourers Funds	495	0	0
Grants from National Agricultural Labourers' Union	20	0	0	Relief	278	16	0
				Migration	262	12	8
				Emigration	51	6	0
Migration Grants Repaid	3	18	4	Northleach District	5	15	11
Donations	8	0	0	Expenses	353	9	2½
Rules and cards	2	6	7½				
	1,552	15	3½*		1,446	19	9½
	1,446	19	9½				
Balance	105	15	6				

(* The total should in fact be £1,552 15s. 2½d. Book-keeping problems plagued the union throughout its life and caused some of the internal disputes which helped to undermine its position.)

Income and Expenditure of the Banbury District for the Year to November 1873

From: *Labourers' Union Chronicle*—15 November 1873

INCOME	£	s.	d.	EXPENDITURE	£	s.	d.
Branches' contributions	877	6	7½	Relief and lock-out	144	11	2
Donations		1	0	Migration	145	1	2½
Migration grants repaid	4	2	0	Emigration	43	10	6
Grants from the National	109	4	11	District Secretary's salary and travelling expenses	122	11	9
				Delegate expenditure	90	0	0
				Executive committee and auditors' expenses, etc.	31	11	2
				Hire of Town Hall, printing, etc.	16	10	0
				Remitted to the National for the year	387	6	9
				Paid to delegates at the affiliation of the Banbury district	9	4	11
				Expenditure over the fourth allowed for the management	28	7	4
	990	14	6½		990	14	6½*

(N.B.* In practice, this total should be £1,018 14s. 9½d.—showing that expenditure had exceeded income by an unexplained £28 0s. 3d.)

VI

Hiring Fairs and Farm Servants' Combinations in Scotland

'If the masters and servants in lock-out districts could agree to hold periodic hirings as we in the border counties do,' remarked the *Hexham Courant* on 6 June 1874 at the height of the East Anglian dispute, 'wages would adjust themselves without any of the evils which must attend lock-outs or strikes.' Some hiring fairs in fact still survived in southern and midland England. But, except in Dorset,[1] they catered only for carters and for unmarried servants boarding in the farmhouses. Such workers were at least partially inhibited from participating in strikes—a number of striking carters were prosecuted in the 1870s for breach of contract. However the great majority of southern English labourers were engaged by the week and paid primarily (though seldom exclusively) in cash. So discontent usually focused on the level of wages; and demands could be backed by collective action, in law provided that a week's notice had been given, in practice even if it had not.

In Scotland and the far north of England the great majority of the regular farm staff was hired by the year or (in the case of unmarried servants) for six months, on the basis of contracts whose breach could until 1880 be punished by imprisonment. Traditionally these contracts were arrived at by a process of individual bargaining between masters and men at hiring fairs; and even when, as was increasingly the case, private agreements were reached before the fairs, they might still have to be modified in the light of wage increases negotiated there. So the fairs were the keys to the whole system.[2] They were held in market towns

[1] In central Dorset ordinary as well as skilled farm labourers were commonly hired by the year, often in families, at the Dorchester Candlemas fair. But this was poorly publicized, and, being the only fair in the neighbourhood, offered only limited opportunities for testing the state of the market. Also there was a distinct uncertainty as to the obligations created by the yearly bond; and magistrates were not really prepared to enforce them against ordinary labourers on strike, though they would against carters.

[2] This was true also of Wales, where unmarried servants slightly outnumbered the married men engaged by the week. Such few combinations as occurred aimed chiefly at the reduction of hours, and

on fixed dates a month or two before engagements entered into force; and they were usually great occasions:

Oldgate Street was thronged with booths, in which were enacted various amusements; and in the Market Place was a large number of stalls, containing various articles calculated to please both the eye and the palate, and all seemed to come in for a good share of favours.[1]

Bargaining could be protracted—it was not uncommon for both masters and men to shop around a number of fairs before finally concluding an agreement, which was usually verbal and was sealed by the formal advance to the labourer of a token sum, a shilling or a couple of shillings according to the locality. Even when matters were concluded within the day the process could still be tense. Thus in 1877 farmers' meetings to urge wage reductions 'had caused great excitement amongst the rural population': so, 'many hundreds' flocked into Alnwick by rail and on foot—'the hirings at the beginning were very slow, there being numerous "nibbles" cautiously offered by the farmers, but no "takes" made'; 'about two o'clock', however, 'engagements were freely effected on the old terms . . .' At such times of excitement even men not seeking a change of master would wish to 'see the market' before making new engagements with their present employer—attendance at the Kelso March Fair in 1866 was unusually high for this reason.

The natural time to discuss wages and conditions of employment was therefore either at the hiring fair itself, or in the period immediately before it. Hence it was agreed at Earlston late in 1894

that the agitation should be conducted with vigour, and that the ploughmen in the district should meet once a month, at least up to the period of the annual hiring, to make the best arrangements for meeting the farmers on that occasion.

Conveniently enough, over the greater part of the country these fairs were held for married servants in the early spring, the engagements reached taking effect at Whitsun. So discussion and agitation could be concentrated into the winter, when, in

---

on achieving concessions they promptly collapsed – P.P., 1893-4 xxxvi, esp. pp. 15-16, 29-30; see also Dunbabin, article cited, pp. 122-4.

[1] *P.P.*, 1893–4 xxxvi, pp. 430, 471; *Morpeth Herald*, 4 May 1872, p. 4 (of the local May hiring).

any case, there was more time for it since the hours of work were necessarily shorter.[1]

Hiring fairs were not popular with the moralists—they attracted bawdy ballad singers, pick-pockets and other undesirables; and they were often occasions for drunkenness. Many also regarded it as derogatory to human dignity for people to expose themselves in the street to be chaffered for like cattle. And the weather in February, March, and April is often unpleasant. So there were recurrent attempts to suppress hiring fairs and substitute something more decorous, like a labour exchange. In the nineteenth century such attempts always failed, partly because people valued the hiring fairs as holidays, often (with Sundays and New Year's Day) the only ones they got, but also because the system had very real merits.

It was, for instance, felt to provide an institutional alternative to strikes and lock-outs. Wages had to be re-negotiated each year, whereas in central and southern England it might be genuinely difficult to get one's employer to consider a wage claim. But, once concluded, the contract gave both parties substantial security. The bargaining, too, could often be spread over a considerable period. And, since it took place some time before the existing contracts ran out, neither party was under any overwhelming pressure to concede too much for a quick settlement— the labourers were therefore very suspicious of all attempts to move the hiring fairs nearer to the date when the new contracts took effect.

Both the bargaining and the contract was on an individual basis between employer and employee, and pay reflected ability more openly than in southern England. At Dumfries in 1873 'first-rate' hands secured £37–£40 p.a., 'ordinary' ones only £34–£36; but in Worcestershire in the 1860s, we are told, such differences could only be reflected by surreptitious variations in 'perquisites' in kind. In any case work on Scottish farms was more specialized and therefore more highly stratified than was that on southern English ones. And the individualism all this gave rise to did not accord well with collective bargaining or unionism. Lastly the hiring system frequently produced a restlessness and a wish to change masters, or, even more commonly, a wish on the part of men's wives to secure other society than that afforded by the isolated cluster of farm cottages in which they had been living. In the early twentieth century the average

[1] *Morpeth Herald*, 10 March 1877, p. 3; *Berwick Warder*, 9 March 1866, p. 8; *The Plough*, Nov. 1894, p. 16.

married man is said to have changed employers every three years. And since cottages went with the job, such changes often involved a considerable displacement, and thus produced the kind of shifting population that is notoriously difficult to organize.[1]

But the hiring system also had a deeper effect. There were three parts to a bargain—cash pay, payment in kind, and conditions of employment. There could be no ambiguity about the first; and it is therefore the cash payment that proved most responsive to changes in the labour market or to improvements in the standard of living. Payments in kind had once constituted the bulk of a labourer's wages. They might well be spelt out in great detail at the fair, but they had a tendency to remain more or less standard over many decades. Lastly hours and conditions of employment were seldom broached during the bargaining; there could be misunderstandings; and where disputes went to law, the justices would interpret the contract in the light of 'the custom of the country' unless they received definite evidence to the contrary. The result was so rigid that the small unions of pre-World War I days despaired of changing it except by Act of Parliament; accordingly they devoted their principal efforts not towards wages but towards the (unsuccessful) promotion of legislation on such matters as half-holidays and the length of engagements.

Three aspects of the system came in for criticism at one time or another. As the nineteenth century drew towards a close, the whole concept of long engagements and payment in kind aroused growing antagonism. For some people came increasingly to take for granted the regularity of employment that it provided, irrespective of the seasons, and irrespective of periods of sickness of up to six weeks. Rising expectations also made people reluctant to risk tying themselves to an uncongenial master for a whole year. More importantly, they came to want a more varied diet than just oatmeal and potatoes. But to sell oatmeal, or exchange it at the grocer's for other goods, was cumbersome.[2] And if people did deal regularly at a shop, it was naturally more convenient to receive their wages in regular cash payments rather than in the customary lump sum at the end of the term of hiring —for one thing it made it unnecessary to buy on credit, an expensive process, and, for another, there was always the possibility

---

[1] *Berwick Journal*, 28 Feb. 1873, p. 4; *P.P.*, 1861 l, p. 501; Jones, Duncan, Conacher and Scott, *Rural Scotland during the War* (1926), pp. 191, 193–5.

[2] As is shown by the roundabout solution sometimes adopted of a farmer paying in kind but guaranteeing a fixed resale price.

that the farmer might find some pretext for seeking to withhold the lump sum.[1] Not that the hiring system's merits were ever unappreciated—many labourers were ready to write in its defence. But it had been particularly well suited to the early nineteenth century; and, if circumstances changed sufficiently, even its merits might eventually become abuses—long hirings remained general until the Second World War, by which time they probably fell into this category.

The other two grievances deriving from the hiring system were more local in their incidence. In all parts of Scotland some unmarried farm servants were engaged in exchange for their board and lodging plus a small sum in cash. Where they were put up in the farm-house itself this arrangement worked fairly well— and its patriarchal nature drew lyrical tributes from old-fashioned observers. But they were often, and more especially in the arable stretch between Tay-side and Kincardineshire, hired in larger numbers, lodged in a sparsely furnished shed ('bothy') as a dormitory, given basic provisions, and left to get on with it without further help or supervision. The men not infrequently relished the absence of supervision and the freedom to stay out as late at night as they pleased. But it is generally agreed that, though women managed to housekeep successfully for themselves, men did not: so outsiders repeatedly denounced the 'bothy system' for its tendency to brutalize and demoralize. Also, at least at the end of the nineteenth century, bothy dwellers had the reputation of being more detached from their employers than other workers, and therefore more restless and more easily discontented.

The bothy system was most wide-spread in arable areas where unmarried farm servants were the rule. But in south-east Scotland and north-east England, though the general pattern of cultivation was the same, the great majority of the regular farm labour force were married. And their families provided an obvious source of outside assistance in busy times. This was the more necessary since the agricultural revolution had tended to displace the rural craftsmen, who had often held their cottages and small pendicles of land in return for providing a 'reaper' at

[1] The Scottish Federal Ploughmen's Union put the annual cost to the Scottish ploughmen of payment by lump sum in arrears at £100,000, and its Secretary claimed that at the end of the May term of 1890 farmers in Fife, Perth and Angus withheld £1,000, at May 1891 more, but in 1892 less since the men had secured a series of favourable Sheriff Court decisions (*The Plough*, April 1893 and Jan. 1894).

harvest. It was usual, therefore, in these districts, for a man to be hired conditionally on his also producing a woman to work whenever the farmer needed her. Initially this was merely during harvest: in 1814 Sir John Sinclair still describes the woman as a 'reaper', and it was long customary for a ploughman's wife to work without pay for 21 days in harvest in exchange for a rent-free cottage. But the whole trend of the new agriculture was to extend the busy season by raising, and tending, a greater variety of crops. So, particularly where turnips were grown, female labour might be in demand for perhaps three-quarters of the year. And it was not easy for a married woman to work so regularly, especially in the districts (principally East Lothian and the Borders) where it was usual for her to keep a cow. Less store therefore came to be set on the wife's obligation to work during the harvest—indeed it had fallen peacefully into abeyance by the 1860s—and more on the obligation of the ploughman to supply a female worker whenever called upon. These workers were generally unmarried; and when a ploughman could not supply one from his own family, he had to hire a 'bondager' from outside—and occasionally farmers were perverse enough to insist on outsiders in any case.[1]

The obligation to hire a bondager from outside the family was, by the 1860s, regarded as objectionable on two counts. On the one hand few, if any, cottages were large enough to afford privacy either to the bondager or to the family that engaged her. On the other, it was widely felt that a family lost money when it was forced to engage a bondager. For the ploughman had to hire and feed her for a lengthy period (generally a year), but the farmer only paid him for the days on which she actually worked. This loss appeared all the greater, too, in that it was no longer remembered that the ploughman got his cottage rent free in return for his bondager's (or wife's) work, not his own. Most observers felt that it was the financial grievance that was the more deeply resented, though naturally the argument from loss of privacy was also deployed against the system.[2] Be that as it may, it is not surprising that bondage was unpopular, or that,

[1] Sir John Sinclair, *General Report of the Agricultural State, and Political Circumstances, of Scotland* (Edinburgh, 1814), iii, pp. 249–250; *P.P.*, 1893–4 xxxvi, pp. 469–70, 484; *Haddingtonshire Courier*, 7 March 1862, p. 3; *Berwick Warder*, 9 Feb. 1866, p. 7; *North British Agriculturalist*, 28 Feb. 1866.

[2] *P.P.*, 1867–8 xvii, p. 113; *P.P.*, 1870 xiii, pp. 226 n, 228, 231, 434, 442.

in districts where it prevailed, strenuous attempts were made from time to time to modify or abolish it.

Most manifestations of discontent or labour unrest were naturally moulded by the factors so far described. Thus people might on occasion attempt direct action, might refuse, for instance, to feed the horses on Sunday. But there was little future in such a course, since the magistrates would generally find that, by the custom of the country, such work had been included in the contract. And it was expensive to be taken before them: for even when, as not infrequently happened, the farmer waived his claim to damages, there would still be legal costs to be paid; moreover the magistrates might authorize the farmer to withhold the cash payment due at the expiration of the contract, or send the labourer to prison if contumacious. Casual labour not bound by contract was, in this respect, better placed. So although strikes by men were virtually unknown, there are occasional instances of strikes by women harvesters for slight increases in pay. These were usually successful; for the season was urgent, and the episodes carried with them none of the traumatic implications of a betrayal by regular employees that accounted for much of the bitterness of, say, the East Anglian resistance to strikes.[1]

In general, though, little was to be looked for from direct action outside the hiring fairs. And a pattern of behaviour was therefore early established that was to last throughout the nineteenth century and beyond. There may indeed have been some attempts at organization even in the eighteenth century—certainly there were frequent complaints that farm servants were holding out at the hiring fairs for higher wages, and we find one reference to a speaker attempting to organize the ploughmen around Stirling in 1751 and one to an Aberdeenshire association formed in 1780 for the purpose of 'reducing the exorbitant wages of servants'. There was a clear attempt at collective action on the part of ploughmen in Perthshire in 1805, but it was suppressed under the Combination Acts. However in 1834 the Carse of Gowrie was again agitated. A meeting at Inchture was requisitioned by 70 ploughmen, attended by 600, and addressed by both ploughmen and Dundee trades unionists. A committee was elected to extend the movement 'throughout Perthshire', and to press its demands (for an 8 to 10 hour day and payment of

[1] This was, of course, not simply a matter of legal circumstance. English farmers took strikes by hop-pickers and other casual hands fairly lightly, but were much less tolerant of such activity on the part of their regular labourers, even though, in law, these too were usually engaged by the week.

overtime) at the next hiring market in a fortnight's time. It was hoped that a further meeting would be held to co-ordinate tactics, and to declare that no farm servant should engage himself on any terms 'differing in the least from the rules, until he shall first have consulted with the Committee'.

The hiring fair in question was difficult, little business being done in view of the 'determined stand made by the farm servants for a reduction in their hours of labour'; but the combination seems to have collapsed, many of its members defying its rules to seek work on the old terms. The whole episode attracted considerable local attention for a couple of months; a number of similar meetings were held, short-lived associations formed, and their leaders black-listed. Also one counter-meeting deprecated 'the idea of dictating to their masters, after the manner of a trades union, in any way to interfere so as to throw impediments in the way of regular operation of agricultural labour'. Instead it petitioned (unsuccessfully) for shorter hours, both by publishing its resolutions as an advertisement in the local newspaper, and by sending them directly to the Perthshire Agricultural Association.[1]

Later agitations were to achieve more, but the essential features were already present—meetings, publicity, petitions, supplemented by some attempt at joint action at hiring fairs. This might be planned by local 'unions' or 'associations'; but, when it came to the point, these bodies could only influence the way in which their members would seek to bargain, not determine the terms for which they would settle. And there was little or no thought of any action outside the hiring fairs.

The next recorded dispute was in 1845, when a Mr. Thompson of Tranent tried to organize a general refusal by the labourers to engage bondagers. Unfortunately, we know very little about the episode, since the local press was far more scanty than it was to become in the 1860s, and its accounts of hiring fairs are rudimentary. But Thompson's organization was clearly quite good —his adherents at the Haddington fair were numerous, and marked out by the wearing of distinctive ribbons. However, the farmers seem to have been unyielding, and no business was done. Many of the labourers are said to have adjourned to the pub,

---

[1] H. Hamilton, *An Economic History of Scotland in the Eighteenth Century* (Oxford, 1963), pp. 344–5; G. Houston, 'Labour Relations in Scottish Agriculture before 1870', *Agricultural History Review*, vi (1958), pp. 34 ff. One of the 1834 meetings (at Forteviot) did also voice a rather imprecise wage demand, but even here the length of the working day assumed greater importance.

'and a lot of them came out like madmen. That was a queer way to strike.' Whether for this reason, or because the hinds would have nowhere to live if they did not re-engage, they eventually caved in, 'tearing the ribbon from our coat after two o'clock on that memorable Friday'. My quotations come from two letters written during the next major agitation some 20 years later. The letters show that, though the events of 1845 attracted little publicity at the time, they made a major impression locally. And the tone of references to them suggests that, at least in East Lothian, they were taken as illustrating the ineffectiveness of a 'strike', that is of an absolute and collective refusal to engage at the hiring fairs unless certain conditions were met. As a leading article in the *Haddingtonshire Courier* put it, 'The demonstration proved a failure so far as its immediate objects were concerned; and there can be little doubt that were [the hinds] . . . again to combine, they would make equally little of it.'[1]

Not that the labourers were always unsuccessful. In 1857 some farmers sought to alter the date of the Haddington hiring fair from early February to early March. But they only told the men a week before the change. And the latter rejected it, refused to hire privately in advance of the fair as progressive farmers would have liked, and all turned up in Haddington on the old day. The farmers were divided on the change, and so it was dropped, though the idea continued to crop up for another couple of years. This episode, too, was much remarked on locally, and led many, though not all, farmers to distrust the currently fashionable idea of replacing fairs with registry offices—'they could not make a change without the servants thinking that there was to be some oppression; and to send them to have strikes and meetings over the country was the worst thing that the . . . [employers] could do.'

Such a reaction perhaps suggests that labour relations in the Lothians were not altogether smooth. And at about this time there was an incipient combination at Dunbar; this collected and banked subscriptions, but seems to have had no effect on the actual hiring fairs. There were, of course, a number of unsettling factors. One may have been the frequent discussion in the press of such topics as unsatisfactory housing, bothies, and the bondage system. The quite extensive construction of new cottages made it easier for farmers to dispense with bondagers, and perhaps led to growing discontent in areas where they were not prepared to do so. More certainly, the low grain prices of

[1] *Haddingtonshire Courier*, 15 Dec. 1865, 26 Jan. and 9 Feb. 1866.

1864 prompted widespread demands in 1865 for a partial switch from grain payments to payments in kind. And a final factor was probably the growing emphasis on efficiency, as evidenced by rising rents, profits, and wages. This involved more frequent changes in farm tenancies; and the new men had fewer compunctions about breaking up the existing staff of servants and seeking to buy 'the stoutest labour in the cheapest market'. Also when, as was often the case, they came from other parts of the country, they might be tempted to sweep away the East Lothian custom whereby keep for a cow was provided as part of a man's wages, or very occasionally even to go further and also forbid him to keep a pig.[1]

In February 1865 this abrogation of Lothian custom was denounced in a strong letter to the *Haddington Courier*. The letter received wide publicity, and set off a prolonged correspondence (in which farm servants joined) on pay and conditions, and on the causes of 'those annual movings that we are now so much accustomed to, but which are profitless alike to both master and man'. The tone was studiously moderate. But some tension must have underlain references to servants ungratefully changing masters, to the growing remoteness of the new monied farmers, and to the resultant 'no-interest-in-each-others-welfare-system'. Surprisingly none of the correspondents raised the 'bondage' question. But it is mentioned, along with that of payment in kind, as having excited more than usual interest in the Dunbar hiring fair.[2]

As always discussion died down during the spring and summer. But in December a movement was set on foot to organize the farm labourers in the immediate vicinity of Edinburgh. The most important external stimulus was probably provided by the Edinburgh stone-masons, who participated actively in the launching of the 'Midlothian Farm Servants' Protection Society', and whose recent struggle for a nine-hour day was cited approvingly at its first meetings. But the movement also owed much

[1] Both animals cost the farmer more than the sum he was credited with in conventional calculations of wages; but, provided his wife was willing to care for them, they were worth at least twice as much to the labourer.

[2] *North British Agriculturalist*, 1860, pp. 230–2; *Haddingtonshire Courier*, 3 Feb.–17 March 1865 *passim*, 12 Jan. 1866; *Weekly Scotsman*, 23 Dec. 1865, p. 8; *Berwick Warder*, 10 Feb. 1865, p. 4; 'The Scottish Farm Labourer', *The Cornhill Magazine*, X (1864), esp. pp. 617–18; T. Johnston, *A History of the Working Classes in Scotland* (Glasgow, 1923), pp. 355–6.

publicity to the fact that the agricultural world had already been turned upside-down by two recent speeches. The first, by Lord Elcho, claimed that the Lowland Scots were leaving farm work and being replaced by the Irish; he also threatened that, if tenant farmers pressed their landlords too far, the latter would be reduced to farming their estates themselves. Both points gave rise to considerable controversy in their own right, and in addition some people saw them as an attempt to invoke a labourers' agitation to counter that of the farmers. The second speech, by Duncan McLaren, fastened on Lord Elcho's contention that the Scots were deserting farm work, and had the temerity to recommend combination and strikes to the agricultural labourers as a means of bettering their condition. In reality the Mid-Lothian Farm Servants' Society had no direct connection with either speech, and prudently renounced McLaren's advice; but many observers remained convinced of the contrary.[1]

The agitation caught on rapidly, and by late January the *Newcastle Chronicle* could write that 'There is a pretty general movement all over the Borders for a rise in wage by farm servants.' It had also spread north of the Forth, and inquiries had been received from ploughmen as far afield as Aberdeenshire and Ayrshire. There was, of course, extensive newspaper correspondence. But its primary vehicle was probably the public meeting—the *Newcastle Chronicle's* report mentioned that three meetings had been held in the Kelso district in the previous week, and that several more were to take place in the current one. At the meetings, discussion of the ploughmen's condition and grievances was generally followed by the passage of resolutions, and sometimes by the election of a committee or the formation of a small local union or 'protection society'. Such societies are to be met with sporadically in most eastern counties from Moray to Roxburgh, and very occasionally in the southwest. They sometimes formed paper links with the Mid-Lothian (later Scottish) Farm Servants' Protection Society, which was thus able to claim 1,200–1,300 members in the Lothians in January 1867;[2] but for practical purposes they were autonomous. They charged an entrance fee and levied small subscriptions. But, as we shall see, their pattern of activity left them little to spend the money on.

[1] *Weekly Scotsman*, 23 and 30 December 1865; *Haddingtonshire Courier*, 8, 15, and 22 Dec. 1865.

[2] *Berwick Warder*, 4 Jan. 1867, p. 7—there had been 7,661 male farm servants over 20 years old in the Lothians in 1861.

The course of events naturally differed from place to place, but the general trend is clear:

The agitation among farm servants for an advance of wages has assumed various phases, and in the south-east of Scotland it has been resolved into a struggle for the abolition of bondage. At some meetings of the hinds it was agreed to ask for a rise of £5 a year in addition, but the major and more reasonable part of the ploughmen ask only for their present gains, with the removal of the bondage grievance.

This concentration on the abolition of bondage is the more remarkable since the question had not figured among the initial aims of the Midlothian society—Edinburgh lay to the west of the bondage district proper—or indeed among those of the 'Border Farm Servants' Protection Association'. But where the bondage system prevailed it was clearly the most deeply felt local grievance: so, at its first meeting, the Border Farm Servants' Association resolved to make the abolition of bondage the society's principal object. This demand was also the one best calculated to appeal to public opinion—some farmers joined in denouncing the bondage system and none openly defended it. So it represented the most promising line of attack.

The Protection Societies' strategy was simple and traditional. They sought to discourage people from engaging (or re-engaging) themselves before the hiring fairs. At the fairs each man should demand certain minimum terms, generally well above the existing ones. Unity of sentiment might be encouraged by meetings, displays of placards, or the wearing of blue ribbons. But there was never any suggestion of collective action in the sense of a joint refusal to engage unless everybody was accorded these terms. Nor did anybody seek to operate outside the hiring fairs.

This approach enjoyed a fair degree of success. Considerable pressure may have been exercised to prevent re-engagements before the fairs—one hind was burnt in effigy outside his cottage by a crowd of some 300 because, although a member of a protection society, he had re-engaged with his employer to keep two bondagers. Such pressure was not always successful; but still the fairs were unusually crowded, and there was a tendency on the part of the hinds to hold out for minimum terms, sometimes even through a number of fairs. In the end, though, men were prepared to settle for what they could get: at the last market of the season in Midlothian rises of two to four pounds a year were obtained fairly readily, ones of five pounds occasionally; but only exceptional men 'got up to the mark of the

Ploughmen's Association, namely, 15s. a week, the well known [union figure] Tam Ewing being amongst the number'.

Bargaining over bondage was more intense. At Selkirk there appeared to be 'a mutual understanding that a struggle for and against the established usage of the hind keeping in bondage was about to take place'. Hinds with daughters willing to work were readily engaged, but, since the remainder refused to supply bondagers, business was slow. However 'the prevailing opinion in the market was that the bondage system was doomed.' This outcome was not invariable—at Hawick a minority of hinds agreed to re-engage with bondagers for an extra four shillings a week, and at Greenlaw in Berwickshire the agitation dissolved at the hiring fair, again in return for increased pay. But at other fairs the farmers showed a greater readiness to dispense with 'the bondage in its old familiar form'; and in many cases they are said to have re-engaged their servants accordingly even before the fairs.

So bondage everywhere received a substantial check. Participants, correspondents and commentators could refer to the 'very general modification' of the system, asserting that the grievance had been 'adjusted by its practical abolition', and the like. But such claims might be exaggerated—one landlord was to be rebuked for taking them too literally and reminded that bondage persisted on two of his own farms. In 1871 a Royal Commission suggested that the eclipse of bondage had been most marked in East Lothian, where the agitation had led a number of farmers to switch over to female bothies, and less complete in Roxburghshire and Berwickshire, where the system had been still more prevalent.[1] Nevertheless bondage had been curtailed even in these counties, and, for a time at least, it seemed as if 'the labourer no longer fights as he did a few years ago against "the bondage" ', now 'that a combination on the part of the hinds has forced up the bondager's wage'.[2]

Of course the agitation of 1866 was not the only reason for the

[1] The Commissioner was not prepared to hazard a guess at the number of hinds who still had to engage bondagers from outside their own families. But, for what this is worth, a newspaper correspondent put it at a quarter of the labourers in northern Northumberland and Berwickshire (*Berwick Journal*, 24 Jan. 1873 p. 5).

[2] *Haddingtonshire Courier*, esp. 26 Jan. 1866 (quoting the *Newcastle Chronicle*), 16 March 1866, 22 Feb. 1867; *North British Agriculturalist*, esp. 31 Jan., 28 Feb., 9 and 30 March 1866; *Berwickshire News*, 28 Aug. 1923, p. 4; *P.P.*, 1870 xiii, pp. 225–8, 442; Houston, article cited, pp. 39–41.

demise of the bondager system,[1] but it had materially hastened the process and must therefore be regarded as quite unusually successful. Success, however, was accompanied by drawbacks. For since the farmers continued to need female labour, they now preferred to engage men who could supply it from within their own families. This preference was already apparent at the fairs of 1866; very occasionally, as around Ecrom in Berwickshire, it even led some of those without daughters to revert to offering bondagers; and it continued strongly to influence hiring patterns for well over half a century. In many ways this preference may have been no bad thing. For, by the time a man had daughters old enough for regular employment, he may have been getting past his prime. But since female 'workers' (the term soon replaced that of 'bondager') were becoming rapidly scarcer, he could be assured of several years continued employment at peak rates. (Though in the Lothians men started in the 1890s to use their daughters' work to bargain instead for their sons' rapid promotion and their own earlier retirement to easier jobs.) But such arrangements did not always look so attractive from the daughters' point of view. And the very idea of women working in the fields became increasingly unacceptable as the century drew on. So, as we shall see, difficulties were to arise in the future on this score.

Still, for the time being, the agitation of 1866 had laid to rest a major grievance. But this deprived it of its principal stimulus. For it always had been very moderate both in tone and content —when a meeting at Kalemouth demanded not only the abolition of bondage but also a wage increase of £5 per annum it was felt to have gone too far, and few men would join the Protection Society it set up. True agitation did not immediately die down; it even extended into Galloway. But it was forced to confine itself to pressing for increased wages and shorter hours, as, of course, it always had been in areas where bondage was not current. In this connection it encountered more hostility from the farmers, none of whom, even when they were ready to concede

[1] A later report described the process thus: 'The increase in the number and improvement in the character of labourers' cottages [which took place between 1850 and 1870 in the Lothians, rather later in the Borders], the gradual but decided migration of women from country to towns, and the extinction or dying out of bondage service seem to have been contemporaneous. Bondagers were common in East Lothian between 1850 and 1860, the system lingered on up to 1875, but since then it has disappeared.'—*P.P.*, 1893–4 xxxvi, p. 484.

an increase in wages, had any use for a combination to extort one. Hence in Castle Douglas, and perhaps elsewhere, farmers were reluctant to engage servants unless they first broke with the Ploughmen's Association. More importantly, though, the hiring system itself, as I have argued above, made it difficult to negotiate collectively on wages, or to negotiate at all on hours and conditions of work. So there was little scope for the Protection Societies beyond providing legal aid, giving financial assistance to the sick or the victimized, and generally serving as a ginger group. Some survived on this basis for a considerable time—the Border Farm Servants' Protection Association was still in existence in 1870, albeit with only 60 members, a quarter of the total that its Secretary considered attainable. But equally some societies were already being wound up for lack of support in the summer and autumn of 1886. And by December 1867 the Chairman of the East Lothian Agricultural Society was able without contradiction to pronounce a post-mortem—'He was happy to say that they heard no more of those meetings.'[1]

His happiness, however, must have been fairly short lived, for agitation was to revive with the new decade. Sometimes this was a reaction to the general inflationary situation: thus a Dalkeith ploughmen's meeting decided, 'in accordance with the general advance which has taken place in the wages of artisans of every class, . . . respectfully [to] request' a rise to 16s. a week payable weekly or fortnightly. Alternatively, the inspiration might be the shorter hours adopted in engineering in January 1872; by April we hear of a 'Farm Servants' Short Time Movement' that circled Glasgow and extended across the western parts of the Lothians—'Other workmen had shorter hours and were better paid, and why should they be bond slaves—they, on whom everything depended?' 1872, of course, saw the sprouting of the most unlikely combinations, so it is not surprising that farm servants were involved too, and over a wide area. There was an ambitious attempt at an Aberdeenshire Agricultural Labourers' Union with an extremely comprehensive programme. The advent of the two summer hiring fairs in Fife inspired numerous recruiting meetings for a Fife and Kinross Ploughmen's Union. This too, sought shorter hours and higher wages (in that order of priority). By September it claimed 500 members; they represented perhaps a tenth of the eligible farm

---

[1] *Berwick Warder*, 9 Feb. and 24 Dec. 1866; *North British Agriculturalist*, 13 Feb. 1867, p. 105; *Haddingtonshire Courier*, 13 Dec. 1867, p. 2; *P.P.*, 1870 xiii, p. 228 n; Houston, article cited, pp. 39–41.

servants, and came mostly from west rather than east Fife, supposedly because of the example of the local miners. Similarly agitation revived in the Borders, mainly through newspaper correspondence, and meetings called in advance of the hiring season by small local societies. The most usual demands were for a pound a week, payment in cash, and, where it still survived, the abolition of the bondage system (which was reckoned to cost the hind anything from £7 to £10 or even £16 a year).

It is possible that this agitation was geographically wider than that of 1866–7. And it certainly aroused some bitter feelings. The Earl of Dunmore is said to have told the Stirling Agricultural Society that the restlessness of the local farm labourers was attributable not to 'the influence of other farm servants, but rather to [that] . . . of a parcel of scoundrels who deserved to be hung', and to have added that 'It was his own firm conviction that every secretary of a trades union society throughout the country ought to be hung.' And in November 1873 at least seven farmers, who had allegedly kept back their men's wages, were mobbed at a hiring fair near Forfar; similar disturbances had been threatened at Brechin but were prevented by a large force of police.

Most of the unions sought some changes in the general system of engagements, such as shorter hours, fortnightly cash payments, and the like. But these were seldom pressed, except in areas where bondage survived and was again attacked with a fair degree of success, and in Fife. Here feeling against the traditional system of engagements was so strong, and alternative jobs so plentiful, that many ploughmen temporarily deserted agriculture at the Martinmas term in 1873. More generally, though, the movement seems largely to have worked itself out at the fairs. We are told that the Berwick market was better attended than at any time since 'the agitation about the bondage system', but also that the ploughmen generally did not accept advice to stand out for a wage of £1 a week, paid exclusively in cash. Instead 'at almost all the recent fairs' they asked, and usually obtained, a slight rise 'in the money item', with the payments in kind remaining as before. In short the unions had little influence over them. And in any case the agitation probably ran less deep than had that of 1866–7. Certainly it was overshadowed, even in the columns of the *North British Agriculturalist*, by the southern English labourers' movement.[1]

[1] *North British Agriculturalist*, esp. 27 Dec. 1871, 3 April 1872, 12 Feb. 1873; *Fife Herald* (Cupar), esp. 1 Aug. and 5 Sept. 1872, 20 and 27 Nov. 1873; *Newcastle Weekly Chronicle*, 15 Feb. 1873;

After the early 1870s there was a lull. But in Scotland, as in England, the late 1880s saw another revival of rural trades unionism. On paper, at least, this was more impressive than its forerunners. It was certainly longer lived, and it enjoyed a wider geographical coverage. Also the Scottish Ploughmen's Federal Union, into which local societies were largely subsumed, possessed the novel assets of a full-time secretary and of its own newspaper, *The Plough*. It was founded in 1889, and, in evidence before the Royal Commission on Labour in 1892, claimed 6,000 members widely distributed around the country.[1] At the same time the still independent Scottish Farm Servants, Carters and General Union (established in 1886) claimed 600 members in Aberdeen City, Aberdeenshire, and Banff; and there were one or two purely local unions, especially in Ross. These figures must be treated as maxima—it is odd that of the 6,000 ploughmen in Perthshire a bare hundred adhered to the Ploughmen's Union, despite its Secretary's residence in Perth; and when the Union came to register with the Registrar of Friendly Societies in 1895, it had only 1,300 members and some five branches still in operation, its take-over of the Scottish Farm Servants' Union notwithstanding.[2]

Despite occasional verbal intransigence in Wigtownshire, neither *The Plough* nor the Royal Commission on Labour ever reported a strike by male agricultural labourers—indeed 'such things can hardly be on farms where yearly engagements bind man and master, and when supply and demand keep pace with each other.' So the agitation of the 1890s bore many resemblances to its predecessors—meetings (especially before hiring fairs to co-ordinate bargaining), appeals to public opinion, the provision of legal assistance, and the like. There was even talk of publishing a black-list of the names of obnoxious employers, just as there had been in the 1860s; but, as in the 1860s, the risks of libel actions (and of charges of union 'tyranny') preven-

---

Berwickshire News, esp. 7 and 14 March 1871, 22 April 1873; *Berwick Journal*, 7 March 1873; Gwenllian Evans, 'Farm Servants' Unions in Aberdeenshire from 1870–1900', *Scottish Historical Review*, xxi (1952), pp. 29–31.

[1] In Caithness, Ross, Angus, Perthshire, Stirling, Dunbarton, Renfrew, Lanarkshire, Ayr, Wigtown, Kirkcudbright, Dumfries, Peebles, Roxburgh and Midlothian.

[2] Admittedly it later revived to a peak membership of 2,390 in 11 branches (in 1897), and struggled on until 1900. But in its later stages it was primarily concerned with city carters. *P.P.*, 1893–4 xxxvi, pp. 360, 363–4; Gwenllian Evans, article cited, esp. pp. 35–40.

ted this. So it is not, perhaps, surprising that one Assistant Commissioner airily dismissed the Scottish Farm Servants' Union as *déja vu;* 'In its failure, if it be doomed to fail, it is only following the fate of three or four predecessors.'[1]

But this was to miss a number of the movement's more novel aspects. Like their counterparts in southern England, the Scottish unions were now far readier to seek legislative intervention to cure their grievances. Indeed the petitioning of Parliament and the pressurizing of M.P.s must have taken up a very fair proportion of their time. As one Ross-shire branch put it,

your petitioners, while urging these reforms [a nine-hour day and a half-holiday on Saturdays] through their Union, despair of getting them carried through by their employers, or by your petitioners' organizations, with the promptitude that the urgency of their case demands, they therefore submit that Parliament should deal with their case.

There was, perhaps, just an outside chance that the Liberal parliament of 1892–5 would do so. True R. B. Haldane declined to introduce a private member's bill against the payment of wages in kind, on the grounds that the ploughmen were themselves divided on the subject. But a bill for Saturday half-holidays was drafted, and attracted much attention in 1894. However the topic eventually came up as an amendment to the Local Government Bill (which the ploughmen's leaders, like many other Radicals, regarded as a panacea that should contain remedies for all ills). The Secretary of State opposed the amendment as not pertinent to the Bill, and its sponsor had to admit that there had been no definite expression of opinion by the ploughmen in its favour. Even so the amendment was only defeated by 20 votes to 15 in the Scottish Grand Committee. This suggests fairly extensive Liberal sympathy for the Saturday half-holiday, a sympathy that the unions sought to foster by assiduously posing test questions at elections and by-elections. The technique was not always effective as it invited counter-pressure; and one candidate's pro-ploughmen stance was alleged to have cost him the Liberal nomination for Forfarshire. But even his rival advanced on the half-day issue under heckling, and *The Plough* could console itself, 'Happy Ploughmen, who can force the hand and regulate the march of Liberal and Tory candidates!'

Such activity was more political than industrial, and neither

[1] *Weekly Scotsman*, 30 Dec. 1865, p. 5; *The Plough*, July 1893, p. 7; *P.P.*, 1893–4 xxxvi, pp. 335, 481.

the Ploughmen's Union nor its critics made any bones about its affiliation. One Perthshire minister told the Royal Commission on Labour that

Ploughmen, from their isolation and pinched circumstances, cannot combine, like some other bodies of men, in self-defence; for the so-called Ploughman's Unions are one-sided shams, got up to catch the agricultural vote, and not for the honest help of the class, to improve their condition.

And the Commission's report on Moray maintained that 'The Ploughmen's Union has made various attempts to get a footing in the district, especially at election times. It has never succeeded the men distrusting its political complexion, and doubting its financial soundness.' Equally the first issue of *The Plough* made it plain that 'The policy of this paper will be Liberal', albeit both independent and advanced, 'our great cry—*Legislation for the benefit of ploughmen, crofters and small holders.*' As 1894 draws on one detects a certain impatience with the Liberal establishment in general, and the Trevelyan administration of Scotland in particular. But it proved fairly easy to close the ranks for the 1895 election. The process, *The Plough* ingenuously remarked after it was all over, had involved the paper's upgrading to a weekly; as such it 'did good work in many of the constituencies during the election. That being now over, the necessity for a weekly paper has considerably lessened.' It therefore reverted to monthly publication, and was discontinued almost immediately. It was no doubt correct in claiming that it had helped to bring the labourers' cause to the attention of parliamentary candidates. And it had doubtless also reinforced the Liberal proclivities of the ploughmen. But it is unlikely that either the Ploughmen's Union or *The Plough* operated on a large enough scale to have any great effect. And the relative political impotence of the movement is shown by its general omission to endorse candidates for seats on the new Parish Councils despite its earlier enthusiasm for the bodies.[1]

Such candidates were only in fact endorsed in Ross and Cromarty, which brings us to another new development of the 1890s, the penetration of trades unions into the far north. This appears to have come in the wake of the Crofters' agitation of the 1880s, and it constituted a natural sequel. For many crofters in fact derived the bulk of their incomes, not from their own

[1] *The Plough, passim* and esp. April and Sept. 1893, April, June, Aug. and Nov. 1894, 28 Sept. and 15 Nov. 1895; *P.P.*, 1893–4 xxxvi, pp. 315, 366.

plots of land, but, especially on the arable stretch along the east coast, from agricultural wages. This must have encouraged the crofters' leaders to turn to the other grievances of 'the people'; and we find one presiding, for instance, in 1894 over the third annual meeting of the Ross and Cromarty Ploughmen's Union. He claimed that branches existed in every parish where there were enough ploughmen. But they were not always very clearly distinguishable from those of the Highland Land League. Thus a local crofter was 'president of the Union and Land League' branch at Knockbain; and a joint meeting of crofters, ploughmen, and labourers produced a similar combination at Culbokie, after its chairman had appealed in the most general fashion for the adhesion of 'the people ..., apart from the landlords, whose interests are antagonistic to those of the people'. In all this the ploughmen were fairly clearly the junior partners— indeed the Caithness farm servants were understandably piqued when the Royal Commission's emissary ignored their delegates and consulted instead 'men connected with the Land League which know little about our grievances'. It was almost certainly from the Land League that the Ross-shire ploughmen acquired their practice of regular monthly meetings (that earned them the widest coverage in *The Plough* of any county). And the example of the crofters' successful pressure in the 1880s for legislative intervention must have strengthened the ploughmen's tendency to look for comparable state action to achieve their own goals.[1]

These goals were mainly related to conditions of employment rather than to the level of wages, a topic that did not figure at all among the Ploughmen's Union's 'Objects', though it received passing mention from smaller societies. We have seen that the ploughmen were far from unanimously in favour of the Bills supported by their unions. For the latter invariably favoured a break with tradition. Their general attitude is epitomized by *The Plough's* rejoinder to a critic of the extravagance and dietary deficiencies inherent in the shift from farm-grown foodstuffs to groceries:

He also deplores the fact that the men are now living like human beings, taking in other articles from the grocer, instead of living on grain and potatoes. But since he is so enamoured of these articles viz. barley scones, pease scones, porridge, potatoes and salt, I should like to ask, how much does he eat of it himself?

[1] *The Plough*, esp. Jan, April, May, Dec. 1894; *P.P.*, 1893–4 xxxvi, p. 248.

In keeping with this modernist spirit, unions demanded cash payment (which was generally though not universally popular), monthly rather than yearly engagements (for which there was also substantial support), and the abolition of hiring fairs (for which there was no support at all). In addition they pressed for a shorter working day, to be achieved by the abolition of such objectionable practices as the 8 p.m. 'suppering' of horses, for a half or quarter-day holiday on Saturday, and for a definite number of whole holidays to be determined in advance (in place of the more patriarchal practice of the farmer allowing his men a day off from time to time). They also denounced the idea of women working in the fields—now more obnoxious than ever both to the spirit of the age and to the women themselves (who had recently taken to wearing heavy veils and to chewing raw rice to keep their complexions pallid).

These demands were better calculated to appeal to the younger men, and to those whose geographical situation enabled them to compare their conditions with those of other workers and 'to look with jealous eye towards the mill holidays and long evenings at home in winter time'. The attraction of convenience foods and dietary adventure is obvious. Some farmers admitted that they insisted on the evening stable work 'more for keeping their young men at home than for the horses' sake; and the case for fixed holidays was occasionally argued on the ground that it would make possible the arrangement of football and cricket matches. So it is not surprising that the reports to the Royal Commission refer, on the one hand, to 'a growing impatience of continued control, and, whether of hours or days, a sharper desire to be free as early as possible, and a longing for more frequent breaks in the round of toil', and, on the other hand, to the belief on the part of older and more settled men that some of the traditional practices gave them greater security. Even the question of women working in the fields may conceal a genera-tion gap, since the older men gained from the practice while younger ones suffered in the hiring markets from their inability to provide female labour.

But it would not do to press the question of age too far. Local factors and preferences were equally influential—for instance, though the idea of payment in cash was generally popular, it was not so in Aberdeenshire even among union members, and the Scottish Farm Servants' Union suffered accordingly. Local grievances are also important: a system analogous to 'bondage' still survived in Ross and Wigtownshire and was duly attacked; but labour relations in south-east Scotland had been greatly improved by the passing of the bondage system; and, although attempts were made to introduce the Ploughmen's Union (with the support, in East Lothian, of 'some few well-known farmers and one large landed proprietor') they met with little success, except, for some reason, around Earlston. Other such peculiarities could be cited.

All told the movement's impact was probably fairly small; certainly ploughmen so informed the Royal Commission in West Lothian, Lanarkshire and the far north. However the unions undoubtedly had some effect in stirring up the rural scene. In some places this secured higher wages, the direction in which the hiring system could most easily accommodate pressure. Sometimes it led to a new, though usually transitory, stiffness in labour relations, and to the farmers blacklisting ('boycotting') the principal movers. And it undoubtedly provoked a fair amount of discussion of the rural labour problem on the part of farmers and landlords.

This discussion occasionally vented itself in individual concessions,[1] or in farmers' meetings that were often steered by a landlord in the same direction. But these were the exceptions— most farmers declined to give and fell back on mechanistic calculations of the cost of change; one even recalled that at emancipation the slave-owners had been paid £22 million compensation, and asked for comparable Government assistance 'as we are in the same position'. Indeed, some labourers felt the agitation to be counter-productive; though the farmers 'did begin tae mak' some show, by gien up a yookin' noo an' again, bein' under nae compulsion, they wud jist cut short the whole affair whenever they thought fit'.[2]

Such change as there was, of course, lay in the direction the unions advocated. But, for the most part, it occurred independently of them, and represented a natural evolution. The sequence in Greenlaw, Berwickshire, was described in 1923. The agitations of 1866 and 1872 petered out at the hiring fairs; but, some time later, one farmer spontaneously raised the wages of his women workers, and the others had, grumblingly, to follow suit. Similarly the 8 p.m. 'suppering' of horses was quietly abandoned; and 'Year by year . . . some slight improvement in

[1] The prospective Conservative candidate for Berwickshire was among the employers who thought it wise to concede a nine-hour day.
[2] *P.P.*, 1893–4 xxxvi, *passim* and esp. pp. 242, 245–6, 250, 273, 289, 298–301, 304, 333, 352, 429–32, 562–3, 571, 605; *The Plough*, *passim* and esp. Jan., May, Oct., Dec., 1894, Jan. and Nov. 1895.

conditions was accomplished, either in the shape of increased wage or relaxation of conditions . . . the chief element in the improvement' being the 'great tide of migration' that set in in the mid-1870s.[1]

The process was very slow, occasionally so slow that attempts were made to prod it along by combination, and to secure a more independent and commercial relationship between farmers and labourers. But innumerable instances show that labourers were conservative as well as farmers. And, broadly speaking, the evolution of conditions kept pace with that of aspirations. So relations with the farmers generally remained either warm or, at worst, passively acquiescent.

Only in the 1860s did a protest movement arouse any real fervour; and this was clearly the product of a major, but finite and therefore curable, grievance—bondage. The unions of the 1890s, despite institutional improvements, failed to arouse comparable enthusiasm for shorter hours and half-holidays. Another union was started to campaign for them in 1912, and bills were again introduced into Parliament. But its achievements before the outbreak of the War were very limited.

For a time the War seemed to transform the situation. Minimum wage regulation, though in fact unwelcome to the Union, at least brought enhanced status, and a great increase in membership from 6,000 in 1916 to nearly 23,000 in 1919). Also, in the atmosphere of war-time co-operation, the union now managed to negotiate voluntary agreements for half-days, shorter hours, and collective bargaining at district level on wage-rates. But the Government's abandonment of price supports in 1921 and the agricultural depression of the late 1920s caused a widespread reversion to earlier conditions. And the comparative immunity of England (where compulsory wage regulation had been retained) led in 1933 to a further union initiative (supported by the Department of Agriculture) for voluntary collective bargaining. This was ultimately rejected by the local branches of the National Farmers' Union, and after a certain amount of parliamentary pressure the Government appointed a Committee of Inquiry. Its Report painted a picture of farm workers' conditions in most ways not unlike those prevailing in the late nineteenth century; but they were no longer regarded with the same approval. And legislation promptly followed in 1937 and 1938 to provide for the compulsory determination of minimum wages and holidays. Hiring fairs still survived, but they were

[1] *Berwickshire News*, 28 Aug. 1923, p. 4.

suspended in 1941 to reduce labour turn-over; after the end of the War it was agreed that they should not be revived and that instead contracts should be subject to a month's notice.[1]

APPENDIX
HIRING FAIRS

An unusually vivid, but otherwise not untypical, picture of a fair is given by the annual reports in the *Fife Herald* of St. James' Fair, Cupar. The format remained fairly constant, though the details of course altered from year to year. This account was printed on 8 June 1872:

ST. JAMES' FAIR—The great annual holiday of the agricultural portion of the community was held here on Tuesday. The weather during the day was most unpropitious, a drizzling sort of rain commencing to fall early in the morning and continuing till afternoon, making the streets very wet and dirty. Notwithstanding, there was a large turn out of farmers, ploughmen, and farm domestic servants. A great number took advantage of the railway, while as usual scores of corn carts might have been seen pouring in from all directions, highly decorated and loaded with every variety of rustic gaiety. In the feeing market, owing to the recent agitation for higher wages and shorter hours of labour, engagements—especially among the young men—were not so readily effected—several of them asking a rise of £4 to £5 on their last year's wages, and, indeed, a good number left the market not engaged. However, their exertions were so far successful as an average rise of from £2 to £3 was got. Good hands received from £20 to £23, and foremen from £25 to £27, with the usual perquisites. For the amusement and entertainment of the rural swains and their sweethearts, there was an abundant supply of stalls for the sale of confectionery and fancy goods. It was in the Fluthers, however, that the greatest provision seemed to have been made for the popular amusement. There was not perhaps so large a collection of caravans as we have seen in former years; but there was an unusually large number of merry-go-rounds, shooting galleries, photographic saloons, panoramas, and all the paraphernalia usual on similar occasions, all of which seemed to do a pretty good stroke of business. In the afternoon the Ceres brass band took up its position on a stand erected at the west end of the Fluthers, and dancing was

[1] *Rural Scotland during the War*, cited above, pp. 141–5 and Section iv; *P.P.*, 1935–6 vii, pp. 395–447, and 1948–9 xi, pp. 50–83.

indulged in with the wonted vigour of the country lads and lasses to the local tune of 'Ceres Green'. Spirituous liquors were no doubt consumed in liberal quantities, but on the whole the behaviour of the crowd was remarkably good. The afternoon and evening trains rapidly thinned the streets. Excellent arrangements had been made at the station for despatching the passengers; and, notwithstanding the boisterous joviality always displayed in returning from the fair, comparatively good order was kept. In the evening the townspeople turned out in large numbers to the market; and the streets, especially St. Catherine Street and the vicinity of the Fluthers, were quite crowded until a late hour in the evening.

The Fife hiring term was peculiar in that it ended at Martinmas. A second fair was held shortly before then (in early November) for men who hoped in a good year to get better wages by holding out, or for those who in a bad one had not yet been able to secure a place. In 1873 many ploughmen declined to hire even in November, preferring general labouring jobs which were in good supply; but they were expected to drift back to agriculture in the course of the winter. However in the less buoyant 1930s, one criticism of the hiring system was that, if a man was not engaged at the fairs, he had little chance of regular work till next season, and so tended to leave for the city.

VII

Northumberland in the 1870s

During the nineteenth century conditions in Northumberland were very similar to those further north. So it is not surprising that some Scottish agitation spilled over the Border. And in the 1860s there was little to differentiate the two districts. Thus in 1866–7 the servants at Belford, like their Scottish counterparts, displayed a marked reluctance to engage bondagers. Further south, at Alnwick, it had already been remarked in November 1865 that, though single men were much sought after, the current abundance of non-agricultural employment 'rendered them indifferent as to contracting permanent engagements'. Next March the servants had the local bellman summon a meeting immediately before the Hiring Fair: one speaker doubted whether the farmers could afford a rise to 15s. a week, and urged the men to concentrate on the abolition of bondage. Apparently, though, they preferred to press for wage increases; these were resisted on the first day of the fair, but conceded on the second; and they were renewed in 1867 with little excitement on either side.[1] But the next major cycle of activity in Scotland and Northumberland, that of 1872, coincided with the larger and more ambitious 'Revolt of the Field' in southern England. This sought to bring the Northumbrian movement within its own orbit, and the result was something of a synthesis of the two traditions. It is therefore worth examining rather more closely.

Northumbrian agricultural labourers were, of course, conscious of the precedent of the miners' unions. And the achievement of a nine-hour day in mining and engineering in 1871 spread similar aspirations among them; it also created a labour shortage that provided an excellent context in which to demand improved wages and conditions. But the main inspiration of the Northumberland hinds' agitation was indubitably Scottish. A speaker at the first meeting to be reported declared that

the movement was not peculiar to their locality, nor even to their country. From information he had received, he found it had swept from the foot of Ben Lomond to the Clyde, from the Clyde to the

---

[1] *Berwick Warder*, 10 Nov. 1865, 9 and 16 March 1866, 8 March 1867; *Haddingtonshire Courier*, 16 March 1866.

Tweed. It was now moving the district from the Tweed to the Tees, and further south their fellow workmen were taking similar action. As an encouragement he recited what had been done by the hinds in the Lothians, and dilated upon the success that had attended their efforts.

The meeting, held in mid-February 1872 at the Plough Inn, Mitford (near Morpeth), was attended by about 200 hinds, 'a large representation of the farm labourers employed in the vale of Wansbeck, for eight or nine miles of its length, and five or six of its breadth, having Mitford for its centre'. It had been arranged a fortnight earlier by a preliminary meeting whose chairman also presided on this occasion. 'The greater part of his address consisted of a rhymed appeal for united effort, and was largely interspersed with allusion to the heroes and heroines of the ancient mythologies and classical history. It was received with rapturous applause.' His more concrete suggestions were that everybody should, at the next hiring, ask for a nine-hour day, with overtime and Sunday work to be paid extra. And it was further resolved, after some difference of opinion, to press for a quarter of a day off every Saturday. A meeting was to be held in Morpeth Market Place early in the morning of the next hiring day to secure 'a general understanding to ask for these terms'.[1]

In the interval before the hiring fairs several gatherings took place in other villages. All were agreed in seeking shorter hours, but they differed slightly on details, and on what further demands should be made, if any. Partly to sort these differences out, and partly to co-ordinate their tactics, 11 districts sent delegates to a meeting in Newcastle early in March; most came from around Morpeth and Newcastle, but some from as far afield as Haydon Bridge (beyond Hexham) and Whittingham (near Alnwick).[2] A 55-hour week, with alternate Saturdays off, was eventually decided on; and the question of forming a trades union was to be put to meetings in the localities. By this time, however, the hiring season had come on and it was too late to construct any such organization. So when the men at the Morpeth fair saw that their demands for shorter hours would not easily be conceded, they reverted to seeking 'engagements under the old form of agreement', but 'at the greatest increase of pay they could obtain'. 'Accordingly', it was later remarked, 'though in

[1] *Morpeth Herald*, 24 Feb. 1872, p. 4.
[2] The districts were: Earsdon, Haydon Bridge, Heddon-on-the-Wall, Horton, Kenton, Lamesley (Co. Durham), Ponteland, Prudhoe, Shield Row, Whickham (Co. Durham), and Whittingham.

the majority of cases higher wages were received, . . . the main objects for which the agitation had originated were temporarily lost sight of'.

Equally, however, the hours and conditions of work had not been changed in a sense unfavourable to the labourers. A number of farmers had reacted to demands for a nine-hour day and payment of overtime by suggesting that the labourers should only be paid for the hours they actually worked, which were necessarily fewer in winter. Also monthly engagements should replace yearly ones; for this would enable farmers to dismiss unsatisfactory servants, and would relieve them from the obligation to continue to pay wages during sickness. Some farmers even went so far as to suggest the abolition of 'privileges' (the free house, row of potatoes, grain or meal, carting of coals, etc.) and the substitution of a simple cash wage.

In deference to such sentiments, farmers' meetings were called at Morpeth, Ponteland, and Newcastle 'to take into consideration the present movement of farm labourers'. But all three resolved against changing the hours of work in either direction, the two latter meetings by large majorities. None felt itself competent to determine wages, which were best left to the bargaining of the parties concerned; but most speakers seemed not too averse to a small rise—the chairman of the Ponteland meeting 'hoped the masters would give the men a little more wage, to content them'.

The dispute was, as we have seen, fought out at the hiring fairs. The chairman of the Morpeth farmers' meeting had noted that 'The men were to have a meeting at the station [on the first hiring day]: but the best plan would be for the masters to keep away, and on the second day the men would come up to their terms.' He proved correct: even on the first day some bargains were concluded; and proceedings on the second day were unusually well attended by both 'hinds and masters, all of whom evidently meant business. A large number of engagements were effected at . . . a general advance from 1s. to 2s., [but] with the other conditions remaining the same'. This was something of a disappointment to the labourers' leaders, who had hoped that both Morpeth hirings would prove abortive, and that a decision would therefore be postponed to the Newcastle hirings. Nevertheless a meeting was held just before business began in Newcastle. But proceedings there resembled those at Morpeth— after pressing their demands on hours in the morning, generally without success, the men began to settle in the afternoon for a wage increase of one to two shillings instead, though 'a considerable number' had not yet come to terms by the time proceedings closed.

At no stage did any of the men suggest action outside the established cycle of hiring fairs, even though there had been some talk of a strike (in the conventional sense of the word) by women in the Morpeth district. The nearest that anybody came to such a course was at the meeting before the Newcastle hirings. Here one speaker did call for a 'strike', but used the term to mean a general refusal to enter into any new engagements at the fair.[1] He argued that since 'the farmers could not do without hands, . . . another hiring would have to be called, when they would get what they wanted': and since sowing was very backward that season, he envisaged success in under a fortnight. But his advice was not taken, and was, in any case, probably misleading—even if the men did refuse to enter into new engagements, they would have had to work out their old ones until Whitsun, so that their action could have had no practical effect for a considerable period.

There had, however, been talk of a number of devices for improving the men's bargaining position. One idea had been to furnish all hinds with printed copies of a model agreement before the hirings began. More commonly men spoke of forming some kind of trades union; one meeting was inclined to seek to join the miners' union; but though most gatherings were in mining areas, they generally favoured a separate organization for agricultural labourers. And, once the rush of the hiring fairs was over, a Northumberland Agricultural Labourers' Union was formed, with headquarters at Horton and with the intention of establishing branches throughout the county. But the Horton membership was confessedly exiguous; and, since the hirings were now over, it was too late in the year to enjoy much success in evangelization—a meeting at Bedlington in July regarded itself as insufficiently representative to form a branch, and the *Morpeth Herald* records no further activity in the course of 1872.[2] It is arguable that this decline in popular interest permitted the new Union to adopt a programme that would not have enjoyed general support. For in addition to payment for all overtime worked beyond nine hours a day and to the abolition of the bondager system, topics often mentioned in the meetings of the earlier part of the year, the union also demanded payment exclu-

[1] This was also the way in which the word had been used during the Lothians' agitation of the previous decade.

[2] By late Feb. 1873, however, the Horton union had branches at Wooler and Walbottle.

sively in cash and the introduction of monthly rather than yearly agreements. Neither of the last two demands were particularly popular; the first seems to have been quietly dropped, but the second survived in the form of an unrealistic, though frequently voiced, opposition to hiring fairs.[1]

'As the term for the re-engagement of farm servants approaches', remarked the *Hexham Courant* the following March, 'there is a renewal of the labour question.' This year saw a concentration on the organization of union branches. And, from the very beginning, the question of affiliation to the Leamington based National Agricultural Labourers' Union was at issue—at the first meeting to be reported (again at Mitford in mid-February) the rules not only of the Northumberland but also of the National Union were read out. Early in March Joseph Arch himself visited Newcastle 'by invitation of the executive of the Agricultural Labourers' Union of Northumberland', and spoke at length to a crowded indoor meeting chaired by Joseph Cowen jr.;[2] proceedings closed with a resolution, seconded by the miners' leader Thomas Burt, in favour of the formation in Northumberland of a branch of the N.A.L.U.

This resolution was put into effect, in a fairly leisurely fashion, in the course of the summer. Thus in late May a large meeting of labourers of the Horton district was held to form a N.A.L.U. branch; two officers and a committee of nine were elected, and a mere 24 names given in for membership. A similar meeting took place in Mitford in late June; it may, from the National Union's point of view, have been only just in time, for in the course of the next three weeks the Mitford Secretary was also approached by the rival Lincolnshire League. However the League attracted no support in Northumberland; and by the end of October eight N.A.L.U. branches were in existence in the county, while it was hoped to establish a further six as soon as possible. But, since eleven districts had sent delegates to the Newcastle meeting of March 1872, eight branches cannot be said to have been a very impressive total. So it is interesting to be told by a N.A.L.U. speaker that 'With very few exceptions, the men who took the leading part in the agitation last year were now against the

[1] For the episodes just narrated, see the *Morpeth Herald*, esp. 2, 9 and 16 March, 6 April and 6 July 1872, and 22 Feb. and 5 April 1873.

[2] The proprietor of Newcastle's leading newspaper, an advanced Liberal sympathetic to organized labour and the working class, Cowen was soon to win a Newcastle seat at a by-election; and at the time, his political stature was at least equal to that of Joseph Chamberlain.

union—at least they advocated independent union for the north of England.' Their opposition, and the fact that the movement of 1872 had in any case been one of public meetings rather than of a defined and subscribing membership, compelled the N.A.L.U. in 1873 to build up very nearly from scratch,[1] even though it continued to be centred in much the same parts of the county.[2]

The opponents of adhesion to the National Union presumably felt that it was too remote from Northumberland to have any particular relevance to local conditions; and it would not be difficult to construct a case to this effect. But, if so, it is surprising that no move was made to affiliate to the highly decentralized Lincolnshire League, or even to remain independent (as did such miniscule unions as the Gloucestershire Agricultural Association and the West Surrey Union). A number of factors may have contributed to the adoption of the opposite course. I have argued that the Northumberland Agricultural Labourers' Union, as set up at Horton after the hiring fairs of 1872, was probably unrepresentative. Also the miners helped the N.A.L.U. to supply full-time 'delegates',[3] whose services may well have appealed to men concerned with union organization. Expectations were undoubtedly entertained, too, of the N.A.L.U's potentialities as an insurance and benefit society.[4] There was a feeling of solidarity

[1] By late Oct., branches existed at Dinnington, Earsdon, Horton, Kenton, Mitford, Springwell, Ulgham and Whalton; they were projected for Felton, Longhorsley, Ovington, Sheepwash, Stannington and Walbottle.

[2] *Hexham Courant*, 22 Feb., 1 March and 14 June 1873; *Newcastle Weekly Chronicle*, 15 March 1873, p. 8; *Morpeth Herald*, 31 May, 28 June, 19 July, 1 Nov. 1873.

[3] Initially a Mr. Robson, delegate for Northumberland and Durham. But he was soon supplemented (and largely overshadowed) by a Warwickshire man, Gardner, who is recorded by the *Labourers' Union Chronicle* of 16 Aug. as working from 'The Miners' Office', Newcastle. Gardner had earlier been involved in an abortive attempt to unionize the Irish agricultural labourers—P. R. L. Horn, 'The National Agricultural Labourers' Union in Ireland, 1873-9', *Irish Historical Studies*, xvii (1971), pp. 340-52.

[4] In his Newcastle speech Arch had undertaken to establish next May an agricultural labourers' benefit society 'from one end of England to another'. The yearly hiring system rendered benefit societies less necessary in the north than in the south, since wages were not stopped for short periods of sickness. But, as a result, this type of insurance was almost completely unknown to the northern countryside.

with, and admiration for, the exertions of the Warwickshire labourers. Lastly it was argued that, since Northumberland was a high wage area 'subject to the influx of labour from other districts', 'the only real security for the agricultural labourers' permanent benefit was to form one union which would embrace the whole of the kingdom'; and in 1874 collections were held in aid of the locked-out union men in East Anglia in the belief that a victory there would reduce the likelihood of southern migrants undercutting local wage rates.[1] (By contrast the *Hexham Courant*, and probably some farmers also, were looking with increasing impatience to major union-sponsored migration from the south to ease the pressure on Northumberland wages.)

The events of 1873 that we have been discussing can only have had a very limited impact. True wages rose sharply that spring—by from 10 to nearly 20 per cent according to the *Hexham Courant*. But the union cannot be credited with much of the increase. For one thing the movement was on a fairly small scale. But, more importantly, its own speakers felt that it could, and should, have little to do with the exact level of wages. Thus a meeting at Mitford was told that

They could not enforce a uniform rate of wages. As far as they were concerned each man must be left to make his own terms when they took to the streets for it and again offered themselves for sale.

'But a fixed scale of hours', it was contended, 'they could enforce if they were only united.' As in Scotland, it was the conditions of work rather than the basic rates of pay that constituted the real *raison d'être* of the movement. So later in the year another Mitford meeting was told

that, though the condition of trade would naturally bring them an advance of wages, there were other things required by them which could only be gained by union—without which they could never obtain shorter terms of labours, and place themselves on a footing with other workmen.

It is, therefore, not surprising that the union had no use for strikes. Again some female workers were more militant—'the women people' harvesting on a farm near Haydon Bridge staged a successful two-day strike for an advance to 3s. a day (probably from

[1] See esp. the *Hexham Courant*, 4 July 1874, p. 5.

2s. 6d.). But I have encountered no masculine counterpart; and the secretary of the Mitford branch 'repudiated the assertion that the Union was formed to support a strike in the South; the only strike there was, was in Fifeshire, and the Union had nothing to do with it.'[1]

Nevertheless, labour relations undoubtedly became increasingly strained as the year wore on. Admittedly there were no farmers' meetings, as there had been in 1872. But the union had to contend with a number of pressures: attempts were made to deny it a place to meet, successfully in two villages, unsuccessfully in one—and the Longhorsley publican decided, perhaps independently, perhaps under coercion, that he would permit no more gatherings in his house. More seriously, at the 1874 hirings at least one leading farmer insisted that, if he hired men, he would not permit them to join the Union; and in the north of the county there was even talk of forming a defence society for farmers and non-unionist labourers. Further, the *North of England Farmer* favoured the movement with a hostile article; and a handful of union leaders and opponents conducted a controversy in the columns of the *Morpeth Herald* with monotonous regularity from September 1873 to July 1874, and at rather greater intervals down to the following November.

Still we should not overrate the importance of trade unionism as such. In December 1873 the *Hexham Courant's* columnist ascribed the 'excited state' of 'our local agricultural atmosphere' rather to the tenant right question. And the undoubted grumblings about labour related chiefly to its high price—unlike East Anglia, where the farmers' public position in 1874 was to be that they did not grudge the money but that they could not submit to union tyranny. Fortunately barley fetched good prices in late 1873, and one farmer remarked, 'We'll be able, after all, to get our hinds paid.' But some arable farmers had been talking of giving up their farms, and 'many' are said to have put rather more land than usual down to grass, or to have cut down their labour force in other ways. There was even talk 'that some farmers find their expenses owing to the increase in wages so great that they cannot afford to give their workers such a treat' as the usual harvest home festivals.[2] And the *Hexham Courant's*

[1] The only strike I have been able to trace in Fife was of *women* at Methil (*Fife Herald*, 22 May 1873, p. 3).
[2] Though the columnist who reported this talk himself believed that the real trouble was 'the falling off of energy in committees' at Bywell and Corbridge; and at Bywell greater collections were taken than in previous years for holidays for sick farm labourers.

reports of those harvest festivals that did occur related them clearly to *local* tensions:

In these days, when the relations between masters and servants are somewhat disturbed, particularly so in the agricultural section of the community, it is pleasing to hear of instances where the parties are evidently on good terms.

A year earlier descriptions of similar festivities had been more confident and more general, the *Morpeth Herald* remarking on one occasion that

It occurred to us that if the admirers of [urban radicals like] Messrs. Odger and Bradlaugh could have witnessed this graceful condescension, and have heard the outburst of honest enthusiasm [that greeted the squire's appearance], it would have dispelled many of their dreamy theories, and have demonstrated to them the fact that our old names are the pure gold yet.[1]

1874 was the first year that Northumberland trades unionism entered upon already firmly organized. It also saw the peak of the economic boom; and, in southern England, it witnessed the greatest numerical extension of rural trades unionism and also the most bitter clashes between labourers and farmers. So it is remarkable that in Northumberland it proved a fairly damp squib, with action (as opposed to talk) rigidly confined to two spheres—the traditional cycle of hiring fairs, and the collection of money for the eastern counties lock-out.

In February some excitement was caused by a proposal to change the date of the Morpeth hiring fair: this failed, and to mark their success the labourers resolved to mount a great demonstration at the fair, with each union member wearing a piece of blue ribbon to show that

> Though lowly be our station,
> 'Unity is strength', we know.

As a result, 'A stranger in Morpeth might readily have fancied the old borough was in the midst of a contested election, and that blue was triumphant.' There is little trace of comparable activity at most of the other hiring fairs, though a number were visited by union officials. But a meeting of about 1,000 was held on the old date of the Newcastle fair and some hiring done; and,

[1] *Hexham Courant*, esp. 22 Feb., 5 April, 17 May, 7 and 14 June, 23 Aug., 4 Oct., 15 Nov., and 6 Dec. 1873, and 10 Jan. 1874; *Morpeth Herald*, esp. 18 Jan., 28 June, 19 July and 15 Dec. 1873, and 4 April 1874; *Labourers' Union Chronicle*, 28 March 1874.

though the official fair was not boycotted as one branch had recommended, attendance there may have been reduced.[1]

With this exception, however, the fairs were crowded, generally a sign of excitement. Bargaining was hard, and protracted from fair to fair by 'the determination of servants to hold out for higher wages'. These certainly increased, by between two and four shillings a week. What is less clear is the success of the union's formal demands for 'the abolition of the "bondage system" ', Saturday half-holidays, and payment of overtime. Newspaper reports seldom mentioned them, which suggests that they occasioned no major confrontation. But bondage, at least, came under attack. For the *Labourers' Union Chronicle* records that, at Hexham, 'the farmers were not well inclined to dispense with women workers'; and a columnist of the *Newcastle Weekly Chronicle* went so far as to claim that the bondage system was being 'broken up'. Accounts of hiring fairs in later years confirm that 'female workers' were getting steadily scarcer, and suggest that hinds without suitable daughters were less willing, or perhaps merely less able, to engage substitutes. The agitation of 1872-4 cannot but have contributed; but (unlike the Scottish movement of 1866) it was never mentioned in this connection; and responsibility for the change was more usually ascribed to such factors as 'the superior education of the present generation, which allows the more superior class [of women] to forsake the fields for situations in our large towns.'

Wages and conditions of employment were obviously local matters. But at the Newcastle meeting the agitation had showed some signs of broadening to include political and religious questions, as it had done in southern England. For Gardner (a Warwickshire man by origin) denounced the Tory Government, recommended the newly published book, the *Revolt of the Field*, and attributed discontent not only to short pay and long hours but also to the Game Laws, the Poor Laws, primogeniture and the preaching of contentment and subjection by the Established Church; and his fellow N.A.L.U. delegate, Robson, thought it worth mentioning that steps were being taken to establish a co-operative farm.[2] But this course of development was interrupted by the great eastern counties lock-out. The farmers hoped that the lock-out would lead to large-scale migration, several arguing at the Hexham fair in late April that 1,000 or 2,000 men should be sent north, and that with cheaper

[1] The *Newcastle Courant* said it was reduced, but the *Hexham Courant* recorded a large attendance.

[2] The reference is probably to an attempt in Warwickshire.

labour they could expand production to the general benefit. The prospect did not appeal to the local labourers, and the union flung itself into the collection of money for the support of the locked-out men, while Gardner issued repeated warnings of high prices, scarcity of lodgings and strikes in Newcastle, all designed to discourage migration. The process certainly kept agitation alive through the summer, and extended it into the towns. But it largely divorced it from any local content— Arch's visit to Newcastle in May, which had been arranged well in advance of the lock-out and had presumably been intended to stimulate the local movement, was reduced to the simple appeal for funds that he had been making in several other large cities.

The National Union's defeat in late July must therefore have come as a considerable blow. And after the harvest several branches debated the question of leaving the N.A.L.U. and reverting to a county union. The decisions, or those recorded in the *Labourers' Union Chronicle*, were always in favour of the National Union. But the dissatisfied let their subscriptions fall into arrears, or, like the secretary of the Mitford branch, dropped out altogether. In the process membership at one branch fell from 35 to 13. Northumberland had never been a large district— it had not been represented at the N.A.L.U. annual conference, presumably because it lacked the necessary 500 members. Now it simply faded away. Perhaps the last straw was the withdrawal of the N.A.L.U. delegate, Gardner, as a result of the financial difficulties that were to split the National Union in 1875. This withdrawal was postponed through the intercession of Joseph Cowen and the generosity of the Northumberland miners, but only temporarily. And nothing came of the hopeful suggestion that, if he could be assisted for six months by the youthful and energetic Horton figure, Mr. Dodds, 'instead of counting the Union men in Northumberland by scores they will be able to count them by hundreds'. Dodds moved to another village in November, and dropped his position in the union. The last reference to trades unionism, or even to labourers' meetings that I have encountered was in December 1874. And the following November a member of the Labour League, the N.A.L.U.'s rival, wrote to the *Morpeth Herald* expressing surprise that 'no union existed at present among the farm labourers', and putting in a bid for the deserted field. His advocacy fell on deaf ears.[1]

[1] *Morpeth Herald*, esp. 28 Feb., 7 and 14 March, 31 Oct., 28 Nov. 1874, 6 March and 27 Nov. 1875; *Labourers' Union Chronicle*, esp.

During its brief revival in the north in 1878, the National Union attributed its earlier collapse partly to Gardner's recall, but chiefly to the fact that it had given no sick benefit. A final reason was probably the state of the labour market. For colliery wages began to come under pressure in the autumn of 1874, the Northumberland coal-owners determining on a wage reduction in October, and the Durham ones securing a 10 per cent cut by arbitration in November. Agricultural wages for single men moved down slightly in sympathy at the November Alnwick hirings, and the big spring hiring fairs of 1875 were attended by a number of colliers seeking to return to agriculture. Proceedings were summed up in the *Hexham Courant* as follows:

There was little change in the wages of the various hirings excepting at Newcastle, where, towards evening, some men had to submit to a reduction, but there was a wonderful difference in tone and demeanour; that devil-may-care sort of swagger, so disagreeably conspicuous twelve months ago, had nearly disappeared, and men talked more like rational beings.[1]

However, not everybody would have been able to go along with the conclusion, 'How wonderfully easy supply and demand regulate themselves.' For in fact agricultural wages remained obstinately high—in February 1876 a Northumberland farmer told John Bright that 'Colliers rose 50 per cent since 1871, and are now fallen to 15 per cent above the wages of that time. Farm labourers keep their 50 per cent advance and no sign of reduction.' It is therefore not surprising that some farmers sought to compel one, especially given the very uncertain profitability of agriculture—grain had been a chancy business for much of the decade and prices were about to collapse, and, though stock prices kept up, 1877 saw a murrain and, perhaps even more ominously, the first sales of American fresh beef at Stockton.[2] The result was, on the one hand, a considerable increase in tenant right sentiment, and, on the other, a growing concern about labour costs.

---

10 Jan., 28 March, 11 April, 19 Sept., 3 and 17 Oct., 5 Dec. 1874; *Newcastle Weekly Chronicle*, 23 May 1874.

[1] *Morpeth Herald*, esp. 10 Oct., 7 and 14 Nov. 1874, 16 Jan., 6 and 13 March, 16 Oct. and 27 Nov. 1875, 16 Feb. and 11 May 1878. *Hexham Courant*, 9 May 1875, p. 5—its columnist was incidentally a fairly advanced Liberal.

[2] *The Diaries of John Bright*, ed. R. A. J. Walling (1930), p. 377; *Newcastle Daily Journal*, 19 Feb. 1877, p. 2.

The winter of 1876–7 accordingly saw a renewed discussion of the agricultural labour question on the part of the farmers, at first in the correspondence columns of the press, and then, as the hiring fairs drew nearer, at public meetings comparable with those of 1872. As in that year, much attention was devoted to the conditions of employment, and many of the same changes were mooted—notably that engagements should be determinable at a month's notice, and that perquisites should be replaced by a cash wage, paid monthly. Many farmers also sought to move the hiring fairs closer to the date on which the old contracts expired and the new ones took effect. And most, though not quite all, suggested that a reduction in wages was due. Here, however, there was an important division: some farmers were prepared openly to advocate combination to bring down wages, or to agree and enforce a scale of wages; while others were honest enough to maintain that

If farmers hold that demand and supply ought only to raise the workmen's wages, then, to be consistent, they must allow supply and demand to lower them also, as no organized union exists among the men to keep wages up to a false level.

The latter view prevailed at the various farmers' meetings; but though these were careful not to take a position on the level of wages, they showed a much greater readiness than in 1872 to advocate payment exclusively in cash, and subject to a month's notice on either side.[1]

When it came to the point, however, the whole thing fizzled out. Thus at Berwick 'One or two attempts were made to enforce the monthly system, but they were not successful'; similarly, at Alnwick, the 'proposal made by the farmers at their meetings of breaking off engagements at a month's notice was not once mooted', and, after some fairly hard bargaining, engagements were eventually 'freely effected upon the old terms, viz. from 20s. to 22s. a week, with "conditions" upstanding from Mayday to Mayday'.

The principal reason for this fiasco was no doubt the opposition of the labourers, to which we must revert. But a subsidiary one was probably division amongst the farmers. The recasting

[1] That at Wooler resolved in favour of both cash payment and of the possibility of giving a month's notice, that at Glendale in favour of cash payment, and that at Alnwick (the best reported) in favour of a month's notice. There were other meetings that I have not found reports of, but, despite some suggestions, meetings do not seem to have been systematically co-ordinated.

of the whole engagement system by permitting the giving of notice and by systematically reducing all payments to cash was a clearly 'modern' approach; and its adherents may have been correspondingly articulate. But an equally natural response was a more limited and curmudgeonly cutting back of specific 'privileges' that had become troublesome—labourers' leaders were to claim that in cases where Saturday time off had been granted it was now withdrawn, and that there was increasing talk of hirings no longer carrying with them payment in time of sickness. Lastly, in this as in earlier depressions, there was a certain swing back from payment in cash (which was short) to a lower money wage supplemented by more corn and by the keep of a cow.

But just as the labourers' movement of 1872 had evoked a farmers' movement in response, so now the farmers' discussion of wages and conditions prompted a revival of the labourers' trades unionism. Many labourers had joined in the newspaper correspondence, amongst them the former union delegate Dodds. Obviously the suggestion of a farmers' combination to reduce wages was provocative: and the prospect that pay might be withheld, or men dismissed, for sickness was frightening, especially as Northumberland did not possess the Friendly Societies that provided some cover against this in the south. So, despite many similarities between the farmers' proposals of 1877 and the earlier union demands, Dodds was able to stand on its head a favourite farmers' argument: if employers persisted in deducting pay for sickness, the men would be forced to claim for overtime, 'and that will be breaking up the good feeling, and also the old custom of "give and take" between master and man.' Another letter urged the hinds to hold meetings, like the farmers, to consider the proposed changes, and concluded: 'What the hinds now want is a union formed on a Provident Sick Benefit principle . . .'

In Northumberland the suggestion was not acted upon immediately. But in County Durham it was. It may be that the farmers' reaction had gone further in the latter county. For the Durham hirings were made terminable at a month's notice, albeit in response to a meeting that claimed to consist of both masters and men. Also the date of the Darlington hiring fairs had been changed in the teeth of strong protests from an enormous meeting of hinds.[1] A meeting at Staindrop (near Barnard

[1] The Stockton Board of Guardians had also recommended changes in the dates of the local hiring fairs—*Newcastle Daily Journal*, 22 Feb. 1877, p. 3.

Castle) wrote to Joseph Arch, and he promised to come (or send a representative) to Darlington to discuss the formation of union for south Durham and north Yorkshire, to be affiliated to the National Union.[1]

But by now it was April, too late to have much practical effect for the remainder of 1877. (Indeed the most obvious consequence may have been the removal of Dodds from Northumberland to Durham, presumably in connection with the new union.) The following February, however, a remarkable frank letter appeared in the *Morpeth Herald* from 'A Well-wisher of the Hinds':

It will be remembered that an attempt was made a year or two ago to establish a branch of the National Agricultural Labourers' Union in Northumberland, but the movement fell to the ground, as the union did not give any sick benefit, and the hinds thought they did not need a trades union, as there was little fear of a strike or a lock-out occurring in the North, the members being all hired yearly at an upstanding fixed rate of wage, which was paid whether the men worked or not; but it seems as if the farmers—by their action last spring—want to do away with this yearly and upstanding wage, and it is a fact that many farmers now hire their men on the principle 'no work, no pay' . . . But there is now a chance for the hinds to improve their position, by becoming members of the National Agricultural Labourers' Union; for it is now established on a sick benefit principle.

He therefore advised the hinds to hold meetings and get somebody to write to the National Union for its rules; they could then organize a strong district.

The author, who may have been Dodds himself, repeated this advice a fortnight later, supporting it by reference to a farmer's letter that had proposed a four or five shilling wage cut and monthly hirings. But nothing seems to have come of his suggestion of a hinds' meeting on hiring morning at Morpeth: indeed attendance at the Morpeth hiring was unusually small, business difficult, and there, as elsewhere, the farmers generally secured a two-shilling reduction in wages. On 30 March, however, Dodds was able to report that the former National Union delegate, Gardner, 'has again been sent down to lead the hinds out of bondage'. He also referred his readers to the advertisement

[1] *Newcastle Daily Journal*, esp. 9 and 29 Jan., 2 and 26 Feb., 5 and 6 March, 2 April 1877; *Newcastle Courant*, esp. 2 and 16 Feb., 1877; *Morpeth Herald*, esp. 6 Jan., 10 Feb., 10 March 1877, and 16 Feb., 30 March and 11 May 1878.

column for a description of the union's sick benefits, invited assistance in getting up meetings and forming branches, and suggested that though unionism would not keep *'wages* up at a false level, . . . I do believe that if the hinds of Northumberland and Durham were in union *it would keep the system of a Saturday half holiday up.'*

Shortly afterwards the National Union held a small meeting at Newcastle on the old hiring day; it began with about 50 men present, and both Dodds and Gardner spoke, the latter stressing *inter alia* the union's potentialities for 'organising political agitation'. Letters to the press continued, and were supplemented by advertisements urging the hinds to 'make some sort of provision for Sickness and Old Age' by joining the union. There are also occasional reports of meetings and even of the formation of branches. But the movement never really caught on. There was, for instance, no counterpart to the agitation over local charities and the 'Battle of the Vestries' that 1878 had witnessed in the south. And already by May Gardner would seem to have again been withdrawn, Dodds remaining as 'secretary' and delegate for Northumberland and Durham. By the following January he had dropped these titles.

Instead he turned to advocating emigration, as, to a lesser extent, he had already done in 1875 after the first collapse of the union. By the end of February 1879 he had organized the departure for South Australia of ten groups of emigrants from the district, numbering in all perhaps about 800 people.[1] There was to be one more ship in March, for female servants only, and then a pause till June. Dodds seemed to have hoped to resume emigration on a large scale (and probably to accompany it himself). For it was given out that an emigration agent would attend all the hiring fairs in the neighbourhood. The promise was not quite kept. But about 2,000 people did meet at the Morpeth fair to hear emigration addresses from Dodds, and also from Henry Taylor (once General Secretary of the N.A.L.U. and now an Inspector of Emigrants for South Australia), who had been in Northumberland helping Dodds for over a month. Though the meeting went off well, the substance, if not the style, of the speeches was disappointing. Dodds delivered a valedictory

[1] Three of these groups comprised respectively: 20 families, 30 single men, and 10 single women; 40 families or 80–100 people; and 10 families, 30 single men and 10 single women, making 80 people in all. Among the advice they were given was that husbands should help with the children on the voyage, instead of leaving everything to their wives as they did at home.

address, again announcing his intention to leave for Adelaide within the year. And Taylor had to conclude his standard speech by saying lamely that free passages out had been suspended and that there were 'no vessels provided to receive them when they were released from their bonds in May'. He could only hope that it would be possible to resume another year.[1]

The demise of the union left a vacuum in Northumberland labour relations. For the 1877 farmers' movement had been a fiasco, and had had no real sequel—there were one or two letters to the press in 1878 urging its repetition, but no meetings; and by 1879 rent reductions and tenant right clearly loomed considerably larger in the farmers' minds than wage cuts. Admittedly it appears to have been widely assumed that wages would again fall by a couple of shillings; and the farmers insisted on this at the hiring fairs. But they did not formally concert their action in advance, still less exert any general pressure for innovations like monthly contracts.

So neither farmers nor labourers had succeeded in securing any drastic changes in the 1870s. Nor did they for the rest of the century. No national trades union again sought to establish itself in the area, though there were occasional attempts at local combination—meetings were held at the 1892 March fair at Alnwick to form a union, 'but very few attended'. The major developments, therefore, were the cumulative results of pressure applied piece-meal over a considerable period of time, and, as such, they had been long predictable. In the late 1860s it had been the custom of northern parts of the country to pay largely in kind: but a shift from corn to cash was already being commented on in Berwick in 1869; by the early 1890s a monthly cash payment was now usual; and, in this, the north of the country was only following the pattern earlier set in the south. One casualty of the change was the practice whereby the men received the food for a cow as part of their wages: this, too, had been general in 1867; but in the early 1870s the Alnwick Cow [Insurance] Club, an institution of some 30 years' standing, was suddenly faced by increasing mortality and falling demand, a process that was expected to lead the ordinary agricultural labourer to abandon it; and by the early 1890s the labourers had largely given up their cows, though they were not altogether

[1] *Morpeth Herald*, esp. 16 Oct. 1875, 16 Feb., 2, 9 and 30 March, 6 and 20 April, 11, 18 and 25 May 1878, 4 and 11 Jan., 1 and 22 Feb., 1 and 8 March 1879.

happy about doing so. Similarly the bondage system had already come under attack by 1867, and its gradual demise was anticipated by the Northumberland report of the Royal Commission on the Employment of Women and Children in Agriculture. As we have seen, 'bondage' was a common target during the agitation of the 1870s. This probably hastened its decline, but the process was protracted over a considerable period, men becoming more and more reluctant to allow their wives to work or to engage bondagers from outside their own families, and women to enter agricultural work under any circumstances. By 1892 it could be said that the old bondage system was dead, that women workers were almost always the hinds' daughters, and that the inability of young men to supply such 'workers' was 'a reason for their seeking employment in towns'; and the virtual replacement of female labour by machines was also being forecast, albeit somewhat prematurely.[1] Cumulatively, then, the Northumberland countryside had experienced considerable change in the late nineteenth century. But the change was still the product of local rather than external forces; and it was not until the governmental intervention of the First World War that the latter were to have a major impact on the local scene.

[1] *P.P.*, 1867–8 xvii, pp. 113, 116–7, 1868–96, p. 658, and 1893–4 xxxv, pp. 420–2; *Morpeth Herald*, esp. 22 Nov. 1873, p. 3, and 5 and 12 March 1892, p. 2.

VIII

Tenant Right in Britain and Ireland

The prosperity of the early 1870s had been accompanied by widespread unrest among farm labourers. It was succeeded by agricultural depression; and this led in the next two decades to farmers' and tenants' movements that faced the Government with problems of a far more acute variety. Of those in Great Britain the most important were the Scottish crofters' agitation, which first became serious in 1882, and the Welsh 'tithe war', which broke out in 1885. But, to understand the context in which they operated, we must first look briefly at the alterations that had already been made in the land laws, and then at the course of events in Ireland, since this was to be cited extensively in Britain either as an inspiration or as a warning.

In the 1840s rural politics in Britain had been dominated by the Corn Laws. The protection these gave had been lost irrevocably, but the agricultural interest had survived and flourished —so much so, indeed, that the decades after the Crimean War were to be seen in retrospect as 'the Golden Age of British Agriculture'. By the late 1870s this had ended; and cattle disease, wet seasons and bad harvests had ushered in the 'Great Depression', while American grain imports prevented prices from rising as they had previously done to off-set such disasters. In purely economic terms, the depth of the depression can be exaggerated. But it was, nevertheless, to affect most types of farming, with important consequences, both psychological and political.[1]

Before the Reform Act of 1885, tenant farmers probably constituted the most numerous element in the rural constituencies. From time to time they had revolted, though often through disgust at landlord pusillanimity and in a Conservative direction. And there had been discussion about various aspects of 'tenant right' off and on for much of the century. But in general British farmers accepted that their interests were closely (even organically) linked to those of their landlords; and since the landlord

[1] See e.g. P. J. Perry (ed.), *British Agriculture, 1875–1914* (1973), esp. Introduction and chaps. 3 and 7.

usually provided the fixed capital needed•for the operation of a farm, there was considerable truth in this. It would be far too much to say that identity of sentiment was destroyed by the Great Depression. But, for a time, it was strained—just as farmers had earlier reproached their labourers for listening to interested outsiders, so now landlords bemoaned their tenants' alienation by political agitators.

The most noticeable manifestations of this new mood were the sporadic and rather capricious intervention of tenant-farmers in parliamentary elections, and the Farmers' Alliance. A number of tenant-farmer candidates appeared at the 1880 General Election without official ties to either party, though in practice inclining towards the Liberals; the most prominent, Thomas Duckham, was triumphantly elected for Herefordshire. In 1881 H. J. Tollemache had some difficulty in retaining the family seat in west Cheshire for the Conservatives in the face of unanticipated tenant dissatisfaction; but later in the year the adhesion of the tenant-farmers 'as a body' to a Protectionist candidate gave the Conservatives a gain in north Lincolnshire. And 1882 saw an epic contest in the North Riding, a constituency which had not previously been fought for years; despite the support of renegade Whig landlords, his own Protectionist leanings and his overtures towards the farmers, the Conservative candidate only just scraped home against 'the representative of the Farmers' Alliance'.

This body had, in the words of its Chairman, been founded in 1879 as 'an association which should represent the tenant farmer's interests from a tenant farmer's standpoint' (unlike the existing Chambers of Agriculture). It was from the outset political, and in the 1880 elections it posed test questions and saw its programme accepted by about 60 candidates. In 1881 it drew up a draft Landlord and Tenant Bill, which was widely distributed through its branches 'and played an important part in the subsequent speeches and elections of the year'. The Alliance was able to mount quite impressive demonstrations—one meeting in London in October 1880 was said to have been 'largely attended by tenant-farmers from all English counties', and another in Aberdeen in December 1881 by between 2,000 and 3,000 people, representing over 40,000 farmers in north-east Scotland. But though it could clearly attract attention and multiply discussion, when it came to the point the Alliance lacked political muscle; and the Government was able to ignore its objections when formulating legislation in 1883.

More important, then, was the groundswell in favour of some

governmental response to the problem of agricultural depression in general and of tenants' rights in particular. Disraeli had not wanted to concede a Royal Commission on Agricultural Depression, but in 1879 House of Commons sentiment left him no option.[1] His Administration also found it expedient to repeal that ancient Scottish grievance, the law of hypothec,[2] shortly before the 1880 elections. But, as the opposition party, the Liberals were better placed to take advantage of the discontent —Lord Hartington conceded that the farmers had generally been Conservative, and explicitly appealed to them 'to give the Liberals their support for one Parliament' on a trial basis. Many must have made the experiment, for the Liberals did better in the counties than at any time since 1835.[3]

Once in office the Liberals began to pay their debts. Some of their measures presented no particular problems—Gladstone's 1880 budget disposed of the much-abused malt tax. But two

[1] In 1882 the Commission attributed the Depression mainly to bad weather and foreign competition, but could suggest little cure for either. However it noted that the parties had invariably contracted out of the Agricultural Holdings Act, 1875, and recommended that the protection this afforded the tenant should be inalienable. This was important, since the Commission's Chairman, the Duke of Richmond, had been chiefly responsible for the Act; and his conversion meant that the Conservatives could not really oppose the Liberal measure of 1883.

[2] Whereby the landlord's claims on a bankrupt tenant's estate had precedence over all others. The law's repeal was to affect the Scottish crofters' movement in two ways. Firstly it encouraged an unwise extension of credit by local shopkeepers—and it was suggested that their extensive involvement in the crofters' agitation was partly due to a wish to protect these debts at the landlords' expense. Secondly repeal discouraged landlords from advancing money to their small tenants; without advances the tenants could not readily stock extensions to their holdings, and the State was not disposed to lend without security. This caused some difficulty when legislation came to be drafted; and the Crofters' Act of 1886 could only adopt the lame expedient of making funds available for landlords who were so minded to borrow and re-lend at their own risk.

[3] The preceding paragraphs are derived chiefly from Trevor Lloyd, *The General Election of 1880* (Oxford, 1968), esp. pp. 61–2, 114–15, and from the *Annual Register*. See also e.g. W. F. Monypenny and G. E. Buckle, *The Life of Benjamin Disraeli* (2 vol. edn., 1929), pp. 1369, 1371–2; A. H. H. Matthews, *Fifty Years of Agricultural Politics*, p. 7; and *P.P.*, 1882 xiv, questions 58, 853–4. The fullest source for tenant-farmer discontent is the *Mark Lane Express* newspaper.

matters in particular raised the important principle of the free-dom of contract, the Ground Game Act of 1880 and the Agri-cultural Holdings Act of 1883. For the former gave occupiers an inalienable right to kill ground game, and the latter made it impossible to contract away the tenant's statutory right to com-pensation for unexhausted improvements to his holding. Of course neither was a revolutionary measure. But the Govern-ment's justification for its novel interference with agricultural contracts—that the parties to them were not on equal footing[1]—was obviously capable of considerable extension. Neither in England nor in Scotland did the Farmers' Alliance ask for inter-ference with the more important contract as to rent;[2] but this interference had already come about in Ireland, and it was to be demanded by farmers in Wales.

The Farmers' Alliance had opposed the Agricultural Holdings Act as inadequate, and continued in existence thereafter. But it went gradually into decline, and suffered an internal split over Protection. Also the Radical politicians who had briefly seen the Alliance as the key to rural success rapidly cooled towards it, and began instead to exploit the forthcoming enfranchise-ment of the agricultural labourers. So specifically tenant-farmer agitation diminished in England and Scotland after 1883, though (as we shall see) it intensified in Wales with the rise of religious nationalism. The depression, however, did not lift, and neither therefore did agitation in general. But it was now diffused over a very wide variety of grievances, from extra-ordinary tithes on hops (until the 1886 Redemption Act) to preferential railway rates for foreign produce, and over nostrums ranging from small-holdings to (in the 1890s) bi-metallism. Such agitation was inevitably confused, and sometimes contradictory. But it was not necessarily inefficacious—the principal success was perhaps agricultural de-rating in 1896. And it meant that, though politics no longer really turned on rural issues, politicians, pamphleteers,

[1] See e.g. A. G. Gardiner, *The Life of Sir William Harcourt* (1923), i, pp. 372–3; W. E. Gladstone, *Political Speeches in Scotland* (revised edn., Edinburgh, 1880), pp. 85–6, 153, 247–51.

[2] For a flat denial of any such wish by James Howard, Chairman of the Alliance in England, see *The Times*, 1 Nov. 1881, p. 7. In Scotland, where most tenants were stuck with long leases concluded in more prosperous days, the Aberdeen meeting did suggest that the tenants on each estate should ask for rent reductions and even that these could if necessary be determined by arbitration, but it did not invoke the State; and rent did not figure among the formal objects of the Farmers' Alliance of Scotland (*The Times*, 2 and 19 Dec. 1881).

and the general public were all constantly being made aware of the existence of a 'Rural Problem' even in the main-stream of England and Scotland. Some of their actions and pre-occupations in the more specific disputes with which we shall subsequently be concerned must be seen against this back-ground.

It is one of the ironies of history that in 1880 Gladstone, who is sometimes regarded as having been obsessed with Ireland, expected no trouble from that quarter. He was to be speedily disillusioned. For though the 1870s had initially been prosperous in Ireland as elsewhere, this had the side-effect of encouraging landlords to raise rents and tenants to over-borrow, and thus stimulated the emergence of Tenants' Leagues in the east. More importantly the decade ended with a run of bad seasons, potato failures, and near famine conditions in the west. From this there resulted in 1879 the far more extreme Land League of [county] Mayo. By the end of the year the two had merged, largely through the determination of the former Fenian, Michael Davitt, to link, for the first time, Irish nationalism and agrarian discontent in a 'New Departure'. This was to be a 'non-violent' movement, operating just within the ordinary law, and subject to the political leadership of Parnell and the advanced wing of the Home Rule party; but it was also to receive financial and other support from the Irish American Clan-na-Gael and from the Irish Republican Brotherhood.

Once established, the movement devoted itself to an educational and electoral attack on 'landlordism' as the source of Irish poverty and subservience, and to good effect—whereas in 1874 it had been an electoral advantage to be a landlord, in 1880 it was the reverse, and in 1885 it was generally fatal.[1] The 1880 elections secured for Parnell about a third of the Irish parliamentary representation, which he used to obstruct government business in an unprecedented fashion and to publicize Irish, and more especially Irish agrarian, grievances. At the same time the Land League sought rent rebates by hampering evictions and by making evicted holdings impossible to relet: would-be takers, and anybody who associated with them, were arraigned before Land League 'courts', fined, and forced to retract on pain of 'boycotting'—the term dates from this struggle; lastly the sentences of these courts might be supplemented by private violence and agrarian outrages.

As time went on both the landlords and the Land League be-

---

[1] J. H. White, 'Landlord Influence at Elections in Ireland, 1760–1885', *English Historical Review*, lxxx (1965), esp. pp. 756–60.

came increasingly impatient, and the worsening condition of the country forced the Government to take notice. A further factor was the report of the Bessborough Commission on the working of the 1870 Land Act; this had been set up in 1880, and its report the following year proved unexpectedly favourable to the League's demands, Fair Rent, Fixity of Tenure, and Free Sale (the 'three Fs'). In 1881 the Government finally grasped the problem, resorting to the usual combination of coercion and conciliation. It broke parliamentary obstruction, proclaimed the Land League, and took powers of precautionary arrest under which 1,083 people were eventually detained. At the same time it passed a new Irish Land Act, substantially conceding the three Fs. The League's coldness towards this act lost it the farmers' support, and its counter to the arrests (an appeal to withhold rent) failed completely. But a semblance of organization survived, and agrarian crime, now wholly unrestrained, rose sharply,[1] till the confrontation was ended by a political bargain between Parnell and the Government, the 'Kilmainham Treaty'.

Unfortunately the 1881 Land Act left a great deal to be desired. For, if stock prices slumped, the judicially determined 'Fair Rents' might themselves become too high; and there was no machinery for revising them. This in fact happened in 1885–7, and it precipitated another round of the 'Land War', similar to that of 1879–82, but more narrowly confined to a few test 'Plan of Campaign' estates on which both the League and the landlords concentrated their resources. Even more fundamentally, the Act, by according the occupier the three Fs, in effect deprived the owner of the bulk of the management of his estate and left him with little incentive to retain the land. Within a few years, all the political parties recognized (though they might not publicly admit) that the only solution was the full transfer of the land to the occupiers.[2] And the real question was the way in which this should be effected, landlords holding out for a high price, agitators promising the tenants that, with patience, they

[1] Though its extent is often exaggerated: in the worst year, April 1881–March 1882, there were 35 murders and 2,434 'agrarian outrages exclusive of threatening letters' (*P.P.*, 1882 lv, pp. 616–17, 1883 lvii, pp. 1048–9); by comparison with the troubles of the twentieth century these figures are low.

[2] State ownership constituted a theoretical alternative, which attracted both Parnell (a Bismarckian Conservative) and Davitt (a Socialist); but it was quite unacceptable to the Irish farmers themselves.

would get possession for virtually nothing, and Governments anxious to bridge the gap if it could be done at reasonable cost. A satisfactory solution was not worked out until 1903.[1]

In the meantime, it was political developments that took the lime-light. The main purpose of the New Departure had in fact been political, the promotion of Irish nationalism; and after Kilmainham Parnell returned to it. In 1885 he emphasized his parliamentary independence by helping to install a Conservative administration on condition that it abandon coercion. And he also secured great success at the General Election—his new National League had devoted much attention to the choice of candidates, and the Nationalists carried four-fifths of the Irish seats. These two successes culminated in a third, the conversion of Gladstone (and through him of the bulk of the Liberal Party) to Home Rule. This represented a startling reversal of the party's previous attitude, and indeed it ran contrary to the instincts of most of the Party's leaders. In the long run it was to have very important results. But in the short run it put an end to Parnell's parliamentary independence—only Gladstone would concede the Nationalists' aspirations, and they therefore could not afford to break with him. The fact was underlined in 1890 when Parnell's liaison with Mrs. O'Shea became public knowledge, and Gladstone, for fear of alienating the English Nonconformists, forced the Irish Parliamentary Party to discard its leader.

All sorts of lessons could be drawn from the Irish experience; but contemporaries seem to have concentrated on four. Perhaps the most important point was that, by persistent agitation, the Irish had induced the State to intervene and turn upside down the hitherto fundamental principles of land tenure—absolute ownership and complete freedom of contract. If the Irish were to be helped in this way, why not the Scots or the Welsh? Secondly the Irish owed their successes in large part to their organization; and the Land League was to have a number of imitations. Thirdly observers noted the formal independence of the Irish Nationalist Party, and admired the way in which it

[1] For the above, see *inter alia*: Michael Davitt, *Fall of Feudalism in Ireland or the Story of the Land League Revolution* (1904); Clifford Lloyd, *Ireland under the Land League* (Edinburgh, 1892); N. D. Palmer, *The Irish Land League Crisis* (New Haven, Conn., 1940); C. C. O'Brien, *Parnell and His Party* (Oxford, 1957); L. P. Curtis, *Conciliation and Coercion in Ireland, 1880–92* (Princeton, N.J., 1963); and the voluminous papers circulated to the British Cabinet (Public Record Office, Cab. 37 series).

played the two major British parties off against each other in 1885–6; but they tended to overlook its subsequent loss of real autonomy. So both the Scottish crofters and the Welsh came to sport their own nominal party organization and their own Whips. Finally we come to the association between agitation and violence, or, as *The Times* had it, to 'Parnellism and Crime'. This was, of course, generally reprehended. Occasionally leaders would nonetheless capitalize on it—Dr. Clark declared that, if the crofters were baulked 'in the legitimate enjoyment of their [electoral] victory', things would be even worse than in Ireland, since they had received military training in the Royal Naval Volunteer Reserve.[1] Fortunately this was empty talk: neither the crofters nor the Welsh farmers could be described as non-violent, but they never took matters much further than the forcible prevention of the service of writs. However not everybody felt able to count on such restraint; and there were always some people who 'concluded they were on the verge of an agrarian revolution, and . . . made up their minds to act promptly . . . and stamp out quickly the first germs of anything like the Irish disease that might show itself on this side of the Channel'.[2] The degree to which the authorities shared these fears strongly influenced their handling of the disturbances, and thus the success of the movements themselves.

[1] Quoted in the *Inverness Courier*, 26 Dec. 1885, p. 3.
[2] Lachlan Macdonald's explanation of the despatch of police to the Braes in 1882, *Celtic Magazine*, vii (1881–2), p. 394.

IX

The Crofters' 'Land War'

In many respects the north-western seaboard of Scotland resembled the west coast of Ireland, where the Land League had originated. Both were inhabited by a largely Gaelic speaking peasantry, holding small plots of land directly from great estates with little or no legal security against eviction. And in both the limited supply of land—and deliberate estate policy—had resulted in land hunger and forced emigration. However, despite many parallels in their objective circumstances, the Scottish crofter's world was very different from that of his western Irish counterpart. Ireland in the 1880s lived in the shadow of the Great Famine, when nearly an eighth of the population had died; and nationalist leaders were determined that there should be no recurrence of a situation when rents were paid though the people starved. But the Scottish crofters remembered not so much the Destitution (the Famine's milder counterpart) as the Clearances, their forcible transplantation from ancestral holdings and the conversion of the land thus vacated into sheep farms.

These were resumed in the 1840s and 1850s, in part at least as a result of the Destitution. And we have seen that they now sometimes encountered opposition which verged on the organized and articulate. Thereafter evictions fell off sharply, and by the 1880s it was rare for a crofter, and *e fortiori* for a whole crofting township, to lose home and cultivated land (as opposed to hill grazing). So not only public opinion but even ordinary landlord practice had come to give some countenance to the crofter's belief that he had a hereditary right to his croft.

There were, however, occasional exceptions. The most important was the resumption in 1880 by a new purchaser of all the arable and pasture lands of Leckmelm (near Loch Broom); for the resultant protest meeting in Inverness in December 'was the real beginning in earnest of the present movement throughout the Highlands in favour of Land Reform'.[1] And, quite

---

[1] The protest was stirred up largely by the local Free Church minister—A. Mackenzie, *The History of the Highland Clearances* (Inverness, 1883 edn.), pp. 314–26.

apart from such exceptions, in the 1870s in Skye writs of removal were still being issued against some sixty families a year.[1] For the threat of eviction was the simplest sanction with which to underpin estate discipline—that is to enforce the payment of rent, to prevent the subdivision of holdings, to restrain anti-social practices, and to protect game. Indeed, since it operated far more powerfully than the penalties prescribed by law, it was even occasionally invoked for such extraneous purposes as to compel attendance at school. In short it put enormous power into the hands of the factor. The threat was only rarely enforced; but it always might be.[2] And the burst of housebuilding in Skye around the turn of the century was supposed to be attributable to the definitive acquisition of security of tenure after the 1886 Act.[3]

Nor, of course, did the decline of evictions mean the undoing of the Clearances. These continued to dominate the economic and social structure of the area. From Argyll to Sutherland most tenants were small men, paying perhaps a little over £5 per annum in rent: but the great bulk of the landlords' income came from the rental of large farms (to which crofters could not hope to rise), and, to a lesser extent, from leases of sporting rights. Only in Lewis did crofters' rents outweigh the other sources of landed revenue, and Lewis was notoriously over-populated and impoverished.[4] This imbalance had two consequences. Firstly crofting rents tended to become fixed at a traditional figure—on the Macdonald estate in Skye at that of 1830,[5] elsewhere quite commonly at the level of 1848. Such traditional rates were widely regarded as just, and any increases

[1] Admittedly the numbers were declining steadily (*P.P.*, 1884 xxxii, Appendix A p. 77).

[2] Joseph Macleod's *Highland Heroes of the Land Reform Movement* (Inverness, 1917), p. 42, records a case on the mainland in 1872: Roderick Mackintosh's sons poached, so 'their father got notice of removal from the proprietor of Skibo. Roderick, in common with the whole countryside, thought that the warning was merely to frighten him, and the eviction would never be carried into effect'; but, on this occasion, it was.

[3] James Cameron, *The Old and New Highlands and Hebrides* (Kirkcaldy, 1912), p. 88.

[4] The average rental of crofts in Lewis was £2 18s. and there were in addition numerous 'cottars' or sub-tenants. In Skye there were 610 holdings at an average of £3, 935 at one of £6, 178 at one of £12, 25 at one of £40, and 33 at one of £52 (*Celtic Magazine*, vi (1881), p. 393).

[5] More precisely, the rental in 1880 was some 4–5% above that of 1830 (*P.P.*, 1884 xxxiii, questions 8295–9).

correspondingly resented. Equally, though increases might well reflect a land agent's valuation, the traditional rates reflected nothing in particular, and accordingly might not be adjusted to compensate for such changes in the holding as the deprivation of hill pasture. This was, of course, an obvious cause of dispute. And in any case the pattern of settlement produced by the Clearances meant that the small crofting tenants were almost everywhere surrounded by land let to the large farms, some of which their ancestors had once occupied. It was only natural, in the event of economic difficulties, to blame them on the loss of the land, and perhaps to seek for restitution as the simplest cure.

In general the 1870s were good years for the Highlands— stock prices were high (enabling crofters to pay their rents from the sale of calves), and so were wages, partly in response to general economic conditions and partly as the result of a local building boom. This prosperity may have served to mask discontent, but to raise general economic expectations. Meanwhile conditions were being prepared, consciously and unconsciously, that would make possible a co-ordinated crofters' movement should the occasion for one arise. 'It is necessary' one author defiantly maintained,

in these times of land reform activity to emphasise that the real pioneers of the great progressive movement which has transformed the Highlands are not, as newspaper and magazine writers persistently declare, the men who have been instrumental in procuring land legislation, but the promoters of the Highland Railway. . . .[1]

Backed by large landlord subscriptions railways were built up the east coast in the 1860s, and across to Strome Ferry in 1870 and Oban in 1880; at the same time steamer services up the west coast developed rapidly. In the 1860s it could still take a week to reach Edinburgh from Skye, a factor that would materially have inhibited external publicity and assistance for the crofters.

At the same time a 'cultural' movement was building up amongst Highland migrants and sympathizers that would, in other circumstances, have been nationalist. Credit is usually given to John Murdoch, who (on his retirement in 1873) turned to the production of a newspaper *The Highlander*. Murdoch had links with Irish nationalism, and favoured a land settlement along Irish lines. He also sought to encourage the Gaelic language and culture. Three years later *The Highlander* was joined by the *Celtic Magazine*, a scholarly journal primarily devoted to litera-

---

[1] *The Old and New Highlands and Hebrides*, pp. 157–9.

ture, history and antiquities, but also to 'the Social and Material interests of the Celt at home and abroad'. It was edited by a leading Inverness figure, Alexander Mackenzie, who the following year started working for the appointment of a Royal Commission on the condition of the Highlands. And in 1878 Mackenzie's ally, Fraser-Mackintosh, the radical M.P. for Inverness, presided over the foundation of the Federation of Celtic Societies: at the outset 13 societies in Glasgow were affiliated, two each in Greenock and Edinburgh, five in various other large towns, and one in Tobermory. These societies were not necessarily political, but the Federation constituted a machine that could be used to work up the Highland question. Among those who tried was the Celtic enthusiast Professor Blackie, who in 1880 treated the Perth Gaelic Society to an inaugural address on *Gaelic Societies, Highland Depopulation and Land Law Reform*, urging them to fight for improvements.

This all witnessed to the continuing concern for the Highlands of people who had left them. Mackenzie himself had been brought up on a croft. So had the successful railway contractor John Mackay of Hereford, who subscribed liberally to a variety of Highland enterprises including *The Highlander*. Mackay's concern can perhaps be traced to his father; he had served during the Napoleonic Wars, and had on his return been so angered by the clearances during his absence that he vowed 'if he had twenty sons, that none, with his approval would serve a country whose laws permitted the Highland chiefs to perpetrate such gross outrages . . .' John Mackay was President of the Glasgow Sutherland Association in 1878; and among the other officers of the society were J. G. Mackay and Angus Sutherland. Sutherland was a young master at Glasgow Academy, whose grandparents on both sides of the family had been evicted. J. G. Mackay worked as a draper in Glasgow, and was 'a vigorous member of all the Highland Societies, Gaelic and otherwise, of that town'; his father is described as an opponent of Patrick Sellar (of the notorious Strathnaver clearances), and his mother as 'a native of the desolated parish of Bracadale, Skye'. Examples could be multiplied.[1]

In short the material existed outside the Highlands for an

[1] H. J. Hanham, 'The Problem of Highland Discontent, 1880–5', *Royal Historical Society Transactions*, 5th series, xix (1969) (subsequently cited as 'Hanham'), pp. 35–40; *Celtic Magazine*, iv (1878–9), p. 36, ix (1884), pp. 270–2, x (1884–5), p. 376; *Highland Heroes*, pp. 59–65; D. W. Crowley, 'The "Crofters' Party", 1885–92', *Scottish Historical Review*, xxv (1956), p. 113.

appreciable agitation. To a certain extent this was even independent of events within the Highlands. Alexander Mackenzie
had been active in canvassing support since 1877, sending copies
of his pessimistic article 'Poetry and Prose of a Highland Croft'
to Argyll and Gladstone, and publishing in 1881 a widely read
pamphlet on the Clearances. And Fraser-Mackintosh, who had
thought demands for a Royal Commission premature in 1877,
decided after the 1880 Inverness meeting about Leckmelm that
it was worth pressing for one.[1]

But obviously his prospects of success were limited while the
Highlands remained quiet. Why they changed in the 1880s is
still not altogether clear. Three types of explanation have been
given: that it was all the fault of external agitators; that it was
the result of a succession of economic disasters; and that it represented a deliberate counter-attack on the part of the crofters.

It was naturally tempting to ascribe all the trouble to outside
agitators. For at least on the surface previous crofter–landlord
relations had been most cordial; and if outsiders were to blame,
there was still nothing basically wrong bar a little thought-
lessness and credulity on the part of the tenants. Highland
landlords were as reluctant to believe that their own crofters
had turned against them as present-day academics to accept
the alienation of their own students. So we are told that

Ireland was certainly the origin of the Skye agitation. The return of
the fishermen from Kinsale immediately preceded the first note of discontent in the Braes, near Portree; an Irish emissary, Mr. McHugh,
followed, and his presence was succeeded by the lawless outbreaks in
Glendale; publications of socialistic tendency were, and still are,
widely circulated among the population through agencies in London
and other large towns, some of which bear to have been printed in
Dublin . . .

And more generally we learn that 'Irish legislation was carefully
watched, and it is known that, on the passing of the Irish Land
Bill, a copy was sent (to order) to a remote part of the Lewis;
this legislation was at the root of the agrarian agitation in the
Highlands.'[2]

There is quite a lot of substance in this position. The Scottish
press gave extensive coverage to Irish developments, and it was

---

[1] *Celtic Magazine*, iii (1877–8), pp. 32–5; viii (1883), pp. 282–3.
[2] *Confidential Reports to the Secretary for Scotland on the condition of
the Western Highlands and Islands*, Oct. 1886 (Lothian Papers—
S(cottish) R(ecord) O(ffice), GD 40/16/32, subsequently cited as
Confidential Reports), pp. 3, 55.

easy to draw parallels between the two countries. So it is not surprising to find the *Glasgow Weekly Mail* reporting that Iona was disappointed in the Duke of Argyll, partly because he had not reduced his rents as expected, but more especially because of his resignation from the Government in protest against the Irish Land Bill—'for they believed the remedy for Ireland was the cure for them, and could not consistently be refused to the Highlands and Islands of Scotland, as they are near akin in their landlordism, factorialism, and industries.' And, from a different point of view, Argyll himself endorsed this judgement: 'The crofting row in Scotland', he told Gladstone, '. . . is in part —and great part—the mere reverberation of the Irish Land Act among a population somewhat similarly situated, and partially in distress this year from a failure of potatoes and of the fishery.' In fact it was only within very definite limits that the crofters identified with the Irish. But they had certainly absorbed the lesson that concessions come only to those who press for them; one witness told the Royal Commission that

I must say I think the Goverment policy has been rather hard on a loyal people like the Orcadians. I have said in joke, but also a good deal in earnest, to some of my friends down south, that if we had been more of a landlord-shooting and outrageous class in Orkney we would have had telegraphic communication long before now . . .[1]

But though the importance of the Irish example seems fairly well established, direct external agitation was at most a merely contributory factor in the earliest outbreaks of discontent. In Skye unrest first showed itself on the Kilmuir estates, and for primarily internal reasons. The small tenants had protested against the rent increases of 1877, but had been persuaded to give them a trial. The proprietor's residence was immediately wrecked by a great flood, which may have been taken as divine condemnation of the changes; and in any case the crofters seem to have been forced to borrow to meet their obligations. They therefore began to press for reductions, especially when the Valtos tenants discovered that their rise had been based on a mis-statement of the number of cattle they were allowed. This had to be corrected, and served as a precedent. There were *ad hoc* rent rebates in 1880. And in 1881 the Valtos tenants refused to pay anything beyond the old rent: they were threatened with

[1] *Glasgow Weekly Mail*, 30 April 1881, p. 2; Argyll to Gladstone, 10 Feb. 1883 (printed in Hanham, p. 32); *P.P.*, 1884 xxxiv, question 24447.

eviction, and offered inducements to leave; but they declined to go and the proprietor climbed down.

These events must have been noted in other parts of the island, and presumably encouraged the belief that boldness paid. They were certainly noted outside. While the evictions were still pending, a meeting of the Irish Land League in Glasgow provided a platform for a speech and motion denouncing them; a second meeting was also held, and a Skye Vigilance Committee appointed.[1] And, despite the rapid settlement of the Kilmuir affair, there descended on Skye a number of land reformers, including John Murdoch. Murdoch's visit to the Braes (near Portree) resulted in a dozen crofters taking out subscriptions to his paper *The Highlander* and thus familiarizing themselves with the more lurid stories of the Clearances. And at least one of the other visitors sought to re-open the local grievance of Ben Lee, a grazing of which the crofters had, in their view, been deprived without compensation in 1865. He did not meet with immediate success, largely because he was regarded as an outside trouble-maker. But in November 1881 the townships of the Braes did petition for the return of Ben Lee; and, when this was refused, they bound themselves to pay no rents until it was handed over. The Kilmuir example was no doubt known, but it is not specifically mentioned. Another reason given for the raising of the question at that time was 'that we were hearing that there were new laws passing about lands'. And a third factor was that the existing lease of Ben Lee was due to expire the following Whitsun; the crofters saw this as a convenient opportunity for Lord Macdonald to redress the wrong that had been done to them during his minority; and some even convinced themselves that this had been the intention all along.[2]

A second type of explanation for the transformation of Highland sentiment in the early 1880s is economic. It has considerable merit. For there certainly was a series of disasters: in

[1] Its members included Angus Sutherland and J. G. Mackay, whose activity on behalf of the crofters at this time nearly lost him his job.

[2] Hanham, pp. 51–3; *Glasgow Weekly Mail*, 30 April and 7 May 1881; Norman Maclean, *The Former Days* (1945), chaps. 4, 7, 8; *P.P.*, 1884 xxxiii, questions 8549 (Kilmuir), 9385 (the Braes). Also *Official Reports and Papers Relating to the Recent Disturbances in the Island of Skye* (printed for possible circulation to the Cabinet, March 1883), Harcourt Papers, Stanton Harcourt, Oxon. (W. V. H., Box Big Key 6)—subsequently cited as *Official Reports*.

1878 Sir James Matheson, the proprietor of Lewis, died, and his enormous private expenditure on the island was cut off, leaving it completely unviable. In the winter of 1881 storms smashed over a thousand boats on Skye, and carried crops out to sea. The following year saw potato and crop failures so serious as to compel resort to Destitution Funds—by the spring of 1883 over a third of the families in Kilmuir are said to have been destitute, and conditions in the Ross of Mull were worse. Finally in 1885 cattle prices collapsed, and a change in the organization of the east coast fishings materially reduced earnings from that source. And besides these specific disasters the crofters may have been facing adverse long-term trends. They frequently claimed that their arable land was exhausted by repeated cropping, and this was probably true. Also changing patterns of living, aided by the prosperity of the 1870s, made them more dependent than before on cash purchases from outside, of tea, meal (their own produce being now fed to their animals), and even of clothes. '. . . . of all incomes derived from labour, that of the crofter is perhaps the most liable to fluctuations'; in a good year he might make at least £10 from the sale of cattle, and £12 or sometimes even £20–30 at the east coast fishings (more if his family went too); 'but bad markets and an unprofitable fishing reverse all this, and having acquired extravagant habits in prosperous years, he falls inevitably into debt and discontent.'[1]

Both the chronology and the incidence of unrest fit this pattern reasonably well. Trouble started in Skye in 1881–3; but it remained largely confined to the island, and to fairly limited districts in the Outer Hebrides, until 1885 when it expanded to cover the greater part of the western sea board. Also though membership of, and sympathy for, the Land League was widespread, actual violence was largely confined to the poorest areas. Of the 14 riots instanced by Lord Lothian in 1888, all but two (Tiree and Dornoch) occurred in parishes that he listed as among the most strikingly overcrowded in Scotland. Most of these parishes had either riots or court cases arising out of disputes over land or rent. And, with the Orkneys, they account for the vast majority of such court cases.[2]

[1] Hanham, pp. 52, 57–8; *P.P.*, 1884 xxxiii, questions 8544–5, 1888 lxxx, pp. 642–3, 647; *The Old and New Highlands and Hebrides*, p. 53; *Confidential Reports*, pp. 18, 78; Sir William Collins to Sir William Harcourt, 2 and 10 March 1883—unless another provenance is given, all letters to Harcourt are cited from the Harcourt Papers.
[2] P(ublic) R(ecord) O(ffice), Cab. 37/22/23, pp. 2–3, 7; *P.P.*, 1888 lxxxii, pp. 1–8.

But one must not take economic determinism too far. The Braes were not affected by the storm of 1881. And it was in precisely the years when cattle prices were at their peak that the agitation became institutionalized in Skye, with affiliation to the London Land Law Reform Association in 1883 and the general adoption of the no-rent movement in 1884. In Lewis, too, it could be stated that initial refusals of rent had been deliberate, though by 1886, after the disastrous east coast fishing, 'the failure to meet their obligations arises in many cases from actual inability'.[1]

The earlier Lewis refusals were said to have been made 'on the ground that pasture land had been withdrawn—a misconception, for the common grazing in the occupation of crofters is as extensive as ever . . .' And whatever the rights and wrongs of it, they represent something of a counter-attack. By all accounts the crofters had accepted the Great Clearances with remarkable docility; resistance was rare, and when it occurred it took the form of direct prevention of the service of writs, not of an attempt to bring counter-pressure on the landlord. But things had now changed. In 1865 the inhabitants of the Braes had fought their loss of Ben Lee in the courts, but had ultimately accepted it for fear of the factor: thereafter they did no more than surreptitiously allow their stock to trespass on it until 1881, when, as we have seen, they suddenly demanded its return on pain of a rent strike; and the following summer they simply re-occupied it. The same trend can be seen even more clearly on the other side of the island in Glendale, which had been planted with fishermen's crofts in the 1840s, and was certainly too crowded for men to derive a living except from the sea. The local fishing may have deteriorated, and by 1882 the whole valley was in arrears of rent. It remained quiet until December 1881. But in the next couple of months a ban on keeping dogs and on trespassing in search of sea-ware proved the last straws. A public meeting was held in the church in February; the tenants resolved that each township should petition for the redress of its grievances, and all undertook in writing not to tolerate any victimization. The petitions were duly sent in, and were quite ambitious. Thus the tenants of Fasach asked for the redress of the 'breaches and harms which had been done to them for the last forty years'; those of Skinidin sought the return of some adjacent islands that had once been part of their farm, but only before its division into crofts; and those of Milvaig demanded that they be rented the neighbouring farm

[1] *P.P.*, 1884 xxxiii, question 88; *Confidential Reports*, p. 16.

of Waterstein. This they had never possessed; but it was about to become vacant, and they sought to take advantage of this opportunity to break out of their cramped conditions.[1]

Such 'opportunities' were fairly common at the time since the great Highland sheep farms were now in decline—Australasian competition was lowering wool prices, and, in any case, they had probably been over-grazed during the years of prosperity. Consequently a number were thrown back into the landlords' hands. They could have been divided among the crofters, but this would generally have meant a marked drop in rental. Moreover it was very doubtful whether the crofters possessed the capital to stock them—the inhabitants of the Braes could not stock Ben Lee when they obtained it, and they were fairly typical.[2] So landlords often preferred to keep the farms in hand, or to convert them into deer forests (which paid better than sheep farms, and actually employed more labour). A particularly good illustration is provided by the mixed deer forest and sheep farm of Park, on Lewis.[3] Feeling against this had been strong at the last change of tenants in the 1860s, and, as the current lease drew to its close, tension mounted. In 1881 and again a year later thirty-two landless cottars petitioned to be established on some former crofts inside it. Their petitions were first ignored, and then rejected on the pretext that the final petition had been accompanied by a threat of violence; a case could, however, be made out for the policy, if not for the manner, of the refusal.[4] So, when the lease expired in 1883 and a new

[1] *Official Reports*, pp. 1–16; P. C. MacVicar's report of 1 April, and Speirs to Ivory, 27 April 1882 (S.R.O., GD 1/36/1 (i)); A. Mackenzie, *The History of the Highland Clearances* (1883 edn.), pp. 415–23.

[2] See e.g. P.R.O. Cab. 37/14/10, p. 3.

[3] For the origins of the Park estate see *P.P.*, 1884 xxxiv, questions 17386–7, 17713–4, and 1902 lxxxiii, p. 449. There had always been a deer forest, part of which was converted into a sheep farm. But the neighbouring crofters had lost their summer shielings with the tighter preservation of game; and the estate had been expanded and consolidated by the removal (principally in the 1830s and 1840s) of, according to the crofters, 106 families, according to the estate, rather over 60. It is agreed that some of these were planted on other farms not previously under crofters. But, with the remorseless growth of population, people still sought for relief from the re-occupation of former crofter holdings.

[4] For a justification of the refusal, see *P.P.*, 1884 xxxii, Appendix A, p. 152. In view of the extreme local congestion the Deer Forests Commission scheduled Park for the extension of existing crofter holdings (almost exclusively by way of rough pasture); but it

tenant could not be found, the estate preferred first to keep the farm in hand and later to convert it to deer. Naturally the neighbouring townships, all grossly overcrowded, deeply resented this. And in 1887 their resentment issued first in an attempt by a body of landless men to take possession of part of the forest, and shortly afterwards in the Great Deer Raid— this had been planned for months in advance (with the cognizance of the *North British Daily Mail*), and 1,100 people were involved; it lasted two days, and 200 (out of a total of 6–700) deer are said to have been killed. The Raid certainly served its purpose of attracting attention to the island; and with attention came increased government help; but only a few men were actually given holdings within the Park peninsula.[1]

So by the early 1880s conditions in the Highlands were ripe for some kind of land movement. There was the Irish precedent, economic pressure, the apparent opportunities presented by the decline of the sheep farms, and, above all, a growing readiness among the crofters to assert themselves. Accordingly we encounter activity over quite a wide area. The successful resistance to eviction at Bernera in Lewis in 1874 is sometimes taken as the beginning of unrest. Apart from this incident the island remained quiet, but by about 1880 the Chief Constable of Ross-shire was anticipating trouble there. Petitions began over Park, as we have seen, in 1881–2, and by 1883 the neighbouring parish of Uig had joined in.[2] Again from 1873 onwards there was a trickle of offences arising out of land disputes in the Orkneys, and the improving activities of a retired general on Rousay occasioned considerable opposition. In Caithness the 'small tenants' joined the Scottish Farmers' Alliance, and parti-

---

remarked that it would not have scheduled comparable land on the mainland (*P.P.*, 1902 lxxxiii, pp. 361–2).

[1] *P.P.*, 1884 xxxii, Appendix A, pp. 152, 179–80, and xxxiii, question 17454; *P.P.*, 1902, lxxxiii, p. 449; *The Old and New Highlands and Hebrides*, pp. 115–19; A. Geddes, *The Isle of Lewis and Harris* (Edinburgh, 1955), p. 252.

[2] As in Park (Lochs), the Uig agitation had its antecedents: we are told that 'the secession in Uig from the Free Church was as much if not more a land question than a church one.' And in both districts 'the move for the land began . . . before there was any word of the matter either by agitators or others.' (*P.P.*, 1884 xxxii, Appendix A, pp. 179–80.)

cipated enthusiastically in the nation-wide campaign for tenant-right; but by 1882 they had become disillusioned with the Alliance as the organ of the larger farmers; so they set up their own organization to press for a maximum limit on holdings, a compulsorily resident tenantry, and some control over rents.[1]

None of this posed any serious threat to the local authorities. But in 1882 in Skye events passed rapidly out of their control.[2] Lord Macdonald's[3] counter to the rent strike at the Braes was to try to persuade the Crown to bring criminal charges of inti-midation. This was refused for lack of detailed evidence. And he was then left with the alternatives of concession or eviction (a *civil* process). In choosing the second he was completely within his legal rights, and he also had a perfectly presentable moral case;[4] his actions, unlike Major Fraser's in Kilmuir, were not questioned by the local and Edinburgh legal establishments, or by the police authorities in Inverness. But the sheriff's officer serving the writs of removal was met by about 100 men and forced to burn them. This deforcement was a *criminal* offence which the authorities could not easily ignore, especially when an unofficial visit by the Sheriff-substitute and the Procurator-Fiscal failed to shake the determination of the Braes people. So arrests were decided upon, and with the more alacrity since it was hoped that they would have a sobering effect in Glendale and elsewhere in the island.

But since the county could only make 19 constables available for service in Skye this was easier said than done. The Chief Constable thought that 20 would suffice, but police apprecia-tions had already proved over-optimistic. Sheriff-Substitute

[1] *P.P.*, 1884 xxxiv, questions 24409, 24464ff., 24955–25103, and 1888 lxxii, pp. 1–8; *Inverness Courier*, 28 Oct. 1882, p. 8.

[2] The following paragraphs are based principally on the Ivory Papers, S.R.O., GD 1/36/1 (i) and on the Harcourt Papers, W.V.H., Box Big Key 6. The authorities' reactions to events in Skye will be further discussed in my Conclusion, pp. 304–6.

[3] In practice the factor, Alexander Macdonald, enjoyed a great deal of independence: but his behaviour was influenced by whether he was acting for Major Fraser, Lord Macdonald, or himself (he had no trouble with his own tenants).

[4] The Braes rents *had* been reduced in the early part of the century when Ben Lee was formally taken from the crofters. Accordingly no further reductions were made in 1865, when the severance became actual (*Official Reports*, Docs 2 and 3). On the other hand Speirs told Ivory that 'These Braes people seem willing enough to submit to arbitration, but I don't think A. McDonald will consent to that.' (13 March 1882.)

Speirs wanted a hundred soldiers instead. And the Lord Advocate decided that the arrests should be made by a surprise force of 50 policemen, mostly borrowed from Glasgow. In the event the force proved insufficient—the commander of the Glasgow contingent was of the opinion that it should have been twice as large. By dint of arriving at 5.30 a.m., the police made the arrests without difficulty, but an attempt to rescue the prisoners resulted in a nasty scuffle, 12 policemen and 7 women being injured; and there was reason to anticipate a raid that night on the Portree prison, though it never in fact materialized.

The episode was splashed across the Scottish newpapers as the 'Battle of the Braes';[1] but, though (as we shall see) it had a considerable effect on the outside world, it totally failed to 'break the back' of the agitation in Skye. Instead the Braes people put their cattle onto Ben Lee at Whitsun, and prevented the service of writs of interdict in September. It is just possible that the writs could have been served by three or four respected local constables. But the local authorities[2] were undisposed to take chances and wanted a force large enough to preclude the possibility of resistance; they also sought a spectacular success, both for its own sake, and in order to cow unrest in Glendale, which was recognized to be far harder to coerce than the Braes. Immediately after the 'Battle' Sheriff Ivory set out to work for the despatch of a gun-boat and marines. By September fear of a general rent strike throughout Skye[3] had brought the Lord Advocate round to his point of view; and on the 21st they jointly applied to the Home Secretary for military aid.

Ivory clearly anticipated no difficulties—in his covering letter he remarked that his personal engagements demanded that the expedition should leave, at latest, by the end of the following week. But by his application he had turned over ultimate control of events to the Home Secretary—and Sir William Harcourt felt that military intervention would merely conjure up a Scottish land question to add to the Irish one; moreover he believed, from personal observation, that the crofters had much to complain of. So he preferred instead to lean heavily on Lord Macdonald to force him to compromise with his tenants; and, with

[1] The original melodramatic despatch in the *Dundee Advertiser* is printed by Hanham, pp. 24–30.

[2] More esp. Ivory (Sheriff of Inverness-shire, Moray and Nairn), Anderson (Procurator-Fiscal, Inverness), Speirs and McLennan (Sheriff-substitute and Procurator-Fiscal, Portree).

[3] By Oct. fears were being voiced that trouble would spread to other parts of the north-west Highlands.

the help of a certain amount of good fortune, he succeeded in holding off a military expedition until the Ben Lee dispute was settled in December.

But the world had not been standing still in the meantime. The news of the Battle of the Braes brought correspondents from at least ten newspapers flocking to Skye.[1] It also led the Land Restoration League to send in its Scottish agent, Edward McHugh, in company with John Murdoch. Less obtrusively, but far more productively, the Glasgow activists established contact with Glendale. Moreover the agitation for a Royal Commission received an enormous stimulus: petitions were signed, meetings held, and attempts made to raise the matter in the House of Commons. And by February 1883 Frazer-Mackintosh could inform the Home Secretary, in an open letter, that the Press were unanimously in favour of a Commission from the (anti-crofter) *Scotsman* downwards, that the 'Landlords and officials in the disturbed districts are not averse', and that a majority of back-bench Scottish M.P.s wanted a Commission, while only four were hostile.

The Government's initial reaction had been to refuse, Harcourt privately believing that things could best be settled by minor concessions on the part of the landlords, and all concerned seeing the danger of 'opening the floodgates of a Highland land question by a Commission . . .'.[2] But events moved out of their control. For though the dispute at the Braes was settled, the inhabitants of Milvaig (in Glendale) continued to occupy the farm of Waterstein in defiance of an Interdict, assaulted and drove one of the shepherds off the farm, and in mid-January 1883 routed a small detachment of police whom it was proposed to station in the valley. This could not be altogether overlooked. Already in early November 1883 Rosebery was pressing forcefully for the re-assertion of the law linked with 'an enquiry . . . into what has caused the state of things which has required the intervention of the military': after the final assault on the police he joined the Lord Advocate in pressing for action, and

[1] *Celtic Magazine*, vii (1882), p. 344.

[2] Harcourt had changed his mind by 25 Nov.; Gladstone still remained hostile to a Commission, but his absence in Cannes in Feb. 1883 may have lessened the force of his warnings. For this and the previous paragraphs, see B(ritish) M(useum) Add. MSS. 44197 fo. 144, 44476 fo. 245; Gladstone to Harcourt, 25 Nov. 1882, and Harcourt to Lorne, 3 Nov. 1884 (not sent) (Harcourt Papers); Agatha Ramm, *The Political Correspondence of Mr. Gladstone and Lord Granville, 1876–86* (Oxford, 1962), ii, pp. 21, 32.

by the end of the month Harcourt had reluctantly decided on the despatch of military force plus a Royal Commission. The military never in fact sailed, since it was decided first to give the wanted men a last chance to surrender—accordingly one Malcolm M'Neill (from the Board of Supervision) was sent to stage a proconsular descent on Glendale from a gunboat. He succeeded in persuading the men to surrender; and, though in all other respects the people remained obdurate, the idea of military action faded away.

That of inquiry, which had originally been its adjunct, survived. Throughout the summer of 1883 (save for an interlude caused by shipwreck) the Royal Commission toured the western Highlands collecting evidence. And, as Malcolm M'Neill rather sourly reported in 1886, it was to be generally believed in Skye that

of all means by which discontent has been fostered, none produced such baleful results as the Royal Commission . . . The crofters entertained the belief that the Commission possessed executive and administrative powers, that the inquiry would issue in immediate action at their instance, and, therefore, that the more they could be induced to receive as evidence the more signal would be the overthrow of the landlords.

Certainly the Commission's procedure was bound to actualize discontent, especially in areas where it had not previously been overt. For it invited delegates from each township or district to state the local grievances. This demanded that they first be rehearsed in preliminary meetings, and left considerable scope for activists to articulate them. These activists might themselves be crofters. Alternatively the preliminary meetings might be prompted by small-town Radicals, or (more particularly in Sutherland) by Free Church ministers. Or the initiative might come from outside the Highlands—John Mackay of Hereford and Angus Sutherland of Glasgow both took an energetic part, and Alexander Mackenzie of Inverness was to be thanked for his important services 'in selecting the most competent witnesses, and encouraging the people to speak fearlessly before the Royal Commission'. In general the process must have served not only to make the crofters increasingly self-conscious, but also to bring them into closer contact with outside sympathizers— Dugald MacLachlan, a banker and Sheriff Clerk Depute in Portree, was later to depose that 'I did not know I had any influence until I went round with the Crofters' Commission and [expressed my views then—deleted] acted as interpreter'; by the end of the year he had been offered the position of principal adviser to the movement on Skye.[1]

For in the course of the autumn and winter of 1883–4 advantage was taken of such contacts to institutionalize the unrest. In Sutherland the moving spirits were, at first, often Free Church ministers, whose part in presenting evidence to the Commission we have already noticed.[2] They had for some time served to distribute charity raised by Edinburgh activists; so the next step of affiliating to the Edinburgh Highland Land Law Reform Association was natural enough. More remarkable was the feat of the London H.L.L.R.A. in enrolling the heart of the agitation, Skye. This owed much to the assiduity of its secretary, Donald Murray, who wrote to everybody who had given evidence to the Royal Commission, and who managed to engage as a paid lecturer the 'Glendale Martyr', John Macpherson.[3] The Edinburgh and London Associations always co-operated, and in September 1885 they merged.

By then the movement was spreading widely—the London H.L.L.R.A. (the larger of the two) claimed 29 Highland branches and 5,000 members in March 1884, 90 branches and 10,000 members in September 1885.[4] The following year Malcolm M'Neill was asked to report on the origin and conduct of the agitation in various parts of the north-western sea board.[5] In

---

[1] *Confidential Reports*, p. 3; *Oban Times*, 28 June 1884, p. 5; 'Notes of Evidence taken by Sheriff Ivory at Portree on 2d February and 21, 22, and 23 May 1885', GD 1/36/1(ii)—depositions of Dugald MacLachlan and Archibald Macdonald, Garafad.

[2] But though individual ministers were prominent in the agitation (especially in Sutherland and the Lowlands), others held aloof even at the cost of alienating their congregations. The Free Church General Assembly confined itself to recommending ministers to secure the presentation of reliable information to the Royal Commission. Similarly the brothers MacCallum, ministers of the Established Church at Waternish in Skye and Strontian in Morven, were the mainstays of the agitation in their respective districts; but the Church as a whole was hostile, as was the Roman Catholic hierarchy.

[3] Sergeant Boyd's report, 10 June 1884 (GD 1/36/2 (i)).

[4] The Edinburgh H.L.L.R.A. claimed 30 to 40 branches and 3–4,000 members in 1885—*Oban Times*, 28 June 1884, p. 5; *The Scotsman*, 3 Sept. 1885, p. 5. (In the counties of Argyll, Inverness, Ross and Sutherland—though the movement spread beyond them— there were over 184,000 Gaelic speakers.)

[5] Chiefly the section from Oban to Lochinver. These *Confidential Reports* were hurriedly compiled from conversations with non-crofter local notables, but they are still of considerable interest.

some places he was told that 'the agitation seemed to originate without external suggestion', or that it sprang from newspaper accounts of similar action elsewhere, or from meetings held to prepare for the Royal Commission. But Skye is frequently mentioned as the source of contagion. And the same (surprisingly few) names crop up again and again as the evangelists of the movement: Mackenzie (of the *Celtic Magazine*), Murdoch (of the *Highlander*), Macpherson the 'Glendale Martyr', Donald Mac-Callum (minister of the Established Church at Waternish in Skye), and to a lesser extent the London barrister, Stuart Glennie.

Conditions had favoured their work. As we have seen, the north-west was badly hit by economic depression in 1885. It was also in the throes of intense political excitement, in 1884 over the House of Lords' rejection of the Franchise Bill, and in 1885 over the elections. These were the first in which the crofters were entitled to vote; 'crofter' candidates came forward to woo them,[1] and except in Sutherland succeeded in defeating the official Liberals. Their opponents naturally maintained that they owed their success to 'sheer Bribery of Promises'; and they do seem to have held out extravagant expectations of a distribution of the land—the popular Radical landlord, Lachlan Macdonald of Skaebost in Skye, was warned privately by Murdoch, Angus Sutherland, Dr. Clark and Mr. Saunders to buy no more land in case he lost it. Certainly the crofters were made aware that some legislation on their behalf was imminent; and they were probably led to believe that only 'Land League' members would be able to take advantage of it. Such hopes were to prove greatly exaggerated—and their disappointment had already caused some disillusionment with the H.L.L.R.A. by the time M'Neill reported in the autumn of 1886. But legislation for the crofters was indeed in the air.[2]

For in April 1884 the Royal Commission had produced a sympathetic report. Its chairman, Lord Napier, recognized that the crofters' principal desire was for 'more land, restoration of

[1] Dr. G. B. Clark (chairman of the London H.L.L.R.A.) in Caithness, J. Mc.D. Cameron (primarily the nominee of local Radicals but also supported by the H.L.L.R.A.) in Wick Burghs, Angus Sutherland in Sutherland, Dr. R. Macdonald (president of the London Gaelic Society) in Ross, Fraser-Mackintosh in Inverness-shire, and in Argyll D. H. Macfarlane (who had previously sat for County Carlow but had earned the nick-name of 'member of Skye').

[2] *Confidential Reports*, p. 26 and *passim*.

land'. And he steered the Commission to a set of recommendations designed to meet these demands (at least for the crofting
township, if frequently not for the individual crofter). These
were, however, generally regarded as over-complicated and as
ruinous to landlords—Harcourt described them as of 'less than
no assistance'. But matters could not be left in this condition—
the Duke of Argyll admitted that 'Governt. after they have
appointed a Commission are half pledged to "do something" ',
and even the Lord Advocate, despite a valiant attempt to
torpedo the Report section by section, eventually reached a
similar position.

Napier had feared all along that the model of the 1881 Irish
Land Act would be followed, and Harcourt came to recommend
this. But he preferred first to exert pressure to induce the principal landlords to come up with proposals, and only then to
legislate to make these compulsory for the rest. Largely as a
result of the abolition of hypothec,[1] he could see no way to meet
the crofters' principal need, for more land, by legislative action,
and therefore had to rely on 'voluntary' landlord co-operation
in this field. So his bill was limited to judicially determined
rents and minor provisions (like the offer of state loans) to
enable landlords to establish new crofter holdings if they so
desired. All this took time—the Cabinet did not approve
Harcourt's bill till March 1885, and the Liberal Government
fell before any progress was made with it.[2] Moreover when it
got out that the terms of the Bill had been discussed with
landlords, but not with the crofters' leaders, the latter were
angry. So they resolved to demand more, and, in the light of
their triumphs at the General Election, they probably genuinely
expected to obtain it.[3]

At this stage it will be convenient to revert to 1883, and to
follow the agitation in northern Skye in rather more detail,
basing ourselves principally on the police reports commissioned
by Sheriff Ivory.[4] M'Neill's descent on Glendale in January had

[1] For the difficulty this caused, see above p. 175n., and also
P.R.O., Cab. 37/14/7.
[2] Napier to Harcourt, 3 April 1884; memorandum by the Lord
Advocate, 29 July 1884; Lochiel to Harcourt, 16 Nov., and Argyll
to Harcourt, 17 Nov. 1884; P.R.O., Cab. 37/14/7 (esp. Docs. 1–3).
[3] See e.g. *The Scotsman*, 3 Sept. 1885, p. 6, and the *Inverness
Courier*, 29 Dec. 1885, p. 3.
[4] See GD 1/36/2(i). The Chief Constable's report of 31 Oct. 1884,

persuaded the men wanted for assault to surrender. But they were only imprisoned for two months; on release they were received as heroes; and one, John Macpherson, promptly acquired the title of the 'Glendale Martyr'. This did not in any way check the local agitation. However for a year and a half local questions seem to have been predominant—quarrels between townships, dissatisfaction with the share of Waterstein allotted to Milvaig as a compromise settlement, grazing disputes, complicated quarrels about the replacement of a shepherd and a miller, and an unreasonable determination to have none of the local factor.[1] Had the Trustees been prepared from the outset to discard him, the rent audits of November 1883 would have gone smoothly in Glendale, as they did elsewhere in Skye; and it is even possible, though I think unlikely, that the agitation would have petered out. Certainly as late as 30 November the Chief Constable of Inverness-shire expected that 'the present excitement will blow over'.

In fact the winter saw the organization of Skye into branches of the London H.L.L.R.A. This could not have happened, of course, if the crofters had not wished it. But it was not universally popular—John Macpherson's neighbours were, for a time, distinctly suspicious of his appointment as a paid lecturer. And the crofters were under a certain amount of pressure from their sympathizers. Thus on 8 October 1883, MacVicar, the local police constable, reported a letter from Edinburgh, and on 10 November, another from a Free Church minister in Greenock 'telling them to renew the agitation, or to form a Land Law Reform Association in Glendale'. Ten days later Murdoch wrote

---

which was based on them, was published (*P.P.*, 1884–5 lxiv, pp. 335ff.) as justification for the subsequent military expedition. It was accordingly strongly attacked—for testimony in rebuttal and reaffirmation see the 'Precognition as to Complaint of John Macpherson' (GD 1/36/1(iii)). With the major exception of the insinuations about secret societies in Glendale—which the local police had in fact already tracked down to an unreliable source—it emerges, in my judgement, substantially intact.

[1] There were 2 estates in Glendale. The smaller was run in an archaic and uncompromising way by a resident doctor and his nephew. The larger was managed by neighbouring gentlemen as factors. The new factor was anxious to extend the crofters' grazings (though not to the full extent of their demands). But he was ill-received from the outset, ostensibly because he was Irish, but in fact because his predecessor had been popular (despite all the complaints made about him), and the people wanted him back.

reproaching them for their absence from a crofters' demonstration in Lewis—he said

the Lewismen had more pluck in them than the Skyemen, and that they were far behind in the agitation; and what about Waterstein? He also advised them to keep meeting and to stick shoulder to shoulder as Highlanders, and that they were sure to be successful.

In the summer of 1884 the police tried hard to find out about the workings of the H.L.L.R.A. It was not difficult to discover the office holders and ring-leaders of local branches. But, on the more interesting question of external assistance, Sergeant Boyd could say only that, though the crofters were no doubt regularly advised 'by people from Edinburgh, Glasgow and Greenock, as well as other places in the South', he could not give their names and addresses, 'because correspondence to and from Crofters is kept strictly private by them'. He was, however, clear that Donald Murray, the Secretary of the London H.L.L.R.A., was the crofters' 'principal leader and adviser, through the medium of John Macpherson, Glendale'. 'The crofters here are all looking to' Macpherson 'as their leader, and he gets his instructions from the H.L.L.R. Association London, who are paying him and also directing him on his lecture tours.' Also it seems that some general co-ordination and supervision of the agitation in Skye was exercised by Dugald MacLachlan and a small group of sympathetic shopkeepers in Portree.[1]

In its operation the H.L.L.R.A. obviously sought to keep up the agitation. Its rules demanded monthly committee meetings of each branch, and it also exerted considerable pressure on its members to attend special rallies. Speakers at these could easily get carried away, and use stronger language than they really intended. Thus Professor Blackie was to claim that he and his companions on a tour in the summer of 1884 had sought to exert a moderating influence and to discountenance dreams 'of the possibility of an Agrarian Law by process of general confiscation'; but he indirectly praised Glendale for having driven off so many policemen; and at Portree he is supposed to have declared, flourishing his walking-stick, that he 'would fight the devil if he came within his reach, and although he was getting an old man, he would not die until he would see the rights of the

[1] The best source for this group is the investigations into, and protestations about, MacLachlan's complicity in urging resistance to the police in Oct. 1884, and over his dismissal a year later from the office of Sheriff Clerk Depute (GD 1/36/1(ii)).

poor established, and the landlords done away with.'[1] On occasion the H.L.L.R.A. probably sought to create trouble. And certainly, if trouble did break out, the Association provided machinery for spreading it—the Kilmuir branch's 'no rent' resolution of October 1884 was published as an advertisement in the very sympathetic *Oban Times.*

The spring of 1884 was dominated by the Royal Commission. There was a slight lull in the agitation pending its Report, and meetings were then called to discuss it. It was at first quite well received, but the prevailing sentiment soon became one of impatience—within a month a meeting decided on a petition to Gladstone, to be signed by every crofter in the three northern parishes of Skye, threatening 'that, unless they would get their wishes immediately that they would take the law into their own hands.' This attitude was apparently encouraged by Donald Murray (of the H.L.L.R.A.), for in late May he instructed Macpherson to tell 'the crofters to take possession of all the hill grazings in dispute to the old march; and if they wanted assistance that they would send them assistance immediately.' The summer saw more talk than action, as most of the men were away at the fishings. But with their return the trickle of land seizures expanded considerably.[2] Some were the result of private disputes.[3] But most were the result of policy. And some of the crofters' designs were quite far reaching. With land seizures went refusals to pay rent. Much of Glendale had already done so in 1883 (though principally through dislike of the factor). And on 25 October 1884 the Kilmuir H.L.L.R.A. published a resolution to withhold rent until Major Fraser had met all its demands. This example was soon copied, and by 8 December there were twelve 'no-rent' townships on Lord Macdonald's estates in Skye.

By now the crofters were becoming increasingly sure of themselves. 'They are under the belief that no soldiers will ever come

---

[1] Blackie to Rosebery, 22 Aug. 1884 (National Lib. of Scotland, RB 60), and the reports of Sergeant Boyd and Inspector Macdonald of 21 and 22 Aug. (GD 1/36/2(i)).

[2] There were also sporadic occupations of land in Tiree, and in the Outer Hebrides, though quite often they were not persisted with.

[3] Thus John Campbell, jr., of Hamaravirein in Glendale, claimed that he had bought beasts on the strength of a promise of land, and had been left stranded when the factor broke his word; he was perfectly prepared to pay rent; and he had been offered some kind of grazing for the beasts until he could sell them. The factor, of course, had a different story.

to the district, and believe that they are quite capable of resisting any other force.' This belief probably derived from the fact that deforcements in early April in Kilmuir and Glendale had (to the general surprise) been allowed to pass off with impunity. And it may explain some of the minor agrarian outrages and the threats of violence to the landlords' agents and partisans that now began to be reported (especially from Kilmuir). Some of these later proved to be fabrications—but they should not all be dismissed, for a number were implicitly confirmed by leading crofters in evidence taken the following year. Amongst other things the intention was expressed of forcibly taking Major Fraser's manager and two other men to a mass meeting and there demanding explanations and recantations. Major Fraser asked that they be protected, and nine policemen were sent to the estate. But, in accordance with a telegram from H.L.L.R.A. leaders in Portree, they were forcibly turned back on 30 October. This proved the last straw. The M.P. for Inverness-shire promptly cornered Harcourt, and the latter reluctantly agreed to send marines.[1]

The expedition to Skye and Tiree, with excursions to Lewis, went off less disastrously than Harcourt had anticipated—arrests were made, the crofters were frightened into withdrawing their beasts from the grazing they had occupied, and the news of the expedition may have made some impact in other areas. But on the whole it was a failure. For one thing information as to the marines' movements was systematically leaked to journalists and to H.L.L.R.A. leaders in Portree, and telegraphed on ahead: so when the force reached its destination it was apt to find the wanted men gone and the rest of the population drawn up in effusive welcome. Also Harcourt steadily refused to use the marines to protect the service of writs for the recovery of rent: the no-rent movement accordingly continued unabated—indeed in the course of 1885 it spread to most of the Islands, though (despite Macpherson's efforts) it was not widely adopted on the mainland. Lastly, against his better judgement, Harcourt allowed the marines to be scattered over the disturbed districts to protect the landlords' partisans. But the danger of outrage had been exaggerated, and the crofters' leaders were also anxious to stamp out such practices. Hence there was nothing for the marines to do except fraternize with the crofters (which led the latter into considerable doubt as to where exactly

[1] See (besides the sources already cited) the correspondence in GD 1/36/1(ii).

the marines and the Government stood). The landlords got tired of putting up their protectors, and came to want their shooting lodges for other purposes. So the force was ignominiously withdrawn amid a welter of recrimination.

It was not a happy precedent. But in August 1885 the new Conservative Home Secretary seemed nevertheless to be anticipating another expedition in November (when rents again fell due). However he distrusted Sheriff Ivory's judgement, and was afraid to give him control of troops. Ivory absolutely refused to appoint a co-adjutor, and the idea of sending a military force was dropped. In its absence Ivory would not protect the service of writs or risk arrests for political crimes, believing that the attempt might well lead to murder. In these circumstances the Skye landlords were reduced to taking a leaf out of their opponents' book, and declined to pay rates on rental they had not received; the crofters also stopped paying rates, though whether from poverty or unwillingness was debatable; and local government, education and poor relief on the island became decidedly precarious.[1]

The 1886 Liberal Government sought for the cure in legislation very much along the lines of the 1885 Bill. This passed without major alteration,[2] and provided for a Crofters' Commission to fix rents and arrears on application by landlord or tenant. While such rents were being determined, and provided they were paid thereafter, the tenant was safe from eviction and sure of compensation for improvements. The process of determining rents was bound to be a lengthy one, during which landlord–tenant relationships were likely to remain in limbo. But matters were not improved by the widespread belief that the Act was inadequate, and the consequent refusal of the Skye crofters to apply to the Commission for fair rents. This meant that they were still indulging in an illegal rent strike, and left them still liable for eviction at six months notice. What the

---

[1] The landlords did in fact guarantee loans for poor relief during the 1885–6 winter; but some schools had to close (*Parl. Deb.*, 3rd series cccv (April–May 1886), 1487).

[2] It is sometimes stated that the original Bill applied only to grazing and not to the crofters' arable holdings. This results from a confusion with the Bill's original provisions for the compulsory enlargement of holdings, which were broadened under pressure from Crofter and Radical M.P.s (but which had only been applied to 40,200 acres—mostly in Sutherland—by 1896). Otherwise the Bill went through fairly easily and substantially intact (*P.P.*, 1886 ii, pp. 117ff., 133ff., 151ff; see also *Annual Register*, 1886, pp. 83–5).

Liberal Government would have done about it is not clear: according to Argyll it had decided to enforce the service of writs for *rates*; but as far as the Inverness-shire authorities knew, it was still following the traditional line that it could give no assurances until they had 'shown by actually failing in the attempt that it is impossible to put the law into force, in the usual manner'. However in its closing moments it did send a large force of marines (backed by a major warship) to Tiree, where a Sheriff's Officer and police had just been deforced in the service of interdicts.[1]

The situation was transformed by the advent of Arthur Balfour to the Scottish Office. Probably after initial consultations with Macleod of Macleod, he suddenly summoned Ivory to London on 24 August, and sketched out proposals for the despatch of marines to Skye to protect the service of writs not only for rates but also for rents and removals.[2] They were to be followed by the Crofters' Commission, which should concentrate on fixing rents in the most disturbed areas. With Salisbury's backing, Balfour pushed these proposals through the Cabinet, and the expedition landed in Skye in early October. Led by Sheriff Ivory, it was conducted with a vigour that was widely claimed to border on brutality, and a tremendous clamour ensued—the high point was the unauthorized pounding of a baby as security for payment of rates;[3] and the story was told, albeit mistakenly, that Ivory instituted 'medals' for the reward of any constable who captured a crofter. Politically, though, the expedition was a success. For, despite a few scuffles, there was no bloodshed; the payment of rates was resumed; and, above all, the crofters had by 18 October been frightened into

[1] The preceding three paragraphs are principally based on the Ivory and Harcourt papers. See also e.g. Cab. 37/16/53 and 54, Cab. 37/18/44, Argyll to Balfour (23 Aug. 1886, B.M. Add. MS. 49800) and to Lothian (11 and 27 Jan. 1888, GD 40/16/35 fos. 24ff. and 27ff.).

[2] Military protection for the service of these writs was no novelty in Ireland. But they differed in kind from the purposes for which soldiers had previously been employed in the Highlands, being disputes not between the state and the subject but purely between private parties.

[3] He was valued at 6d., less than a collie also pounded at the same time: the baby was not, of course, taken away from his mother, but he qualified for inclusion in Macleod's *Highland Heroes* (p. 210). For the general question of outrages see the copy of Charles Cameron's *The Skye Expedition of 1886: Its Constitutional and Legal Aspects* (Glasgow, 1886), annotated by Ivory (GD 1/36/2(ii)).

applying for the protection of the Act they had recently despised.

This enabled Balfour to place increasing emphasis on conciliation—by the end of the month he was exerting his influence privately to stay proceedings for eviction, and by January 1887 he was taking a surprisingly tolerant attitude towards recent deforcements 'especially as the chief culprit seems to be an idiot'. Also he refused point-blank to mount another coercive expedition in January (the landlords having largely omitted to take advantage of the earlier one and now finding themselves on the verge of bankruptcy). Instead he preferred to rely on the determination of rent by the Crofters' Commission. This was a slow process, not substantially complete in Skye until 1889; and it was not without incident—Lord Macdonald at first refused to acknowledge the Commission's competence to interfere. But, in the end, rents were reduced by from 20 per cent on the Macleod estate to 39 per cent in Waternish, and from about half to three-quarters of the outstanding arrears were cancelled. In economic terms the reduction of arrears probably was a boon, though that of rent cannot have made much difference to the crofters. But politically the changes were far more important— the reductions were taken to justify the antecedent agitation,[1] and the new levels were accepted as being fair. The island thus gradually began to calm down.[2]

At first it seemed that the agitation had been checked in one place only to flare up in another. 1887 saw considerable trouble at Clashmore (near Lochinver in Sutherland), made dramatic by the ability of Hugh Kerr, the 'modern Rob Roy', to evade arrest for several months by taking to the hills: in fact trouble in Sutherland was largely localized to Clashmore, but by December the Duke's Commissioner was convinced that, if it was not firmly checked there, raids would break out on the Forest of Reay. They would have been imitations of the Great Deer Raid of Ballalan in Lewis in November 1887, which we have already encountered, and which was followed in January by the chasing of stock from, and the attempted occupation of,

---

[1] Various local disputes were also settled. That of Ben Lee was resolved in the crofters' favour, which partly accounts for the unusually large rent reductions accorded to the Braes.

[2] The preceding three paragraphs are based principally upon the Ivory Papers (esp. GD 1/36/1(iv)), the Balfour Papers (esp. correspondence with Ivory, Sir Francis Sandford, and Sheriff Brand, B.M. Add MSS. 49800, 49801, 49871), and the reports of the Crofters' Commission (*P.P.*, 1888 lxxx, 1890 lviii).

sheep farms at Aignish and Galson, near Stornoway. These last produced the tensest scenes of the whole movement, since not enough troops were sent to control the crowd, and there was a serious danger of their having to open fire. Not surprisingly Balfour's successor, Lord Lothian, was that month considering a memorandum which looked forward to an indefinite period of outbreaks in widely scattered districts, followed by the despatch of troops, the restoration of order, and then the repetition of the cycle when the troops were withdrawn; to meet this it was proposed to keep three to four gunboats and 300 marines on the west coast 'for a period of about a year at any rate and longer if necessary'.

However the memorandum proved unduly pessimistic. In fact the marines were withdrawn from Lewis in September 1888, and, to many people's surprise, they did not need to return. Indeed the catalogue of Lothian's papers contains no further references to disturbances after 1888. And the improvement can perhaps be explained. Already by the late summer of 1886 M'Neill had found the movement generally in decline. Now the most riotous areas (Tiree, Skye, Lewis) had been dealt with militarily: and the unusually heavy sentences of 9 to 15 months passed on the Clashmore and Aignish rioters may have served as a further deterrent (though the sudden death of the judge imme- diately after the Clashmore case rather spoilt the effect).[1] There was little to be gained from the Unionist Government by further rioting. And, on the other hand, the Crofters' Commission was directed to Lewis as it had been to Skye, the proprietrix, Lady Matheson, remarking that

were a *single township* even dealt with, the present discontent would be much allayed, and further the Factor fully believes the rents would begin to come in; at present they pay nothing and openly announce their intention of so acting until the Commissioners arrive.

Lastly there was a slow, but definite, improvement in economic conditions.[2]

---

[1] The Tiree rioters had received 4–6 months; no other sentence had exceeded two months, and most had been far lighter. (*P.P.*, 1888 lxxxii, pp. 1–8). The High Court in Edinburgh tended to sentence more severely; and the venue of the trial lay largely in the hands of the Crown.

[2] Lothian Papers, S.R.O., esp. GD 40/16/12–13 fos. 23–6, 33–4, 41–8, 62–9, GD 40/16/18 fo. 31; *The Old and New Highlands and the Hebrides*, pp. 115–28; *Highland Heroes*, p. 31.

Meanwhile the whole context of discussion was changing. The Napier Commission had not confined itself to land, but had also made recommendations on such topics as emigration, communications, harbours and fisheries. These featured prominently in the landlord meetings Harcourt had inspired in early 1885, but they were on the whole passed over—though the Liberal Government had allocated some money for fisheries, the extension of telegraphs, and a new mail service from Oban to Uist and Barra. Matters were given a new impetus when the Great Deer Raid attracted attention to Lewis: Sheriff Fraser and M'Neill were sent over, and in January 1888 reported sombrely (in fact too sombrely) that actual starvation had only been prevented by an unusually good potato crop, and that it was almost certain before the next season's became available:

... we should fail in our duty if we omitted to point out that the disaster which was averted by the growth of a new industry subsequent to 1851, must certainly befal the Lews, and that soon, unless either employment can be found for the inhabitants, or the population is greatly reduced.

And the message was rammed home in April by a very able memorial from the principal Highland landlords: this proved that (at least in the Outer Hebrides) there was just not enough land to go round, called for 'a well-planned scheme of [overseas] colonization by families' and for a Report on which to base a coherent scheme of public works; and it dumped the problem firmly into the Government's lap—

The day has passed when individuals can attempt to deal with poverty in the Highlands or to remove its causes. The events of the past, and the necessities of the present, and the dangers of the future are before your Lordship and the Government. The responsibility now rests with them ...[1]

Salisbury took the matter up personally with Lothian. The newly introduced scheme for assisted emigration to smallholdings in western Canada was expanded, and attempts were

[1] Landlords had earlier adopted a very similar attitude in the aftermath of the Destitution. In 1850 they had pressed chiefly for government assistance to emigration, which they obtained. But they also asked for special help with drainage (beyond the terms of the current Drainage Act) and 'that the government should extend to the proposed railway to Oban, assistance similar to that given to railways in Ireland'. (*P.P.*, 1851 xxvi, pp. 1093–6, and Prebble, *op. cit.*, pp. 211–18.)

made in 1888 and 1889 to recruit emigrants. However the project was a failure, and in 1899 the two Canadian settlements contained only some 250 people. The disappointment was due partly to the crofters' reluctance to emigrate (especially when the Highland Land League told them it was not necessary), partly to Government insistence that the scheme should be largely self-financing, and partly to a lack of capital that made it difficult for the emigrants to farm satisfactorily on arrival in Canada.

More came of the pressure for public works. In June 1889 Lothian made a lightning tour of the Islands, accompanied by an experimental trawler, and by a Royal Engineers Colonel who was to report on the proposals suggested. The tour was a great success. Ostensibly Lothian was on a non-political visit indicating only the Government's concern to do 'what they could to ameliorate the condition of the inhabitants'. So people of all persuasions felt free to co-operate—thus the 'Glendale Martyr' came on board to point out the best fishing banks in Loch Poltiel; and though some crofters' meetings and delegations still gave priority to the land question, all thanked Lothian for coming and made practical suggestions. This attitude was clearly more likely to produce results. And by November Chamberlain's protégé Alexander Morrison (of the Lewis Crofters' and Cottars' League) had come to praise the Government's public works as 'a generous measure', to explain that 'Lord Lothian . . ., when recently in the Lewis, stated that the present Government did not intend to interfere with the land question', and to conclude that 'there is no use occupying your attention with this subject meanwhile, and we had therefore better discuss the proposed railway and harbour scheme.'

Railway politics proved almost as engrossing as land reform, but less explosive. They also had the side effect of dividing the western Highlanders against themselves, depending on which railway line they expected to benefit from. The machinery of government (including another Commission) continued to grind on, and in December 1890 the Chancellor of the Exchequer was in a position to accept a package of £61,500 for capital works to improve fisheries, 'a modest measure' of telegraphic extension, and a steamer subsidy of £6–7,000 per annum for five years. The following March the Cabinet formally sanctioned negotiations for a new State-supported railway line from Garve to Ullapool (though in the end the route from Fort William to Mallaig was chosen instead).[1]

[1] *Parl. Deb.*, 3rd series cccii (Jan.–March 1886), 1319–20, ccciii

Meanwhile the crofters' movement gradually died away. In Morven, Argyllshire, for instance, the local branch of the Land League stopped meeting in 1889, and finally died in 1892. Elsewhere organization survived longer, but its social and political aspects became increasingly pronounced. For the 1886 Act had met all the crofters' basic demands, with the single—though major—exception of that for more land; and it was only a matter of time before they realized this. During the 1886 election campaign Angus Sutherland had denounced it as 'a landlord's bill both in conception and in the appointment of officials to carry [it] out . . . It was simply to help the landlords'; but a little over two months later, he found himself forwarding a petition (from Kilmuir crofters afraid of eviction) that described the Act as 'an instalment of justice', albeit 'not sufficient to remedy the grievances under which we suffer'. This line became increasingly common; by 1889 J. G. Mackay, while still maintaining that the distribution of the land was necessary, nevertheless conceded that 'the benefits secured under the Crofters' Act were great'. And in 1894 the now fairly moribund Land League was even ready to defend the Act against the criticisms of its erstwhile spokesman Dr. Clark.

The first test of the League's continued power came in 1890 with the elections to the new County Councils, which were said to have caused more excitement in the Highlands than in the rest of Scotland. But it was successful only in Sutherland, where 'Of the 19 elected members, 17 are Land Leaguers'; in Ross, on the other hand, the Land League candidates were 'severely defeated, to their own intense surprise and amazement, and to the gratification of sensible men'. Overall, individual crofters' leaders, and even crofters, were returned, but of more importance was a sharp swing back to the landlords—these formed comfortably the largest group on the Ross-shire Council and Sir Kenneth Mackenzie became Convenor; similarly Lochiel became Convenor of the Inverness-shire Council. And the pattern was broadly repeated at the 1892 elections.

By now the Liberals had returned to office at Westminster,

(March 1886), 165; *P.P.*, 1888 lxxx, p. 675, 1899 lxxviii, pp. 175–6; Lothian Papers, GD 40/16/24–5 fos. 2–11, 26–31 and *passim*, GD 40/16/29 fo. 2, GD 40/16/42 *passim; Liverpool Daily Post*, 5 Nov. 1889. Extraordinary government expenditure on development in Lewis was perhaps less in volume, but more productive in outcome, than that of the former proprietor, Sir James Matheson (*P.P.*, 1902 lxxxiii, esp. pp. 301, 340).

which might have been expected to revive interest in the land question. But it was buried under a Royal Commission, the so-called Deer Forests' Commission, appointed to schedule land suitable for the expansion of crofter holdings. This reported in 1895, scheduling some 1,200,000 acres, but the tottering Rosebery administration took no notice. And such dissatisfaction as this caused merely took the form of crofter abstentions sufficient to give the Unionists the otherwise safe seat of Inverness-shire. Land agitation was to revive in the Highlands from time to time. But its most important cycle was over.[1]

[1] Gaskell, *op. cit.*, p. 100; *Inverness Courier*, 25 June and 7 Sept. 1886, 31 Jan., 7 and 11 Feb. 1890, 9, 13 and 20 Dec. 1892; *The Scotsman*, 13 June 1889; *P.P.*, 1895 xxxviii, p. 22.

X
The Welsh 'Tithe War'

1886 was a bad year for outbreaks. While *The Times* was proclaiming that 'There is war in Tiree', the *Daily News* launched an account of the difficulties in Denbighshire under the equally sensationalist headline, 'The Tithe War in Wales'.[1] Superficially the two 'wars' were fairly similar. But though Welsh unrest took much the same outward form, it was handled differently and was accordingly far less successful.

Between 1880 and 1885 the Welsh land question and, still more, that of the disestablishment of the Anglican Church in Wales came to be worked intensively by journalists, preachers and politicians (often the same people). This may have led to individual refusals to pay tithe;[2] and in May 1886 Christ Church, Oxford was told that Nonconformist complaints on grounds of principle against payment 'have very much increased in the last year or two'. But tithes as such did not feature at the 1885 elections; and there seems no reason to doubt the finding of an Inquiry in 1887 that

The commencement of the disturbances . . . was contemporaneous with the agricultural depression which became acute when the price of stock fell in the years 1885 and 1886 . . .

The tithe rentcharge had been regularly paid up to the end of 1885, when the farmers demanded from the titheowners a reduction similar to that which they had received from the landlords. It was demanded as a matter of right, and when so demanded was refused. . .

There existed in Wales from old times a strong feeling amongst the Nonconformists that the tithes were improperly claimed and taken by the Church of England, and a desire has grown up . . . that they should be applied to some lay purpose for the benefit of the Nation. This feeling has arisen from causes partly religious, partly social, partly national, and partly political, and, although it had formerly been to a great extent passive, it became active and aggressive when the demand of the farmers for the reduction of the rentcharge had been refused.[3]

[1] *The Times*, 24 July 1886, p. 9; *Daily News*, 23 Aug. 1886, p. 3.
[2] The Tithe Commutation Act of 1836 had transferred liability for tithe to the *owner*, but in practice it was usual for the tenant to contract to pay it.
[3] Christ Church, MS Estates 50 fo. 1779; *P.P.*, 1887 xxxviii, p. 293.

Trouble seems to have started in January 1886 with occasional demands for tithe rebates, especially at Llandyrnog (Denbighshire). Here a delegation of large farmers asked the rector for a reduction, and he promised to speak to his agent about it; but when told the next day that nobody would pay without a rebate, he declined to act under duress. So no reduction was offered at the tithe audit, and the farmers therefore left in a body. Three subsequently volunteered to stand out and compel the rector to distrain on their stock, if the others undertook to compensate them. At this point, however, the rector saw his mistake, and started negotiating about rebates; so matters did not come to a point until the autumn. Moreover he was personally popular; and public attention was monopolized by the Home Rule question. So the disputes remained purely local.

The next half-year's tithes were due in late summer, and again there were sporadic demands for reductions. The critical confrontation came at the isolated and overwhelmingly Nonconformist village of Llanarmon-yn-ial. Here the rector came of fairly humble Dissenting stock; such men lacked social prestige, and were always suspected of having apostasized for personal gain. After receiving the usual notice that tithe was now due, his parishioners held a meeting and sent the rector a delegation that abruptly demanded a 25 per cent reduction in tithes; he refused, the tithe-payers resolved to stay away from the audit, and a solicitor was instructed to distrain on them. They therefore sent the rector a more conciliatory delegation, though there is a conflict of evidence as to whether they reduced their demand to 10 per cent. In any case the rector still refused, and the delegation withdrew shouting scriptural imprecations. A further meeting was then held, and a letter sent comparing the rector to Pharaoh, and telling him

... he was useless, had done no good in the parish, and was animated by a spirit contrary to that of our Saviour. They looked upon the agitation as a stepping stone to the disestablishment of the Welsh Church, and said that as he had appealed to Caesar (meaning the law) to Caesar he should go.

The usual procedure for the recovery of tithes from defaulters was to visit the farm in question and, if payment was still refused, serve a ten-day notice of intent to distrain. This would be followed by a second visit during which stock or agricultural produce sufficient to cover the liability would be 'seized': the seizures were usually left on the farm, often on trust but occasionally under the care of bailiffs. And a third visit would be made not less than a week later to sell them, generally by auction if their owner refused to buy them in beforehand.

This process was cumbersome at best, and it readily lent itself to disruption. For a bailiff had no right to force his way in, and farms might be so thoroughly fortified that he could not reach them. If he distrained on cattle, as was usual, these might be hidden when he returned to sell them; or large crowds might so chase them round the farm as to prevent his catching and bringing for auction the beasts he had distrained on. The auction would certainly be conducted in the face of a large and hostile crowd, and might well be broken up or the auctioneer otherwise intimidated. There could also be a general refusal to bid at the sales. And it could be made physically impossible to remove the stock from the farm. Lastly, when all these obstacles were overcome at one farm, it would be necessary to go through everything again at the next, in a hostile countryside where farms were widely separated and scattered around almost at random.

At Llanarmon the first distraints were made on 17 August. A month later three sales had been conducted successfully; on a fourth farm one cow had been sold, but the other could not be found; and on a fifth all sales had been prevented. 'The farmers calculate that if the agitation and the clerical reprisals go on as at present, it will take them with two enforced sales per week exactly five years to recover tithes already in arrears.' In fact tithes became legally irrecoverable after two years. And the eventual extraction of £30 from the five farmers in question cost the Rector about £100, for which he had to pledge his cows, pony and furniture as security.

This was a good beginning for the anti-tithe agitation, especially as events at Llanarmon were dramatic and continuous: in addition to repeated meetings, negotiations and demonstrations, bailiffs were driven out of the area; sales were attempted on four separate days, once in the presence of 40 and once of over 80 policemen; and the rector himself was briefly accorded police protection. All this was avidly and extensively reported by the press. Within a month farmers had 'almost unanimously struck against tithes' in four parishes (including Llandyrnog), and Llanarmon had become a name to conjure with: at Llantysilio a speaker declared that 'They admired the spirit in which their brethren at Llanarmon were fighting the battle, and they would most certainly follow their example unless very substantial reductions were made in the tithes.' The movement spread rapidly, though not universally, through North Wales, and was frequently successful in securing reductions of the order of 10 per cent.[1]

Of the parishes affected, we are perhaps best informed about Meifod in Montgomeryshire.[2] Here the tithes were divided between several owners, but the greater part was held by Christ Church, and most of the rest by the incumbent, Archdeacon Thomas. The disturbances at Llanarmon had occasioned discussion, and one of the churchwardens suggested that Meifod should follow suit. Also a large farmer, Joseph Richards, was asked by colleagues in a neighbouring market town to try to get something going in his parish. The upshot was a tithe-payers' meeting, attended by a landowner, Captain Mytton, and by Archdeacon Thomas. Thomas formed the impression that he constituted the principal target, and that Christ Church would be left till later.[3] So he undertook to do whatever Christ Church did in the way of rebate; and it was resolved to ask all the tithe-owners for a reduction of 10 per cent. Only one agreed, and this was felt to contrast unfavourably with the 15 per cent rent reductions given by many local landlords. Thomas urged Christ Church to concede, reminding it that the depression was real, and also that 'We who live among our people are placed in a more difficult position than yourselves . . .' But the college preferred to stand on the legal position that the tithe was the first charge on the produce of the land, payable 'so long as any margin of profit was left'.[4] This reply did not commend itself to the tithe-payers, and the issue continued to seethe over the winter, Captain Mytton organizing a further petition. Christ Church held firm; but Archdeacon Thomas eventually gave the

[1] *Daily News*, Aug.–Sept. 1886 *passim*; N(ational) L(ibrary) of W(ales), SA/Tithe/No. 75.

[2] My account is derived mainly from the Christ Church estate papers (MS Estates 50 fos. 1771–1843) and *Letter Books*, and from the *Inquiry as to Disturbances connected with the levying of Tithe Rent Charge in Wales* (*P.P.*, 1887 xxxviii).

[3] Though Captain Mytton is said to have spoken up for the local clergy, but to have suggested that Christ Church could well afford a rebate.

[4] The Tithe Commutation Act, 1836 had established this priority, and had reduced the sum receivable by tithe-owners to reflect the improved security of payment. The Act also related the sum payable in any given year to the average grain prices over the previous seven. And since grain prices fell ahead of stock in the 1880s, this meant that the level of tithe due in 1887 already reflected the agricultural depression that had only recently struck Wales.

rebate, confessedly because he would otherwise get no payment at all. The manner of this concession was not calculated to win popularity, and he made matters worse by his frequent letters to the press over the next two or three years.

Christ Church's February tithe was not well paid, and by April 1887 it was pressing its agent, David Owen, to distrain. Probably the college anticipated little difficulty—its Treasurer had remarked in March 1886 (though admittedly in an English context) that 'the recovery of Tithes is always possible by extreme measures.' However it was to be disappointed. There was some difficulty in finding auctioneers, since the usual ones declined to act against old friends, and the first substitute dropped out because his wife thought it too dangerous. Six distraints were made; but when Owen returned to check that the beasts were still on the farms he was hooted and prevented from doing so. His presence at the sales on 11 May was expected to cause trouble, and he avoided them. But a large crowd still assembled, and declined to permit the beasts to be brought out for auction. After trying at two farms, the auctioneer gave up.

Christ Church then pressed the county authorities strongly to provide proper protection, and 130 policemen were laid on (at a cost of £140) for a second attempt on 27 May. In addition all the eligible farmers were sworn in as special constables to keep them quiet. On 26 May the beasts were sold by private treaty to a Welshpool butcher, who was to drive them away if the farmers still declined to buy them back for the full value of the tithe. This would have been a serious matter, as they were worth considerably more than the tithe due. And at the second farm visited—the first settled in full—a crowd of about 800 yelled so ferociously that Christ Church's special representative called the whole thing off to avoid 'a running fight for the eight miles to Welshpool'. Other men might have been bolder, but both the Chief Constable and Edward Griffiths, a Calvinist methodist minister, thought he was wise. The butcher appears to have made a further attempt to repossess the beasts by night which created a great disturbance. He was told to keep his bailiffs away 'or their lives would not be safe'; and at the subsequent inquiry, Griffiths, Joseph Richards' son-in-law, was not prepared to discount the threat.

There followed considerable recrimination between the county authorities and Christ Church, which would have liked them to call in the military. But in fact there was some doubt as to the legal position. And one of David Owen's guarantors—Christ

Church's agents were 'bonded'—pulled out, probably for political reasons. It was late September before a replacement, G. D. Harrison, could be found. So the summer was passed in negotiations: the county authorities, and other would-be mediators, suggested compromises; one landlord paid on behalf of his tenants, another induced two of the six ring-leaders to pay by returning the 10 per cent rebate to them out of his own pocket; and Christ Church approached the Ecclesiastical Commissioners to make sure that the two bodies were proceeding along the same lines. On appointment Harrison pressed the college hard to allow some rebate, and it is possible that, but for the Ecclesiastical Commissioners, Christ Church would have done so. Instead it sent an unsuccessful appeal to Captain Mytton, suggesting that the landlords assume the payment of tithe in accordance with a current Government Bill. And Harrison proceeded to clear up the legal mistakes Owen had left, with a view to taking proceedings to recover any arrears outstanding in January 1888.

The county authorities had little sympathy with Christ Church's position, and the prospective Conservative candidate for Montgomeryshire was strongly opposed. So a neighbouring Unionist M.P. got the new Chief Constable's wife to write to the Home Secretary, and himself suggested that tithe was far too high. The Home Secretary passed the letters on to Christ Church with expressions of his anxiety as to 'the possible developments of this Tithe agitation in Wales'. But the college declined to be leant on, though it affirmed its readiness to make individual allowances in cases of *bona fide* poverty.

The other half of Major Godfrey the Chief Constable's strategy was an attempt to reduce the scale of confrontation at sales. This involved a sympathetic appeal to the farmers:—

I am fully aware that you have no wish to oppose the law (!) and are fighting for a principle (!!), and I hope that you will assist me in averting from the county the discredit of a lawful protest (!!!) being made the occasion of violence and lawlessness.[1]

In exchange for such assistance he undertook to bring only a token force of police to the sales. Instead he sought to enlist the assistance of dissenting ministers, professional men, radical gentry, and others whom he believed to have local influence:

it is only through the leading men that an impression can be made,

[1] I quote from the Dean of Christ Church's copy of the circular of 11 June 1888.

and then it has to filter down through the Farmers till it reaches the real rioters, the irresponsible farm labourers and others.[1]

This strategy came to be known as 'moral suasion', and, as we shall see, it was to enjoy a considerable vogue. By and large it proved successful in preventing serious trouble in Montgomeryshire. But at Meifod it proved a very near thing. At Godfrey's suggestion the sales were postponed until late August 1888, after the hay harvest. And, in the view of A. C. Humphreys-Owen, one of the 'leading men'[2] who attended to calm them down, it was a continuous strain keeping things within bounds and, at the last farm, touch and go. Only six out of 23 sales could be conducted; and the remaining 17 were highly problematic, since the leading men could not attend on every occasion, and 'Even if we did our influence would get stale or an accident would bring on a scuffle and then the mischief would be done.'[3]

Harrison himself believed that he would need more protection another time. And, probably for this reason, the actual collection under distraint was eventually entrusted to specialists from London, Messrs. Stevens and Peterson. These seem to have had a fairly easy time of it when finally they got round to Meifod in the summer of 1889. 26 farmers were now in arrears. But this time Major Godfrey and Martin Woosnam (a local solicitor who had long acted for the Anti-tithe League) persuaded them, much against their inclination, to insist on sales only at seven farms, and elsewhere to pay under protest at the distraint stage. All seven sales were carried through successfully in late July, though Peterson was knocked about a bit in the process. And a pattern was set, for the future, of merely token resistance.

By November 1889 perhaps seven-eighths of Christ Church's Welsh tithes had been paid in full.[4] Before selling up the remainder, an interview was arranged with the county M.P., Stuart Rendel, who was also Chairman of the Welsh Parliamentary Party; but, though Rendel found the Christ Church case unanswerable, there was no practical outcome. Meanwhile

[1] Major Godfrey to Stuart Rendel, 19 April 1890—N.L.W. MS. 19450 no. 201.
[2] A local squire, J.P., and railway director, he ran the Montgomeryshire Liberal Association, and in 1889 was to become chairman of the county council.
[3] A. C. Humphreys-Owen to Rendel, 24 Aug. 1888—N.L.W. MS. 19463 no. 449.
[4] They held tithes in five parishes, of which three seem to have given trouble at one time or another.

Humphreys-Owen had again been working to prevent trouble, and the sales were so timed that they could be carried through in three days. They met with no disturbances beyond some egg throwing.

Christ Church's success in recovering tithe seems to have diverted pressure back on to Archdeacon Thomas, who had in 1889 suspended his rebate as tithes now stood at 20 per cent below par. Accordingly he received only a third of the sum due;[1] and considerable trouble was anticipated in 1890 when he seemed about to distrain—there were rumours that 150 Birmingham police would come to help at the sale.[2] In fact Thomas seems to have restricted himself to an open correspondence with Joseph Richards, accusing him of breaking the rules of his sect by defaulting on his contract to pay tithe. The actual sales were held over until shortly after Christ Church's in December 1890: both were token affairs. In 1891 tithe activity in Meifod appears to have been confined to lectures. In April it was taken as a matter of course that the previous precedent of token sales (for Archdeacon Thomas) would be followed. And thereafter the topic seems to have faded from the local newspaper, the *Montgomeryshire Express*.

One point that emerges very clearly from the events at Meifod is the divergence of interests between local and external tithe receivers. Local receivers, like Archdeacon Thomas, might derive the greater part of their income from the tithe of the parish, and might not be in a position to risk losing the lot by insisting on payment in full. So rebates were quite widely conceded: it would seem that in the dioceses of St. Asaph and Bangor general rebates were given in nearly two-thirds of the parishes. Such rebates might be spontaneous—the incumbent of Gresford

felt so grateful to the tithe-payers for not having troubled me in 1886–7 when I was ill, and when there was difficulty in so many parishes, that I offered 10 p.c. reduction in 1887–8 simply as a token acknowledgement of their kindness.

And they might reflect the advice of the bishop: the rebate of 15 per cent at Llawr y Bettws 'was a mistake, but it was a sequel to an order from our late Diocesan's Charge at Corwen to treat tithe defaulters with all generosity . . .' But the most common pattern was of a 10 per cent reduction given at a

---

[1] 117 people were in arrears (N.L.W. SA/Tithes/147).
[2] R. Lloyd to Rendel, 5 April 1890 (N.L.W. MS. 19450 no. 201).

number of audits as a condition of securing the remainder: 'I found that the farmers were all unsettled, and that I should have a lot of trouble unless I gave the 10 p.c. So I feel *compelled* to give way.'[1]

Such concessions generally, though not invariably, resulted in satisfactory payment. There were cases, much publicized by the champions of the Church, where they were treated simply as a spring-board for futher demands;[2] but these were unusual. There was, however, a tendency for concessions to become general, farmers in one parish seeing no reason why they should not obtain as much as their neighbours. To a certain extent greater prosperity, and the continued fall through the sliding scale of the level of tithe payable, led to a reduction of demands in 1889. But attempts to discontinue rebates could lead to resistance, as at Llanelian and Llangwyffau. And in many parishes there were individuals or groups who obstinately declined to pay at all.

So it is possible that the level of tithe would have been permanently diminished but for the intervention of the nonresident tithe-owners. Their interests were often very different from those of residents. Christ Church, Stuart Rendel was told, 'depends to the extent of £24,000 a year on tithe. Concession of abatement in Wales would mean concession elsewhere.'[3] Of the £24,000 only a little over £2,000 came from Wales; and, though the college met with no open refusals in England, some of the delays in payment were too long and too repeated to be accidental. More important than the Oxford colleges were the Ecclesiastical Commissioners. We have seen that they played a major rôle in stiffening Christ Church's determination in 1887; and as they received nearly a fifth of all Welsh tithes their operations were fairly widespread. Lastly there was the Clergy Defence Association, formed in October 1886 as a counter to the Anti-tithe League. This claimed to draw principally on Welsh

[1] R. E. Prothero, *The Anti-tithe Agitation in Wales* (1889), pp. 16–17. The questionnaire on which his calculations for St. Asaph are based is preserved in the National Library of Wales (SA/Tithe/Nos. 1–207). My perusal of it makes me sceptical of the possibility of meaningfully tabulating the arrears, as Prothero seeks to do.

[2] At Cwm, according to the Dean of St. Asaph, 15% was extracted in 1886, 20% demanded in 1887, and the vicar 'was told frankly that it was the intention of the tithe-payers to ask for a reduction every year until nothing was left'—*The Times*, 7 Feb. 1838.

[3] Rendel to A. C. Humphreys-Owen, 19 Nov. 1889—N.L.W., Glansevern Collection, no. 470.

support, but by January 1887 it had supposedly received £5,000 worth of English subscriptions. It actively supported incumbents in resisting demands for abatement, but to what effect is not altogether clear—one vicar suggested that the Defence Fund of 1887 'was worse than wasted'.[1]

Both the Ecclesiastical Commissioners and the Clergy Defence Association started to distrain in 1886, and Christ Church joined them in 1887. They met with considerable resistance and often failed to achieve their object. By June 1887 police protection had been required at Meifod, Whitford (Flintshire), and Llanarmon, Llanfair, Pensarn, Llangwm, Bodfari and Mochdre (Denbighshire); at the last two places the police had been supplemented by soldiers, since the Chief Constable did not wish to borrow from other counties at that time of year. The trouble at Llangwm and Bodfari was fairly serious: and at Mochdre inadequate crowd control precipitated a scuffle in which 50 civilians and 34 policemen were injured. The upshot was an inquiry, before which the rights and wrongs of tithe and tithe-collection were fought out again.[2]

Partly for this reason, and partly because they vainly hoped that the question would be settled by legislation, the tithe-owners suspended operations for the rest of the year. They resumed in December to prevent tithe becoming two years overdue, and therefore irrecoverable. By now they were becoming increasingly professional, generally using Stevens and Peterson in place of local agents. Indeed the whole process became ominously like a campaign: in January 1888 in Flintshire 50 hussars, 50 police, and the 20 Irish 'emergency men' (in 'semi-military attire', and armed with batons and occasionally cutlasses) were engaged on the collection of some £300 to £400; the cavalcade might also contain carts and haycutters to remove the stacks distrained upon.[3] A distaste for such proceedings, and still more for the way in which Peterson had treated the police, led Major Godfrey to develop his new approach of conciliating the farmers to induce them to accept responsibility for the safety of the distraining party. More brusquely Major Leadbetter, the Chief Constable of Denbighshire, told Alun

[1] *P.P.*, 1894 lxiv, p. 959; 1896 xxxv, question 76164; Frank Price Jones, 'Rhyfel y Degwm', *Transactions of the Denbighshire Historical Society*, ii (1953), p. 91—I am indebted to Mr. Rhys Price Jones for translating this article; Stanley Leighton, M.P., to Lord Salisbury, 22 Jan. 1887 (Salisbury Papers, Christ Church); N.L.W. SA/Tithe/ 131.　　　[2] *P.P.*, 1887 xxxviii, esp. pp. 294–7.

[3] *The Times*, esp. 12, 16, and 19 Jan. 1888.

Lloyd, the solicitor for the Anti-tithe League, that he would prefer to leave the protection of the party to the farmers, but that he would act if necessary: he received the disquieting reply that all members of the League were of course 'in favour of law and order, but there is one thing to which they entertain the strongest aversion, and that is to pay their tithes without a "vigorous" protest.' And so it proved. Half the Denbighshire farms in arrears were visited without serious incident. But at Llanefydd the mob made proceedings impossible when two, and again when 12, policemen escorted Mr. Stevens. The following day 33 policemen returned, and were met and escorted by an enormous crowd. A scuffle led to general fighting, and the injury of 19 members of the crowd and two of the distraining party.[1] Matters were tense for the rest of the day; and on the next visit, though there was no violence, the work of the distraining party was effectively hampered. So Leadbetter applied for military assistance.

This seems to have constituted a turning point. The hussars proved unexpectedly popular—'They will give us fair play, and are too much men to knock us whilst on the floor': they were cheered repeatedly, and at one sale money was collected to give them a drink. The crowds dwindled and vanished at Llanefydd; this 'was attributed on the one hand to the presence of the military . . . On the other . . . to the counsel of the leaders, but which is the correct version we cannot vouch.' Certainly, after the collision at Llanefydd, Alun Lloyd enjoined the crowd to keep ten yards away from the nearest policeman, and himself walked between the two so as to be sure who was responsible for any future trouble. And the remaining farms in Denbighshire were safely visited. Thereafter the cavalcade proceeded into Anglesey, though on one occasion in that county even the presence of soldiers did not ward off a riot and the prevention of distraint.[2]

[1] A man who had been beating a tray next to Stevens' ear may or may not have struck him. Stevens grabbed the man, who raised his stick (in offence or in self-defence, depending on whom one believes). The crowd pushed forward to protect him and/or to attack Stevens, and may or may not have struck an emergency man. It was dispersed by the police with batons, but rallied, attacked the police and was routed.

[2] N.L.W. 19462 nos. 406–7; George G. Lerry, 'The Policemen of Denbighshire', *Transactions of the Denbighshire Historical Society*, ii (1953), pp. 131–3; *Denbigh Free Press*, 5 and 10 March, 12 May–7 July 1888.

By and large, however, it had been an impressive demonstration—615 farms had been visited in Denbighshire alone; and this must have reinforced the advice Alun Lloyd and others were coming to give, that so long as tithes were legally due they would have to be paid, albeit under protest. Also the unpleasantness of the whole business inclined all parties to seek to avoid confrontations. Major Godfrey pioneered the conduct of agreed token sales only; by June 1889 he could claim that his technique had been adopted in Cardiganshire, Denbighshire and Pembrokeshire; and Merionethshire followed suit later in the year.[1] This usually succeeded in calming matters down: by July 1889 the *Baner*, the mouth-piece of the anti-tithe agitation, admitted that distraints were causing less unrest than they had a year ago.

But 'moral suasion' was not a panacea—after further trouble at Llanefydd in 1890 the military were again called in.[2] And in Cardiganshire the policy served considerably to prolong the conflict. It was adopted after riots in 1889, when the police had disarmed 17 men of their pitch-forks by knocking them down, and, after being stoned in a narrow lane at the next farm, had cleared the hedges, cracking 50 heads in the process. The Chief Constable was somewhat abruptly dismissed—in Cardiganshire the elected county councillors controlled the new police authority through the casting vote of its chairman. For political reasons it proved difficult to agree on a replacement,[3] and the new Constable, Howell Evans, did not take over till 1891. Evans stuck to the policy of 'moral suasion' even after its abandonment by the neighbouring counties of Pembrokeshire and Carmarthenshire had brought resistance there to an end. And he played it according to rigid rules: he would personally accompany Lewis, the tithe-collector, and, if Lewis succeeded in getting foot in a farm-yard without pushing, would intervene to protect him. But pushing Lewis back, often roughly and with threats of personal injury, whenever he tried to leave the road, was legitimate. This attitude was re-inforced by a striking

[1] Flintshire did not, and there were a number of disturbances in the autumn of 1889.

[2] The decision to do so was retrospectively criticized by an inquiry of the county's Standing Joint Committee, chaired by Thomas Gee (T. Gwynn Jones, *Cofiant Thomas Gee* (Denbigh, 1913) p. 492).

[3] The Standing Joint Committee would not have a churchman; and two of its proposed candidates were vetoed by the Home Secretary.

reluctance on the part of magistrates to convict on charges of assault; and the result was a fairly localized back-log of 100 to 200 unenforced court orders for the payment of tithe. Asquith, the Home Secretary, began to take an interest in mid-1893, and in 1894 he insisted on more substantial police protection. There followed renewed attacks on the police, and the Chief Constable had to recommend borrowing from other county forces. Asquith enforced this by threatening to withhold the police grant. And, in the summer of 1895, resistance to tithe collection ceased in the face of 75 policemen, though litigation dragged on for another four years.[1]

Asquith's was the first direct intervention of any consequence on the part of the central Government. The Conservative administration in 1886–92 had accorded the local authorities military aid on demand, but had largely left them to handle matters themselves. The only exception was its intervention in the trial of 31 Llangwm rioters, which was transferred from magistrates to the Assizes, and which it sought to transfer to Queen's Bench in 1887, presumably as a political demonstration. In general, though, the Government tried to resolve the problem through legislation, but did so with a singular, and perhaps uncharacteristic, incompetence.

Admittedly the task was not easy. The Church was desperate for a transfer of tithe liability from tenants to landlords and for a more satisfactory way of enforcing payment; but, especially at first, it grudged any reduction in the amount payable. However such a reduction, or 'equitable adjustment', was strongly demanded by the arable south-east of England, which had suffered most from falling prices. This 'agricultural interest' constituted an important section of the Government's majority, and parts of it were in touch with such extreme Welsh M.P.s as Thomas Edward Ellis. Another important group, the Liberal Unionists, were ambivalent towards the whole question. The Welsh were predictably hostile.[2] And despite Gladstone's goodwill, Harcourt threw his weight strongly into the opposite scale: he wished to stake his claim to the reversion of the Liberal leadership, he was worried about the possibility of alienating the Welsh, and he was anxious to drive a wedge between the

[1] *Montgomery Express*, 4 and 25 June 1889, 3 June and 23 Dec. 1890; 'Rhyfel y Degwm', p. 95; N.L.W. 19450 nos. 197–201; Prothero, p. 23; Rev. R. Lewis, *The Tithe War in West Wales* (N.L.W. 15321), *passim*.

[2] Though in 1889 they were partly restrained by their desire for the passage of the Intermediate Education Act.

Conservative county members and the tenant farmers. Lastly the Government's whole legislative programme was heavily overloaded, and was facing systematic opposition.

All things considered, the first attempt in 1887 was over-optimistic: it provided for the transfer of liability from tenant to landlord, for the enforcement of payment by County Courts, and for the compulsory redemption of tithe. In introducing it, Lord Salisbury admitted that he was not certain it could pass into law that session; and, despite a last minute attempt to restrict its scope, it was duly dropped. Salisbury's revised proposals of 1888 fared no better. In 1889 an avowedly interim measure, confined to the enforcement of payment, was hopelessly mismanaged; and though the Home Secretary wrote that 'almost any sacrifice of tithe which the party will bear is preferable to the discredit of abandoning' the Bill, its withdrawal was forced by a procedural device. Next year the Bill was again altered, this time to conciliate the agricultural interest whose cavalier neglect in 1889 by an urban Home Secretary and Attorney General had moved Harcourt to great glee. But it still ran into trouble; and it was caught up in a general back-bench revolt that led the Cabinet to over-rule Salisbury and jettison the entire legislative programme. The proposals of 1891 favoured the tithe-owner less than any of their predecessors, and they were given absolute priority. So at long last they were carried into law, though shorn of the sanction of imprisonment.[1]

The new Act left much to be desired. It scarcely touched the method of calculating the tithe payable, and so had to be amended in 1918 and 1925. More seriously it did not much improve the machinery for distraining on obdurate landlords or owner-occupiers. This was part of the explanation of the long continuance of the agitation in Cardiganshire, where small freeholders were common.[2] It also left the door open for a quite extensive revival of the tithe question in the early 1930s in

---

[1] Viscount Chilston, *Chief Whip* (1961), pp. 179–82, and *W. H. Smith* (1965), esp. pp. 257–60; A. G. Gardiner, *op. cit.*, ii, pp. 109–12; Lady Gwendolen Cecil, *Life of Robert Marquis of Salisbury*, iv (1932), pp. 153–6; *Annual Register, sub anno; Parl. Deb.*, 3rd series cccxii (March 1887), 1458; Matthews to Salisbury, 16 Aug. 1889, and Hicks Beach to Salisbury, 16 Nov. 1890 (Salisbury Papers).

[2] Like the Caernarvonshire quarrymen, they could also complain that tithe had been capriciously apportioned between the various small-holdings and that liability for it had 'often been kept somewhat in the background' at the time they bought them.

parts of eastern and southern England (and to a lesser extent in Wales).[1] Still, for the time being, the 1891 Act seems to have put an end to disturbances in most of Wales. And there can be no doubt that the delaying of legislation for five Parliamentary sessions had considerably prolonged the agitation.

In the meantime the Church turned to the landlords for relief. Sometimes it sought to bully them—in the winter of 1887–8 the Clergy Defence Association tried distraining (under a little-known section of the 1836 Act) on the land itself rather than on the tenant's property; but to no great purpose. More usually landlords were merely begged to intervene, or warned that if the attack on tithe were successful one on rent would follow immediately. Their reaction was mixed. Some saw no reason to get their fingers burnt in a quarrel that did not directly concern them. Others had no sympathy with the Church and regarded tithes as undesirable, or at least untenable, imposts: a conference at Rhyl in 1889 carried a resolution that Wales needed not so much a Tithe as a Church Discipline Bill to provide a cheap way of reforming abuses.

But many landlords took a different attitude. Prothero believed that, in two-thirds of the cases in North Wales where tithes were paid without arrears or abatements, the landlords were responsible. Their simplest course was to re-assume liability for the payments of tithe—where this was done without any corresponding increase in the rent, wrote Archdeacon Thomas somewhat naïvely, all had been quiet; he mentioned Lord Penrhyn in this context, and might have mentioned the Marquis of Anglesey. Few landowners could afford to be so generous; but a fair number renegotiated the liability for tithe with or without

[1] This was triggered by falling prices (which since 1925 no longer reduced the level of tithe). They were felt particularly by former tenants who had, as was quite common, bought their holdings too dearly in the immediate aftermath of the War. Resistance to tithe was not, perhaps, as tense as during the Welsh Tithe War, but both sides used the same methods. And the situation was not improved by the interventions of Mosley's Blackshirts. Matters eased with agricultural recovery, but the Government had to take up the question again. In 1936 it bought out the tithe-owners with gilt-edged stock, and partially recouped itself by continuing to collect tithe at a reduced rate for a further 60 years. This appears to have succeeded in putting 'an end to a secular controversy'—Royal Commission on Tithe Rentcharge in England and Wales, *Report* (*P.P.*, 1935–6 xiv) esp. Part I, and *Minutes of Evidence* (1934–5); *Annual Register*, 1934 and 1936; Colin Cross, *The Fascists in Britain* (1961), p. 107.

concessions to the farmers,[1] and others simply paid when their tenants defaulted and recouped themselves through the rent. Others again preferred to bring pressure to bear on the tenants to compel them to pay: 'Mr. Heskett only allows an abatement on the rent to tenants producing their last tithe receipts, a perfect antidote.' And the questionnaire on tithe arrears in the diocese of St. Asaph asked the incumbents to list not only the names of defaulters but also those of their landlords. Not everyone thought it would be helpful to report defaulters in this way, but the method obviously had considerable possibilities:

I never had any trouble from Sir Watkin's tenants, but some of Mr. West's tenants have been for years ring-leaders of the Anti-tithe League, and I have given him a list of their names, and since then they have been a little more reasonable in their demands for abatement.

So it is not surprising to find comments like 'Through Landlord influence opposition [to tithe] is decreasing.'[2]

Prothero attributed the success of such stands by landlords to the fact that 'The tenancies are for the most part yearly, and in Wales, whatever may be the case in England, no difficulty is experienced in letting land at present rentals.' At least one landlord gave his tenants notice to quit, and then relet their holdings to them with the tithe merged in the rent. But there were, at most, only four cases where coercion was pushed to the extreme of eviction. And when Nathaniel Watkin did so lose his holding, probably as a result of pressure from the rector of Manafon (near Meifod), he managed to find another farm in the neighbourhood, and continued active in the local agitation. Other farmers, like Joseph Richards, the Meifod ring-leader, merely defied their landlords with impunity. Nor, of course, did all landlords actively intervene against the agitation; at Meifod only two are supposed to have done so, while Captain Mytton actively encouraged it. In any case some tithe-payers had no landlords.[3]

[1] They included, according to Prothero, 'several of the largest landlords in Wales'.

[2] *Daily News*, 23 Sept. 1886, p. 3; *The Times*, esp. 1 Dec. 1887 and 16 Jan. 1888; *Montgomeryshire Express*, 10 Dec. 1889, p. 3; Prothero, p. 17; N.L.W. SA/Tithe/esp. nos. 26, 59, 73, 80, 97, 193, 207.

[3] Prothero, pp. 29–30; *P.P.*, 1896 xxxiv, p. 538; N.L.W. MS. 19462 nos. 341, 344; N.L.W., Glansevern Collection, Rendel to Humphreys-Owen, 11 April 1887; *The Times*, 1 Dec. 1887, pp. 13–14; *Montgomeryshire Express*, 4 Dec. 1888, 23 Sept. 1890.

So the decline in agitation that was widely, though not universally, observed in 1889 must have been due to other causes besides landlord pressure. One was certainly the recovery of prices towards the end of the decade. Another was probably boredom: in one parish we are explicitly told that the 'labouring population', in another that the farmers themselves, were tiring of the agitation. Some farmers may also have been a little worried by the violence they had unleashed. Humphreys-Owen thought this to be the case in Meifod in 1887; and Cornwallis-West, M.P. for West Denbighshire, believed that many tithe-payers, though still insisting on sales, were 'strongly averse to the assembly of mobs'. Events in Flintshire and Denbighshire in 1888 must have strengthened these fears, and also have shown that violence could not always prevent the recovery of tithe. Such factors presumably assisted the adoption of Major Godfrey's 'peaceful policy', even though it meant that tithe would in fact be paid.[1]

So it probably seemed in 1889 that, if the agitation was to be kept going, it would need some political stimulation. Hitherto it had in fact been largely local. Admittedly this was not always realized. For the movement was assiduously puffed by the leading Welsh-language newspaper, Thomas Gee's *Baner*. And Gee's circle had set up first a 'League of those oppressed by the tithes' in 1886, and then a 'Welsh Land, Commercial and Labour League' the following year. Many people therefore saw Gee as 'the responsible source and cause of the troubles which have agitated Wales during recent times': the authorities vainly translated the *Baner* in the hopes of finding material for a prosecution; and at least one clergyman wrote a grovelling letter to Gee imploring him to persuade his parishioners to accept a $7\frac{1}{2}$ per cent rather than a 10 per cent rebate.[2]

But, in my opinion,[3] a closer look suggests that, despite Gee's undoubted prestige, the real centres of decision were more local. For in some areas, like Meifod in 1887, the agitation deliberately did not affiliate to the central Anti-tithe League. And the 1888 report of the Welsh Land League claimed only that in the previous two years over 300 of its farmer members had been distrained on; yet, as we have seen, 615 farms were visited in Denbighshire alone in 1888. Indeed the unusual violence of

---

[1] N.L.W. SA/Tithe/nos. 63, 76; N.L.W. MS. 19462 no. 370; *The Times*, 15 July 1887, p. 5.
[2] *The Times*, 6 Oct. 1887, p. 13; 'Rhyfel y Degwm', p. 97; N.L.W. 8306 fo. 97.
[3] For another view see 'Rhyfel y Degwm', esp. pp. 97–102.

Llanefydd in that year was attributed to the people's greater independence of the anti-tithe officials. Humphreys-Owen was quite clear

That the idea of an organization existing which could be controlled by me or anyone else was nonsense; that the movement was spontaneous and the only connection between different parts of Wales where it had taken place was one of general sympathy . . .

This was perhaps a slight exaggeration. For the League recompensed its members for financial losses incurred by insisting on sales. Its representatives attended most sales, and also the Commission of Inquiry into the 1887 disorders. It offered legal advice and assistance. But it clearly declined to advise local branches on what rebates to claim from the tithe-owners. And though its officers, and particularly John Parry of Llanarmon, its president, went on speaking tours, their reception varied sharply from parish to parish, and could on occasion be extremely hostile.[1]

Before 1889 such backwardness met with little but journalistic rebukes and exhortations to follow the example of Tal, Llangwm and Clwyd. But a certain unrest was apparent among southern Welsh politicians. By May 1889 Gibson of the Aberystwyth *Cambrian News* was accusing the Liberal leaders of killing the tithe movement in Montgomeryshire with flowery speeches. And in July the Secretary of the South Wales Liberal Federation urged on Rendel 'an Anti-tithe Relief Fund to indemnify farmers who are sold up for principle'. The South Wales Federation continued to force the pace, and was joined by Gee, who had hitherto rather ostentatiously kept his League independent of the Liberal Federation. The question was considered at a joint meeting of the North and South Wales Federations' executives at Llandrindod on 3 September. Here Gee secured a formal commitment to the idea of paying tithe only under compulsion, and the appointment of a committee to frame rules for resistance. But he did so only by undertaking privately that assistance should be confined to selected tenants. Also the committee was dominated by moderates, and the rules themselves would have to be submitted to constituency associations before they were adopted.

Humphreys-Owen was nevertheless worried. We find him writing to Rendel that, if they were 'to go in earnest into the

[1] *P.P.*, 1887 xxxviii, pp. 299–300, and 1896 xxxiv, pp. 174–5; *Oswestry and Border Counties Herald*, 16 March 1887; *Denbigh Free Press*, 19 May 1888; N.L.W. 19462 no. 406.

business', they would have to take advice on the law of conspiracy and maintenance; he also suggested that he and Rendel faced the alternatives of guiding the movement, however unpalatable, or watching it pass into other hands that would either eclipse them or plunge it into violence. But he need not have been so concerned. Gee had over-reached himself and his son Howel made matters worse through impatience. The moderates rebelled, and Gee suffered a series of stinging rebuffs from the North Wales Federation. As North Wales was the home of the tithe agitation, that was more or less the end of the affair; Gee's League was wound up without any real replacement.[1]

But opposition to tithes had been only part of a much larger movement that encompassed many causes. Chief amongst these was probably the Disestablishment of the Anglican (or 'alien') Church, with which went a drive to expand and secularize education and to develop a Welsh university. But disestablishment was often run close by the 'land question', the attempt of hard-pressed tenant farmers to unload some of their economic burdens and, with the slogan 'the land is stronger than the lord', to escape from what many perceived as the tyranny of the landlord and his agent. Arising out of, and also inspiring, these campaigns was a vague cultural and political nationalism articulated by the *Cymru Fydd* (or 'Young Wales') societies. So the Principality remained full of combustible material. And indeed the economic respite, afforded by the 1889–90 recovery of agricultural prices, proved only temporary. Unrest therefore continued; but the failure of the tithe agitation showed that further progress could come only from politics, not from direct action.[2]

This had always been Humphreys-Owen's feeling—as he told Rendel, 'Welsh farmers cannot play the Irish game there are too few of them they are not united enough and they are too close to striking distance of the party of law and order.' Rendel viewed himself 'as pioneer of the conversion of Liberal Cabinets to the cause of Wales'. A personal friend of Gladstone's, he was not unnaturally determined to work within the Liberal Party. And by December 1890 he claimed to have achieved 'the treaty of Wales with the English Liberal Party under which that

[1] N.L.W. MSS. 8306 fos. 121, 130, 19451 no. 237, 19463 esp. nos. 484, 498, 505, 509–17, 19464 no. 521; *South Wales Daily News*, esp. 4 and 17 Sept. 1889; Prothero, p. 25; *P.P.*, 1895 xl, p. 324.

[2] The lesson was perhaps underlined by the passage in 1889 of the Welsh Intermediate Education Act, which went far towards establishing a system of non-denominational secondary education.

Party has guaranteed Wales the 2nd place in the General Liberal Programme'.

The Welsh opportunity came with Gladstone's assumption of office in 1892; and the Welsh M.P.s unanimously resolved that Disestablishment should have that second place. Rendel was later to claim he had never believed that Disestablishment was attainable; he was concerned with it only as 'a clear and effective issue with all Anglicizing influences in Wales, and a practical declaration of the case for Welsh Nationalism[1] outside Wales'. And he was content simply to see a *'Government* Bill on the Stocks and in its due place in the Government programme'. After some involved politics he was to have this satisfaction. But other M.P.s were less tolerant of governmental delays; and Lloyd George's intrigues (over the management of the property the Church was to lose) played a significant part in bringing down the Rosebery Government. Still the Liberal Party had been irrevocably committed to Disestablishment. And once the fatal obstacle of the Lords veto was removed in 1911, it returned to the task—symbolically Lloyd George kept a portrait of Thomas Gee in the hall of 11 Downing Street.[2] The outbreak of the 1914–18 War further delayed things, but he finally piloted a measure through in 1919. Some of the participants in the anti-tithe agitation had regarded it as 'a stepping stone to disestablishment and disendowment of the Church'; and their hopes were thus eventually fulfilled.

The same cannot be said of the land question. This had fewer connections with the anti-tithe agitation than had Disestablishment—indeed efforts were initially made to keep the two distinct. But both intimately concerned farmers, and both tended to be worked by the same people at the same time: in Flintshire, for instance, the Holywell Farmers' Club and the Whitford Anti-tithe League were interlocking bodies. And in 1887 Gee merged the Tithe League into the Welsh Land, Labour and Commercial League he had always wanted.

Though Ellis and Bryn Roberts had brought the land question up quite often in the preceding Parliaments, the Welsh demand in 1892 was not for action but for a Royal Commission on the Irish or crofting model. Gladstone was unenthusiastic, partly because he did not like the analogy, but also because Royal Commissions had many deficiencies, not least the time they took. Instead he suggested a more expeditious Select Com-

---

[1] Literally 'Nationalisation' (F. E. Hamer, *The Personal Papers of Lord Rendel* (1931), pp. 305–6).

[2] H. Du Parcq, *Life of David Lloyd George* (1912), p. 73.

mittee. Rendel, who was never very keen on the land question, would have accepted this; but he was overborne. In part it was simply a question of status. However Ellis also stressed that only a Royal Commission could travel round Wales and take evidence on the spot. And his correspondents seem to have looked to the preparation of such evidence as both an occasion and a tool for the 'working' of the countryside.[1]

They got their reward. A Commission was appointed, and it took six volumes of evidence, which had a valuable purgative effective on rural discontent. But it did not report until the Liberals had fallen from office; bulk apart, its conclusions were unimpressive; and it split predictably along political lines on the crucial recommendation of judicially determined rents. The Conservatives ignored it. And by the time of their demise in 1905 the real return of prosperity had buried the agitation. Unlike the traditional religious issues, the Welsh land question was scarcely mentioned at the 1906 elections. Lloyd George admittedly remained acutely conscious of a land problem, but he no longer approached it on a purely Welsh basis. And the War supervened before his massive Land Inquiry Committee could lead to any practical results.[2]

[1] N.L.W. 8308 fos. 265, 276, 19462 no. 396; Thomas Edward Ellis Collection, esp. nos. 820, 1268, 1402, 1404; *Cofiant Thomas Gee*, p. 575; *P.P.*, 1887 xxxviii, pp. 419–21.
[2] For a fuller treatment of the topics touched on in the last five paragraphs, see K. O. Morgan, *Wales in British Politics 1868–1922*, esp. chaps iii–iv.

XI

Ideas and Arguments—
Farm Servants

Of the early nineteenth century protest movements discussed in Chapter II, none was coherently organized; and only the Rebecca Riots (or rather the public meetings into which these developed) were in any real sense articulate. For the remainder, we can only reconstruct their participants' beliefs from their actions, and from the threatening letters and appearances in court that Dr. Peacock has utilized. By the second half of the century all this had changed. Rural protest was now sufficiently open to seek to enlist the support of public opinion, and its leaders were educated and self-confident enough to do so by speaking and writing at some length. Nor, generally, did they lack outside assistance—indeed the crofters in the 1880s and the English agricultural labourers in the 1890s had it positively thrust upon them. Lastly the local press was now more voluminous than ever before or since. So, though there are many pitfalls, it is perhaps possible to analyse more closely the concepts and arguments put forward, and worth doing so for the light they shed on the general evolution of nineteenth-century political culture.

In this chapter we shall be concerned with the Scottish and English farm servants, and in subsequent ones with the crofters and the Welsh anti-tithers. But two common features are perhaps worth noting at the outset. First the importance of singing: most contemporary accounts of the English agricultural labourers print, and give considerable prominence to, the songs they so regularly sang at meetings to popular or hymn tunes;[1] the Highland Land Law Reform Association soon came to reinforce its attractions with 'social meetings' resembling ceilidh's, and in Mary MacPherson it came to possess something very like an official bard; and the Welsh tithe sales were often enlivened by the singing either of hymns or of specially commissioned and rather scurrilous 'anti-tithe ballads'.[2]

[1] For examples, see e.g. Howard Evans, *Songs for Singing at Agricultural Labourers' Meetings* (London and Leamington, no date). It should, of course, be remembered that most villages of any size had their band, and that these bands played a far greater role in community life than their successors do today.

[2] In Ireland, too, scarcely a Land League meeting 'came off in the

More wide-spread still was the influence of religion. The various movements may have operated in very different contexts, but they all drew arguments and imagery from the Bible. This should not altogether surprise us; for, in Olive Anderson's words, 'The temptation to claim the primacy of religious and historical ideas over political and economic ones in mid-nineteenth century politics . . . probably ought not to be resisted, except where the . . . élites are concerned'.[1] And even at governmental level the direct intervention of the Almighty in terrestrial events was more frequently seen than it is today. But as the century wore on, other arguments came to supersede the religious at least in economic questions. In 1839–46 the case against the Corn Laws had been deliberately presented as religious even more than commercial, but in the early twentieth century such dialectic was seldom invoked either for or against Tariff Reform. So it is significant when we find our agitators resting their position heavily on divine or biblical authority, as, for instance, 'Land Reform Justified: THE BIBLE AND THE LAND QUESTION', Chapter I of Joseph Macleod's *Highland Heroes of the Land Reform Movement*.[2]

The earliest movement which falls to be considered here was that of the Scottish farm servants in the 1860s. Its most vivid portrayal is afforded by some reminiscences of Greenlaw written shortly after the First World War. There, we are told, the bondage grievance was ventilated at a public meeting. The chair was taken by a gentleman, and the schoolmaster also said a few words. But the labourers themselves provided the chief speakers.

The bulk of their imagery and appeal was almost entirely from Holy Writ; no reference whatever being made to writers on econo-

---

West or South which had not its singer with some "lament" of a hero of agrarian repute, or a versified malediction upon an evictor or other obnoxious enemy of the cause'—Michael Davitt, *The Fall of Feudalism in Ireland*, p. 166.

[1] 'The Political Uses of History in Mid Nineteenth-Century England', *Past and Present*, xxxvi (1967), p. 87.

[2] Macleod (who had personally participated in the agitation of the 1880s) remarks that 'there are many who try to escape from the teaching and force of Old Testament Writ, by saying we are not under Moses—an excuse which I claim should have little weight in a country where the Fourth Commandment has been applied so rigorously to the first day of the week' (p. 9).

mics, probably for the very good reason that they knew nothing of them. They knew, however, the economics taught in Deuteronomy, which, after all, was a very good text book with its restrictions and prohibitions against harsh or unjust treatment.

The principal orator . . . was a hind . . . named Johnston. If oratory is the art of persuasion and conviction of the audience, Johnston was entitled to take the first place. His presentation of the case, marshalling of the facts personal and pointed illustrations, and his concluding appeal to the Supreme Tribunal was most powerful and dramatic. . . . The appeal was further increased by a humorous, though unconscious, touch. Proceeding step by step in denunciation of the bondage system he would, at the end of each in solemn tones, ask, 'And what does the Lord our God say to that?' This he would answer in an apt Biblical quotation. The effect was electric, and through the mist of years I see the old schoolroom, the crowded building, the excited figures roused to an enthusiasm almost as wild as followed the appeals to liberty, equality, and fraternity, made in the cafes of Paris in the time of the Revolution. But there was this difference: the enthusiasm of the gathering in the Free Church School was inspired by the belief in an All Wise Providence in place of the phantasm of a Goddess of Reason.[1]

This quotation has a somewhat archaic feel. And the impression is heightened by the fact that the Scottish farm servants' movement was unique in having no political overtones at all. For it antedated the great expansion of the electorate by the Second Reform Act, and political involvement on the part of the farm labourers was, as yet, inconceivable.

But this does not mean that the movement was out of touch with its times. It was perfectly possible to combine a Biblical frame of reference with a surprisingly mundane approach to the questions at issue. Thus one correspondent of the *Haddingtonshire Courier* began his letter by ascribing the current outbreak of rinderpest to the Lord:

'Behold the hand of the Lord is upon thy cattle, upon thy oxen, and upon thy sheep;'[2] and so it is, whether it be murrain or rinderpest. Surely, then, there is a cause; and why may it not be oppression? . . . 'For the oppression of the poor, and the sighing of the

[1] *Berwickshire News*, 28 Aug. 1923, p. 4.
[2] Exodus 9 : 3—the same text was chosen later in the year by Canon Girdlestone for his celebrated sermon denouncing the farmers in his congregation and inaugurating a policy of raising rural wages in Devon by encouraging migration to Lancashire.

needy, now will I arise, saith the Lord.' And who doth not see that the Lord hath risen!

But the letter goes on immediately to deprecate a strike, favouring instead a deputation to talk things over with the farmers; it continues with a balanced discussion of methods of payment, assumes a two shilling a week rise in wages, and argues that the farmers would in fact find this cheaper than trying to make do with inferior hands.

The second half of this letter reflects another facet of the farm servants' movement, the reasoned appeal to the masters' generosity. As a leader in the *Haddingtonshire Courier* put it,

So far as the agitation has proceeded here, it has altogether been confined to our own columns . . . The hinds of this county . . . have no desire to combine for the purpose of forcing up the price of their labour. They have hitherto refrained from getting up meetings, at which irritating language, if we may judge from what has taken place in Midlothian, would be most likely to be indulged in, and are seemingly content to throw themselves on the generosity or justice of their masters, in the hope that an appeal so made will be generously responded to.

The leader then proceeded to discuss the merits of the men's case, and concluded that 'there would be a general feeling of satisfaction throughout the county should the farmers next Friday see their way to make the small advance of wages now so respectfully requested.' This hope was largely realized. And one hind, perhaps the writer of our earlier letter, expressed his satisfaction with the labourers' tactics. For a 'strike' would only have injured the more honourable men, who would have been left stranded when others backed out and took the first opportunity of hiring themselves. But 'the letters have done good; for this reason, the farmers see we have been asking nothing amiss, and they have opened their hearts and given us more. So I hope all the hinds will agree with me in returning thanks to them for their kindness.'[1]

Such an attitude may seem dangerously meek. But there was, in fact, quite a lot to be said for it. The nineteenth-century countryside was strongly hierarchical—as somebody wrote of the suggestion that both masters and men should be obliged to furnish certificates of good character at the hiring fairs:

There would be superior and inferiors as to social position as long

[1] *Haddingtonshire Courier*, 26 Jan. 1866, pp. 2–3, 9 Feb., p. 3.

as the world lasted, and it would be reversing the law of nature for masters, who are superiors, to bring certificates to servants.

In such a society abusive language was frequently, perhaps even usually, counter-productive. And this was sometimes stated quite plainly: 'With the view of making the movement generally successful', the chairman of one meeting advised his audience to seek 'to preserve those feelings of harmony and friendship which had hitherto existed between them and their masters.' Many subsequent movements realized the wisdom of this advice; but few were as successful in moderating their tones.[1]

But that farm servants should speak out at all was something of a novelty, and reflected a growing sense of their own value. Thus one writer to the *Haddingtonshire Courier* praised those farmers 'who spoke so well of us as a class at the late Farmer's Club meeting', but commented that others were too free with 'talk of "foggies" and rubbish amongst us . . . it would be better if there were more kindness shown, even if it were but a smile—for I have seen that alone turn what they call rubbish to good advantage.' Another correspondent expressed concern about the *relative* status of agricultural labour, observing that 'Although we poor hinds are an honest hard-working respectable looking class of men, still we are degraded by all other trades-men. They seem to think that we poor hinds are so ignorant that they [sic] know nothing—they have scarcely common sense.' And he went on to urge collective effort to 'better our condition in life and be no longer jeered and laughed at by our fellow brethren for our simplicity'.

However these sentiments did not amount to a rejection of the prevailing social and economic conditions, apart from the single institution of bondage. I have encountered only one suggestion that 'there must be something radically wrong with the system, as scarcely a single ploughman brought up his sons to the same profession.' Far more typical was the declaration of one of the most outspoken figures of the Midlothian Farm Servants' Protection Society, Tam Ewing, that 'We want no revolution, nor yet the broken fiddle strings of Fenianism. All we want is a few more shillings to support ourselves and our wives and families.' And with this conservatism in ends went a conservatism in means also. As we have seen, the movement revolved around the traditional structure of hiring fairs: indeed its whole tactics were directed towards inhibiting the prior conclusion of bar-

[1] *North British Agriculturalist*, 14 March 1866, and 1868, p. 761.

gains in private; and the idea of 'registry offices' (or employment exchanges), the reformers' perennial alternatives to the fairs, was firmly dismissed as a trick. The Scottish farm servants' movement was, in short, the least radical and most limited in its objectives of those that we shall be considering; but it was also one of the most successful.[1]

It is harder to generalize about the English agricultural labourers' agitation of the 1870s, since this extended more widely and lasted longer. Clearly it had many resemblances to the Scottish movement we have just described: both, after all, occurred at broadly the same time and in fairly similar environments; and both represented an attempt on the part of farm workers to extract better conditions from their employers through a combination of collective action and appeals to public opinion. So it is not surprising that, for instance, our account of the meeting in Greenlaw (Berwickshire) can be largely paralleled from one of a similar gathering in Tysoe (Warwickshire).[2]

Indeed the atmosphere in and around Herefordshire, chronologically among the earliest of the English labourers' movements, was initially not unlike that of Scotland. There was a succession of meetings called for the labourers 'to state their grievances, and to discuss the question of their condition, and how it may be improved'. A variety of speakers bore witness to their hardships, generally in what was intended to be the most respectful language.[3] And the union's secretary, Thomas Strange, summed up. He frequently claimed divine sanction for the movement, or declared of its demands, 'This is not philanthropy, this is justice.' But at the same time Strange deprecated strikes and was genuinely anxious to remain on good terms with the farmers—he had originally sought to link his agitation with their demands for lower rents and local taxes; and he also stressed that, since Herefordshire labourers were too underfed to work as well as their northern colleagues, the farmers might actually gain by conceding higher wages, 'for a farmer had said

[1] *Haddingtonshire Courier*, 29 Dec. 1865 and 26 Jan. 1866; *North British Agriculturalist*, 10 Jan. and 21 Feb. 1866.
[2] M. K. Ashby, *Joseph Ashby of Tysoe* (Cambridge, 1961), pp. 59–62.
[3] Unfortunately farmers often disputed their facts, and the cases were used as ammunition for a rather sterile newspaper correspondence between landlords and farmers.

to him . . . that he would rather have three well-fed men than four half-fed ones.' However Strange's olive branches were rejected, and his meetings physically interrupted by farmers in a way that I have not encountered in rural Scotland.[1]

Also Strange was himself somewhat unusual in discountenancing strikes for higher wages. The other major leader to do so was Alfred Simmons, secretary of the Kent and Sussex Labourers' Union. And it was probably significant that Strange was a school-teacher, Simmons a journalist. By contrast Joseph Arch, a jobbing farm labourer, made his reputation through a strike mounted within about three weeks of his union's foundation. And the Lincolnshire League, which largely eschewed middle class assistance, made special provision in its rules for strikes to drive wages up to 18s. a week and (rather more circumspectly) beyond. In short, once they were roused, southern English labourers were generally more militant than their Scottish counterparts. They had, of course, to surmount fewer institutional barriers to strike action, since they were mostly engaged by the week and were not usually housed by the farmers. But it is also likely that they were more discontented, and therefore readier to denounce the farmers and contemplate the modification of supersession or the entire agricultural system.

A variety of factors may have contributed to this difference in contentment. As the map opposite shows, wages were rather lower in the south; and the difference seemed all the greater since the shorter southern hours and higher piece work and harvest earnings were often overlooked. Coal (and thus heating, clothes-drying and cooking) was dearer; and the more numerous Scottish cooked meals[2] probably resulted in a better diet. Also the more extensive employment of women, and the practice of 'double-hinding' (engaging father and unmarried son on the same contract) both raised *family* income considerably and secured for the head of a Scottish family a more skilled and attractive job than that of his English counterpart. Lastly

[1] *Hereford Journal*, 9 March 1872; *Hereford Times*, esp. 18 March 1871, 27 April and 18 May 1872. Farmers interrupted labourers' meetings in other parts of England too; but things were perhaps worst in Herefordshire, a county that also had unusually rowdy meetings at the time of the 1889 county council elections.

[2] It was usual in much of England to work straight through the day, taking time off for a hurried lunch in the fields; in Scotland to work longer hours but to return home for a break and a cooked meal at mid-day (see e.g. *P.P.*, 1870 xiii, pp. 218–19, 1893–4 xxxvi, p. 468).

HEBRIDES

LEWIS

'AVERAGE TOTAL WEEKLY EARNINGS OF ORDINARY
AGRICULTURAL LABOURERS'
(including the estimated value of
allowances in kind) ... IN 1902.'
(*P.P.* 1905 xcvii, p. 348.)

CAITHNESS 13s.7d.

SUTHERLAND
15s.10d.

Moray F.

ROSS AND CROMARTY
'mainland'
16s.10d.

NAIRN 18s.1d.

ELGIN
17s.10d.

BANFF 18s.2d.

ABERDEEN
19s.5d.

INVERNESS 17s.8d.
'mainland'

KINCARDINE
19s.6d.

FORFAR
20s.8d.

MULL

PERTH 19s.11d.

Firth of Tay

FIFE 20s.5d.

Firth of Forth

Y 19s.6d.E

ARRAN

STIRLING
22s.0d.

HADDINGTON
19s.6d.

EDINBURGH 20s.10d.

DUMBARTON

RENFREW

LANARK

PEEBLES
20s.7d.

SELKIRK
19s.5d.

BERWICK
19s.9d.

*Firth
of Clyde*

AYR 20s.10d.

DUMFRIES
18s.10d.

ROXBURGH
19s.5d.

KIRKCUDBRIGHT
18s.6d

WIGTOWN
17s.8d.

Solway F.

CUMBERLAND
20s.0d

NORTHUMBERLAND
21s.7d.

DURHAM
22s.2d.

R. Tees

WESTMORELAND

ISLE
OF
MAN

NORTH RIDING 18s.10d.

IRISH SEA

EAST RIDING
19s. 2d.

WEST RIDING
19s.10d.

LANCASHIRE 20s.7d.

R. Humber

ANGLESEY
16s.7d.

FLINT 19s.5d.

DENBIGH 17s.8d.

CARNARVON 19s.8d.

CHESHIRE
18s.9d.

DERBY 20s.7d.

NOTTS.
19s.9d.

LINCOLN
18s.8d.

*The
Wash*

MERIONETH
17s.8d.

STAFFORD
18s.4d.

LEICESTER
17s.4d.

RUTLAND

NORFOLK 15s.3d.

MONTGOMERY
16s.0d.

SALOP
18s.0d.

HUNTS
16s.2d.

CAMBRIDGE
16s.1d.

CARDIGAN 15s.8d.

RADNOR
16s.10d.

WORCESTER
16s.5d.

WARWICK
16s.4d.

NORTHAMPTON
16s.2d.

BEDFORD
16s.6d.

SUFFOLK 15s6d.

BRECKNOCK
18s.6d.

HEREFORD
16s.3d.

OXFORD
14s.6d.

BUCKINGHAM
16s.2d.

HERTS
17s.2d.

ESSEX
16s.11d.

PEMBROKE
16s.7d.

CARMARTHEN
17s.9d.

MONMOUTH
18s.10d.

GLOUCESTER
15s.5d.

MIDDX
20s.4d.

LONDON

R. Thames

GLAMORGAN
21s.3d.

BERKS
15s.11d.

SURREY
20s.0d.

KENT 19s.7d.

BRISTOL CHANNEL

WILTS
15s.8d.

HANTS
17s.9d.

SOMERSET 16s.11d.

DORSET
15s.6d.

SUSSEX 17s.7d.

DEVON 17s.1d.

CORNWALL 17s.4d.

there are stray indications that southern English farmers may have under-rated the skills and abilities of their men.[1]

However this may be, it is quite clear that, subjectively, most Scottish labourers were convinced that they were far better off than the English: thus in 1894 a union meeting in Ross-shire dwelt on

the disparaging and backward state of the agricultural workers in the principal English counties, and the extremely low rate of re- muneration paid compared with the rate at present current in the north of Scotland [actually there was little difference in earnings]. The lengthy account of a strike . . . on one of the principal farms in Essex . . . afforded a fit and suitable subject for a brief discussion by several members present.[2]

It was also common to contrast the manly independence of the north with the servility and insecurity of the southern 'Hodge'. This, too, had some substance, since the hiring system guaran- teed employment in bad weather and in sickness. But it also gave the northern farmer far more control over his men's housing than his southern counterpart.

Another important difference lay in the degree of land hunger present in southern England. This varied markedly from place to place. But there was a wide-spread demand for allotments, and a rather lesser demand (exaggerated by the labourers' allies and political sympathizers) for small-holdings. These constituted a major theme of late nineteenth-century rural radicalism, and they could only be obtained at the expense of either farmer, squire, or parson. However in Lowland Scotland, as the Royal Commission on Labour observed with some surprise, this theme found no echoes outside Galloway. For the Scottish farm ser- vant worked very long hours, and tended, if anything, to receive rather too much of his payment in kind. Since he usually lived on a farm, rather than in a village, his cottage always had a garden already: and the practice of keeping a cow was in decline. So he had no occasion to seek for more land, and this removed a very major bone of contention.

Lastly the English and Scottish movements differed in organi- zation. The English 'Revolt of the Field' often began with a spontaneous mushrooming of local meetings and associations, but these soon coalesced into organizations solider and more

[1] This is, of course, not capable of objective proof: the best discus- sion I have encountered is in *P.P.*, 1919 ix, pp. 76–9, 470; see also *P.P.*, 1893–4 xxxv, pp. 688, 885.
[2] *The Plough*, Dec. 1894, p. 15.

firmly directed than the Scottish Farm Servants' Protection Society of the 1860s—the three major English unions of the 1870s, for instance, all at some stage published their own newspaper. Such organization was naturally designed to make the movement permanent; and it both caused and reflected the adoption of a variety of goals rather than the concentration on a simple and limited grievance, like bondage. Organization also demanded full-time officials, a new departure in the history of British rural discontent. Some of these had to be borrowed from outside the ranks of the agricultural labourers, and, together with the progressive gentlemen whose advice and assistance was also solicited, they introduced a new awareness of the trends and political controversies of the outside world.

Accordingly we find the major rural trades unions registered with the Registrar of Friendly Societies. Some of their leaders attended meetings of the Trades Union Congress. And the Lincolnshire League, in particular, also organized industrial workers in Scunthorpe and in north-east England. So it is not surprising that one strand of the 'Revolt of the Field' was strongly marked by the prevailing spirit of mid nineteenth-century unionism. This has been characterized by Dr. Hobsbawm as a conscious, though partial, adjustment on the part of skilled workers to the rules of a self-regulating market economy. The typical policies of such 'new model' unionism 'aimed at the creation of a permanent scarcity of skilled labour, so as to raise its market price'. And workers as well as employers 'tended to favour the shortest possible forms of hiring contract so as to enable either side to bargain for better terms with the least possible delay'.[1]

Mutatis mutandis this description would fit the agricultural labourers of the 1870s surprisingly well. For all low wage areas fostered migration to better paid jobs in the north and in towns; and all areas, though not all leaders, favoured emigration. In Dorset, indeed, the mere threat of such a policy was expected to prevent the farmers from retaliating against union members during the slack season after the harvest. And in Herefordshire, the West of England Union relied exclusively on shifting 'the men off until the farmers felt the want of them and came to their price'; for, as we have seen, Strange felt that strikes, quite apart from their other drawbacks, did not cure the fundamental superfluity of labour.[2]

[1] *Labouring Men* (1964), p. 350.
[2] *Dorset County Express*, e.g. 4 June, 9 July, and 19 Nov. 1872; *Hereford Times*, e.g. 23 March and 20 April 1872.

There was, too, an instinctive hostility to long contracts, and an emphasis on the paramount need for the labourer to be free to take up the most advantageous offer as it came along. Thus Arch told the Richmond Commission on Agricultural Depression that a 'yearly engagement was always too good a security to me', and he spent a long time emphasizing that regardless of the season of the year or the inconvenience to his employer, the labourer 'ought to have the fullest liberty to take his labour where he can to make the best market'. Also, in marked contrast to Simmons (of the Kent and Sussex Labourers' Union), Arch firmly declined to speculate on the wages and conditions that would remove all grounds for complaint:

I do not go on such paternal lines. I teach the labourer never to be satisfied while there is a chance of advancing in life. To teach a man to be content is to teach a man to curse himself; that is to say, you should increase within his mind a just discontent for every year of his life to make himself a better man, and his family more intelligent, and better fed, and better clothed . . . I teach him he must never be satisfied so long as there is a better prospect before him, and he thinks he has intelligence and brain and perseverance to reach after it.[1]

Arch was, of course, a highly skilled itinerant workman. And his attitude was perhaps less appropriate, even during an economic boom, to the ordinary southern agricultural labourer, who was neither a very skilled nor a very mobile man. Still the 'Revolt of the Field' did come during an inflationary period, when the labourers were not only pushed by rising prices but were also able to make out quite a good case for a wage increase in terms of supply and demand. A number of their sympathizers held that agricultural wages had been kept below the market level by the labourers' isolation and individual weakness, and that the function of the unions was to enable the labourers to test the market. Thus the Radical politician Edward Jenkins declared that, 'As they at present stood, none of the men could make a fair bargain with their masters; and the object of the Union was to enable them to do so': and at another union meeting the philosopher T. H. Green said of the law of supply and demand, 'the farmer could not and would not give more than he could afford, and the way to find out what he could afford was by common action, and with the Union at their back.'

But there were limits to the gains that could be expected

---

[1] *P.P.*, 1882 xiv, questions 60564, 60606–12, 60616–19, 61242.

from the operation of supply and demand economics. These limits were underlined by the East Anglian farmers' success in dispensing with union labour even at harvest time. Indeed one stock way of rebutting union demands was to invoke 'those great laws of political economy'. So it is not surprising that many unionists were inclined to appeal instead to a higher principle.

To Arch this principle was justice. 'Now if demand and supply regulate the price of labour, if because a few men are out of work, a farmer takes advantage of this and screws down the labourers' wages I maintain it is not just to do so'. This opinion was very common—the *Labourers' Union Chronicle* is full of attacks on the pretended 'law' of supply and demand. And the first N.A.L.U. secretary, Taylor, bluntly took issue with T. H. Green's espousal of it:

There was no greater fallacy in the minds of the public. Why should the law of supply and demand regulate the wages? . . . Were not the resources such as to give every man a living? and a good living too at the worst of times? Why should a man in a slack time receive 5s. a week less than in a busy time? A man . . . in the busy time of the year might employ 100 men at a pound a week, but why should he lower his men's wages when he employed only half the number. If he did so, he had the advantage of the slack time as well as the busy. But when they got the whole of the labourers combined then the law of supply and demand would not operate, inasmuch as the one would not undersell the other . . . and he contended that the labourers themselves ought to be the judge of the value of their labour.[1]

If successful, this would merely have constituted an inversion of the widespread practice whereby the principal landlords, farmers and local worthies met once or twice a year to decide, in the light of changes in seasons and prices, on a 'fair' local wage rate. Indeed the labourers often cited such gatherings as precedents for their own combinations. But the idea of a 'just wage' might look either backwards or forwards. For it had underlain much of the first phase of urban trades unionism, persisting in Coventry until about 1860.[2] And, in the form of state-enforced minimum wage-rates, it was again to be implemented in agriculture for the greater part of the twentieth

[1] *Hereford Times*, 27 April 1872, p. 10; *Oxford Journal*, 26 Oct. 1872, p. 8; *Dorset County Express*, 23 July 1872, p. 4.
[2] John Prest, *The Industrial Revolution in Coventry* (Oxford, 1960), pp. 53–5, 123.

century. This channel of development, however, never occurred to Arch (or his colleagues); and, when it was put to him as an academic question, he replied, 'I do not see how legislation is to regulate my wages.'[1] His successors in the 1890s had no such inhibitions.

This is not to say that the agricultural labourers had no political ambitions in the 1870s. By July 1872 union speakers were already declaring that they wanted not only higher wages but also the franchise, and that they intended 'to send working men to represent our interests in . . . Parliament'. In November, Arch attended a Conference of the Electoral Reform Association, and the following year it was anticipated that he would contest the borough of Woodstock at the next General Election. By June 1873, indeed, the N.A.L.U. newspaper, the *Labourers' Union Chronicle*, put the acquisition of the franchise second only to higher wages—'it is quite time that [the labourer] . . . should be on a political equality with the land-owner, his old oppressor. Taxation without representation is tyranny.' No taxation without representation is, of course, a very old slogan. And there was little theoretical novelty in the other arguments propounded—that the poor man was as good as the rich, that all interests should be represented, and then the labourers would no longer be the victims of such unjust legislation as the Game and Poor Laws and Enclosures. Except for the last, all these points turned on considerations of status; and, like many other nineteenth-century groups, the agricultural labourers were to pursue the franchise at least as much as an end in itself as for any ulterior purposes—'we teach the men that, as citizens (at least they ought to be citizens, but they are not), they ought to have political power.'[2]

But though the labourers' reasons for wishing the vote were not particularly novel, the mere fact that they did so was. Earlier involvement in national politics on the part of English rural labourers had been infinitesimal. We have seen that the Scottish movement of the 1860s had no political overtones, even though it coincided with the opening of the struggle over the Second Reform Bill. And in March 1867 John Bright himself had believed that a £10 or £12 franchise in the counties

[1] *P.P.*, 1882 xiv, question 60362. Equally Arch did not favour the legislative limitation of working hours (60588).

[2] *Dorset County Express*, 9 July 1872, p. 2; Pamela Horn, *op. cit.*, pp. 73–4; W. Wing, *Parliamentary History of the Borough of Woodstock during the Present Century* (Oxford, 1873), pp. 1, 6; *Labourers' Union Chronicle*, 7 June 1873, p. 1; *P.P.*, 1882 xiv, question 59961.

would encounter no agitation 'for a *very long period*'.[1] But he was mistaken—the dichotomy between household suffrage in the boroughs and a restrictive franchise in the counties was too glaring to be tenable, especially when certain boroughs like Morpeth and Woodstock in fact extended deep into the surrounding countryside. The agricultural labourers were probably less important than the miners in bringing such anomalies to an end. But their leaders certainly worked persistently for the vote; and, as Mrs. Horn has shown above, they signed in large numbers the annual petitions that Trevelyan submitted to Parliament in the 1870s and that had secured the conversion of the Liberal leadership by the end of the decade.

In the process, the agricultural labourers' unions were irrevocably committed to the Liberal Party. Nonconformity, and opposition from farmers and landlords, would probably have driven them there anyway. But the process must have been assisted by the fact that virtually all their external support came from left of centre (mostly from the political orbit either of Birmingham or of the London Trades Council), and very little of it shared Canon Girdlestone's reluctance to identify 'the cause of the peasantry with any one particular party, either religious or political'. There was, indeed, a faint possibility that the movement would drift still further to the left into active republicanism: for William Banks, the man who emerged in control of the Lincolnshire League, had been a republican lecturer,[2] and prominent external sympathizers included Auberon Herbert and Sir Charles Dilke, both notoriously of that persuasion. To its opponents this was enough to damn the whole agricultural labourers' movement as republican; but most union speakers vigorously repudiated the charge. And, though they were initially highly critical of the 1886–74 Gladstone government,[3] the events of 1874–80 duly brought them, in common with most other Radicals, to a firmer Liberal allegiance.

But the programme of the *Labourers' Union Chronicle*, as we have seen it enunciated in the issue of 7 June 1873, included not only higher wages and the vote but also land reform— broadly the paper demanded the division into small-holdings of

[1] To Disraeli, printed in G. M. Trevelyan, *The Life of John Bright* (1913), pp. 381–2.
[2] Information from Mr. F. Cossey.
[3] Over e.g. the Criminal Law Amendment Act, 1871, the despatch of soldiers to get in the harvest in 1872, education, and the excessive tenderness shown in disendowing the Irish Church.

waste and of all state forests, the expropriation (with compensation reducing over 20 years) of the land of non-educational charities and corporations, and the appropriation of a tenth of all gifts or legacies of land exceeding 100 acres. One may doubt whether the ordinary agricultural labourer was wedded to these particular proposals.[1] But there was clearly an extensive desire to obtain some land; and the National Union's inability to provide it helped to precipitate its first big split, that of 1875. Such aspirations were usually couched in very general language, but they can perhaps be discussed under three headings: allotments, that might supplement wages but would not replace them as the labourers' principal livelihood; small-holdings or co-operative farms, that would render their owners independent of the neighbouring farmers; and the division of the land, that would extinguish these farmers altogether.

The need for allotments was a constant theme of late nineteenth-century rural debate, and had, of course, been expounded much earlier—the provision of allotments had been one response to the shock of the Swing Riots in 1830, though they may have dwindled away again in the course of time. In the 1870s allotments commanded a premium over and above the rent for agricultural land,[2] which suggests an unsatisfied demand for them. The local landlords could certainly have made more land available, as they did later in the century. And it could be argued (as at Littlemore, Oxfordshire) that they might even gain by doing so, since this would enable the labourers to keep their families out of the work-house in old age, and would thus reduce the rates. The idea was clearly believed to have appeal, for a fortnight later the National Union's General Secretary descended on Littlemore and promised that

If they showed themselves to be sober men, there was no power on this earth that could prevent their getting a small portion of land. They could apply to the land-owners for land, with the Union to back them up, and if the landowners refused to allow them any, they had only to say to the Legislature, 'You must take the land',

[1] They probably derived from W. G. Ward, an eccentric on the Union's Consulting Committee—see Howard Evans, *Radical Fights of Forty Years* (London, n.d.), p. 38.

[2] Even 20 years later it could be remarked that allotments were generally rented at double the average of agricultural land; the difference was partly, but not entirely, accounted for by their superior quality, by the risks and costs of letting land in small portions, and by the inclusion of a sum to cover rates and taxes (*P.P.*, 1893–4 xxxv, p. 190).

and then they would get a portion of it. The time would soon arrive when they would get allotments . . .

But, however alluring this prospect, it might be easier to concentrate on charity lands, since these were already in a special position. As the local union secretary at Littlemore told the labourers, 'they did not stand much chance of getting' land that came on the market in the usual way, 'for these land monopolizers stepped in and beat them. He thought that land, in which the poor had an interest, should be "fished" out.' So he suggested that they petition the Charity Commissioners to divide into allotments one small farm that 'rightly belonged to the poor', and another plot that must do so too since no individual ownership could be traced.[1]

At that time charities owned over half a million acres in England. So most villages had such plots of land; and tablets in most churches commemorate the gift of the odd piece, the rent of which was to be applied to the benefit of the poor. But in the course of time disputes could well arise as to the manner of this application—there might be misappropriation or neglect (as at Swinbrook) or unfounded traditions of local rights (as at Yarnton). Or, as at Tysoe, latent resentment against the way in which control of the 'Town lands' had passed to the vicar and a group of self-coopting Trustees, might suddenly become articulate when a change was made in the traditional way of distributing their proceeds.[2]

Such disputes were of considerable local importance; and they were probably more frequent than usual at this time because of a general tendency to rationalize ancient bequests, often diverting them in the process from their original beneficiaries to such socially useful purposes as education, or even middle-class education. No labourers' movement could have ignored the topic. And it would be easy to complement Dr. Horn's illustrations with examples from other counties—in 1879 Banks of the Amalgamated Labour League claimed to be investigating the charities of no fewer than 40 parishes.[3]

Involvement with local charities and village politics reflected

---

[1] *Oxford Journal*, 3 and 24 Aug. 1872; *Oxford Chronicle*, 3 Aug. 1872.

[2] James Caird, *The Landed Interest* (1870), p. 140. For Swinbrook and Yarnton (both in Oxon.) see the notices in their churches; *Joseph Ashby of Tysoe* contains a full account of the protracted controversy over the Tysoe 'Town Lands' or 'Charity Estate'.

[3] *The Labourer*, 1 Jan. 1879.

a distinctive mental outlook. In purely economic terms there may be some justification for describing the 'labourers in husbandry' as 'the only real Marxian proletariat that England ever had'. But in practice they often thought in terms of their localities—during the celebrated Ascott-under-Wychwood strike in 1873 one of the blacklegs, 'a determined non-unionist', was allowed through, presumably because he was a former native of the village, and the trouble (whatever it was) only arose over other strike-breakers, who were not. Again great store was set by 'rights' derived from the past—it really mattered to, say, the inhabitants of Shipton-under-Wychwood that an eight-acre fuel allotment should be recognized not as a charity but as compensation for the 1851 enclosure. And, in an extreme case, a whole life-time after the enclosure of Otmoor its villagers were still more interested in re-hearing that saga than in any of the more contemporary propaganda brought to them by the future Viscount Samuel.[1]

This sort of local concern helps to explain the great rôle that anti-clericalism played in both agricultural trades unionism and rural radicalism in general. As one writer puts it, with especial reference to Norfolk in the 1870s:

The village radical placed disestablishment and disendowment of the church first in his programme. Religious differences had nothing to do with this . . ., except in isolated parishes where 'high church' practices had offended. It came because the parson stood in the way of any great alterations in the administration of public business. He controlled the vestry and the management of public charities, as a guardian he administered the hated Poor Law, and his influence in the village school ensured that education should take place in an atmosphere favourable to the existing social order. He personified the impediments to reform, and upon him was concentrated the full force of the radical attack. Any grievance served as an outlet for angry feelings.

It is, therefore, not surprising that the *Labourers' Union Chronicle* should have included on its mast-head the slogan 'Freedom from Priestcraft', or that Christopher Holloway, the first chairman of the Oxford District, should have wished 'to see the time when Churches are turned into barns and parsons into threshing men'.

But naturally the parsons were not the only targets—earlier in the same speech Holloway had declaimed 'Let them . . .

[1] *Oxford Journal*, 7 June 1873; information from Mr. A. F. Thompson.

have a revolution rather than go back to the dark ages and be serfs and slaves of the farmers.' And the farmers had to encounter a steady stream of abuse, the more hair-raising items of which were assiduously collected by 'One of the Threatened' for the edification of his Oxfordshire colleagues:

You, the Farmers of England, have been denounced rightfully and truthfully as a public nuisance. It does seem that you are really quite ignorant of your own history and history of agriculture in our country. England was happy England when there was not a farmer in the land; as the office of farmers has increased happiness has died out: they have covered the land with their influence, and their influence has been the doom of the labourer . . . A *slavedriver* grinding up the flesh and blood of the labourer into rent . . . When can we get rid of him?[1]

Of course the labourers never did 'get rid of him'. But from time to time they tried. There were, for instance, sporadic attempts to establish co-operative farms 'in connection with the Union', and on occasion the National Union itself rented a farm. But nothing much came of this; and in fact shortage of capital would have precluded any major developments along this line. The acquisition of small-holdings was slightly more feasible. A number of union districts formed Land Societies to obtain them. And the National Union's inactivity in the matter led in 1875 to the establishment of the break-away 'New Union', whose main purpose was the securing of land for its members.

But success was very limited. So it is to aspiration rather than performance that one should look when considering the labourers' hopes of major land reform.[2] And there can be no doubt that aspirations were high: Arch was to recall that 'a lot of the men were craving for the land; as some one said, they were properly "land mad" '; and 'One [union] official told me he had been asked for money to buy an old thrashing machine!' But he himself regularly played up to this sentiment—at a great meeting in Dorset in 1872 he promised that he would never rest till each man had two-and-a-half acres of land; a year later,

[1] L. M. Springall, *Labouring Life in Norfolk Villages* (1936), p. 112; *Oxford Journal*, 10 Aug. and 21 Dec. 1872.

[2] They did, of course, support the standard radical assault on the Land Laws: but though the reform of these might make farming more profitable and thus raise wages, and might eventually break up the great estates and so weaken the aristocracy, it could not be expected to provide many labourers with land or diminish their general dependence on the farmers.

at the National Union's conference, he was speaking of the labourers each having 'a good sized allotment . . ., say, two, three, four or five acres', and twenty years later he was still deprecating quarter-acre allotments—'it was not a quarter enough; it would make the men slaves. They wanted from three to four acres to work properly.[1] This was more than most men could cultivate (even with family and hired help) on top of a regular job as a farm worker, and so must be seen rather as a demand for small-holdings.

Some labourers undoubtedly went farther. Harris, one of the men sent from Warwickshire to help establish the union in Dorset, admitted that 'the farmers say they cannot afford to give' the wages demanded; 'Well, then, let them leave their farms, and let the land-owners divide the farms into from 8 to 20 acres each; then more people would make a good living, the land would be a better cultivated, and more would be produced, which would be a national benefit.' In Berkshire a Thomas Rouse voiced ideas that, to the *Oxford Journal,* seemed

to be of a slightly communistic type, for he recommended his 'brothers all' to hold well together, and he reckoned that in five years time they would be in a position to dispossess the farmers of their lands and take to them themselves.

Rouse was one of the two delegates chosen by the meeting to attend the National Union's inaugural conference. Lastly, in Suffolk, an able pamphlet written to justify the 1874 Lock-out claimed that:

In most cases the [discharged men's] reply amounted to this: 'Well, sir, we have no fault to find with you; you are a very fair master and mean right: but these union folks do say they are going to do away with this Queen and have a Republic, and that the land will all be divided equally among us'. Combat such notions as we might, so firmly were they impressed with the belief that they decided in large numbers to 'stand by the Union'.

There was certainly some encouragement to entertain such delusions. The National Union's General Secretary, Henry Taylor, held that 'the land of this country was held of the Queen for the good of the people, and if that trust was forfeited the land must revert to the people'; and the *Labourers Union*

---

[1] Joseph Arch, *The Story of his Life* (1898), pp. 278, 297–8; *Dorset County Chronicle,* 25 July, p. 12; *Labourers' Union Chronicle,* 7 June 1873, p. 4; *Bury [St. Edmund's] Free Press,* 10 Oct. 1891, p. 7.

Chronicle frequently voiced such sentiments.[1] They probably lost nothing in the telling—after all George Edwards was, years later, to recall Chamberlain's carefully qualified programme of 1885 as 'ransoming the land back to the people'. And in 1874 the *Times* correspondent, Clifford, concluded that 'in some of the villages . . . agitators in the course of the struggle must have led the Unionists to believe that a division of the land was imminent.'[2]

In theory Parliament could have effected this. And in 1878 unions in south Norfolk petitioned, praying that 'a bill may be framed giving all cultivable land into the charge of a special representative body, compensating present owners . . .' This petition was probably inspired by propaganda rather than by faith. But faith played an enormous rôle in the movement as a whole, and not unnaturally—the sudden success of 1872 could be attributed at least as convincingly to divine intervention as to any more mundane causation, and only divine intervention could realize the labourers' most extreme hopes. The Dorset secretary even dared to apply to his movement Acts 5: 38–39— 'Refrain from these men and let them alone; for if this counsel or this work be of men it will come to nought. But if it be of God ye cannot overthrow it; lest haply ye be found even to fight against God.'[3]

Of course the use of religious language was only to be expected—many, perhaps even most, union leaders were Nonconformist lay preachers, for the movement had 'found it desirable to get Christian men and teetotallers as officers'. Speeches at the inauguration of the National Union 'were punctuated with cries of "Amen", "Praise Him", and other devout utterances'. In decline, the Lincolnshire League considered partial amalgamation with the Primitive Methodists, calling on those 'who are earnestly preaching salvation for the souls of men to assist us save their bodies also'. And in the 1890s the leading

[1] They were still current in the 1890s: the National Union's Essex organizer, for instance, condemned the existing system of large farms for divorcing men from the land, and asked 'Will not God visit us as a nation for this? I know he will; and the sooner our nation repents by restoring the land to the people again, the better it will be'—*English Labourers' Chronicle*, 26 Nov. 1892, p. 5.

[2] *Dorset County Express*, 9 July 1872, p. 2; *Oxford Journal*, 1 June and 24 Aug. 1872; George Edwards, *From Crow-Scaring to Westminster* (1922), p. 53; Clifford, pp. 92, 154—Clifford's sympathies were slightly on the labourers' side in the lock-out, but, on the other hand, he got most of his information from large farmers.

[3] Springall, p. 115; *Dorset County Express*, 24 Sept. 1872, p. 4.

figures in at least two of the three major unions were of that denomination.[1]

The language of redemption was therefore regularly used—'When he heard of the movement in Warwickshire, his soul moved within him and he knew the day of redemption had come'—and language suggestive of some apocalyptic transformation of society not infrequently: 'he believed that they would soon see the dawning of a better day, when the poor should be made rich and when all should have plenty.' This faith might be retained regardless of set-backs. Arch, in his old age, saw in the Countess of Warwick's readiness to edit his autobiography:

a sign of the grand union that is coming, when prince and peer and peasant shall combine and cooperate for the good of one and all . . . the world in union! That is what is coming, that is what all must work for . . . as sure as the sun shines in the heavens the great and glorious day when the world will be in union will dawn at last.

Significantly, a Lincolnshire unionist, in reproducing this prophecy, preceded it with an expression of his belief that

the time is not far distant when God will send restored apostles and prophets to his Church who will visit the aged poor and investigate how they live on three shillings a week . . ., and enter a strong protest against such cruelty and preach with much force the gospel of God, that it will kill or cure barren or fruitless professors . . .

And he qualified Arch's description of universal co-operation with the words, 'As many as are led by the spirit of God and they only.'

Some of these utterances may have been mere bombast, and others intended to be taken figuratively. But it would be difficult to interpret them all away, and more natural to accept that the expectation of divine assistance was an important factor in maintaining the labourers' confidence and cohesion; indeed it was sometimes invoked precisely for this purpose:

The farmers have tried to stop the Union, but they may as well empty the sea with a tea-spoon; for you have got the Union not only in your hands but in your hearts . . . I would rather die than

[1] *Labourers' Union Chronicle*, 29 Nov. 1873, p. 6; E. Selley, *Village Trades Unions in Two Centuries* (1919), p. 47; Russell, p. 125; *The Memoirs of Josiah Sage* (1951), chap. vii; George Edwards, esp. pp. 29, 36.

give up advocating the cause of the Union. I know that we are advocating a cause which has the blessing of God.[1]

Divine sanction was most usually looked to. But, if the movement's opponents are to be believed, other authority might occasionally be invoked. Thus one old man is supposed to have told his employer that 'it had been predicted in the year 1774 that the labourers would get the better of their masters in 1874, and they meant to fulfill the prophecy by means of the Union.'[2] Such attitudes were undeniably antiquated by the 1870s, which was why they were retailed as propaganda. But other 'backward-looking' practices were more serious. The traditional resort to arson to pay off grievances was not yet dead. And there is some evidence that it increased in the aftermath of the eastern counties lock-out, as it had after the collapse of the Swing riots: for instance a Cambridgeshire farmer, who had closed his coprolite works to release black-leg labour for the 1874 harvest, duly lost his stacks; other cases are not hard to come by, and they prompted fears 'that the old scenes of rick burning . . . might be repeated'.[3] On the whole, however, they were not, or not sufficiently to have any impact on the national crime rate.

Violence was, I think, quite genuinely anticipated at first. At the start of the first major lock-out in Oxfordshire, the farmers circulated a repeat of a handbill 'issued during the noted riots of 1845 under the auspices of the [still exant] Agriculturalists Protection Association', guaranteeing each other's property against damage and offering rewards for information as to the 'villain or villains' responsible—the term gave offence, and had to be modified to 'person or persons' to suit a politer age. They also summoned 'a strong force of police' to attend the labourers' first demonstration 'stating that they expected a riot leading to the destruction of machinery and to other depredations'.

Most union speakers took pride in the movement's moderation and exhorted their audiences to keep the peace. But there were occasional attempts to play on these fears of violence. Thus the eccentric W. G. Ward, a member of the National Union's Consulting Committee, declared in its newspaper that

If the farmers were now to succeed by their lock-out in exhausting the Union Funds . . . they would find that they had suppressed a

[1] *South Eastern Gazette* (Maidstone), 7 May 1872, p. 3; *Hereford Times*, 27 April 1872, p. 10; Arch, pp. 405–6; Russell, p. 138; *Dorset County Express*, 23 July 1872, p. 4.   [2] Clifford, p. 66.
[3] A. J. Peacock, 'The Revolt of the Field in East Anglia', work cited, p. 165.

moderate and legitimate agitation only to arouse agrarian anarchy . . . that the success would be signalled by midnight surprises, by beacon fires from one end of England to the other. There are circumstances that justify war, even civil war.

The passage attracted general, though not universal, censure at the Union's 1873 Conference. But its sentiments were largely repeated the following year by the Bishop of Manchester, who asked 'in language more forcible than Episcopal',

Are the farmers of England going mad? Can they suppose that this suicidal lock-out . . . will stave off for any appreciable time the solution of the inevitable question, what is the equitable wage to pay the men? The most frightful thing that could happen for English Society would be a peasant's war. Yet that is what we are driving to, if insane counsels of mutual exasperation prevail.[1]

Fortunately the Bishop was mistaken. Many people had realized this all along—the venerable J. W. Henley, M.P., told the Oxfordshire Agricultural Society in 1872 that

Old men who remembered what this country was many years back would be thankful to deal with this subject in a quieter manner than that in which they had had to deal with it something like thirty or forty years ago. Since then, however, wages had increased nearly 25 per cent. . . . He had no doubt that some could recollect the 'Swing' riots about forty years ago. . . . We had reason to bless ourselves now that, instead of the question being raised by breaking machinery and burning their homesteads, the persons had come forward more quietly, though in some instances they had had agitators among them. It was, however, a blessed change to see the way in which parties approached each other from what they did in those days . . .[2]

Naturally the movement was not impeccable—besides the arson we have already noticed, there were occasional cases of threatening letters, intimidation, and scuffles with black-legs. However these were both rare and wholly peripheral to the main purposes of the unions. By contrast even the mildest of previous rural outbreaks in England had taken the form of riotous assem-

---

[1] This was not the only episcopal blunder—earlier the Bishop of Gloucester had had some difficulty in explaining away an apparent call to duck agitators in the nearest horse-pond.

[2] *Oxford Chronicle*, 13 July 1872, pp. 7–8; A. Clayden, *The Revolt of the Field* (1874), pp. 145 ff.; Russell, pp. 60–61; *Oxford Journal*, 25 May 1872, p. 8.

blies and the forcible destruction of threshing machines: and the whole tactics of the Scottish crofters and of the Welsh 'League of those oppressed by tithes' in the 1880s were to hinge on paralysing the machinery of the Law by making it impossible to serve writs or conduct distraints. Instead the agricultural labourers of the 1870s concentrated on collective bargaining (backed by selective strikes), on playing the labour-market through the encouragement of migration and emigration, and on self-help through co-operatives and benefit societies. The language used at meetings may often have been archaic and backward-looking, as were many of the motives and expectations of the participants. The unions' actions were not—and those few Minutes that have survived portray perfectly conventional, albeit rather incompetent, trade union organizations.

They operated in an environment in which neither the agricultural labourers nor their employers found it easy to combine. So, in the long run, the economists were right: '. . . no matter what agitators wanted to do or what kind-hearted people wanted, the supply and demand would settle the price of labour as it had settled the price of everything else.' The agricultural unions, like their contemporaries in unskilled industry, were formed on the surge of an economic boom, pushed wages up, and then went into rapid decline with the change in the trade cycle. Arch subsequently declared that 'since 1875, when the depression set in, I have advised the labourers, thousands of them, when they were under notice of [wage] reduction to accept it. I said, "You must take it; the situation of the farmers is not at all good." '[1] Admittedly there were a number of strikes against wage reductions (especially on the part of the Kent and Sussex Union in 1878–9); but, for the time being, the militant phase of rural unionism was over.

Accordingly the agricultural unions, or those of them that survived, increasingly busied themselves with other matters. Above all there was a turning to politics—further campaigns to gain the vote, campaigns to secure the return to Parliament of Liberals in general and (from 1880) of Joseph Arch in particular, campaigns against Turkish atrocities in Bulgaria, against the Zulu War, and against the retention of flogging in the British army. These brought the agricultural labourers into the mainstream of politics even before they got the vote. And many people thought that, after their enfranchisement in 1885, they

[1] *P.P.*, 1882 xiv, question 58562.

might constitute the key to these politics. Schnadhorst, the Secretary of the National Liberal Federation, was already telling Joseph Chamberlain in June 1883 that

As regards the new voters especially in rural districts the question that arouses them is land. The labourers will vote for the party which they think will better their condition—it is a matter with them not of sentiment but of bread and cheese.[1]

Jesse Collings gave similar advice. And Chamberlain responded by seeking to enlist rural support and pitching his programmes accordingly. Indeed it was on a rural Amendment to the Address that the Salisbury Government was brought down in 1886. The practical benefits this brought the labourers were not great.[2] But it made it reasonable for them to hope to secure their aims through the political process, rather than through industrial action.

Much of the revival of rural unionism in the 1890s accordingly proceeded along these lines. 'The newer labourers' unions', remarked the Land Restoration League, '. . . differ in some important respects from the "National Union", founded in 1872 by Joseph Arch.' Besides being more localized, cheaper, and free from the incubus of a 'benefit section',

They avowedly discountenance strikes, and look rather to the use of the VOTE for the improvement of social conditions. . . . Above all, they see much more clearly than ever that the quarrel of the labour is not so much with the working farmer, as with the system of private ownership of land, under which both farmer and labourer are oppressed and robbed.[3]

This description is naturally most applicable to the shadow unions that the League itself set up.[4] But it does not greatly mis-

---

[1] Chamberlain Papers, University of Birmingham.

[2] Though indirectly the heightened awareness of the rural question certainly stimulated the provision of allotments; between 1873 and 1886 these grew in number by over 40 per cent; the rate of increase then almost doubled between 1886 and 1890; and thereafter it fell back sharply, perhaps because the demand had been substantially met—*P.P.*, 1896 lxvii, pp. 520-1, 584.

[3] English Land Restoration League, *Special Report, 1892* (1893), p. 8.

[4] Notably the Berkshire, the Warwickshire, and the Herefordshire Agricultural and General Workers' Unions, the Hertfordshire and Bedfordshire Land and Labour Leagues, and the somewhat more genuine Wiltshire General and Agricultural Workers. For

represent the two more substantial unions with which it cooperated, the Norfolk and Norwich Amalgamated Labour Union and the Eastern Counties Labour Federation. George Edwards, the future secretary of the Norfolk and Norwich, had read a number of Henry George's works in the 1880s and had become 'a convert to the principles contained therein'. This convinced him that 'if there was a revival in the Labour movement amongst the rural workers, the leaders would have to lift the men's thoughts above the question of the mere raising of wages and would have to take political action and seek to remove the great hindrance to man's progress.' And he said as much to the initial delegation that asked him to form a union in November 1889. He also 'started out with the idea of avoiding strikes'. This was not always possible; but though the Norfolk and Norwich spent appreciably on disputes in 1891, it spent only lightly thereafter. In 1893 the unions failed to halt the reduction of wages, and thereafter politics again offered the only promising avenue. Edwards had just failed to secure election to the Norfolk County Council in 1892; but the advent of District and Parish Councils in 1894 launched him and his wife, and more briefly a number of his followers, into local government. As councillors they were able to spot-light abuses, especially in poor relief, and to secure for the District Council's roadmen wage rates slightly above those of the ordinary agricultural labourer.[1] But Edwards still remained convinced that 'nothing will ever prove effectual but the abolition of our present land system'; and when his union finally collapsed in 1896 he did a tour of lecturing with the Land Restoration League's peripatetic Red Van in Wiltshire.[2]

The Red Van lectures had been launched in 1891 at the invitation of the Eastern Counties Labour Federation, 'The labourers' leaders feeling that the Land Question was at the bottom of the Labour Question.' In this connection, the Federation's secretary, Joseph Robinson, was to write in a book review:

Of course an Act for the compulsory cultivation of the land is not the only reform needed, as a reform in the land laws is quite as important. The land should be purchased by the State at a nominal value—not at a fancy price—and let off to the farmer at a rent 50

Warwickshire, see Pamela Horn, 'The Warwickshire Agricultural and General Workers' Union, 1893–97', *Midland History*, i (1972), pp. 23–36.

[1] Though not the 15 shillings a week they had tried for.

[2] George Edwards, p. 53 and chaps. 5–8.

per cent below the present price. Another important reform would be for the State to purchase the railways so that rates for the conveyance of agricultural produce might be greatly reduced. With these alterations of our present system we venture to think the condition of both labourers and farmers would be far more prosperous than at present.[1]

This was a formidable list. But it was only an abbreviated version of the Federation's 'programme', which ran from parish councils, payment of M.P.s, abolition of the Boards of Guardians, old age pensions, farming companies and co-operative societies, and the taxation of uncultivated lands, to arbitration in place of strikes and of wars, county council farms and construction of steam tramways, municipal workshops and work for the unemployed.[2] In fact it was a hodge-podge of contemporary progressive thought.

This is not surprising. Land Reform had always played a rôle in politics, and in radical expectations, quite out of proportion to the direct importance of the measures advocated; and, as time went on, the spectrum it covered broadened progressively in response to growing intellectual sophistication and to the widening range of backgrounds from which reformers were drawn.[3] No sooner had the English agricultural labourers started to move in the 1870s than they had assistance pressed upon them from a great variety of politicians, intellectuals and eccentrics, many of whom were fascinated by some kind of peasant farming. In the 1880s the whole land question became more acute with the onset of the so-called 'Great Depression'. For this certainly resulted in a reduction in the intensity of arable culti-

[1] English Land Restoration League, *Special Report, 1891*, p. 5; *Bury Free Press*, 4 March 1893, p. 6.
[2] The other items were: 'More scientific farming wanted. Compulsory cultivation of land. Co-operative farming and [Eastern Counties Labour] federation trading. Labour representatives on all public authorities. A proportion of working men as magistrates. Religious equality. Tax mansions and deer forests to their full value. Land-law reforms; fixity of tenure; State to own the land. Better wages for agricultural labourers. Better homes for the workers; excessive rents reduced.' (*P.P.*, 1893–4 xxv, p. 339.)
[3] A full history of the movement remains to be written; but see e.g. F. M. L. Thompson, 'Land and Politics in the Nineteenth Century', *Royal Historical Society Transactions*, 5th series xv (1965), pp. 23–44, and John Saville, 'Henry George and the British Labour Movement', *Bulletin of the Society for the Study of Labour History*, v (1962), pp. 18–26.

vation which many—and not least the rural trades unions—regarded as immoral. It also coincided with a major exodus from the country to the towns, which alarmed urban workers whom it threatened to undercut, and which contributed towards the slum conditions that were just being publicized. At the same time Ireland came to the boil with the sudden success of the Land League and of the Nationalist Party; the land question really was one of the two fundamental Irish problems, and people could easily come to believe that it was as important in England. Scotland and Wales occupied an intermediate position, and both saw movements of a vigour and importance eclipsing those of England. Progressive opinion tended to support all indiscriminately; and accordingly it coalesced into an amorphous collection of overlapping societies devoted to land reform, of which the basically Henry George-ite and Christian Socialist Land Restoration League was one. Symbolically this employed for the evangelization of Northamptonshire and Bedfordshire not only the rising Warwickshire villager, Joseph Ashby, but also the elderly fore-runner of crofting unrest, John Murdoch, who had more recently presided at the formation of the Scottish Parliamentary Labour Party.[1]

One common speaker at meetings of the Eastern Counties Federation described Welsh *methods* of tithe resistance, and declared that 'What they wanted to do was to adopt the tactics of the Irish and Welsh in the Eastern Counties.'[2] But political action apart, the Federation did not in fact borrow tactics, only arguments and objectives. Its position was therefore not comparable to that of the Irish and the crofters, who had contributed towards their successes by presenting the Government with a problem of law and order. Rather it resembled the contemporary Scottish farm servants' unions in looking to the state to secure for them objects that they were not strong enough to achieve in their own right.[3] But unlike them it did not concentrate on pushing for specific and minor changes, like the

[1] 'The Warwickshire Agricultural and General Workers' Union', esp. pp. 28–9; Hanham, article cited, pp. 35–6; Peacock, thesis cited, pp. 176–8.

[2] *Bury Free Press*, 4 and 11 March 1893.

[3] One meeting was rather optimistically told that they should be able to place the prospective district councils 'absolutely under the control of the labour organization. Trades Unions could in this manner use their votes to raise wages' by forcing the councils to embark on a large programme of public works at high wages, which the farmers would then have to come up to (*ibid.*, 15 April 1893, p. 5).

Saturday half-holiday;[1] instead it diffused its efforts very widely. In the event neither tactic proved successful, but the Scottish one was the more promising.

However the English unions were larger and rather more self-reliant than the Scottish. Besides looking to legislation, Robinson also followed the old will-of-the-wisp of seeking to place men on the land through the Federation (partly with the profits that might be expected from the sale of 'Federation tea'); then 'if there was a dispute with a farmer, the Federation would set the men to work on a Federation farm at a better wage.' And he looked to combination to increase wages. At first his experience was fortunate. In the rising market of the spring of 1891 the Federation approached farmers where it had branches, and (according to the Land Restoration League) succeeded in obtaining 'practically without a strike and almost without friction, an extra one or two shillings a week'.[2] Combination might also assist in controlling the supply of labour—the urban section of the Norfolk and Norwich Amalgamated Union prevented the Norwich townsmen from undercutting rural labourers at the 1891 harvest, though it was less effective in Yarmouth where strike-breaking was a local industry. But then the tide turned, and in 1892 and 1893 the boot was on the other foot, farming being no less unprofitable but labour more plentiful. Again the Federation claimed to have checked the reduction of wages, saving the labourer one to two shillings a week, an excellent return on his three-farthings subscription. There was some truth in this; and in 1892 and 1893 the Federation was reluctantly drawn into strikes to prevent wage cuts, though only a small proportion of its members were involved.[3] In general, though, it failed to prevent reductions in the spring of 1893, the season when a wage increase was more usual; and thereafter it virtually abandoned strikes.[4]

[1] Admittedly the Ploughmen's Union newspaper treated all aspects of the land question in a style not markedly different from that of the Eastern Counties Federation; but the Union itself concentrated on the conditions of employment and payment—see above, pp. 146–50.

[2] Though the Land Restoration League may be exaggerating the reluctance of the Federation's members (as opposed to its officials) to pressure the farmers by threatening a strike—see Peacock, thesis cited, p. 177 n.

[3] 117 out of 16,900 members (some probably urban) in 1892, and 100 out of 11,300 in 1893 according to (possibly incomplete) returns to the Board of Trade.

[4] *Bury Free Press*, 4 Feb. 1893, p. 8; Land Restoration League,

The experience of Joseph Arch's National Union, now substantially confined to Norfolk and Essex, was not dissimilar. It forced wage increases in 1890–1, and struck to prevent reduction in 1891–3. These disputes were clearly on a much smaller scale than in 1870s, but they may well have been more numerous than those of its contemporaries. Certainly N.A.L.U. officials approached them far less reluctantly than did their counterparts in other unions—Zacharias Walker, the N.A.L.U.'s Norfolk organizer, wrote regularly of 'our little scraps' in his reports in the *English Labourers' Chronicle*. Expectations were probably not as high as in the 1870s—after his initial successes in 1890 Walker told branches not to go in for further advances at the moment: 'do not rush at things. . . . Don't be striking every week. That was where you got blamed last time.' But his general tone was both militant and matter-of-fact: he was thankful, he wrote, that he had made some farmers in North Creak 'feel uncomfortable, and I will make ten shillings per week so stink that if the men keep united the next high wind shall take it away, or the North fever [migration] shall clear their farms.' Admittedly in late 1892 Arch did suggest to the Norfolk Farmers' Federation the joint settlement of wages rates through an arbitration board, as in a number of other industries. But there would have been no likelihood of the National Union's inviting *farmers* to join, so as the better to agitate for legislation on tithe, the land tax, free silver, pure beer, and cheaper land transfer, as did three branches of the Eastern Counties Federation in January 1891.[1]

Not that political action was ignored. The labourers were often reminded that they had the vote now. In one of Walker's speeches, he reports, 'The interest of the Union and the Liberal cause was well maintained, and I feel sure that both social and political questions go well together.' Arch himself had been an M.P. from 1885–6 and again from 1892, and he never let anybody forget it. But his horizons were more restricted than those of his younger rivals. He continued to look to an expansion of the franchise, to the disestablishment of the Church and the abolition of tithes, and to village councils, which would control charities and have powers of compulsory purchase to secure

---

Special Report, 1891, p. 11; Springall, pp. 100–1; *Bury and Norfolk Post*, 7 Feb. 1893, p. 8.

[1] *English Labourers' Chronicle*, esp. 14 and 25 Jan. 1890, 8 Oct. and 19 Nov. 1892; *The Memoirs of Josiah Sage, passim*; *Bury Free Press*, 7 Jan. 1893, p. 3.

land for the labourers. What Arch wanted, though, was not county council farms subsidized out of general taxation (as Robinson had suggested[1]), but rather that every labourer should have access to as much land as he could cultivate, which would enable him, if offered too little pay, simply to refuse to work for the farmer.[2] He remained a partisan of 'self-help and liberty, order and progress' as opposed to 'Present-day Socialism'; and he was to be unkindly described as 'simply a Liberal of moderate John Bright views taken more or less second-hand'.[3]

Also, like John Bright himself in his old age, Arch came to dwell extensively on the improvements he had witnessed in the course of his life-time. Some union speakers ascribed this amelioration of rural conditions to Arch personally, some to the union. Set-backs, and in particular the decline in *money* wages since the great days of the 1870s, were always attributed to the backsliding of the labourers themselves. And so it was when the brief revival of the 1890s was over and the National Union finally collapsed; in 1895 Arch told George Edwards never to 'trust our class again. I am getting old, I have given all the best years of my life in their service, and now in my old age they have forsaken me.'[4]

[1] *Bury and Norwich Post*, 11 Oct. 1892, p. 7.
[2] See esp. *English Labourers' Chronicle*, 17 Dec. 1892, p. 5.
[3] *English Labourers' Chronicle*, 16 Jan. 1892, p. 5; Joseph Arch, p. 204; F. E. Green, *A History of the English Agricultural Labourer 1870–1920* (1920), p. 176.
[4] The following year Edwards explained the collapse of his own union in similar but more biblical language—Edwards, pp. 90, 92–3.

XII

Ideas and Arguments—Crofters

Tradition played a far greater rôle in the lives of Scottish crofters than in those of English agricultural labourers, and it strongly influenced the ways in which they came to assert themselves. Even in England, the catalyst of a number of combinations in the 1870s had been a defensive concern for the preservation of local charities. But the impetus behind trades unionism was more usually a desire for higher wages; and most village leaders set their faces firmly against the older forms of resistance through direct or illegal action, and struck out on new paths. By contrast the initial stages of the crofters' movement were almost entirely confined either to the obstruction of landlord alterations to the status quo (like the raising of traditional rents), or to attempts to undo recent encroachments on what the crofters regarded as their traditional rights.

Highland memories were assisted by a lively culture of oral Gaelic story-tellers, and could stretch back a very long way: a verse celebrating the trouncing of a sheriff's party at Durness in 1841 harked back to the local victory of Drium na Cùb in the early fifteenth century.[1] But the great disturbances to the traditional way of life, the Clearances, were in fact of fairly recent origin—many were well within living memory, and almost all had occurred within a century. So, once the crofters' initial successes had shown that the clock could be set back, there were sporadic attempts to do so, at the expense not only of landlords but of any other interlopers on township lands. Thus when in 1885 a small Uist township imprudently petitioned the *factor* for more land, North Boisdale men demolished its boundary dyke, telling one complainant 'that I was very bold in going to the factor for more land—that the land was theirs' since it had once been part of the North Boisdale common; the complainant added, 'I have had my croft for 16 years. If ever the North Bois- dale people had anything to do with the land it was long ago.'[2]

[1] 'When the heroes saw the weapons unsheathed, the tongs and the sickle, the stake and the flail, they leapt with fear and some of them said, "this is worse for the Sutherland men than the fight of Drium na Cùb." '—Ian Grimble, *Chief of Mackay* (1965), p. 42.

[2] GD 1/36/2 (ii).

There were, of course, limits to this determination to revert to the past. I have encountered the attempted resumption of an island that had been lost for half a century. But I have not met any desire to return to the open-field system of 'run-rig', though this, too, had only been superseded in the early part of the nineteenth century (sometimes in connection with clearances), and though its surviving vestiges were idealized by the crofters' sympathizers. Also, like other people, crofters had selective memories; so there were, in fact, two sides to many of the more celebrated disputes, like Ben Lee in Skye or the Park Deer Forest in Lewis.

But in general the crofters secured the acceptance of their fundamental contention, that they had formerly occupied a far larger share of the land (which was true), with customary, though not legal, rights of individual security of tenure (which was more doubtful); and that it was these rights which had been extinguished, legally but unjustly, by the Clearances. So when Gladstone was asked by Harcourt in January 1885 to find a rationale for the concession of fair rents and security of tenure, he replied by describing the crofters' case as 'not only actually, but historically, exceptional':

The Highland proprietors of these Parishes were the Chiefs of clans, and the produce which they sought to raise from their lands was not rent, but men. From time immemorial these men had been upon the ground with them, recognized in general as kinsmen . . . in point of moral title to live upon the land, enjoyed uniformly *ab antiquo*, I scarcely know how to distinguish between the Chief and his followers. It was might, and not right, which was on his side when, during the half-century or more which followed the '45, he gradually found that the rearing of men paid him in a coin no longer current, and took to the rearing of rent instead, backed by the law, which took no cognizance of any rights but his . . .

. . . it is, after all, this historical fact that constitutes the crofters' title to demand the interference of Parliament. It is not because they are poor, or because there are too many of them, or because they want more land to support their families, but because those whom they represent had rights of which they have been surreptitiously deprived to the injury of the community.[1]

Gladstone had in fact used very similar language about Irish land; and he may have been partly influenced by the need for

[1] Cab. 37/14/7 no. 5. See also E. D. Steele, 'Gladstone and Ireland', *Irish Historical Studies*, xvii (1970), pp. 82–4.

a principle on which to confine legislation to the West High-lands—'for no one intends to change at this moment the Land Laws in general for the sake of the crofter parishes.' But he was voicing a very wide-spread sentiment that 'The people in this part of the country were not like those in the South—they possessed a hereditary right.' And his picture of the Clearances had been drawn, albeit rather less elegantly, by a doggerel poster in Glendale, Skye:

> *Their fathers bought the land with their life's blood,*
> *And served their landlord chiefs with hardihood.*
> *The Chieftains mingled with the southern lords.*
> *And not content with their old Highland board,*
> *Got in deep debt and their estate mortgaged,*
> *Cleared off their tenants whether old or aged.*

This interpretation was not universally accepted—in his Second Reading speech on the 1886 Crofters' Act, Argyll seemed re-signed to legislation but determined to put the Government right on its historical blunders. Balfour, too, believed that 'the whole of these historical foundations of the Crofters' Act rests on pure fiction.' However as Secretary of State he kept such doubts to himself, and readily included disputed areas (like the Ork-neys) within the scope of the Act. So, for practical purposes, the crofters' view of their history was vindicated.[1]

In Lord Napier's view, the burden of the crofters' complaints to his Commission was 'removal or eviction, generally, and reduction of common pasture. To protect themselves against those oppressions they want fixity of tenure, and more land, restoration of land.'[2] Fixity of tenure presented few problems—evictions were becoming unfashionable. Restoration of land was less easy; but of the intensity with which it was demanded there can be no doubt. Direct action was sometimes tried, most ambitiously in Glendale; here a meeting in September 1884 resolved to re-divide the valley over the course of the next six months, and also decided that the people who had originally come from Bracadale Parish should go back, since there 'were no farms in the neighbourhood [of their present township] to take possession of'. The implementation of this programme was inter-

---

[1] Alexander Morrison of Stornoway, *Inverness Courier*, 24 Sept. 1886, p. 5; P. C. Macvicar's report, 7 Dec. 1882 (GD 1/36/1 (i)); *Parl. Deb.*, 3rd series cccv (April–May 1886), 1480–92; Balfour to Sir Francis Sandford, 20 Oct. and 1 Nov. 1886 (B.M. Add. MS. 49871).

[2] Napier to Harcourt, 3 April 1884 (Harcourt Papers).

rupted by the despatch of marines to Skye. And the following year it was more usual to rely on political action: the Highland Law Reform Association's annual conference resolved 'to continue the agitation till the people are reinstated on their ancient holdings'. So it is not surprising to learn that 'The Skye crofters are in great expectation of the passing of a measure in the new Parliament which will restore to them the lands of which they have been deprived at a merely nominal rent, judicially fixed.' Indeed the spread of the H.L.L.R.A. was commonly attributed to its threat that, unless men joined it, 'they would receive no share of the land when it came to be divided, and this was believed.'[1]

In practice the effect of such a division of the land would have varied enormously from place to place. It would have been sheer folly in Morven, even though the district had been notoriously depopulated. For in the later part of the century it was being restored to prosperity by estate expenditure, financed from outside; to break up the estate would have been to cut off the supply of golden eggs. But, in Inverness-shire and Ross and Cromarty at least, this was not usual. Such expenditure had stopped in Lewis in 1878 with the death of Sir James Matheson, though it continued in Harris; and on Skye M'Neill found it confined to Skaebost (and to Kilmuir, where it was directed principally towards large farmers). More generally the landed proprietors who memorialized the Government in 1888[2] declared that 'those Proprietors and others who, until lately, used to expend large sums in improvements, have been compelled to refrain from any further outlay.'[3] In such circumstances the transfer of land to the crofters might have been of immediate benefit to them (and still more to the landless cottars), *if* they could manage to stock it.[4] And, in all, the Deer Forests Com-

---

[1] Macvicar's report, 6 Oct. 1884 (GD 1/36/2 (i)); *The Scotsman*, 3 Sept. 1885, p. 6; *Inverness Courier*, 29 Dec. 1885, p. 3 (reprinting the *Dundee Advertiser*); *Confidential Reports*, p. 49.

[2] They included the Duke of Sutherland, though I think he may have been doing himself an injustice.

[3] Gaskell, *op. cit.*; *Confidential Reports*, pp. 3, 8–9, 63; *P.P.*, 1902 lxxxiii, p. 302; GD 40/16/24 fos. 2–5.

[4] This was a very serious difficulty—Ben Lee remained unstocked for years after its transfer to the Braes; and land without the means for stocking it would merely have burdened crofters with the rates. Reformers admitted that most crofters would not be able to stock additional land, and had to rely rather vaguely on the prospect of assistance from relatives in the towns, landlords, or the state. How-

mission in 1895 scheduled about 1,200,000 acres as physically suitable for new holdings or the extension of existing crofts, among them the coveted farm of Waterstein in Glendale. Lewis, however, it regarded as so hopelessly congested that 'were the whole forest and farm lands in the Island . . . made available for crofters . . ., this step, while it might allay or mitigate the more serious evils arising from the existing condition of matters, would not effect a permanent remedy, and would only relieve the urgency for a limited number of years.' Here some other course would have to be found.[1]

Also, even if in most areas land could (at an undetermined cost) have been distributed among the crofters, the future consequences were not all clear. Argyll devoted great efforts to proving that confiscation could not be confined to the property of Highland lairds, but would menace all kinds of property throughout the country; and in any case the Highlands, like the rest of Scotland, owed their progress from barbarism to the abolition of Celtic laws and tenures and to the spread of freedom of contract. Even the (comparatively limited) Crofters' Act of 1886 would have been better described as 'a Bill to arrest agricultural improvements in certain counties of Scotland', since it would prevent him from raising the more enterprising crofters into viable small farmers.[2] Lochiel, too, was worried at the prospect 'of fixing the people in a condition from which they ought to be "gently but firmly withdrawn".' This reflected an awareness that standards of living had changed and would continue to do so. Accordingly the proprietors pushed not only for their traditional remedy of emigration, but also for *large scale* public works, avowedly to change the occupation structure of the Highlands. The secretary of their 1885 Inverness meeting told Harcourt that 'I believe it has been the all but universal experience that a good arterial railway never fails to tap and draw off

---

ever after the 1886 Crofters' Act the new security of tenure led many crofters to rebuild their homes, so their financial resources may have been rather greater than anticipated.

[1] *P.P.*, 1895 xxxviii, pp. 22–4, and xxxix part 2 (Maps); nearly 550,000 acres were also scheduled as suitable for the creation of 'moderately sized farms rented at over £30 p.a.' (the limit beyond which the Crofters' Act, 1886, did not apply).

[2] For Argyll's view, see e.g. *Celtic Magazine*, iii (1878–9), pp. 32–3; *The Nineteenth Century*, xvi (1884), pp. 681–701; *Parl. Deb.*, 3rd series cccv (April–May 1886), 1480–92; Argyll to Lothian, Jan. 1888 (GD 40/15/35 fo. 24 ff.).

the surplus labouring population among whom it penetrates', that 'the more population which can be drawn from the present congested localities to new and thriving self-supporting communities, devoted to fishing alone, and in no way dependent on the land for their living, the better.' He added, 'After all, the crofter interest is not the primary or most valuable one in the Highlands,'[1] which were best adapted 'not for agriculture or for manufacturers' but for recreational pursuits: and it would be disastrous to destroy the Highlands' unique attractions, 'and so to divert from them that annual stream of visitors which brings with it so much material welfare in which all classes participate.'[2]

The crofters definitely did not see things in this light. One banner at the Golspie demonstration in September 1885 read,

> Ill fares the land, to passing ills a prey, when deer
> Accumulate and men decay.[3]

Even as to fishing, their evidence to the Napier Commission suggests that they would have preferred to be able to rely on their holdings for a living, and not to have had to supplement them by earnings at the fisheries or in the south.[4] Understandably they did not greatly worry about the future—they had immediate problems enough. Nor, on the whole, did their sympathizers, who generally took the line that there was land enough somewhere in the Highlands for everybody, and who accordingly campaigned quite effectively against the emigration scheme inaugurated by Lord Lothian in 1888. The future looked to by both crofters and their sympathizers was often an idealized version of the pre-Clearance past—one old man said he 'would like to be the way I was before, if it were possible; that is, I should like to have a croft and my cows back again as before'. Similarly in recounting the resettlement of

---

[1] In purely financial terms, this was certainly correct.

[2] Lochiel to Harcourt, 26 Jan. 1885 (Cab. 37/14/10). There had been similar pressure for exceptional Government aid for emigration, drainage, and railway construction (to Oban) in the aftermath of the Destitution; but emigration had bulked far larger than public works, and it was to this demand that the Government proved responsive—*P.P.*, 1851 xxvi, esp. pp. 1093–9, and Prebble, *op. cit.*, pp. 211–18.

[3] *Invergordon Times*, 2 Sept. 1885, p. 3.

[4] Though, as things were and had been for decades, the greater part of their income came from wages, not the produce of their crofts.

Strathnaver, Sellar's most notorious clearance, Joseph Macleod records that the crucial steps were taken

on the very day that the last hoof of the Sellars' stock was disposed of. . . . Thus was fulfilled the prophecy, made years before, that 'when the last hoof of the Sellars was cleared out of the County, then would the sons of the evicted return to the lands of their fathers'.[1]

Even John Mackay of Hereford, whose solution (the gradual creation of indivisible hundred acre holdings, with younger sons 'to be well educated for *Swarming*') probably did not greatly differ from Argyll's, saw it not as an innovation but as the restoration of the Sutherland crofters to their moral and material condition of before the Clearances.[2]

Most crofters, then, thought in traditional terms of the restoration to them of adequate holdings, for which they were prepared to continue to pay traditional or 'reasonable' rents, or rents fixed by a Land Court. This was, however, too tame for a number of their sympathizers, who believed in the fashionable progressive causes of land nationalization or restoration. If they were prudent,[3] such men sought to introduce their doctrines to the crofters under the sanction of that other traditional authority, the Bible. John Murdoch (of *The Highlander*) used to say, 'The Highlander believes in the Bible; we must teach him the land question from the sacred book.' And one of the inflammatory documents put about in 1882 by MacHugh of the National Land League of Great Britain (and printed for circulation to the Cabinet) consisted basically of a string of Biblical quotations, like 'The earth hath he given to the children of man' (Psalm cxv: 16), 'And they shall build houses and inhabit them; and they shall plant vineyards and eat the fruit of them. They shall not build, and another inhabit; they shall not plant, and another eat' (Isaiah lxv: 21–3). Even this did not suffice to win Mac-Hugh himself much of an audience. But the approach undoubtedly helped to overcome the crofters' natural respect for the

[1] *P.P.*, 1884 xxxv, question 36134; Joseph Macleod, *op. cit.*, pp. 200–1.

[2] Both relied on landlord action, but Mackay would have had the Government compel this act of restitution, which would take at least 20 years to carry through. Also there was an unusual quantity of land available in Mackay's native Rogart—Mackay to Blackie, National Lib. of Scotland MS. 2635, esp. fos. 46, 105, 209.

[3] Norman Maclean narrates the discomfiture in the Braes of a Glasgow agitator who began by attacking Lord Macdonald in person, and of Henry George who unwisely criticized St. Peter's treatment of Ananias (*The Former Days*, pp. 50–5, 135–8).

lairds and the religious quietism that kept, for instance, the Lewis leader Ruaridh Ban for years from joining the movement. And it came to be the 'favourite doctrine' of John Macpherson, the Glendale Martyr, 'that all men being equal in the sight of God, all are equally entitled to the use of the land upon which he has called them to live,[1] and that Highland crofters in standing up for their ancient rights were asserting the rights of all men.'[2]

Under cover of such quotations it was possible, though certainly not necessary, to advance proto-socialist doctrines of land nationalization. The crofters' agitation attracted support from all kinds of progressive opinion, and by 1884, at the latest, these supporters had become mutually competitive. Thus Professor Blackie claimed that he, and his companions on a yachting tour, had been 'instructing the natives on the philosophy of the *Land Laws*, which will do them a great deal of good, as some of them have been seduced by a few wild men to dream of the possibility of an Agrarian Law by process of general confiscation.' And the Skye police observed that, with the spread of the Highland Land Law Reform Association of London, 'Some that used to write and agitate them from Glasgow, Greenock etc., in former times such as last year, are not heeded as much now'; in particular Shaw Maxwell of the Scottish Land Restoration League found his spring lecture tour disappointing—'They don't, in general, approve of Mr. Shaw Maxwell's theory, because they don't want to go as far as land restoration . . . but just land law reform.'

But, by 1885, the pendulum was swinging in the other direction. Land nationalizers and restorers attended the H.L.L.R.A.'s annual conference in significant numbers. Though attempts were made to confine them to an evening meeting after the main business had been transacted, Stuart Glennie of London secured the amendment of the resolution on the Crofters' Bill. His amendment demanded that the agitation continue until the restoration of *all* 'Highland forests, moorlands, and hill grazings', to the crofting township if they had formerly possessed them, but otherwise 'to the community generally'. That evening he and Angus Sutherland went on to secure the demanding of

[1] However when asked by Sheriff Ivory whether this doctrine applied equally to his salary as an agitator and to his carriage and pair, Macpherson 'answered that God had made the land, but not the carriage'.

[2] *The Old and New Highlands and Hebrides*, pp. 30, 49, 66, 82; *Official Reports*, pp. 17–18.

'general relief to the community, by again placing on land the burdens that have been transferred by landlord agitation to commerce and industry'. John Mackay of Hereford regarded this as a take-over, and 'felt the time had come to make a stand on the platform of *Practicability*, and dissent from that which no sane man would advocate.' Accordingly at the next general election he supported the candidature of the Duke of Sutherland's (very progressive) heir in opposition to that of Angus Sutherland. And in the course of the next year a number of other sympathizers, notably Free Church ministers, merchants, and Professor Blackie himself, withdrew from the movement, thereby weakening it, but also strenghtening the influence of the land restorers.[1]

These were mostly to be found in Glasgow (and to a lesser extent in Sutherland). They overlapped with enthusiasts for disestablishment, labour representation, and advanced politics generally—several of the highland 'agitators' were connected with the formation of the Scottish Labour Party in 1888.[2] At least in the Highlands, their actual contribution to events was probably slight. For the crofters could only hope for reform if they were recognized as a special case. But land restorers instead tended to view them as 'engaged in a struggle which aimed at the emancipation of the poorer classes of the community throughout the whole country'. Many of the evils of the day, including 'much of the degradation and immorality that at present exists in our great cities', were attributable to the private ownership of land. In theory land nationalizers believed in expropriation with compensation, while land restorers sought to tax land values until they were completely eroded. But this was not fully worked out until the end of the decade; and in any case platform utterances, especially those of Henry George in his celebrated lecture tours of 1884 and 1885, were aimed at securing acceptance rather than precision.

[1] Blackie to Rosebery, 6 March 1884 (N.L.S., RB 60); Mackay to Blackie, 20 Nov. 1886 (N.L.S., MS. 2636 fo. 315); Sergeant Boyd, Dunvegan, 24 April and 19 June 1884 (GD 1/36/2(i)); *The Scotsman*, 3 Sept. 1885, pp. 5–6; *Confidential Reports*, esp. pp. 3, 18, 55, 75.
[2] This general ferment is discussed in (*inter alia*) J. G. Kellas, 'Highland Migration to Glasgow and the Origin of the Scottish Labour Movement', *Bulletin of the Society for the Study of Labour History*, xii (1966), pp. 9–11; D. C. Savage, 'Scottish Politics, 1885–6'; *Scottish Historical Review*, xl (1961), pp. 118–35; and Hanham, article cited.

The most tangible result was probably the intensification of the movement's hostility to game. Deer forests were always easy to attack; but, apart from a *cause célèbre* in Kintail, it was not until 1885–6 that the question of game as such assumed major proportions. The Dingwall conference in 1884 merely sought to tax deer forests more heavily, limit their expansion, and to give crofters the right to kill deer that trespassed onto their own holdings. Next year at Portree the official H.L.L.R.A. motions were silent on the topic. But it was raised by D. H. Macfarlane, M.P., who boasted of poaching 140 sea trout in a night. It was then taken up by the land restorers, Stuart Glennie saying 'he might compress' one of his speeches 'into a single sentence, "Down with deer forests." ' And at Bonar Bridge in 1886 the Game Laws came second only to the restoration 'to the Highland people [of] their Native Land'.

M'Neill's *Confidential Reports* of the same year contain several references to 'a new departure by those who direct the proceedings of the Land League, viz. a design to prevent the exercise of sporting rights, with a view to the depreciation of Highland property': in Lewis there had been 'daily' interference with game, and 'when remonstrance is made, the people now reply that the game is their own.' But, on the whole, this did not amount to much more than occasional poaching, destruction of hotel boats, and the like. There were fears that the organized destruction of game would spread to Sutherland, but in fact it was confined to the very special case of the Park Deer Forest in Lewis. In Torridon the general sentiment was said to be against those young men who obtained guns. And understandably so. Deer forests were bad neighbours. But at the same time they provided considerably more employment (and interest) than sheep farms; and large tracts of the country really were suitable for little else. So feeling against them gradually subsided into grumbles.[1]

In much the same way, the crofters' attitude towards landlords was temporarily sharpened by the teachings of the land restorers, but without permanent consequences. One Skye landlord reckoned in 1866 that only seven of his 75 tenants shared his views of land ownership: 'the people are wholly opposed to the payment of rent, they regard rent as an unjust exaction.' And, under the sub-title of 'Henry Georgeism in Skye', a special

[1] *Celtic Magazine*, ix (1884), p. 573; *The Scotsman*, 3 and 4 Sept. 1885; *Invergordon Times*, 29 Sept. 1886, pp. 3–4; *Confidential Reports*, pp. 7, 13, 78, 91.

correspondent had concluded the previous year, that 'At heart, the Skye crofters

are of opinion that, having paid rent for so many generations, the time has now come when payment of it should practically cease. They argue in this way. The landlord, when he has purchased the land, has done so by paying down 20 or 25 years' rent, and he pays no more in acknowledgement to the Government, while the crofters, apart from the natural rights they conceive they have to their lands, think they have been paying long enough to entitle them to absolute ownership.'[1]

But in fact this did not go very deep. 'When the choice was given, only the Glendale township demanded and were granted peasant proprietorship—a decision they have long since regret-ted.'[2] In stating their grievances to the Napier Commission, the crofters had always given priority to the inadequacy of their holdings, their insecurity of tenure, and their liability to rack-rent; peasant proprietorship or state ownership of land was only mentioned at the very end, if at all. The 'no rent' movement never caught on on the mainland; and even the advertisement of the Kilmuir branch of the H.L.L.R.A. that inaugurated it declared a willingness to pay rent at the traditional level, while the H.L.L.R.A.'s official policy was to demand the fixing of rents by a land court.[3] The subsequent inflation of demands may have reflected little more than the natural tendency of any agitation, when successful beyond its wildest dreams, to escalate until it meets a check. Balfour administered such a check, while at the same time the Crofters' Commission stood ready to offer at least security of tenure and fair rents. Thus controlled, landlords could continue to help, but could no longer hurt, their small tenants.

In any case landlords and large factors were only spasmodi-cally unpopular. Certainly they were much abused. But senti-ment was often mixed. A leading figure in the Braes is supposed to have said at the height of the Ben Lee episode, 'One side of me is for Lord Macdonald and another side of me is for the poor people. The flesh warreth against the spirit and the spirit against the flesh: but which is flesh and which spirit I do know.' And loyalty to Lord Macdonald, admittedly one of the few surviving clan chiefs, probably explains why subsequent agitation there

[1] *Confidential Reports*, p. 26; *Inverness Courier*, 29 Dec. 1885, p. 3.
[2] D. W. Crowley, 'The "Crofters' Party", 1885–1892', *Scottish Historical Review*, xxxv (1956), p. 119 n.
[3] *Oban Times*, 20 Sept. and 25 Oct. 1884.

was only moderate. But in 1882 and 1883 even the tougher Glendale still wanted the return of the recently retired factor, despite all the charges they made against him to the Napier Commission; a poster entitled 'The Glendale Crofters Wrongs' summed him up thus:

> *Tormore the Factor thirty years ago*
> *Began his office and was good or so*
> *Though good and kind of land he was greedy*
> *But after gave meal to poor and needy*
>
> *But he insulted by Milvaig folks*
> *Took to his heels and we'll see him no more.*

Similarly in 1884 the Kilmuir H.L.L.R.A. branch publicly declined to have any further dealings with Alexander Macdonald as factor, partly because he was suspected of pressing the Government for military intervention; but the following year he was returned at the head of the poll for Stenscholl, 'the hot-bed of the agitation', probably in recognition of his own, and still more his grandfather's, kindness. Landlord crofter relations were obviously strained at the height of the agitation; but whereas in Ireland they never recovered from the propaganda of the Land League, in the Highlands they gradually re-asserted themselves despite the diffusion of the new ideas.[1]

If the crofters' attitudes towards the landlords were ambivalent, those towards the police were correspondingly so; for according to Lord Lovat, the Convenor of the Inverness-shire Police Committee, 'The people believe that the police are only the servants of the proprietors and factors, and have no moral influence.' The police were in fact extraordinarily thin on the ground; and whether the people obeyed them depended largely on their own views of right and wrong. As one Sutherland constable put it:

There is hardly any crime of the kind which occurs elsewhere, and if a case of theft or assault were reported, a single constable would have no difficulty in apprehending the offender. But it is otherwise with such matters as offences eg. under the Education Acts, which the people do not regard as offences at all.

All offences in connection with the land agitation fell into this category; in January 1883 Macvicar tried to persuade some

[1] *The Former Days*, pp. 65–6, 68–9, 98, 129–33, 147–9; GD 1/36/1 (i), 7 Dec. 1882; *The Old and New Highlands and Hebrides*, p. 51.

men who had assaulted a shepherd to accompany him to Portree
for trial; they declined 'as it was connected with the farm of
Waterstein, but in any other crime not connected with Waterstein . . . they were quite willing to go with me as they used . . . in
former years.'[1]

If they would not co-operate, there was very little the police
could do about it. The paralysing of the machinery of the law
by the forcible prevention of the service of writs was not new in
the Highlands. And though agitation began with the more
modern device of passive resistance through non-payment of
rent, when faced in 1882–3 with writs of removal or even merely
of interdict, the inhabitants of the Braes and of Glendale reverted to force.[2] Token police escorts were brushed aside; and a
party of six outside policemen was driven out of Glendale by
a large mob. Such actions were either not punished, or punished
only lightly, and the practice not unnaturally spread. Indeed
the crofters' friends in Portree and elsewhere not only notified
them by telegraph of the departure of police expeditions, but
also at least once explicitly urged that they be turned back. On
this occasion the crofters brought their local constable along to
show that no additional force was needed to keep the peace,
'that they did not break the law, and if they did that they had
a policeman of their own with them, with whom they would
willingly go to Portree, to be punished, if required': this said,
they roughly chased the police expedition of nine off the estate,
while promising to bring 'our policeman' 'back safe, and take
care of him'.[3]

But troops were a different matter. Balfour was undoubtedly
correct in telling the Cabinet that though the people held the
police 'in the uttermost contempt', there was wide-spread agreement that they 'will never for an instant attempt to resist the
forces of the Crown; partly for fear of the results, and partly
because they recognize in them what they decline to recognize

[1] Cab. 37/16/54; *Confidential Reports*, p. 93; GD 1/36/2(i), 10
Jan. 1883.

[2] The 'no-rent' policy continued to be widely used in the Islands,
especially after 1884, by which time it had become clear that it
would not lead to eviction. But 'no-rent', and still more the occupation of disputed grazings, were only viable if backed by a readiness
to deforce the servers of writs.

[3] *P.P.*, 1884–5 lxiv, esp. p. 343; see also 'Evidence taken by Sheriff
Ivory' and 'Correspondence between the Home Secretary, the Lord
Advocate, and others and Sheriff Ivory in regard to Skye', GD
1/36/1 (ii and iii).

in the police, *ie.*, that they are the emissaries of the central authority.' Governments were usually careful to deploy overwhelming force, even at the cost of looking ridiculous, rather than risk having to open fire. But the consideration of legitimacy was probably the more important: Macleod of Macleod believed that ten marines would suffice to restore order to Skye in 1886; and on a previous occasion the constable at Dunvegan had reported that, though the people would resist unescorted police to the end, 'Should only a few soldiers come among them, they say they will not lift a hand against them.'[1]

This respect for the central government stemmed partly from simple patriotism, and partly from an old-fashioned belief that, if the Queen and the Government only knew what was going on, they would see justice done. Both attitudes are apparent at a meeting at Kilmuir, reported by the *Celtic Magazine* as being typical 'of what is going on in almost every township in the West'. Arguing against wholesale emigration, one speaker asked:

if the French or Russians should invade the country would the landlords shake themselves like so many Samsons against the Philistines, and put the enemy to rout with an army of factors, ground-officers, tacksmen, and Cheviot rams. Even with all those they would not be able to stand up for Queen and country as the men of Skye did seventy and eighty years ago. The crofters were not met to plot against life or property, but to consider what should be done to secure redress of their grievances, and he hoped our gracious Queen and her councillors would seriously consider the matter, and put an end for ever to the oppression and cruelty with which her loyal subjects were being treated in Skye.

Such views were natural enough. Local government was firmly in the hands of factors or of men who believed in the simple enforcement of the existing law, which came to much the same thing. So, if the crofters were not satisfied with the concessions the factors offered, their only hope lay in the central government. Nor were they disappointed. As Balfour rather acidly observed,

the people have got hold of the idea that the landlords have no *moral* right to their rent, and that if they have a *legal* right, it is not one which the Executive Government seriously intends to support. This latter view, it must be admitted, derives some plausibility from

[1] Cab. 37/18/44; P. C. Boyd, enclosed in the Lord Advocate's letter to Harcourt, 1 Feb. 1883.

the inactivity displayed in enforcing civil obligations in the last five years.

There was, no doubt, an element of self-interest in this appeal to the Government, which sometimes found expression in rather quaint attempts to bargain—a Glendale meeting in 1884 resolved that none of the young men should attend the Royal Naval Volunteer Reserve drills 'until they would get justice from the Government on the Land question'.[1] But a basic fund of loyalty to the Government as such still remained available for Lord Lothian to tap in his tour of the north-west in 1889, having survived disappointment with the Crofters' Act and with the 1886 expedition to Skye (which was, in any case, like its predecessor, largely blamed on Sheriff Ivory instead).[2]

Nevertheless there was an important change in attitude in the course of the agitation. To begin with the crofters themselves, at least in Skye and probably more generally, had fairly modest expectations: they were doubtless unsettled by news of the Irish Land Act of 1881, and by the belief that 'there were new laws passing about lands', and they may have hoped eventually to benefit in this way. But in the immediate future they probably wished only to be left alone to settle their localized disputes with the landlords without fear of coercion—they believed 'that Mr. Gladstone sympathizes with them and that Govt. have refused *under any circumstances* to send troops'. The agitation for a Royal Commission was largely external to the Highlands; and Mackay of Hereford, for instance, was afraid that the crofters would not take proper advantage of it. Accordingly he wrote 'to many of the [Free Church] ministers of Sutherland to convene meetings for the purpose of getting into the minds of the people the vast import of being prepared with evidence, and men marked out to give it'. Things went well; and towards the end of 1883 he could write that

Associations are being formed . . . in various parts of the Highlands, defensive and offensive. The people now see who are friends and foes, and are now determined in consequence. Lairds and factors

[1] This approach had been anticipated during the Crimean War; one meeting declared itself 'resolved that there shall be no volunteers or recruits from Sutherlandshire. Yet we assert that we are as willing as our forefathers were to peril life and limb in the defence of our Queen and country were our wrongs and long-endured oppression redressed . . .' (Prebble, *op. cit.*, pp. 322–3).

[2] *Celtic Magazine*, ix (1884), pp. 337–40; Cab. 37/18/44; Macvicar's report, 6 Oct. 1884, GD 1/36/2 (i).

have declared themselves, and hence the people see they can no longer be trusted. This was the inevitable result of the Inquiry.[1]

Mackay was chiefly concerned with Sutherland, a militant county but not one that contained many 'disturbed districts' where actual clashes with the law were to be feared. The Napier Commission had spread the agitation well beyond its places of origin. It had also given a stimulus to formal organization. At first this had not been necessary; the original townships had acted together as a result of local meetings, supplemented by a little intimidation. From their outside sympathizers they could expect warnings of the despatch of troops or police, and they also received advice, sometimes unsolicited but sometimes at their own request. This advice, though, was on local problems, like whether or not to surrender for trial or to withdraw their beasts from disputed grazings. However in the aftermath of the Napier Commission, the Highland Land Law Reform Associations of London and Edinburgh established a formal network of branches in the Highlands, transforming themselves from urban pressure groups into a coherent movement. They still, of course, continued to give local advice; but each branch was committed to adopting the constitution of the parent body, 'The chief points' of which 'were—the appointment of a Land Court, with judicial and administrative functions, empowered to fix fair rents, award compensation for improvements, regulate the extension of existing townships, and the formation of new ones, and regulate the formation of any occupying proprietary.' In other words they were now committed to securing positive action by the Government.[2]

That meant involvement in politics. Some people had urged this on the crofters all along. Thus in tracing the advent of *The Sutherland Democracy* a contemporary pamphlet gave pride of place to Angus Sutherland's speech in Helmsdale in 1882. He had been sent down by the Glasgow Sutherlandshire Association, and he sought to generalize what had hitherto been a mere grazing dispute (conducted in a low key) into a challenge to a system that he represented as unchanged since the memorable Clearances. His practical advice was that the crofters should

[1] Rev. Donald Mackinnon to Sheriff Ivory, 23 Nov. 1882 (GD 1/36/1(i)); Mackay to Blackie, 3 and 14 April and 25 Nov. 1883 (N.L.S. MS. 2635, esp. fos. 46, 105).
[2] For the rules of the London, H.L.L.R.A. see Macvicar's report, of 14 Aug. 1884 (GD 1/36/2 (i)); for its objects, see the *Oban Times*, 20 Sept. 1884, p. 6.

organize. And he drew attention to the inadequacy of the existing northern M.P.S, telling the crofters not to forget it when
they got the vote.[1]

But it was the situation in 1884 that really encouraged the
spread of political consciousness. For the report of the Napier
Commission was not immediately followed by Government
action. Yet at the same time Gladstone was seen to be trying to
get the crofters the vote and to be meeting resistance. So the
conclusion was drawn that satisfaction could be obtained, but
only if the crofters themselves worked for it:

Mr. Gladstone said in Edinburgh a few days ago that he would deal
sympathetically with them as soon as he could. But Mr. Gladstone,
powerful though he was, could not make good laws unless the people
demanded them. He [D. H. Macfarlane, M.P.] could name several
members who sat behind the Prime Minister who were his opponents
on the land question. It remained with themselves to make the next
House of Commons different from the present one. If at the next
election they would send up fifty members pledged up to the neck
on the land question they might depend on something being done
for them.

Accordingly the H.L.L.R.A.'s Dingwall conference passed resolutions pledging itself to secure the return of Land Law Reform
candidates, approving of Gladstone's Franchise Bill, and urging
the ending of the Lords' power of veto. Moreover the message
went home: next year one demonstration banner confidently
claimed,

The voters cross each sore will cure,
Quacks have no chance at Gartymore.[2]

There was, in fact, little else for the H.L.L.R.A. branches to
do, outside the 'disturbed districts', besides concentrate on
politics. 'At the ordinary meetings', said the first annual report
of the Alness branch, 'members discussed the iniquitous land
and game laws, and the ruin they have wrought on the Highlands'; and it went on to boast of having 'done not a little to
arouse public interest in political subjects, both by the discussions at the meetings, the publication from time to time of the
discussions, and the consequent perusal by the public generally
of those papers wherein sound Radical doctrines are set forth.'

[1] D. W. Kemp, *The Sutherland Democracy* (Edinburgh, 1890), esp.
pp. 38–42; *Northern Ensign* (Wick), esp. 24 Aug. 1882, p. 5.
[2] *Invergordon Times*, 10 Sept. 1884 and 2 Sept. 1885.

Nor was this as dull as it sounds. For the land question was one of obvious immediacy. And the business was, in any case, skilfully managed, being often inaugurated with Gaelic prayers, and brightened up with tea, bag-pipes, and songs—Mary Macpherson, 'The Skye Poetess', was much in demand for 'Land League' occasions and is said to have contributed 'In quantity ... as much as almost all the other 19th century [Gaelic] poets put together.'[1] To these attractions should be added some imposing processions (generally featuring rather cheerful banners), and, above all, elections in 1885 and 1886. The first election was, of course, a novelty: many crofters arrived at the polling booths in Portree before they opened, while in North Uist the crofters marched off to vote in a body; though the second was rather less exciting, the poll remained high.[2]

In the end this was bound to pall; and with the emergence of new issues like Disestablishment, the crofting vote was eventually to prove quite volatile. But to begin with it was strongly committed to Gladstone personally—as an 1886 banner put it,

> Dornoch crofters—
> *Gladstone will back you*
> *If needs be with swords,*
> *To give crofters their rights,*
> *And abolish the Lords.*

This loyalty survived in the face of a number of counterattractions: the Henry George-ism or proto-socialism of many of the crofters' most energetic external sympathizers; the Liberal-Unionism of Fraser Mackintosh and of Joseph Chamberlain (the only first-class politician to stump the Highlands); and the belief that the crofters should copy the Irish independence of both major parties. True each of these attractions caused splits. And the third seemed to be strikingly vindicated by the 1885 elections, when 'crofter candidates' defeated the official Liberals in five constituencies. But though they thus adopted a stance of independence, it was always rather hollow—as Dr. Clark, the new M.P. for Caithness, put it in December 1885, 'while we will support a Tory Government that will' meet the crofters' demands, 'we only hope to get them from a Liberal Government.'

[1] S. Maclean, 'The Poetry of the Clearances', *Transactions of the Gaelic Society of Inverness*, xxxviii (1939), pp. 319 ff.; see also *The Old and New Highlands and Hebrides*, chap. 22 ('The Bards of the Movement').

[2] *Invergordon Times*, 22 Sept. 1886, p. 3; *Inverness Courier*, 5 Dec. 1885, p. 2.

So by 1892 the crofters' movement (or what remained of it) had been almost completely re-absorbed into official Liberalism.[1]

In exchange progressive views on the land question became the local Liberal gospel. This was something of a triumph for the land agitation. For in the early 1880s the president of the Inverness-shire Liberal Association had been Major Fraser, the rack-renting proprietor of Kilmuir in Skye. And the change can be seen in Joseph Macleod's collection of vignettes on *Highland Heroes of the Land Reform Movement*: a number of the earlier ones were crofters who had genuinely risked eviction for the cause; but the heroism of younger men (like Duncan Mackintosh a large Inverness draper and an influential member of the local Burgh and County Liberal Associations) appears to have consisted only of holding 'most advanced' views 'on all questions, but particularly in regard to the land'.[2] Accordingly the next major installation of land reform came not as a result of another crofters' revolt (like that of the 1880s in Skye), but through the insistence of a former pupil of Angus Sutherland's, Lord Pentland, and the energetic backing afforded him by the Scottish Liberal Association.[3]

[1] *Inverness Courier*, 26 Dec. 1885, p. 3, and 24 Sept. 1886, p. 5.

[2] Hanham, article cited, p. 51; *Highland Heroes*, pp. 121–2.

[3] The 'Pentland Act' of 1911 extended to all small tenants in Scotland protection analogous to that afforded within 'crofting parishes' by the 1886 Act; it also went far beyond the genuflections of previous legislation in compelling the provision of new small holdings—see John Brown, 'Scottish and English Land Legislation 1905–11', *Scottish Historical Review*, xlvii (1968), and D. W. Crowley, article cited, p. 26.

XIII

Ideas and Arguments— the Tithe War

The first distraint for tithe at Llanarmon, the cradle of the Welsh agitation, took place in mid-August 1866. In early September, at a farmers' meeting in Ruthin, there was formed a 'Society for supporting those who suffer under tithe distress' (or 'Anti-Tithe League'). And a fortnight later it put out a manifesto (in Welsh and English) that is worth quoting at length: 'About nine months ago', it begins,

owing to the great depression in the price of agricultural produce, an informal meeting of farmers was held in Llandyrnog to consider the situation, as it was painfully apparent that the farmers could not pay their way any longer unless something was done to diminish to a material extent their outgoings. They had, all of them, previously applied for a remission in the amount of their rent, and their landlords to some extent acquiesced in their application, and in almost all cases had allowed 10 per cent, and upwards, off the rent. That being the case, it was thought that an application should also be made to the rector of the parish for a reduction of 10 per cent. in the amount of the tithe. This application was accordingly made, but it was refused, the rector demanding the whole of the tithe . . .

The manifesto then proceeded to give its version of events at Llandyrnog, Llanarmon and elsewhere, and concluded that 'it will be readily seen that the disestablishment and disendowment of the Church was not the primary object of the League.' The League's original objects, it claimed, had been limited to supporting farmers' appeals for tithe rebates, compensating them (as far as its funds allowed) for losses incurred by refusal to pay except through forced sales, and providing information about tithe law.

But the manifesto went on to say that the League did not favour the solution of transferring liability for tithe from tenant to landlord; for this would help neither party.

Besides, with the view of avoiding further complications the members of the League are anxious that all questions which may arise between agricultural tenants and landowners should be dealt with entirely apart from the question of tithes.

The League was not formed with the object of securing the disestablishment and disendowment of the Church, but it must be admitted that the depressed state of agriculture, and the refusal of the clergy to listen to the reasonable and respectful appeals which were made to them by the farmers for reductions in the tithe rent charge, and also the unmerciful and unchristian spirit evinced in insisting upon a forced sale of their stock, together with a lively sense of the misappropriation and maladministration of the tithes (which they consider to be national property and ought to be devoted to national purposes) have so influenced the minds of the members of the League that they consider that a louder demand than heretofore should be made for the disestablishment and disendowment of the Church of England, especially in Wales. And whenever the Church is disendowed, it is earnestly hoped that no such deceptive and unsatisfactory a measure of disendowment will be proposed as was applied to the Irish Church; but such a measure only as will secure to the country the greatest amount possible from the tithes, the whole, or a large portion of which should remain in each parish or district, to be applied to educational and other local purposes, whereby ratepayers will be relieved from many burdens which are now felt to be extremely oppressive.[1]

The agitation, then, claimed to be basically economic. As the great journalist Thomas Gee put it at the inaugural meeting of the Anti-Tithe League,

The price of agricultural produce and stock had fallen in the markets of the country fully fifty per cent., and the farmers were compelled to seek relief. There were only three classes who depended directly on the land—the landowners, the farmers themselves, and the clergy, and as farmers had felt the pinch and had contracted their expenses in every direction, as the landowners had also returned sums varying from 10 to 30 per cent of their rents, it was but natural for the farmers to turn to the clergy and appeal to them for a reduction in their tithes.

And when the tithe-owners refused, it was equally natural to dwell on the iniquity 'of money wrung from these poor, hard-driven farmers going to provide champagne and claret for the common room of the wealthiest colleges in the world', or even to suggest that 50 pounds a year 'was quite enough for a clergyman.'[2]

---

[1] *Daily News*, 8 and 23 Sept. 1886; *P.P.*, 1887 xxxviii, pp. 299–300.
[2] *Daily News*, 25 Aug. and 8 Sept. 1886; Osborne Morgan, quoted by *The Times*, 30 Nov. 1887, p. 3.

Simple disinclination to pay played a considerable rôle in the agitation, and presumably accounts for the participation of a number of Anglicans. It was duly exploited: as one politician wrote to another, 'You will not, of course, be misled if there is an outcry for the abolition of tithes—tithes cannot be abolished, but I should not be surprised if there is a demand. We can only work through the tithe-payers[1] & they will clamour for abolition.' Even when they were reconciled to paying, people preferred their money to be spent locally. So there was a good deal of grumbling about the vast sums drawn by such bodies as the Ecclesiastical Commissioners, and spent not only outside the particular parishes in question but allegedly also outside Wales. Indeed absentee tithe-owners in general found things more difficult than local ones. Hence the Anti-tithe League's promise that once the tithe had been converted to national purposes it would mostly be spent where it was raised.[2]

However the actual agitation crystallized round demands for tithe reductions of about 10 per cent. These would have cost resident clergy, at least, less than they often protested, had they been readier to collect their tithes themselves and so save the 5 per cent charge usually made by their agents. Nevertheless the demands were not very compelling. For, since the 1836 Tithe Commutation Act, tithe had been payable no longer in kind, but as a money rent-charge based by a sliding-scale on the average corn prices over the last seven years. It had therefore, as the tithe-owners repeatedly pointed out, already fallen by 17 per cent since the beginning of the decade.[3]

This was usually passed over in silence by the anti-tithers. But when the point was taken up, it led necessarily to an attack on the whole basis of the commutation under the 1836 Act. Thus on one occasion Joseph Richards of Meifod claimed, 'They would be paying much more than the real tithe when they paid it minus ten per cent'; and another speaker declared that, though the parsons only 'said they owned the tenth part of the earth', they 'now claimed more than the tenth. They claimed nearly one-half of it.' Such contentions perhaps verged on the rhetorical. But they could be supported by three kinds of argument. The system of sliding-scales based on corn averages was

[1] By a slip of the pen Gibson actually wrote 'tithe-owners' (to Rendel, 8 May 1887—N.L.W. MS. 19450 no. 170).

[2] *P.P.*, 1887 xxxviii, p. 294; R. E. Prothero, *The Anti-tithe Agitation in Wales* (1889), pp. 8–9.

[3] In 1881 the scale stood at £107·14, in 1887 at £87·44 (*The Times*, 6 Jan. 1887, p. 9).

subjected to plausible, but specious, technical criticism.[1] Next
undoubted anomalies were pointed out: some land was exempt
from tithes; some districts were more heavily tithed than others;
at commutation landowners had been free to apportion their
tithe as they pleased between their different fields in any given
parish; and in any case the relative value of different types of
land had sometimes changed since then. Lastly there was widespread confusion as to what the tithe represented. For since it
was still called 'the tenth' (*y Degwm*), there was a general feeling
(supported by confused remembrances of the pre-Commutation
practice) that it ought to *be* a tenth. What it should be a tenth
of was less clear, and witnesses before the 1887 Inquiry into
tithe disturbances were frequently incoherent on the point.
Probably they felt that the tithe should be a tenth of the rent,
or of the 'gross annual value'; such an attitude recurred in the
English agitation of the 1930s, and the Royal Commission on
Tithe proved sympathetic towards it. This association of tithe
with a tenth of the gross annual value was emphatically not
accepted by Lord Salisbury's Government[2]—after all tithe had
originally been a tenth not of rent but of produce (or at least
of certain kinds of produce). But, once the association was made,
it was no doubt quite easy to find instances of land that had
been over-tithed.[3] Even so, these were probably unusual: at
Meifod, according to Archdeacon Thomas, tithe came to about

---

[1] As in the 1840s, men often complained because Welsh corn was
less valuable than the English corn that determined the averages;
but it was never suggested that its value did not fluctuate in sympathy with the English. Tithe commutation had been based on a
protected market, not on the lower prices obtaining under free trade.
But in fact the price of other produce had fallen less than that of
corn; Wales was not a great corn-producer, and so gained from the
tying of tithe to corn rather than to produce in general. Lastly the
system of basing tithe on septennial rather than triennial averages
was attacked; but though in earlier depressions this system had
resulted in tithe moving against the general trend of prices, this
time it did not. The real trouble was that since corn fell earlier than
stock prices (which were what chiefly mattered in Wales), the tithe
had already come down before stock collapsed; so there was no
sudden reduction to compensate for this collapse.

[2] This would go no further (in its 1891 Act) than to provide that
liability for tithe should not exceed two-thirds of the Schedule B
estimate of the gross annual value of the land; the provision was in
fact seldom to be invoked (*P.P.*, 1935–6 xiv, pp. 876–7, 887).

[3] *P.P.*, 1887 xxxviii, e.g. pp. 307–8, 357, 377 (a fourth of the
produce of the land), p. 312 (a fourth of the rent).

a thirteenth of the rent;[1] and, as the following table shows, the general average was only slightly higher.

TABLE I: *Tithes in 1887 as a % of gross Schedule B Income Tax assessments, 1887–8*[2]

		Monmouthshire	9·2
Flint	10·7		
Denbigh	10·4	Essex	18·6
Anglesey	9·8	Suffolk	17·7
Brecon	9·7	Hampshire	17·3
Glamorgan	8·8	Norfolk	15·9
Radnor	8·7	Kent	14·7
Cardigan	8·3		
Montgomery	8·2	England	9·1
Carnarvon	8·0		
Pembroke	7·7		
Merioneth	6·5		
Carmarthen	6·4		
Wales	8·7 (excluding Monmouthshire)		

It will be seen that south-east England was more heavily tithed than Wales; and, since corn was more important there, agricultural depression was worse. Yet opposition to tithes in late nineteenth-century England never approached the Welsh scale. So economic difficulties alone cannot explain the 'Tithe War'. True the farmers of the Vale of Clwyd, in the heart of the agitation, were supposed in 1887 to be paying their debts out of capital. But the tithe-owners' offers of individual rebates to farmers in genuine straits were seldom taken up. And the general reduction that was demanded instead (10 per cent on tithe, or a fraction of 1 per cent of out-goings) could not have been of any very great assistance. Indeed some of the leaders of the agitation did not even pay tithes, and many participants paid only very small sums. 'What is a clergyman to do', asked Vincent with only slight exaggeration, 'when a tithepayer comes down to the parsonage asserting magnificently that he will consent to pay on a reduction of 25 per cent being granted, and then is driven to confess that the amount due from him is only 4d.?'

[1] *The Times*, 1 Dec. 1887, pp. 13–14.
[2] Derived from *P.P.*, 1887 lxiv, pp. 572–3, 1892 xlviii, pp. 252–5: for a discussion of Schedule B tax assessments, see J. C. Stamp, *British Incomes and Property* (1916), chap. 2.

Sectarian and political animosities lay only a very little way below the surface; and, as the Anti-Tithe League's manifesto declared, the non-compliance of the Anglican clergy brought them instantly into play.[1]

One South Wales farmer calculated that, over the last forty years, he had paid £800 in tithe to a church he had never entered. In Llanarmon rather over £360 per annum was payable, but there were only 30 Anglican communicants out of a population of 1600. And in Anglesey there were alleged to be 27 inland parishes without a resident minister, three or four of which never had services and eight or nine had services less than once a week. On such figures Nonconformists based a very understandable reluctance to support the 'alien Church' through compulsory tithes. In reply Anglicans reminded them, *ad nauseam*, that such was the law of the land, and that furthermore the tithe was really a tax on landlords, which tenants had freely contracted to pay as the landlords' agents. Strictly speaking, this was correct. But the conclusion that liability to tithe had been taken into consideration in assessing the rent was not. Often tithe was simply not mentioned when the terms of a tenancy were discussed; and, by the custom of the country, this was tantamount to the tenants' contracting to pay.[2]

A further stir to the cauldron was given in early 1887 by Thomas Gee's action in holding a census of attendance of religious worship. Predictably both sides cheated; and there was a suspicious gap before results could be published. From this it was concluded that the Church had made an uncomfortably good showing. For it probably was larger than any single Nonconformist denomination; and it may have been expanding in South Wales, and in the small towns, though not the upland countryside, of the north. It was this reviving strength, the champions of the Church went on to contend, that really worried the Calvinist Methodists, and led them to bend every nerve to secure its destruction, especially where it was doing a good job. Be that as it may,[3] things were not improved by Gee's subsequent patronage, later that year, of the composition of tithe ballads to be sung (in Welsh) to popular tunes:

[1] *Letters from Wales* (1889), pp. 25, 37, 212–3.
[2] *Daily News*, 24 Aug. and 28 Oct. 1886; N.L.W. SA/Tithe/no. 73, Thomas Edward Ellis Collection no. 677a; *Letters from Wales*, chap. xv.
[3] The sect probably did provide the principal opposition to tithe. But it was far from monolithic—some Calvinist ministers actually helped local vicars to get the tithe in.

> *Apostolic priests, indeed!*
> *Judases in heart and deed;*
> *Traitors steeped in fraud.*[1]

Such ballads were intended principally for tithe distraint sales, which were often considerable occasions. In Merionethshire some were enlivened by a mock parson in a donkey cart: the cart was placarded, 'Religious Equality for Wales. Tithes for the people. The parson to feed himself. Justice up; tithes down. The voice of the people'; and the 'parson' repeatedly went through the following chatechism:

Q. What is your name?   A. Parson Degwm [tithe].
Q. What are you?   A. A poor [i.e. incompetent] preacher.
Q. Where do you come from?   A. From England.
Q. Where are you going?   A. To Rome.

Hostility to the clergy and their ritual could also be expressed in a less jocular fashion. Haystacks that were to be seized for tithe were often surmounted with clerical effigies and placarded with slogans. At Henelwys in Anglesey a distraining party encountered 'a straw figure . . . with a table in front, with chopped turnips, and a small tin cup . . . intended to represent a celebration of the Holy Communion.' In Cardiganshire a retired Baptist minister erected a figure inscribed ' "I am the oppressor and the destroyer" say the people. "For thy people are as they that strive with the priest." ' And in Cwm (near St. Asaph) an effigy of the vicar was carried round by a crowd of farm labourers, preceded by a man chanting anti-tithe ballads, and then knocked to pieces with sticks. Even where things were less personalized, it was usual to convert distraint sales into meetings to demand Disestablishment and Disendowment.[2]

If the Church were disendowed, the tithe would then become national property. And though some farmers simply demanded the abolition of tithes, most at least professed a readiness to pay them were they diverted to national purposes.[3] These pur-

[1] T. Gwynn Jones, *Cofiant Thomas Gee*, pp. 461–4; J. Cynddylan Jones to Gee, 4 March 1887 (N.L.W. MS. 8306 fos. 122 (a) and (b)); *Letters from Wales*, pp. 40–6, 82–5, 99; *Denbigh Free Press*, 24 Dec. 1887, p. 4.

[2] *Montgomery Express*, 24 Dec. 1889, p. 7; *The Times*, 27 Jan. and 28 March 1888; Rev. R. Lewis, *The Tithe War in West Wales* (N.L.W. MS. 15321, p. 13–punctuation added).

[3] However tithe agitation revived in the 1930s in very much the same districts, though not with the same intensity, as in the 1880s; and by then Disestablishment *had* converted the tithe into 'national property'.

poses were never very clearly defined, but there was a general understanding that the bulk of the money would go towards education. This had its drawbacks. For a high proportion would be spent in the towns, which did not appeal to a number of hill farmers. Besides it enabled apologists of the Church to claim that the net effect would be the collapse of the voluntary schools and a consequent *increase* in local taxation. They also maintained that tithes payable to bodies like church schools and Oxford colleges were already being devoted to educational purposes, and that the recalcitrants were therefore being, at best, illogical. This charge prompted Gee to ascertain from Professor Rhys that All Souls' services to education were inconsiderable, and led to lengthy wrangles over Christ Church's educational clientele and as to whether the college should be regarded as a clerical or a lay impropriator.[1] Moreover in many quarters the voluntary schools maintained by the Church were regarded not as a service to education but as an additional grievance; for many Nonconformists had no option but to expose their children to them, especially at the secondary level.[2]

Indeed, though its ritualist proclivities and apostolic pretensions were heartily disliked, the main objections to the Established Church were that it was English and that it was privileged. For most of the century the entire superstructure of Welsh society—local administration, justice, higher education, and the like—had been under the control of Anglican and English speaking landlords, clergymen and their dependents. As time went on this stranglehold had been increasingly challenged. And occasionally the challengers had been punished, notably after the 1859 and still more the 1868 elections, when some hundred farmers had been evicted for voting the wrong

---

[1] Legally it was a lay impropriator, but as the tithe demands were headed 'The Dean and Chapter' this did not carry much conviction. It was widely believed in Meifod that only the sons of peers were admitted (and that after a free education they were then rewarded with large sums of money screwed out of poor Welsh farmers); alternatively 'it was becoming more and more a training college for young English parsons', and a Puseyite one to boot; anyway it was exclusively Anglican. In reply the college ascertained that in 1889 five dissenters, two sons of dissenting ministers, and one Hindu held awards, and that seven dissenters and one minister's son (who became an Anglican) had only recently left (MS. Estates 50 esp. fos. 1787, 1815, 1838–9; *The Times*, 28 June 1887, p. 2.)

[2] *The Anti-tithe Agitation in Wales*, p. 6; N.L.W. MS. 8308 fo. 286; *Daily News*, 17 Nov. 1886, p. 5.

way.[1] Since the 1872 Ballot Act such tactics were largely (though not entirely) things of the past. Landlord pressure certainly remained possible, and was indeed exerted during the Tithe War; and some landlords may still have shown a preference for Anglican tenants when letting vacant holdings. But radical pamphleteers were seldom able to find convincing examples of recent victimization, and so tended to flog old horses. However resentment still continued; and the progress of democracy made its expression (and stimulation) steadily easier. The Tithe War was an episode in this process.

Thus a meeting after sales at Manafon in December 1888 was told that 'The Welsh people had been trampled upon too long by unprincipled clergymen, but they were beginning to lift up their heads. The [newly constituted] County Council was a step in the right direction, by means of which the common people could attain power.' Another speaker added that 'Formerly the three greatest men in a parish were the parson, the squire, and the steward! What a change had come to pass! . . . The parson used to be a very formidable man, but now he was going down and the people were coming up.' Resolutions were then passed in favour not only of disestablishment but also of the election to the county council of 'farmers and other men of democratic principles'. Next month the voters took this advice: all things considered, landlords did not do badly, but the Liberals achieved a commanding position in every county but Breconshire and Radnorshire. The new men, some of them prominent anti-tithers, had been established locally as at least on a par with the Justices.[2]

There were some who hoped that the anti-tithe agitation would be equally effective in forwarding Welsh progress at a national level. In early 1887 Gibson, of the *Cambrian News*, dwelt repeatedly on the prevailing political apathy, and saw the anti-tithe movement as the only redeeming feature. And the young Lloyd George asked Ellis, 'Do you not think that this tithe business is an excellent lever wherewith to raise the spirit of the people?' The previous autumn a Welsh undergraduate at Cambridge had reminded Thomas Gee that 'It is interesting to compare the beginning of the Irish and Welsh movements. In Ireland (as in Wales) the first circumstance of importance was

[1] For a discussion of the evictions see *P.P.*, 1896 xxxiv, pp. 162–72, and K. O. Morgan, *Wales in British Politics*, pp. 20, 25–7. T. E. Ellis was a nephew of one of the victims.

[2] *Montgomeryshire Express*, 4 Dec. 1888; *South Wales Daily News*, 29 Jan. 1889.

the refusal to pay tithes . . .' Gee did not need the reminder. In
the autumn of 1885 he had been planning to establish a Welsh
Land League on the Irish model, with Michael Davitt to address
its inaugural meeting. But the Home Rule crisis had supervened; Gee broke with Gladstone, underestimating Welsh
loyalty to him, and the following summer had to make an
exceedingly ignominious return to the fold.[1] Perhaps to cover
this retreat he resumed plans in late June for a Welsh National
League. The tithe agitation burst before it got off the ground,
so Gee took up the Anti-tithe League instead, his son Howel
becoming joint secretary. And a little over a year later this was
merged into the Welsh Land, Commercial and Labour League:
the new body had an ambitious programme, including disestablishment, a national fund for the payment of M.P.s on the
Irish model, and collective action to force rent reductions that
would in practice have been tantamount to boycotting.[2]

It is hard to say how much this amounted to. Gee was seeking to tap a quite genuine vein of nationalist sentiment. This
was largely cultural. But it was also fed by the belief that
independent action on the Irish model was the key to political
success, by exasperation with the muffling of Welsh radicalism
in a generally Conservative Parliament, and by the repression of
the tithe agitation. There were shouts of 'Home Rule for Wales'
at a number of tithe sales; and T. E. Ellis wrote that the use
of police in Cardiganshire made him understand the Irish feelings about Dublin Castle. From 1888 Welsh M.P.s sat as the
'Welsh Parliamentary Party'; and though in practice this enjoyed little more independence and cohesion than the 'Crofters'
Members', there was a major row when Ellis accepted office in
the 1892 Liberal Government. The failure of that Government
soured many radicals; and Lloyd George concluded in 1895 that
'all our demands for reform, whether in Church, Land, Education, Temperance or otherwise, ought to be concentrated in one
great agitation for national self-government.' Gee agreed.[3]

But within months Lloyd George's *Cymru Fydd* movement

---

[1] His reconversion to Gladstonian Liberalism was widely believed
to be a direct result of the decline in the circulation of his newspaper,
the *Baner*.

[2] N.L.W. MS. 19450 nos. 168–70; N.L.W. Thomas Edward Ellis
Collection no. 679; N.L.W. MS. 8306 fo. 94a; P. Jones-Evans, 'Evan
Pan Jones—Land Reformer' *Welsh History Review* iv (1968), pp. 152–3;
Letters from Wales, pp. 8–9; *Denbigh Free Press*, 31 Dec. 1887, p. 8.

[3] 'Rhyfel y Degwm', p. 105; K. O. Morgan, *Wales in British
Politics*, chaps. iii and iv.

had collapsed in a welter of personal and regional recrimination. Politicians could not be taken at their face value. Gee had already shown this when he had to eat his words on Home Rule in 1886, and was to do so again in 1889 when he failed to induce the North Wales Liberal Federation to take over his tithe agitation. Indeed Stuart Rendel was to prove fairly accurate in his claim, made in 1887 with particular reference to the tithe and land agitations, that 'Wales generally gets to learn that the forward party are the smoke of the movement, fierce and almost fiery at the chimney's-mouth, vapourous and ineffectual, however spread-eagling and magnificent, in mid air and certain to come down in the end as mere soot.'

For the Welsh farmers were able to look after themselves. True they lapped up the purple passages of the *Baner* and similar newspapers, and enjoyed listening to the harangues of politicians. They also used the legal and public relations services of the Anti-tithe League and the South Wales Liberal Federation. But though Gee demanded the three Fs, most farmers made it clear that they had no use for the third, free sale of the occupier's interest in the farm. Similarly they always gave a very frosty reception to the land nationalizer, Dr. Pan Jones, and to his Irish friend Michael Davitt. And when the Liberal agent for Flintshire tried to horn in on the anti-tithe agitation, he was firmly excluded.[1]

It is therefore interesting to note the difference between the land and the tithe movements. The former never departed from the cycle of agitation, Royal Commission, and (hopefully) legislation, despite the precedent of the Rebecca Riots (which had been at least partly agrarian). The latter certainly did not neglect this cycle. There was much debate on the origin of tithes.[2] In 1887 the Anti-tithe League managed to secure the

[1] Rendel to A. C. Humphreys-Owen, 5 Nov. 1887 (N.L.W. Glansevern Collection no. 357); Thomas Gee, *The Welsh Land, Commercial and Labour League and its Objects* (Denbigh, 1888), p. 7; P.P., 1896 xxxv, p. 757; P. Jones-Evan, article cited, pp. 152–4, 157; P.P., 1887 xxxviii, p. 425.

[2] Lloyd George once scored a dialectical triumph over an unwise curate by challenging him to produce a copy of the 'deed or will giving the Church a right to the tithe' (H. Du Parcq, *The Life of David Lloyd George*, i, pp. 201–4). Another line of argument ran that tithe had been introduced by King Offa in penitence for the murder of Aethelbald; that it had originally been devoted to the maintenance of the poor, and only misappropriated to its present owners under Henry VIII; and that if the then Parliament could transfer tithe, the present one could restore it again to national purposes.

appointment of an *Inquiry as to Disturbances connected with the levying of Tithe Rentcharge in Wales*, and induced it to go beyond the disturbances themselves and receive evidence on all aspects of the tithe grievance. And the agitators certainly looked for legislation to disestablish the Church and transfer the tithe to national purposes. But at the same time they took direct action to prevent the levying of tithe in a way that was never attempted with regard to rent. For parsons were both less popular than landlords and far more vulnerable.

Direct action meant arranging that some, or all, of the tithe-payers should decline to pay and thus force the owner to collect his tithe (at maximum expense to himself) through distraint and sales. In so doing, they claimed that they were merely agitating 'against what they considered an injustice', and following the precedent of the earlier refusal to pay church rates (which had done much to make Thomas Gee's own reputation). Moreover, Gee maintained, everybody 'had the option, according to law, of paying his Tithe, either voluntarily, or by distraint'; and the farmers were only choosing the latter alternative. Two judges endorsed this view in *obiter dicta*. But it is hard to fault Prothero's reply that, on this reasoning, 'all the sanctions by which the law seeks to enforce a particular line of conduct are only alternatives. Every lawbreaker may therefore justify his conduct by the plea that he has only exercised the option which the law provides.'[1]

Sometimes the tithe-payers were content with token and unresisted distraint sales; on one occasion when the regular auctioneer failed to arrive, an anti-tither even conducted the sale himself, donating the fee to League funds. Often, too, the farmers did not go beyond passive resistance, like removing from their premises everything susceptible to distraint or tendering payment in pennies; and at times they may have resented the tendency of crowds to gather at the sales, especially when these proceeded to chase the cattle to prevent the auctioneer from picking out the beast he had distrained on. Often, however, the movements of auctioneers were watched; and crowds of several hundreds were summoned deliberately, by gunshots, horns, flags or even newspaper advertisements. A high point was reached at Llangwm in May 1887: a lane was blocked to prevent the removal of cattle sold in default of tithe; patrols were mounted at night in case the bailiffs returned for them; and when the auctioneer came back two days later, he was captured,

[1] *Montgomery Express*, 4 Dec. 1888; *Cofiant Thomas Gee*, pp. 482–3; *The Anti-tithe Agitation in Wales*, p. 24.

forced to sign a paper promising never to go on similar business anywhere in the country, and then paraded for some miles with his coat turned as a sign of repentance.[1]

The attitude of the leaders to this sort of thing was ambivalent. Formally, they condemned violence. And unlike, for instance, such leading Scottish crofters as John Macpherson the 'Glendale Martyr', they did not (with one exception) themselves commit assaults. Indeed they went to considerable lengths personally to restrain the crowds and protect the auctioneers. But at the same time they denied responsibility for the conduct of the mobs they had called into being, and exonerated individuals who did lapse into violence. Instead they preferred to blame it on disproportionate distraints (largely a non-issue[2]), or on the 'provocative' use of police to escort auctioneers, which was to put the cart before the horse.[3] For they had, in fact, embarked on a policy that could only succeed through the disruption of sales, since, if peace was preserved, the tithe-owners would simply collect their dues and the farmers would be landed with additional costs. So, even if they often baulked at the means, the anti-tithe leaders willed the ends. As Rendel reminded Gee, to talk of throwing 'every constitutional obstacle' in the way of collection 'would be merely playing with language if they did not mean to introduce something like disturbance or menace'.[4]

The result was rather half-hearted. Situations were created in which collisions were likely: but violence as such was not planned. There was some talk of paying tithe according to a Plan of Campaign: but no co-ordinated scheme was ever agreed on for the withholding of all tithe, as opposed to the demanding of local rebates. There were sufficient threats and 'social pres-

[1] 'Rhyfel y Degwm', pp. 81–9.

[2] For various reasons distraints were often levied on objects worth more than the tithe due. This did not harm the farmer, if, as was usual, he exercised his option of buying them in at the auction for the amount of his debt. But it did in the rare cases where he refused, and another buyer had to be found. Also the *Baner* alleged that there were occasions when the farmer was not even given the option to repurchase. On the other hand legal remedies existed for excessive distraint, and the Anti-tithe League was quite capable of taking them.

[3] Violence to auctioneers antedated police protection; and the absence of police did not, at any stage, necessarily prevent it, though such absence could sometimes be bargained against a peaceful sale. Specialist London tithe agents and 'emergency men' were certainly not always conciliatory. But they never did anything serious enough to lead to a successful criminal prosecution by the Anti-tithe League.

[4] *South Wales Daily News*, 4 Sept. 1889, p. 2.

sure' to make some farmers pay their tithes by subterfuge or at night: but nothing very serious happened to anybody who paid openly. Exclusive dealing was used to prevent innkeepers assisting auctioneers or police; and bailiffs were certainly chased out of a number of villages. But this was fairly pointless, since bailiffs could be dispensed with and auctioneers could provide their own conveyances if they had to.

A great deal therefore depended on the attitude of the crowd at any given sale. This varied with the crowd's composition. Farmers certainly felt very strongly about sales—they frequently hung up in their houses the horns of beasts that had been distrained on. And they sometimes assaulted the auctioneer or emptied buckets of filth over him, or, more irresponsibly, let bulls loose—these were fairly impartial as to whether they charged the auctioneer or the crowd, and it is surprising that they never killed anybody. But the farmers were not usually the 'real rioters'. Godfrey, the Montgomeryshire Chief Constable, described these as 'the irresponsible farm labourers and others'; and Humphreys-Owen wrote that the main risk in Montgomeryshire was of 'lads beginning horse play and so provoking fighting. This would be checked much more effectively by their own masters than by the police.' In Meifod in 1888 trouble came partly from the Welsh small-holders, but principally from the labourers at the more English end of the parish who 'are eager for the task of mobbing the auctioneer and the respectables'. At Llanarmon, at the beginning of the agitation, a procession of Minera lime-burners turned up on the day fixed for a sale, armed with sticks; the crowd cheered them, 'but the leaders counselled peace and stolid opposition'; and the auctioneer told the *Daily News* that the farmers themselves would not resist the sale 'as they are anxious to enter their protest only against paying tithes to the Church; it is the colliers who constitute the rough element.' In Flintshire their places were taken by the lead miners, whose numbers probably help to explain the unusual prevalence of disturbances in that county. In short, sales differed from place to place with the nature of the crowd and the way it was handled.[1] And the fortunes of the anti-tithe movement varied accordingly.[2]

[1] Major Godfrey prided himself on his ability to turn sales 'off into a laugh', thereby excluding 'the dangerous element'.

[2] George G. Lerry, 'The Policemen of Denbighshire', *Transactions of the Denbighshire Historical Society*, ii (1953), p. 134; N.L.W., MSS. 15321, pp. 21–2, 149, 19430 no. 201, 19463 no. 449; *Daily News*, 24 Aug. 1886, p. 6.

But a movement that relied principally on forcing sales had no real possibility of development. Either the tithe-owners would find it impossible to recover tithe in this way, or they would succeed and the writing would be on the wall. And since some, at least, of the movement's roots were economic, better times would work against it and make the farmers' resistance to tithe less determined. The agitation was not exactly archaic— indeed the aim of scaling down tithe, reforming its assessment, and applying the proceeds to the relief of rates was rather modern. But the agitation did draw inspiration from the resistance to church rates of 20 years earlier,[1] and it preferred to adopt similar tactics instead of embarking in earnest on violent and organized boycotting and Plans of Campaign on the contemporary Irish model. The choice is very understandable. But it is ironic that a movement whose members were better able to look after themselves than the agricultural labourers or the crofters, and whose leaders were certainly more sophisticated and articulate than any we have previously encountered, should nevertheless had adopted a less developed form than either.

[1] In Cardiganshire inspiration may also have been drawn from the Rebecca riots of over 40 years earlier—'Becca' put out one notice in the traditional form, and the press noted that the most persistent centres of opposition to tithe had also been conspicuous in the earlier disturbances.

XIV

Conclusion

In conclusion it is perhaps worth looking briefly at the factors that determined the success or failure of the movements we have discussed. In the first half of the century these movements were overwhelmingly local in their incidence. Very occasionally they might petition Parliament or the Government, or (especially when prompted by outsiders) might deliberately appeal to public opinion at a more general level through public meetings, pamphlets, or letters to the press. But, for the most part, they sought either to persuade (or coerce) local farmers and magistrates into paying better and employing more, or else themselves to right local grievances by direct action—like destroying machinery, fences or toll gates, driving poor law overseers from the parish, or forcibly preventing the service of writs. Their success therefore depended in the first instance on the reaction of the local establishment, and secondly on the degree to which the central Government was prepared to support it in case of trouble.

Clearly the local establishment could, on occasion, be persuaded or intimidated. The initial Rebecca riots of 1839 procured the removal of the new toll gates against which they had been directed. One or two clearances were dropped because of the resistance they encountered, though the great majority were not. And the most widespread of the southern English labourers' outbreaks, that of 1830–1, did succeed in raising wages in many districts. But in a formal sense no individual outburst lasted very long, though, as Dr. Peacock has shown, in some areas a propensity to resist was more or less endemic. So the problem was not only to secure concessions during the disturbances but also to keep them afterwards.

We can perhaps see this most clearly in connection with wages and employment in southern England; for agricultural labour was in widespread surplus, a factor underlying many of the riots, fires and threatening letters. The Select Committee on Agricultural Distress of 1836 asked a number of witnesses not only whether wages had been raised 'by intimidation' in 1830, but also what had happened since. They were often told that the demand for labour from railway construction and public works had served to keep agricultural wages up; but there had also been many reductions in sympathy with the fall in prices. Only one man mentioned any check, the Chairman of the Agricultural Association of Cambridge. He declared that 'we are paying 50 per cent more for labour than we ought to do, as a sort of premium of insurance to prevent our farms being burnt down . . . in the village near me we had 13 fires in one year and a half'; and in 1837 he added that he himself had 'two men employed for no other reason than they should not rob on the highway, they having declared to me, that rather than go to the poorhouse they would rob'.[1]

But the force of such arguments seems to have been limited. For it was in fairly low wage areas that they were chiefly to be met with, and they must therefore have had less effect on wages and employment than the existence of alternative job opportunities. Also, though there were other grounds for objecting to the institution of a proper rural police, the most usual one was that the existing state of affairs was tolerable and not worth going to great expense to improve. So it seems likely that the fear of disturbance was most influential when it confirmed (rather than conflicted with) the feelings of farmers and landlords.

In general their predisposition was to spread employment rather than to raise wages, since 'Those in any parish have to maintain all in that parish, either in the field or in the workhouse . . .'. For this reason 'They *cannot*, even if they would, employ only a few, and "feed" them well.'[2] Accordingly there had always been some uneasiness about the threshing machines that cut into winter employment. In 1830 farmers had been ready to acquiesce in their destruction, and they were not reinstated for perhaps a decade in East Anglia and two in other parts of southern England. Even at a lower level of technology, farmers in Kent were conscious that the introduction of the

[1] William Thurnall of Duxford, *P.P.*, 1836 viii Part I, pp. 121–5, 133, and 1837, v p. 127—he also said that the village in question had had no further fires since the execution of an incendiary.

[2] J. C. Morton, *Handbook of Farm Labour* (1868 edn.), p. 76. Large landlords owning whole parishes could, however, restrict the population by controlling the number of cottages, and drawing any extra labour they needed from the uncontrolled (and poorer) 'open villages' in the vicinity. In the early 1860s an attempt was made to check this by spreading the burden of poor relief to the whole poor law union. But in practice farmers and landlords continued to offer jobs and housing on a largely parochial basis.

scythe in place of the sickle 'has, on all occasions, excited the ill-will of the labourers to a very dangerous extent . . .'; and Dr. Collins has shown that as late as the 1860s the choice of harvesting tools was largely determined by the availability of hands. Pressure from the labourers thus reinforced the social code of their superiors. And that there was nothing inevitable in this development is shown by the example of Scotland; for there farmers made the opposite choice of a smaller but more productive and highly-paid regular work force,[1] supplemented by purely casual or immigrant labour at peak seasons.[2]

However, if the fear of rural disturbances had some influence on local men, it had virtually none on the central government. This did not perhaps despatch troops quite as freely as some magistrates would have wished; but its opposition to the 1830 riots was firmer than that of the generality of J.P.s; and it was almost invariably prepared to check sustained disorder by force. Naturally ministers were not indifferent—Wellington's 1830 King's Speech deplored the recent riots, and Graham regretfully confided to Peel in 1843 that 'South Wales bids fair to rival Ireland';[3] but they did not tailor their policies to avoid trouble in the countryside. Thus Eliot Yorke warned of violence if the Corn Laws were repealed and wages fell, and there was also talk of farmers riding on London behind black banners; but Peel's actions were determined by other considerations.

The Poor Law provides an even clearer illustration. A bill to extend employment by permitting the levying of a labour rate was introduced in April 1830, backed by a labourers' petition attributing their distress to Poor Law administration. It made no progress; and the Swing riots the following autumn were sometimes attributed to the neglect of such petitions. Accordingly when Parliament re-assembled there was successful pressure for an inquiry into the poor law administration. But though the Agricultural Labourers' Employment bill was re-introduced

---

[1] One observer noted that in the late 1860s 2,314 servants (including 941 women) were employed on 61,000 acres of lowland eastern Scotland, as against 3,236 (including 526 women) on a fairly comparable sample of central southern England— he added that the disproportion in the number of *families* involved was even greater (*P.P.*, 1870 xiii, pp. 239–40).

[2] Hobsbawm and Rudé, *op. cit.*, pp. 298–9; *P.P.*, 1836 xxxiv, p. 639; E. J. T. Collins, 'Harvest Technology and Labour Supply in Britain, 1790–1870', *Economic History Review*, 2nd series xxii (1969), esp. pp. 464–73.

[3] J. T. Ward, *Sir James Graham* (1967), p. 213.

in both Houses, it fared no better; and it also failed the following summer despite an attempt to play on the fear of outrage. In 1832 it was passed—as a purely temporary measure pending the report of the Poor Law Commissioners—because of the personal conversion of the Duke of Richmond. But though he in his turn presented its renewal in 1833 as a safeguard 'against the recurrence of those outrages and that system of terror which, in the Autumn of 1830, disgraced the fairest portion of England', it was lost in the Commons by 17 votes to 29: clearly the question was regarded as of no great importance.[1] The real reform of the Poor Laws, of course, proceeded on quite different lines; and in rural England the policy of denying out-door relief to able-bodied males was pushed through with remarkable resolution in the face of some riots and of widespread discontent.[2]

The Rebecca riots, however, had a rather different outcome, partly because they were more articulate and more concerned to appeal to public opinion. They were, of course, put down by force. But both the Colonel sent to suppress them and the Carmarthenshire magistrates pressed for the appointment of Commissioners to inquire into 'the causes of insubordination', in the belief that this would have a calming effect. The Government agreed, and inquiries were made first privately and then publicly. Rioters were induced to give evidence, and some at least of their grievances were then met by legislation.[3]

This pattern of inquiry, hopefully followed by legislation, was to recur quite often. But it was not one that farm servants and agricultural labourers sought to follow in the 1860s and 1870s. Scottish farm servants had occasionally combined to work the hiring fairs before the 1860s, but they now did so on a much larger scale. However they never tried to go outside the system of the fairs; and, as we have seen, this tended to accommodate pressure through higher wages rather than through changes in the conditions of employment. In the single instance of 'bondage', though, considerable changes were made in these

[1] *Annual Register*, 1830; *Parl. Deb.*, 2nd series, xxiii (April 1830), 3rd series, i (Oct.-Dec. 1830), iv (June–July 1831), xiv (July 1832), xviii (June 1833), xix (July 1833), xx (Aug. 1833).

[2] It might be thought that the survival of out-door relief as the principal form of poor law assistance represented a substantial concession possibly extorted by fear. But such relief was concentrated on widows and on the sick, and only comparatively rarely accorded to the most dangerous class, able-bodied adult males (see e.g. *P.P.*, 1844 xix, pp. 290–5, 1851 xlix, p. 95).

[3] David Williams, *op. cit.*, pp. 228, 275.

conditions—partly because it aroused deeper opposition among the servants than any other employment practice, but also because many large farmers and landlords were themselves unhappy with it.

In 1872 the English labourers were still dealing directly with their employers and with the local gentry, but now 'with the Union at their back'. Organizations like the *National* Union of Agricultural Labourers sprang up and sought to transcend the previous framework of relations by enabling 'the whole power of England . . . [to] be thrown into any district that the necessities of the case shall require'.[1] Indeed not only of England. For the N.A.L.U. also promoted combination in Ireland in a vain attempt to limit competition from migrant workers; and all unions enlisted the services (and prestige) of colonial governments to encourage emigration and thus raise the wages of those who stayed behind.[2]

The rural unions of the early 1870s were undoubtedly impressive—in 1875 the N.A.L.U. could claim the largest membership (though only the seventh largest income) of any then registered.[3] But they were less strong than they had hoped. This was partly a function of the poverty, dispersion and organizational inexperience of the class they represented; and such factors might lead to failure even in fields, like insurance, where the unions did not encounter much external opposition. But more important was the fact that most farm workers (and potential harvesters) remained outside the movement. Some admittedly sympathized with their union colleagues. But others did not, and were quite prepared to take the places of those on strike. So indeed were a number of union members, as minute books make clear.

Combination by labourers on a more than local and ephemeral

[1] *Oxford Journal*, 26 Oct. 1872, p. 8; *Hereford Times*, 25 May 1872 p. 9.
[2] See Pamela Horn, 'The National Agricultural Labourers' Union in Ireland, 1873-9', *Irish Historical Studies*, vii (1971), and 'Agricultural Trades Unionism and Emigration 1872-1881', *Historical Journal*, xv (1972). During the Swanbourne, Bucks, strike in Feb. 1873, emigration leaflets, headed 'By Authority of H.M. Govt. of Queensland' and adorned with the royal coat of arms, were liberally distributed, and even enclosed with written wage demands (Bucks Record Office, D/FR/109 and 133). Such practices may explain the charge that union meetings had been called in Berks and Hants 'by printed handbills headed with the Royal arms and the words, "By authority of Her Majesty's Government" ' (*The Times*, 28 March 1873, p. 11). [3] *P.P.*, 1877 lxxvii, p. 144.

level was a novelty that was to be bitterly resented. What really rankled was the intervention of 'outsiders'—'What right has Mr. Banks, or Mr. anybody else to interfere between you and your employers?', they were asked. And it was put to them that, by joining a union, they had ceased to be free agents: 'you are slaves to your Union and must do as you are told.' This was, of course, not the case; but the farmers' suspicions derived at least a certain plausibility from the National Union's practice of accompanying wage claims with demands for a general conformity to its rules. And if farmers felt that the advent of unionism had transferred their relationship with their employees out of local context, it was, at least in theory, always open to them to combine in reply. In practice this might not prove so easy—disorganization and landlord coolness effectively thwarted the attempt in Oxfordshire. But in East Anglia farmers' defence associations materialized whenever the pressure from the labourers' unions became substantial, that is both in 1872–4 and in 1891–3. They generally bound their members to help each other out in the event of a strike, to stick rigorously to the current rate of wages for the district, and not to employ unionists.[1] This last could mean the countering of strikes in detail through more extensive lock-outs. And though the labourers might be successful in the early stages of a cycle (when market trends were generally favourable), combination by farmers was fully capable of restoring the balance.[2]

The direct effect of the agricultural labourers' unions was therefore limited.[3] Indeed we have seen that in the eastern counties, where they were most developed, wages actually rose more slowly than in the rest of the country. Indirectly, however, they were more influential. They certainly strained social relationships, in some ways to the labourers' detriment.[4] But

[1] The labourers maintained that farmers had always co-operated unofficially to get rid of trouble-makers and to fix local wage rates; and to that extent the new associations merely constituted a formalization of existing practice.

[2] Russell, *op. cit.*, p. 62; F. Clifford, *The Agricultural Lock-out of 1874*, Introduction and pp. 59–63, 83, 162–3; Pamela Horn, 'Farmers' Defence Associations in Oxfordshire—1872–4', *History Studies*, i (1968); *P.P.*, 1893–4 xxxvii Part 2, p. 164.

[3] Though they must have been of enormous importance in the lives of many emigrants, some union officials, and some men who lost jobs or houses in strikes or lock-outs.

[4] The Wiltshire writer Richard Jefferies recorded that 'the kindly old habits' (like allowing labourers the freedom of the farmers'

they also served notice of the existence of a rural problem.
Further reminders were provided by the 'flight from the land'
that set in with the depression of the later 1870s. The new
Liberal Government addressed itself to this problem in 1880.
At first it thought principally of the tenant farmers. But the
Ground Game Act of 1880 benefited the labourers as well; and
the Allotments Extension Act of 1882 directed that land belonging to village charities should if possible be let as allotments, thus meeting one of the labourers' common demands.[1]
Moreover the Liberals were also committed to giving the agricultural labourers the vote. And from 1883 onwards Joseph
Chamberlain came increasingly to look to them, rather than to
the tenant farmers, in his attempt to extend his personal political base into the countryside; for good measure he also added
the Scottish crofters. In so doing, he was clearly influenced by
the contrast between the Radical enthusiasms of the labourers'
and crofters' leaders and the Tory 'prejudices' of the farmers.[2]
With his 'Unauthorised Programme' of 1885 Chamberlain
established certain rural aspirations, notably allotments and
small-holdings, as significant political issues. And the following

---

kitchen to sit and dry their clothes, or giving them breakfast on
Sundays) 'are dying out before the hard-and-fast money system and
the abiding effects of Unionism, which even when not prominently
displayed, causes a silent, sullen estrangement.' (*Hodge and his
Masters*, 1890 edn. p. 307.)

[1] Howard Evans gives a (not altogether reliable) account of the
Act in his *Radical Fights of Forty Years*, pp. 50–3. It was largely the
work of Jesse Collings, but could not have passed without Government endorsement. Despite last-minute assistance from the Lord
Chancellor, it was badly drafted; its administration gave rise to
complaint, and in 1884 Collings secured its investigation by a
Commons Committee (for whose report see *P.P*, 1884–5 viii, pp. 1 ff.).

[2] From 1876–81 Chamberlain had often talked in terms of 'a
definite bid from the Radicals to the Tenant Farmers'. But in 1885
he explained to Thomas Gee that the latter were not interested;
large English farmers depended on landlords for improvements to
their holdings, and did not relish the prospect of fixity of tenure if
it meant themselves assuming the burden of improvements. In
Chamberlain's view nothing would alter the prejudices that led
them to support the Conservatives in hopes of protection; but he
added politely, 'In Wales no doubt it is different; and probably the
question there may some day be presented for settlement in a separate form' (24 Jan. 1885, N.L.W. MS. 8305 no. 14). Later in the year
Bright also turned down Gee's overtures (*ibid.* no. 11).

year Randolph Churchill countered from the Conservative side with the not dissimilar 'Dartford Programme'.

As *electors* the agricultural labourers were sufficiently numerous, and uncommitted, to make it worth the political parties' while competing for their votes. Thus in the run-up to the 1892 elections both parties held conferences on much the same aspects of the rural question;[1] and some legislation naturally resulted from this competition.[2] This cannot but have encouraged the labourers' unions in both England and Scotland, during their rather sickly revival in the 1890s, to look for satisfaction very largely to Government and Parliament. This was a great change from the 1860s and 1870s; for the Scottish unions had then been largely a-political, and the English ones had been more concerned to *prevent* interference by the State, agitating against the despatch of troops to break harvest strikes and against the discriminatory Criminal Law Amendment Act of 1871. But however startling the transition, it did not produce much in the way of results. This was partly because the unions now represented only a tiny minority of the labourers, and because in England, though not in Scotland, their demands were impossibly far-reaching. More important, though, was the fact that agricultural labourers never gave rise to any problem urgent enough to force itself on the Government for immediate attention. Thus no printed paper was circulated to the Cabinet about them until 1913; and though the employment of women and children in agriculture prompted a Commission of Inquiry and legislative interference in the 1860s, the *Parliamentary Papers* do not reveal any comparable concern for the class as a whole.

But, by their forcible resistance to the law, both the Scottish crofters and the Welsh anti-tithers posed more immediate questions. They were not, admittedly, of the first importance, and so scarcely feature at all in the private correspondence of politicians. But they both demanded decisions from those responsible, and these decisions in turn influenced the further development of the two agitations.

Trouble first became acute in the Highlands, as we have seen, when the inhabitants of the Braes started a rent strike to compel the return of Ben Lee, and then deforced the sheriff's officer who was seeking to serve writs of removal. For the county

[1] *The Times*, 11 Dec. 1891 and 30 Jan. 1892.
[2] Notably the 1886 Allotments and the 1892 Smallholdings Acts. The machinery these created was not much used ;but the voluntary provision of allotments and small-holdings was enormously stimulated—*P.P.*, 1896 lxvii, pp. 520–1, 584.

police force was too small to handle the affair without outside assistance. Professor Hanham feels that the authorities should simply have overlooked the matter, thus leaving the Macdonald estate no option but to give way. (And certainly the estate was pressurized later in the year into accepting a disadvantageous compromise.) But this would have been, for the nineteenth century, a very high-handed approach, and there could be no certainty that Lord Macdonald would stand for it. Also it would presumably have been seen in Kilmuir, Glendale and elsewhere as an open invitation to copy the Braes.

In fact the only alternatives considered by the county authorities and the Lord Advocate were the despatch of an outside police force or the sending of troops. And in April 1882 the Lord Advocate decided on a surprise expedition by what turned out to be an inadequate police force. This led to the 'Battle of the Braes'; and as Professor Hanham points out the massive press publicity this engendered drew in outsiders 'to provide the leadership necessary to make out of isolated grievances a political movement'.[1] Also arrests by *police* did not suffice to damp the local agitation. But Speirs and Ivory had always wanted *troops*, whose prestige was very different. And in the limited context of Skye they were probably right—by the late autumn, at least, there was widespread, though not quite universal, agreement on the island that soldiers would not be resisted. Certainly in their absence events passed increasingly out of control.

But Harcourt, the Home Secretary, was exceedingly reluctant to sanction their despatch. In great part this stemmed from sheer emotional repugnance, which no doubt led him to exaggerate the difficulties attending their use. But he was also conscious of, and indeed in touch with, a widespread public opinion that would have been outraged by such an expedition. This led him to conclude that it would prove fatal to the landlords: 'It will infallibly bring up the Scotch land question in a form which they will bitterly repent and you will find the Scotch Members [of Parliament] compelled to make common cause with the Land League.' And it is true that most of the landlords outside Skye whom Harcourt consulted deprecated the despatch of troops.

The prospect of military repression added impetus to the campaign that had already been mounted for an Inquiry to establish how matters had come to such a pass. Initially the Government had been opposed. But Harcourt later changed his

[1] Article cited, esp. pp. 64–5.

mind, partly because he felt that resistance to the law was fostered by local middle class recognition 'that the Crofters have much to complain of', partly because of the imminence of famine, and partly because of the sentiments of Highland M.P.s. Eventually Harcourt had his way in the absence of the Prime Minister, perhaps the only man who could have challenged him on a departmental matter not of the first importance. Moreover though a Commission was often suggested as the counterpart of a re-assertion of the law, it was in the end adopted largely as an alternative to taking military measures. In some quarters, at least, this seemed a Government endorsement of the agitation.[1]

Even within the Administration opinions were divided as to whether the Commission would vindicate the landlords or the crofters. Certainly the Cabinet could not claim to have met Gladstone's pre-requisite for its appointment, 'that there ought to be in view some fair probable solution of the question with which it has to deal'.[2] Yet they nevertheless conceded a prestigious Royal Commission ranging over the whole of the West Highlands, instead of merely a restricted inquiry into events in Skye. In so doing, they abandoned the initiative to the Commission itself. And this considerably altered the context of the dispute, firstly (as we have seen) by providing an occasion for the spread of agitation, and secondly by the way in which it conducted its hearings: each township was invited to send delegates to state its 'grievances', but factors were not permitted to cross-examine them and were sometimes even discouraged from giving evidence in rebuttal of specific points.[3] The effect was to establish that it was the landlords who were in the wrong and who would have to make concessions.

Political circles widely discounted the Commission's actual recommendations as impractical, but it was accepted that the Government would have to frame substitutes. This was in fact done in consultation not with the crofters' leaders but with the

---

[1] Equally it was represented to Harcourt that the despatch of troops would constitute an endorsement of the landlords. This and the previous paragraphs are based principally on the Harcourt and Ivory papers; see also Harcourt to Gladstone, 25 Nov. 1882 (B.M., Add. MS. 44195 fo. 144), and Harcourt to Rosebery, 3 Oct. 1882 (N.L.S. MS. 10034 fos. 142–51).

[2] See Gladstone to Granville, 8 Feb. 1883, and Granville to Gladstone, 6 and 24 Feb. 1883 (printed by Agatha Ramm, *op. cit.*, ii, pp. 19, 21, 32).

[3] See *P.P.*, 1884 xxxiii, pp. 588, 591, 597.

more enlightened of the landlords, since Harcourt believed that only with their good-will could more land be made available to the crofters. Understandably the H.L.L.R.A. was angry; and its rapid expansion at the time of the 1885 election encouraged the crofters to hope for considerably more. But they were to be disappointed, the 1886 Act being very similar to the 1885 proposals. And the new Act provided the necessary conditions for a new Government to re-establish order through rent reductions and military expeditions.

This outcome proved fairly satisfactory, indeed probably the best that could have been obtained. But it had been reached by a largely fortuitous process, and things could clearly have turned out differently. Perhaps the most important determinants were: the inability of the county authorities to control events without military assistance; Harcourt's personal reluctance to send troops; the nature and standing of Scottish public opinion, which made coercion far more unpalatable than it would have been in an Irish context; and the handling of the Napier Commission. All this forced Governments of both parties to take action that they would not otherwise have contemplated. Some was of immediate benefit to the crofters; and it also established the principle, still current today, that the crofting counties constitute a special case. But once Government had made up its mind, it could not be seriously deflected. The effects of the independent political phase of the agitation were essentially marginal, though further gains were to be made in the long run through the permeation of the official Liberal Party.

The Welsh opposition to tithe also intruded itself on public attention by presenting a problem of law enforcement (in a way that the contemporary English movement did not). Fundamentally it was a more serious matter than the crofters' unrest because of its separatist overtones, of which the Prime Minister was well aware.[1] But in the short run it did not demand such difficult decisions since the local authorities were more competent to handle it themselves.

As we have seen most resident Welsh clergy conceded the rebates requested of them. But non-residents did not, and they demanded protection in the exercise of their legal rights. Some county authorities were rather unhappy about providing it, but only in Cardiganshire between 1889 and 1894 did they per-

[1] Cf. Matthews to Salisbury, 31 May 1887, 'It certainly does look as though the spirit of nationality, which has united Germany and Italy, were operating to disintegrate this country' (Salisbury Papers, Christ Church, Oxford).

sistently refuse.[1] And they were better able to give protection than had been the Inverness-shire Commissioners of Supply, partly because they had far larger police forces and partly because communications were more developed than in Skye. Even so they had occasionally to seek military assistance. But there was no disposition on the part of the Conservative Government to withhold it. Matthews, the Home Secretary, may occasionally have had his doubts, notably in connection with Christ Church, but he did not have anything like the political standing of Harcourt; and the despatch of troops in support of the civil power seems to have been virtually automatic, as indeed Sheriff Ivory and the Lord Advocate had expected it to be in their own case.

In 1887 there were, however, a number of collisions between police and crowds, and Welsh M.P.s seized on them to force a Commission of Inquiry. This was a fairly low level affair, conducted by a London police magistrate; but the Anti-tithe League clearly hoped to widen it into a general inquest on the whole question of tithe. However the Commissioner did not fulfil their hopes. He found briskly that the blame for the injuries lay with those who had caused the crowds to assemble. And though he was prepared to hear general evidence as to tithe, the League gained little by it. For the established classes in Wales, unlike the Highland landlords,[2] combined to brief publicists and lawyers to defend them.[3] These lawyers were permitted to cross-examine witnesses both before the 1887 tithe inquiry and later before the Royal Commission on Land in Wales; and they gave a good account of themselves. Within the Principality they might not be able to compete with the vernacular press, but

[1] There might have been more trouble had the peak of the agitation not already passed before the partial democratization of county government in 1889. But police, and even troops, were deployed after that date outside Cardiganshire. And Cardiganshire itself had eventually to change its policy for fear of losing its police grant.

[2] The Duke of Argyll sought to found a 'Landowners Truth Defence Association', but did not succeed in arousing much interest —to Balfour, 27 Oct. 1884 (B.M. Add. MS. 49800).

[3] The 'North Wales Property Defence Association' was formed in Dec. 1885; it sponsored such writings as Vincent's *Letters from Wales*, and his extremely effective *Tenancy in Wales, A Reply to 'Landlordism in Wales' by Adfyfr* (1889). We have already encountered the 'Clergy Defence Association' of Oct. 1886. And Prothero's *The Anti-tithe Agitation in Wales* was based on questionnaires circulated to all incumbents in the dioceses of St. Asaph (where the new bishop was very militant) and Bangor.

outside it they probably had the better of the debate, especially on tithe where their opponents' case was inherently weak. It is, of course, difficult to assess their influence, but they certainly precluded the emergence of a public opinion consistently hostile to Welsh landlords and tithe-owners. And at least as regards tithe-owners, such a development was a distinct possibility, since tithe was also an English grievance felt on both sides of the House.

But even if the Government was not seriously constrained by public opinion, it could not remain indifferent to disorders in Wales. So in 1887 it decided to prevent them by transferring liability to tithe from occupier to owner. Its proposals were tactically mishandled in Parliament and enjoyed low priority, so they dragged on from year to year. But though they aroused some Tory criticism and no great enthusiasm in any quarter, they were bound to pass eventually, since they did not encounter systematic opposition from the English Liberal Party. Once again a protest movement had been able to force the Government to act, but not to control the manner of its action.

By the 1890s the tithe question had become almost wholly subsumed in that of Disestablishment (which implied the secularization of tithe along with other church property). This and land reform were now pursued entirely through conventional political channels. The key to success lay in establishing that Wales constituted a case distinct from England and therefore capable of separate treatment. The 1892 Liberal Government acknowledged this for the Church by bringing in a Disestablishment measure. It also bowed to the wishes of Welsh farmers (who enjoyed considerably more weight in the Party than did English agricultural labourers) by appointing a Royal Commission on Land in Wales; and the majority duly found that the prevalence of great estates, small farms and land hunger sufficiently differentiated the Welsh agricultural system from the English to warrant the judicial fixing of rents. The second Salisbury Government had been prepared to countenance separate treatment for Welsh Intermediate Education. But land was another matter, and the Church was central to the Conservative creed. So changes were scarcely to be expected after the Tory landslide of 1895, especially as the internal collapse of *Cymru Fydd* and the Welsh Liberal Federation removed all significant pressure for them. So both the church and the land questions sank into a slumber from which the latter never revived.

To sum up, in nineteenth-century Britain unrest sometimes

passed beyond the control of the local establishments but never beyond that of the central Government. So where concessions were made from weakness (as was the forced return of 10 per cent to Welsh tithe-payers), they were most likely to be the work of local men. Similarly the central Government did not frame its policies with a view to the avoidance of rural unrest. But such avoidance was one of the factors behind the southern English tendency, in the half-century after Waterloo, to spread work rather than to maximize productivity. Yet even in southern England people generally reacted to events rather than anticipated them. Thus the Swing riots of 1830 led to the extensive abandonment of threshing machines and to widespread pay increases. The 1872 'Revolt of the Field' was countered in the eastern counties by the formation of farmers' defence associations. Later, in response to the 'flight from the land' and the agricultural labourers' acquisition of the franchise, the propertied classes stepped up the provision of allotments and of other amenities designed to keep the 'peasantry' contented.

All this was primarily the work of local men. For the State did not usually intervene unless the local authorities were unable to enforce the law, or unless it was subjected to considerable political pressure. During the first part of the century such inability to enforce the law was not uncommon in the absence of a proper rural police; and so soldiers were often despatched to contain comparatively minor episodes, like the levelling of fences on Otmoor or the riots at Great Bircham in Norfolk.[1] Interventions of this kind never wholly ceased. But in later years they became less common, and therefore more conspicuous.[2] Even in the early 1840s such a substantial deployment of troops as was conjured up by the Rebecca riots had to be defended, and the Government thought it wise to promise an investigation into the grievances behind them. By the second half of the century the various rural disturbances were able to command far more sympathizers in Parliament, and were, in any case, better able themselves to appeal to public opinion. An inquiry thus came to be viewed as a natural concomitant to the use of the military, and as an almost inevitable step if this inflicted casualties.

Certainly inquiries could prove a useful weapon in the arsenal

[1] See pp. 20–1, 37–8 above.

[2] Churchill's reluctant decision to send troops to Tonypandy in 1911 has attracted considerable notoriety. A century earlier it would have been taken for granted.

of agitation. The crofters' urban friends began pressing for one at a very early stage; and its concession made legislation inevitable, albeit not quite the legislation they would have preferred. Later in the decade the Welsh sought to follow this example.[1] The inquiry into tithe disturbances proved a disappointment, but that into Welsh land might have brought results had it worked faster, or had the Liberals not fallen from power. There was no pressure for a comparable inquiry into the conditions of the agricultural labourers.[2] But this may have been a tactical error. For when Lloyd George established a Liberal Party Land Enquiry Committee shortly before the First World War, it came up with what were—from the labourers' point of view—attractive recommendations. And but for the advent of the War, the late nineteenth-century land question might have had something of a swan song. Yet though Lloyd George was deeply rooted in this tradition—he had been secretary of the South Caernarvonshire Anti-tithe League—he was also uniquely sensitive to the changing needs of the future. So his Land Campaign, had it really got under way, would have provided an interesting bridge between the ideas and aspirations we have discussed in this book and the conditions of a new century.[3]

[1] There was also an Irish precedent—the passage of the 1881 Land Act had been much facilitated by the Report of the Bessborough Commission on the working of the 1870 Act.

[2] The chief reason for this omission must be trades union suspicion of state intervention, which was particularly strongly felt by Arch and men of his generation. Also the farm workers' unions were not pleased with the investigations undertaken in 1890s in connection with the Royal Commission on Labour.

[3] For Lloyd George's land policy before 1914, see H. V. Emy. 'The Land Campaign: Lloyd George as a Social Reformer' in A. J. P. Taylor (ed.), *Lloyd George: Twelve Essays* (1971).

Index

Index